Fodor's 2000

Seattle & Vancouver

USED

W9-AYQ-088

The complete guide, thoroughly up-to-date

Packed with details that will make your trip

The must-see sights, off and on the beaten path

What to see, what to skip

Vacation itineraries, walking tours, day trips

Smart lodging and dining options

Essential local do's and taboos

Transportation tips

Key contacts, savvy travel advice

When to go, what to pack

Clear, accurate, easy-to-use maps

Books to read, videos to watch

Fodor's Travel Publications, Inc. • New York, Toronto, London, Sydney, Auckland
www.fodors.com

Fodor's Seattle & Vancouver

EDITOR: Jennifer Levitsky Kasoff

Editorial Contributors: John Doerper, Julie Fay, Sue Kernaghan
Editorial Production: Nicole Revere
Maps: David Lindroth, *cartographer*; Rebecca Baer and Robert Blake, *map editors*
Design: Fabrizio La Rocca, *creative director*; Guido Caroti, *art director*; Jolie Novak, *photo editor*; Melanie Marin, *photo researcher*
Production/Manufacturing: Mike Costa
Cover Photo (Gas Works Park, Lake Union, Seattle)**:** Morton Beebe/Corbis
Cover Design: Pentagram

Copyright

Special Sales

Fodor's Travel Publications are available at special discounts for bulk purchases for sales promotions or premiums. Special editions, including personalized covers, excerpts of existing guides, and corporate imprints, can be created in large quantities for special needs. For more information, contact your local bookseller or write to Special Markets, Fodor's Travel Publications, 201 East 50th Street, New York, NY 10022. Inquiries from Canada should be directed to your local Canadian bookseller or sent to Random House of Canada, Ltd., Marketing Department, 2775 Matheson Boulevard East, Mississauga, Ontario L4W 4P7. Inquiries from the United Kingdom should be sent to Fodor's Travel Publications, 20 Vauxhall Bridge Road, London SW1V 2SA, England.

PRINTED IN THE UNITED STATES OF AMERICA

10 9 8 7 6 5 4 3 2 1

Important Tip

Although all prices, opening times, and other details in this book are based on information supplied to us at press time, changes occur all the time in the travel world, and Fodor's cannot accept responsibility for facts that become outdated or for inadvertent errors or omissions. So **always confirm information when it matters,** especially if you're making a detour to visit a specific place.

CONTENTS

Contents

Maps

ON THE ROAD WITH FODOR'S

EVERY Y2K TRIP is a significant trip. So if there was ever a time you needed excellent travel information, it's now. Acutely aware of that fact, we've pulled out all the stops in preparing *Fodor's Seattle & Vancouver 2000*. To guide you in putting together your Pacific Northwest experience, we've created multiday itineraries and neighborhood walks. And to direct you to the places that are truly worth your time and money in this important year, we've rallied the team of endearingly picky know-it-alls we're pleased to call our writers. Having seen all corners of Seattle & Vancouver, they're real experts on the cities and the beautiful areas surrounding them. If you knew them, you'd poll them for tips yourself.

During the more than 20 years **John Doerper** has lived in the Pacific Northwest, he has explored every nook and cranny of this vast and beautiful region by car, on foot, by boat, and on horseback. But even though nature is beautiful and wild here, he always feels himself drawn to the region's great cities, where wilderness merges with civilization. He loves watching eagles and orcas as much from the dining patio of a waterfront restaurant as he does from his kayak, and he enjoys listening to birds in urban parks as much as he does on an alpine trail. But most of all he loves Seattle and Vancouver for their big-hearted people, as well as for their great restaurants, museums, theaters, opera houses, and symphony halls. John wrote the introductory essay for this book.

Freelance writer **Julie Fay,** who revised the Seattle and Side Trips from Seattle chapters, is a former caterer who has contributed to several Fodor's projects. A Seattle native and fifth-generation Washingtonian, Julie lives with her husband and two children in Seattle, but spends much of each summer at her family's beach cabin in the San Juan Islands, revisiting favorite haunts and combing the north Puget Sound region for new ones. Julie enjoys hiking, biking, and camping. She is afraid of bears and used to enjoy gardening.

Vancouver-born freelance writer **Sue Kernaghan** lives on Salt Spring Island—a place she discovered while researching the Side Trips from Vancouver chapter. A fourth-generation British Columbian, Sue also enjoyed getting reacquainted with her hometown while updating the Vancouver chapter.

Don't Forget to Write

We love feedback—positive and negative—and follow up on all suggestions. So contact the Seattle & Vancouver editor at editors@fodors.com or c/o Fodor's, 201 East 50th Street, New York, New York 10022. Have a wonderful trip!

Karen Cure
Editorial Director

The United States

ONTARIO

CANADA

QUÉBEC

NEW BRUNSWICK

Fredericton

Québec

Montréal

MAINE

Augusta

Ottawa

Montpelier

VT.

N.H.

Concord

Boston

MINNESOTA

Duluth

MICHIGAN

Lake Superior

Lake Huron

Toronto

Lake Ontario

Buffalo

NEW YORK

Albany

MASS.

R.I.

Providence

WISCONSIN

St. Paul

Green Bay

Milwaukee

Lansing

Lake Michigan

Hartford

CONN.

New York

Minneapolis

Madison

Detroit

Cleveland

Lake Erie

PENNSYLVANIA

Harrisburg

Trenton

N.J.

Philadelphia

Chicago

Pittsburgh

OHIO

Columbus

Baltimore

MD.

Dover

DEL.

Annapolis

Washington, D.C.

IOWA

Des Moines

Omaha

ILLINOIS

Springfield

Indianapolis

INDIANA

Cincinnati

WEST VIRGINIA

Charleston

Frankfort

Richmond

Norfolk

VIRGINIA

Topeka

Kansas City

Jefferson City

St. Louis

Louisville

KENTUCKY

Raleigh

MISSOURI

Nashville

TENNESSEE

NORTH CAROLINA

Tulsa

ARKANSAS

Memphis

Columbia

SOUTH CAROLINA

Little Rock

Birmingham

Atlanta

GEORGIA

Savannah

ATLANTIC OCEAN

MISSISSIPPI

Jackson

Montgomery

ALABAMA

Savannah

Houston

Baton Rouge

New Orleans

LOUISIANA

Mobile

Tallahassee

FLORIDA

Jacksonville

Orlando

Bahama Islands

Gulf of Mexico

Miami

Nassau

N

0   500 miles

0   800 km

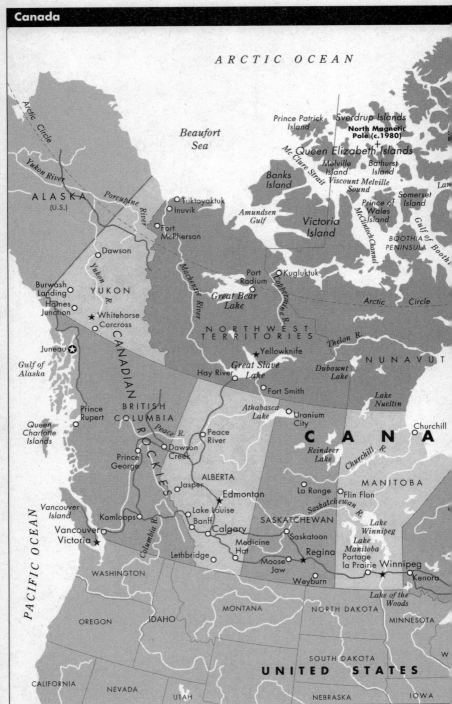

ARCTIC OCEAN

Arctic Circle

Yukon River

Porcupine

ALASKA
(U.S.)

Beaufort
Sea

Prince Patrick
Island

Sverdrup Islands

North Magnetic
Pole (c.1980)

Queen Elizabeth Islands

Mc Clure Strait

Banks
Island

Melville
Island

Bathurst
Island

Viscount Melville
Sound

Lan

Somerset
Island

Prince of
Wales
Island

McClintockChannel

Tuktoyaktuk
Inuvik

Amundsen
Gulf

Victoria
Island

BOOTHIA
PENINSULA

Gulf
of
Booth

Fort
McPherson

Porcupine
River

Dawson

Yukon R.

Mackenzie River

Port
Radium

Kugluktuk

Coppermine R.

Burwash
Landing

YUKON

Great Bear
Lake

Arctic   Circle

Haines
Junction

Whitehorse
Carcross

CANADIAN

N O R T H W E S T
T E R R I T O R I E S

Thelon R.

N U N A V U T

Juneau

Yellowknife

Dubawnt
Lake

Lake
Nueltin

Gulf of
Alaska

Great Slave
Lake

Hay River

Fort Smith

Prince
Rupert

BRITISH
COLUMBIA

Athabasca
Lake

Uranium
City

C A N A

Churchill

Queen
Charlotte
Islands

ROCKIES

Peace R.

Peace
River

Reindeer
Lake

Churchill R.

Dawson
Creek

Prince
George

ALBERTA

La Ronge

Flin Flon

MANITOBA

Jasper

Saskatchewan R.

Kamloops

Columbia R.

Lake Louise

Banff

Edmonton

SASKATCHEWAN

Saskatoon

Lake
Winnipeg

PACIFIC OCEAN

Vancouver
Island

Vancouver
Victoria

Calgary

Medicine
Hat

Lake
Manitoba

Portage
la Prairie

Winnipeg

Lethbridge

Moose
Jaw

Regina

Kenora

WASHINGTON

Weyburn

Lake of the
Woods

OREGON

IDAHO

MONTANA

NORTH DAKOTA

MINNESOTA

W

CALIFORNIA

NEVADA

UTAH

SOUTH DAKOTA

U N I T E D   S T A T E S

NEBRASKA

IOWA

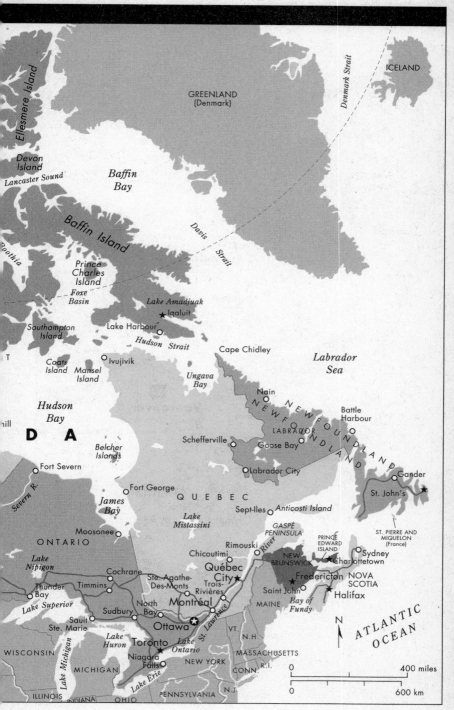

ICELAND

Denmark Strait

GREENLAND
(Denmark)

Ellesmere Island

Devon
Island

Lancaster Sound

*Baffin
Bay*

Baffin Island

Davis Strait

Boothia

Prince
Charles
Island

Foxe
Basin

Lake Amadjuak
★ Iqaluit

Southampton
Island

Lake Harbour ○

Hudson Strait

Cape Chidley

*Labrador
Sea*

Coats
Island

Mansel
Island

Ivujivik ○

Ungava
Bay

Nain ○

Battle
Harbour

T

*Hudson
Bay*

D   A

Belcher
Islands

N E W F O U N D L A N D

LABRADOR

Scheffervile ○

Goose Bay ○

chill

Fort Severn ●

○ Labrador City

Gander ●

Severn R.

*James
Bay*

Fort George ●

Q U E B E C

Sept-Iles ●   Anticosti Island

St. John's ★

Moosonee ●

*Lake
Mistassini*

GASPÉ
PENINSULA

ST. PIERRE AND
MIQUELON
(France)

ONTARIO

Rimouski ●   River

PRINCE
EDWARD
ISLAND

Sydney ●

*Lake
Nipigon*

Chicoutimi ●

NEW
BRUNSWICK

★ Charlottetown

Cochrane ●

Québec
City ★

Fredericton ★

NOVA
SCOTIA

Thunder
Bay ●

Timmins ●

Ste.-Agathe-
Des-Monts ●

Trois-
Rivières ●

Saint John ●

★ Halifax

Lake Superior

Sudbury ●

North
Bay ●

Montréal ●

*Bay of
Fundy*

MAINE

Sault
Ste. Marie ●

Ottawa ☆

St. Lawrence

VT.

N   *ATLANTIC
OCEAN*

WISCONSIN

*Lake
Huron*

Toronto ★

*Lake
Ontario*

N.H.

MICHIGAN

Niagara
Falls ★

NEW YORK

MASSACHUSETTS

Lake Michigan

Lake Erie

CONN.   R.I.

0   400 miles

ILLINOIS   INDIANA   OHIO

PENNSYLVANIA

N.J.

0   600 km

Seattle and Vancouver

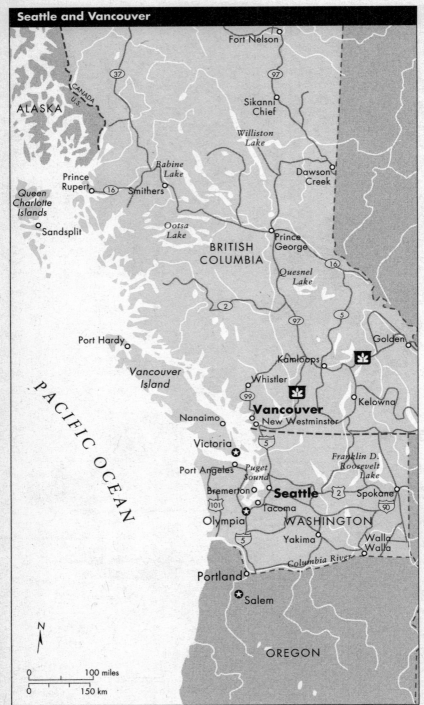

ALASKA

Fort Nelson

37

97

CANADA
U.S.

Sikanni
Chief

Williston
Lake

Babine
Lake

Prince
Rupert

16

Smithers

Dawson
Creek

Queen
Charlotte
Islands

Sandsplit

Ootsa
Lake

BRITISH
COLUMBIA

Prince
George

16

Quesnel
Lake

2

97

5

Golden

Port Hardy

Kamloops

Vancouver
Island

Whistler

99

Kelowna

Vancouver

Nanaimo

New Westminster

5

Victoria

Port Angeles

Puget
Sound

Franklin D.
Roosevelt
Lake

PACIFIC OCEAN

Bremerton

101

Olympia

5

Tacoma

Seattle

2

Spokane

90

WASHINGTON

Yakima

Walla
Walla

Columbia River

Portland

OREGON

Salem

N

0   100 miles

0   150 km

ESSENTIAL INFORMATION

AIR TRAVEL

BOOKING YOUR FLIGHT

When you book **look for nonstop flights** and **remember that "direct" flights stop at least once.** Try to avoid connecting flights, which require a change of plane.

CARRIERS

For information about airline service to particular areas covered in this book, *see* the A to Z section at the end of the city chapters or the Essentials section following the coverage of each region in the side trips chapters.

➤ MAJOR AIRLINES: **Air Canada** (☎ 604/688–5515 in Vancouver; 888/247–2262 in Canada; 800/776–3000 in the U.S.). **Alaska** (☎ 800/426–0333). **American** (☎ 800/433–7300). **America West** (☎ 800/235–9292). **British Airways** (☎ 800/247–9297). **Cathay Pacific** (☎ 800/268–6868). **Continental** (☎ 800/525–0280). **Delta** (☎ 800/221–1212). **EVA Airways** (☎ 800/695–1188). **Hawaiian** (☎ 800/367–5320). **Japan** (☎ 800/525–3663). **Northwest** (☎ 800/225–2525). **Thai** (☎ 800/426–5204; 800/668–8103 in Canada). **TWA** (☎ 800/221–2000). **United/United Express** (☎ 800/241–6522). **US Airways/US Airways Express** (☎ 800/428–4322).

➤ SMALLER AIRLINES: **Canadian** (☎ 800/426–7000). **Horizon Air** (☎ 800/547–9308). **Reno Air** (☎ 800/736–6247). **Southwest** (☎ 800/435–9792).

➤ REGIONAL AIRLINES: **Air B.C.** (☎ 604/688–5515, or 800/776–3000 in the U.S.; 800/663–3721 in Canada). **Harbor Air** (☎ 800/359–3220). **Harbour Air Ltd.** (☎ 604/688–1277 or 800/665–0212). **Helijet Airways** (☎ 604/682–1468 or 800/665–4354). **Kenmore Air** (☎ 425/486–1257 or 800/543–9595). **Pacific Spirit Air** (☎ 250/537–9359; 800/665–2359). **West Isle Air** (☎ 800/874–4434). **Westjet** (☎ 800/538–5696).

➤ FROM THE U.K.: **American** (☎ 0345/789789). **Canadian** (☎ 0345/616767). **British Airways** (☎ 0345/222111). **Delta** (☎ 0800/414767). **United** (☎ 0845/8444–777).

CHECK-IN & BOARDING

Assuming that not everyone with a ticket will show up, airlines routinely overbook planes. When that happens, airlines ask for volunteers to give up their seats. In return these volunteers usually get a certificate for a free flight and are rebooked on the next flight out. If there are not enough volunteers, the airline must choose who will be denied boarding. The first to get bumped are passengers who checked in late and those flying on discounted tickets, so **get to the gate and check in as early as possible,** especially during peak periods.

Always **bring a government-issued photo ID to the airport.** You may be asked to show it before you are allowed to check in.

CUTTING COSTS

The least-expensive airfares to Seattle and Vancouver must usually be purchased in advance and are nonrefundable. It's smart to **call a number of airlines, and when you are quoted a good price, book it on the spot**—the same fare may not be available the next day. Always **check different routings** and look into using different airports. Travel agents, especially low-fare specialists (☞ Discounts & Deals, *below*), are helpful.

Consolidators are another good source. They buy tickets for scheduled international flights at reduced rates from the airlines, then sell them at prices that beat the best fare available directly from the airlines, usually without restrictions. Sometimes you can even get your money back if you need to return the ticket. Carefully read the fine print detailing penalties for changes and cancellations, and **confirm your consolidator reservation with the airline.**

When you **fly as a courier** you trade your checked-luggage space for a ticket deeply subsidized by a courier service. There are restrictions on when you can book and how long you can stay.

➤ CONSOLIDATORS: **Cheap Tickets** (☎ 800/377–1000). **Discount Airline Ticket Service** (☎ 800/576–1600). **Unitravel** (☎ 800/325–2222). **Up & Away Travel** (☎ 212/889–2345). **World Travel Network** (☎ 800/409–6753).

ENJOYING THE FLIGHT

For more legroom **request an emergency-aisle seat.** Don't sit in the row in front of the emergency aisle or in front of a bulkhead, where seats may not recline. If you have dietary concerns, **ask for special meals when booking.** These can be vegetarian, low-cholesterol, or kosher, for example. On long flights, try to maintain a normal routine, to help fight jet lag. At night **get some sleep.** By day **eat light meals, drink water** (not alcohol), and **move around the cabin** to stretch your legs.

FLYING TIMES

Nonstop flying time from New York to Seattle is approximately 5 hours; flights from Chicago are about 4–4½ hours; flights between Los Angeles and Seattle take 2½ hours. Flights from New York to Vancouver take about 5½ hours nonstop; from Chicago, about 4½ hours nonstop; and from Los Angeles, about 3 hours nonstop.

HOW TO COMPLAIN

If your baggage goes astray or your flight goes awry, complain right away. Most carriers require that you **file a claim immediately.**

➤ AIRLINE COMPLAINTS: U.S. Department of Transportation **Aviation Consumer Protection Division** (✉ C-75, Room 4107, Washington, DC 20590, ☎ 202/366–2220). **Federal Aviation Administration Consumer Hotline** (☎ 800/322–7873).

AIRPORTS & TRANSFERS

The major gateways are **Sea-Tac (Seattle-Tacoma) International Airport** and **Vancouver International Airport.** For information about airport transfers to downtown, *see* the A to Z sections at the end of the Seattle and Vancouver chapters.

➤ AIRPORT INFORMATION: **Vancouver International Airport** (✉ Grant McConachie Way, Richmond, ☎ 604/276–6101). **Sea-Tac International Airport** (✉ Pacific Hwy. S [Hwy. 99], ☎ 206/431–4444).

BOAT & FERRY TRAVEL

Ferries play an important part in the transportation network of the Pacific Northwest. In some areas, ferries provide the only form of access into and out of communities. In other places, ferries transport thousands of commuters a day to and from work in the cities. For visitors, ferries are one of the best ways to get a feel for the region and its ties to the sea.

BRITISH COLUMBIA

BC Ferries operates ferries between the mainland, Vancouver Island, the Gulf Islands, and elsewhere, carrying passengers, cars, campers, RVs, trucks, and buses. Peak traffic times are Friday afternoon, Saturday morning, and Sunday afternoon, especially during summer months and holiday weekends. Vehicle reservations can be made on some routes.

Black Ball Transport's MV *Coho* makes daily crossings year-round, from Port Angeles to Victoria. The *Coho* can carry 970 passengers and 100 cars across the Strait of Juan de Fuca in 1½ hours. Advance reservations are not accepted.

Victoria Clipper operates three passenger-only jet catamarans between Seattle and Victoria. One makes the trip in two hours, another makes it in three hours, and the third, which takes the scenic route, makes it in five hours. The company also operates the *Princess Marguerite III* car and passenger ferry between Seattle and Victoria, with one round-trip daily from mid-May to mid-September. The sailing time is 4½ hours each way.

➤ FERRY COMPANIES: **BC Ferries** (✉ 1112 Fort St., Victoria, BC V8V 4V2, ☎ 250/386–3431 in Victoria and outside British Columbia; 888/223–3779 everywhere in British Columbia except Victoria). **Black Ball Transport** (✉ 430 Belleville St., Victoria, BC V8V 1W9, ☎ 250/386–2202 in Victoria; 360/457–4491 in Port Angeles). **Victoria Clipper** (✉ 2701 Alaskan Way, Pier 69, Seattle, WA 98121, ☎ 250/382–8100 in Victoria; 206/448–5000 in Seattle; 800/888–2535 elsewhere in the U.S. or in Canada).

WASHINGTON

If you are planning to use the Washington State Ferries, try to **avoid peak commuter hours.** The heaviest traffic flows are eastbound in the mornings and on Sunday evening and westbound on Saturday morning and weekday afternoons. The best times for travel are 9–3 and after 7 PM on weekdays. In July and August, you may have to wait up to more than an hour to take a car aboard one of the popular San Juan Islands ferries. Walk-on space is always available; if possible, **leave your car behind.**

➤ FERRY COMPANY: **Washington State Ferries** (✉ Colman Dock, Pier 52, Seattle, WA 98104, ☎ 206/464–6400; 800/843–3779 in WA).

BUS TRAVEL TO AND FROM SEATTLE AND VANCOUVER

Greyhound Lines operates regular intercity bus routes to points throughout the Pacific Northwest. **Gray Line of Seattle** has daily bus service between Seattle and Victoria via the Washington State ferry at Anacortes. Smaller bus companies provide service within local areas. One such service, **Pacific Coach Lines,** runs from downtown Vancouver to Victoria (via the British Columbia ferry system). **Quick Shuttle** provides bus service between Seattle's Sea-Tac Airport and Vancouver's major hotels and cruise terminal.

➤ BUS INFORMATION: **Greyhound Lines** (☎ 800/231–2222; 800/661–8747 in Canada). **Gray Line** (☎ 206/624–5077 in Seattle; 250/388–5248 in Victoria). **Pacific Coach Lines** (☎ 604/662–8074 or 800/661–1725).

Quick Shuttle (☎ 604/940–4428; 800/665–2122 in the U.S.):

BUSINESS HOURS

Most retail stores in Washington are open from 9:30 to 6 daily in downtown locations and later at suburban shopping malls. Downtown stores sometimes stay open late Thursday and Friday nights. Normal banking hours are weekdays from 9 to 6; some branches are also open Saturday morning.

In British Columbia, most stores are open from Monday through Wednesday and on Saturday between 9 AM and 6 PM, on Thursday and Friday from 9 to 9, and on Sunday from 11 to 6. Normal banking hours in Canada are from 9 to 4 on weekdays and, in residential areas, from 9 to 3 on Saturday. Some branches may be closed on Monday, and most downtown Vancouver branches are closed on Saturday.

CAMERAS & PHOTOGRAPHY

The natural splendor of the Pacific Northwest will vie for the attention of your camera lens. The water and islands, along with the urban centers and small villages, are all worthy of your attention. Seize the sunny times of day for the clearest shots.

➤ PHOTO HELP: **Kodak Information Center** (☎ 800/242–2424). *Kodak Guide to Shooting Great Travel Pictures,* available in bookstores or from Fodor's Travel Publications (☎ 800/533–6478; $16.50 plus $4 shipping).

EQUIPMENT PRECAUTIONS

Always **keep your film and tape out of the sun.** Carry an extra supply of batteries, and **be prepared to turn on your camera or camcorder** to prove to security personnel that the device is real. Always **ask for hand inspection of film,** which becomes clouded after successive exposures to airport X-ray machines, and **keep videotapes away from metal detectors.**

CAR RENTAL

➤ MAJOR AGENCIES: **Alamo** (☎ 800/327–9633; 020/8759–6200 in the U.K.). **Avis** (☎ 800/331–1212; 800/879–2847 in Canada; 02/9353–9000

SMART TRAVEL TIPS A TO Z

in Australia; 09/525–1982 in New Zealand). **Budget** (☎ 800/527–0700; 0144/227–6266 in the U.K.). **Dollar** (☎ 800/800–4000; 020/8897–0811 in the U.K., where it is known as Eurodollar; 02/9223–1444 in Australia). **Hertz** (☎ 800/654–3131; 800/263–0600 in Canada; 020/8897–2072 in the U.K.; 02/9669–2444 in Australia; 03/358–6777 in New Zealand). **National InterRent** (☎ 800/227–7368; 0345/222525 in the U.K., where it is known as Europcar InterRent).

CUTTING COSTS

To get the best deal **book through a travel agent who will shop around.** Also **price local car-rental companies,** although the service and maintenance may not be as good as those of a major player. Remember to ask about required deposits, cancellation penalties, and drop-off charges if you're planning to pick up the car in one city and leave it in another. If you're traveling during a holiday period, also make sure that a confirmed reservation guarantees you a car.

Do **look into wholesalers,** companies that do not own fleets but rent in bulk from those that do and often offer better rates than traditional car-rental operations.

➤ WHOLESALERS: **Auto Europe** (☎ 207/842–2000 or 800/223–5555, ℻ 800–235–6321).

INSURANCE

When driving a rented car you are generally responsible for any damage to or loss of the vehicle as well as for any property damage or personal injury that you may cause. Before you rent see what coverage your personal auto-insurance policy and credit cards already provide.

For about $15 to $20 per day, rental companies sell protection, known as a collision- or loss-damage waiver (CDW or LDW), that eliminates your liability for damage to the car. In most states you don't need a CDW if you have personal auto insurance or other liability insurance. However, **make sure you have enough coverage to pay for the car.** If you do not have auto insurance or an umbrella policy that covers damage to third parties,

purchasing liability insurance and a CDW or LDW is highly recommended.

REQUIREMENTS & RESTRICTIONS

In British Columbia, your own driver's license is acceptable, children six and under must use a child seat, and car rentals incur both a 14 percent sales tax and a $1.50 per day social services tax. In Washington State you must be 21 to rent a car, and hold a major credit card. Rates may be higher if you're under 25. You'll pay extra for child seats (about $3 per day), which are compulsory for children under five, and for additional drivers (about $2 per day). Non-U.S. residents will need a reservation voucher, a passport, a driver's license, and a travel policy that covers each driver, in order to pick up a car.

SURCHARGES

Before you pick up a car in one city and leave it in another **ask about drop-off charges or one-way service fees,** which can be substantial. Note, too, that some rental agencies charge extra if you return the car before the time specified in your contract. To avoid a hefty refueling fee **fill the tank just before you turn in the car,** but be aware that gas stations near the rental outlet may overcharge.

CAR TRAVEL

FROM THE U.S.

The U.S. interstate highway network provides quick and easy access to the Pacific Northwest in spite of imposing mountain barriers. From the south, Interstate 5 (I–5) runs from the U.S.-Mexican border through California, into Oregon and Washington, and ends at the U.S.-Canadian border. Most of the region's population lives along this corridor. From the east, I–90 stretches from Boston to Seattle. I–84 runs from the midwestern states to Portland.

The main entry point into Canada by car is on I–5 at Blaine, Washington, 30 mi south of Vancouver. Three highways enter British Columbia from the east: Highway 1, or the Trans-Canada Highway (the longest highway in the world, running more than 5,000 mi from St. John's, Newfoundland, to Victoria, British Columbia), Highway 3, or the Crowsnest Highway, which crosses southern British Columbia, and Highway 16, the Yellowhead Highway, which runs through northern British Columbia from the Rocky Mountains to Prince Rupert.

Border-crossing procedures are usually quick and simple (☞ Passports and Visas, *below*). Every British Columbia border crossing (except the one at Aldergrove, which closes at midnight) is open 24 hours a day. The I–5 border crossing at Blaine, Washington, (also known as the Douglas, or Peace Arch, border crossing) is one of the busiest border crossings between the United States and Canada. The peak traffic time at the border northbound into Canada is daily at 4 PM. Southbound, delays can be expected evenings and weekend mornings. Try to plan on reaching the border at off-peak times.

ROAD CONDITIONS

➤ WINTER ROAD-CONDITION REPORTS: **British Columbia** (☎ 604/660–9770). **Washington State** (☎ 888/766–4636).

RULES OF THE ROAD

The speed limit on U.S. interstate highways in Washington State is 65 mi per hour in rural areas and 60 mi per hour in urban zones, 55 mi per hour on secondary highways. In Canada (where the metric system is used), the speed limit is usually 50 kph (30 mph) in cities. Secondary roads and mountain highways have limits of 50 to 80 kph (30 to 50 mph), and freeway speed limits range from 90 to 110 (56 to 68 mph).

WINTER DRIVING

In coastal areas, the mild, damp climate contributes to roadways that are frequently wet. Winter snowfalls are not common (generally only once or twice a year), but when snow does fall, traffic grinds to a halt and the roadways become treacherous and stay that way until the snow melts.

Tire chains, studs, or snow tires are essential equipment for winter travel in mountain areas such as Leavenworth, Washington, or Whistler, British Columbia. If you're planning

to drive into high elevations, be sure to check the weather forecast beforehand. Even the main highway mountain passes can be forced to close because of snow conditions. During the winter months, state and provincial highway departments operate snow advisory telephone lines that give pass conditions.

CHILDREN IN SEATTLE AND VANCOUVER

There's plenty for kids to enjoy in both Seattle and Vancouver—from green spaces, to the waterfront, to urban adventure. Nearby each city are islands, beaches, inlets, and mountains to explore. If you are renting a car, don't forget to **arrange for a car seat** when you reserve.

FLYING

If your children are two or older **ask about children's airfares.** As a general rule, infants under two not occupying a seat fly at greatly reduced fares or even for free.

Experts agree that it's a good idea to use safety seats aloft for children weighing less than 40 pounds. Airlines set their own policies: U.S. carriers usually require that the child be ticketed, even if he or she is young enough to ride free, since the seats must be strapped into regular seats. Do **check your airline's policy about using safety seats during takeoff and landing.** And since safety seats are not allowed just everywhere in the plane, get your seat assignments early.

When reserving, **request children's meals or a freestanding bassinet** if you need them. But note that bulkhead seats, where you must sit to use the bassinet, may lack an overhead bin or storage space on the floor.

LODGING

Most hotels in Seattle and Vancouver allow children under a certain age to stay in their parents' room at no extra charge, but others charge for them as extra adults; be sure to **find out the cutoff age for children's discounts.**

SIGHTS & ATTRACTIONS

Places that are especially good for children are indicated by a rubber duckie icon in the margin.

CONCIERGES

Concierges, found in many hotels, can help you with theater tickets and dinner reservations: a good one with connections may be able to get you seats for a hot show or prime-time dinner reservations at the restaurant of the moment. You can also turn to your hotel's concierge for help with travel arrangements, sightseeing plans, services ranging from aromatherapy to zipper repair, and emergencies. Always, **always tip** a concierge who has been of assistance.

CONSUMER PROTECTION

Whenever shopping or buying travel services in Seattle and Vancouver, **pay with a major credit card** so you can cancel payment or get reimbursed if there's a problem. If you're doing business with a particular company for the first time, **contact your local Better Business Bureau and the attorney general's offices** in your state and the company's home state, as well. Have any complaints been filed? Finally, if you're buying a package or tour, always **consider travel insurance** that includes default coverage (☞ Insurance, *below*).

➤ LOCAL BBBs: **Council of Better Business Bureaus** (✉ 4200 Wilson Blvd., Suite 800, Arlington, VA 22203, ☎ 703/276–0100, FAX 703/525–8277).

British Columbia Better Business Bureaus (✉ 788 Beatty St., Suite 404, Vancouver V6B 2M1 ☎ 604/682–2711 for mainland British Columbia; ✉ 1005 Langley St., Room 201, Victoria V8W 1V7, ☎ 250/386–6348 for Vancouver Island). **Washington Better Business Bureau** (✉ Box 68926, Sea-Tac 98168-0926, ☎ 206/431–2222).

CRUISE TRAVEL

Cruise ships travel the Inside Passage and Gulf of Alaska from mid-May to late September. The most popular ports of embarkation are Vancouver and Seward (port city for Anchorage), but cruises also leave from San Francisco and Seattle. One of the best ways to see the region is to combine your cruise with a land tour.

CUSTOMS & DUTIES

When shopping, **keep receipts** for all purchases. Upon reentering the country, **be ready to show customs officials what you've bought.** If you feel a duty is incorrect or object to the way your clearance was handled, note the inspector's badge number and ask to see a supervisor. If the problem isn't resolved, write to the appropriate authorities, beginning with the port director at your point of entry.

IN AUSTRALIA

Australia residents who are 18 or older may bring home $A400 worth of souvenirs and gifts (including jewelry), 250 cigarettes or 250 grams of tobacco, and 1,125 milliliters of alcohol (including wine, beer, and spirits). Residents under 18 may bring back $A200 worth of goods. Prohibited items include meat products. Seeds, plants, and fruits need to be declared upon arrival.

➤ INFORMATION: **Australian Customs Service** (Regional Director, ✉ Box 8, Sydney, NSW 2001, ☎ 02/9213–2000, FAX 02/9213–4000).

ENTERING CANADA

American and British visitors may bring in the following items duty-free: 200 cigarettes, 50 cigars, and 14 ounces of tobacco; 1 bottle (1.1 liters or 40 imperial ounces) of liquor or wine, or 24 355-milliliter (12-ounce) bottles or cans of beer for personal consumption. Any alcohol and tobacco products in excess of these amounts is subject to duty, provincial fees, and taxes. You must be 19 or over to bring alcohol or tobacco into British Columbia. You can also bring in gifts (not including advertising material, alcohol, or tobacco products) up to the value of $60 (Canadian) per gift. A deposit is sometimes required for trailers (refunded upon return). Cats and dogs must have a certificate issued by a licensed veterinarian that clearly identifies the animal and certifies that it has been vaccinated against rabies during the preceding 36 months. Seeing-eye dogs are allowed into Canada without restriction. Plant material must be declared and inspected. There may be restrictions on some live plants, bulbs, and seeds. With certain restrictions or prohibitions on some fruits and vegetables, visitors may bring food with them for their own use, providing the quantity is consistent with the duration of the visit.

Canada's firearms laws are significantly stricter than the U.S.'s. All handguns and semiautomatic and fully automatic weapons are prohibited and cannot be brought into the country. Sporting rifles and shotguns may be imported provided they are to be used for sporting, hunting, or competition while in Canada. All firearms must be declared to Canada Customs at the first point of entry. Failure to declare firearms will result in their seizure, and criminal charges may be made.

RETURNING TO CANADA

Canadian residents who have been out of Canada for at least seven days may bring home C$500 worth of goods duty-free. If you've been away less than seven days but more than 48 hours, the duty-free allowance drops to C$200; if your trip lasts 24–48 hours, the allowance is C$50. You may not pool allowances with family members. Goods claimed under the C$500 exemption may follow you by mail; those claimed under the lesser exemptions must accompany you. Alcohol and tobacco products may be included in the seven-day and 48-hour exemptions but not in the 24-hour exemption. If you meet the age requirements of the province or territory through which you reenter Canada, you may bring in, duty-free, 1.14 liters (40 imperial ounces) of wine or liquor *or* 24 12-ounce cans or bottles of beer or ale. If you are 16 or older you may bring in, duty-free, 200 cigarettes and 50 cigars. Check ahead of time with Revenue Canada or the Department of Agriculture for policies regarding meat products, seeds, plants, and fruits.

You may send an unlimited number of gifts worth up to C$60 each duty-free to Canada. Label the package UNSOLICITED GIFT—VALUE UNDER $60. Alcohol and tobacco are excluded.

➤ INFORMATION: **Revenue Canada** (✉ 2265 St. Laurent Blvd. S, Ottawa, Ontario K1G 4K3, ☎ 613/993–0534; 800/461–9999 in Canada).

IN NEW ZEALAND

Homeward-bound residents 17 or older may bring back $700 worth of souvenirs and gifts. Your duty-free allowance also includes 4.5 liters of wine or beer; one 1,125-milliliter bottle of spirits; and either 200 cigarettes, 250 grams of tobacco, 50 cigars, or a combination of the three up to 250 grams. Prohibited items include meat products, seeds, plants, and fruits.

➤ INFORMATION: **New Zealand Customs** (Custom House, ✉ 50 Anzac Ave., Box 29, Auckland, New Zealand, ☎ 09/359–6655, FAX 09/359–6732).

IN THE U.K.

From countries outside the EU, including the U.S., you may bring home, duty-free, 200 cigarettes or 50 cigars; 1 liter of spirits or 2 liters of fortified or sparkling wine or liqueurs; 2 liters of still table wine; 60 milliliters of perfume; 250 milliliters of toilet water; plus £136 worth of other goods, including gifts and souvenirs. If returning from outside the EU, prohibited items include meat products, seeds, plants, and fruits.

➤ INFORMATION: **HM Customs and Excise** (✉ Dorset House, Stamford St., Bromley Kent BR1 1XX, ☎ 020/7202–4227).

IN THE U.S.

Non-U.S. residents ages 21 and older may import into the United States 200 cigarettes or 50 cigars or 2 kilograms of tobacco, 1 liter of alcohol, and gifts worth $100. Meat products, seeds, plants, and fruits are prohibited.

RETURNING TO THE U.S.

U.S. residents may bring home $400 worth of foreign goods duty-free if they've been out of the country for at least 48 hours (and if they haven't used the $400 allowance or any part of it in the past 30 days).

U.S. residents 21 and older may bring back 1 liter of alcohol duty-free. In addition, regardless of your age, you are allowed 200 cigarettes and 100 non-Cuban cigars. Antiques, which the U.S. Customs Service defines as objects more than 100 years old, enter duty-free, as do original works of art done entirely by hand, including paintings, drawings, and sculptures.

You may also send packages home duty-free: up to $200 worth of goods for personal use, with a limit of one parcel per addressee per day (and no alcohol or tobacco products or perfume worth more than $5); label the package PERSONAL USE, and attach a list of its contents and their retail value. Do not label the package UNSOLICITED GIFT, or your duty-free exemption will drop to $100. Mailed items do not affect your duty-free allowance on your return.

➤ INFORMATION: **U.S. Customs Service** (inquiries, ✉ 1300 Pennsylvania Ave. NW, Washington, DC 20229, ☎ 202/927–6724; complaints, ✉ Office of Regulations and Rulings, 1300 Pennsylvania Ave. NW, Washington, DC 20229; registration of equipment, ✉ Resource Management, 1300 Pennsylvania Ave. NW, Washington, DC 20229, ☎ 202/927–0540).

DINING

The restaurants we list are the cream of the crop in each price category. Properties indicated by an ✕🏨 are lodging establishments whose restaurant warrants a special trip.

RESERVATIONS & DRESS

Reservations are always a good idea: we mention them only when they're essential or are not accepted. Book as far ahead as you can, and reconfirm as soon as you arrive. We mention dress only when men are required to wear a jacket or a jacket and tie.

DISABILITIES & ACCESSIBILITY

➤ LOCAL RESOURCES: The **Seattle King County Convention Visitor Information Bureau** (✉ 520 Pike St., Suite 1300, 98101, ☎ 206/461–5800) notes the wheelchair-accessibility of attractions and lodgings in its Seattle Visitor and Lodging Guides. If you drop by the **Vancouver Tourist Information Centre** (✉ 200 Burrard St., ☎ 604/683–2000), you can look in the Centre's General Information binder

for a list of area attractions that are wheelchair-accessible. You can also call 800/663–6000 for a free copy of the *Super Natural British Columbia's Accommodations Guide,* which notes the accessibility of lodgings in the province.

LODGING

When discussing accessibility with an operator or reservations agent **ask hard questions.** Are there any stairs, inside *or* out? Are there grab bars next to the toilet *and* in the shower/tub? How wide is the doorway to the room? To the bathroom? For the most extensive facilities meeting the latest legal specifications **opt for newer accommodations.**

➤ COMPLAINTS: **Disability Rights Section** (✉ U.S. Department of Justice, Civil Rights Division, Box 66738, Washington, DC 20035-6738, ☎ 202/514–0301; 800/514–0301; 202/514–0301 TTY; 800/514–0301 TTY, FAX 202/307–1198) for general complaints. **Aviation Consumer Protection Division** (☞ Air Travel, *above*) for airline-related problems. **Civil Rights Office** (✉ U.S. Department of Transportation, Departmental Office of Civil Rights, S-30, 400 7th St. SW, Room 10215, Washington, DC 20590, ☎ 202/366–4648, FAX 202/366–9371) for problems with surface transportation.

TRAVEL AGENCIES

In the United States, although the Americans with Disabilities Act requires that travel firms serve the needs of all travelers, some agencies specialize in working with people with disabilities.

➤ TRAVELERS WITH MOBILITY PROBLEMS: **Access Adventures** (✉ 206 Chestnut Ridge Rd., Rochester, NY 14624, ☎ 716/889–9096), run by a former physical-rehabilitation counselor. **Accessible Vans of the Rockies, Activity and Travel Agency** (✉ 2040 W. Hamilton Pl., Sheridan, CO 80110, ☎ 303/806–5047 or 888/837–0065, FAX 303/781–2329). **Care-Vacations** (✉ 5-5110 50th Ave., Leduc, Alberta T9E 6V4, ☎ 780/986–6404 or 780/986–8332) has group tours and is especially helpful with cruise vacations. **Flying Wheels**

Travel (✉ 143 W. Bridge St., Box 382, Owatonna, MN 55060, ☎ 507/451–5005 or 800/535–6790, FAX 507/451–1685). **Hinsdale Travel Service** (✉ 201 E. Ogden Ave., Suite 100, Hinsdale, IL 60521, ☎ 630/325–1335).

➤ TRAVELERS WITH DEVELOPMENTAL DISABILITIES: **New Directions** (✉ 5276 Hollister Ave., Suite 207, Santa Barbara, CA 93111, ☎ 805/967–2841 or 888/967–2841, FAX 805/964–7344). **Sprout** (✉ 893 Amsterdam Ave., New York, NY 10025, ☎ 212/222–9575 or 888/222–9575, FAX 212/222–9768).

DISCOUNTS & DEALS

Be a smart shopper and **compare all your options** before making decisions. A plane ticket bought with a promotional coupon from travel clubs, coupon books, and direct-mail offers may not be cheaper than the least expensive fare from a discount ticket agency. And always keep in mind that what you get is just as important as what you save.

DISCOUNT RESERVATIONS

To save money **look into discount-reservations services** with toll-free numbers, which use their buying power to get a better price on hotels, airline tickets, even car rentals. When booking a room, always **call the hotel's local toll-free number** (if one is available) rather than the central reservations number—you'll often get a better price. Always ask about special packages or corporate rates.

➤ AIRLINE TICKETS: ☎ **800/FLY–4–LESS.** ☎ **800/FLY–ASAP.**

➤ HOTEL ROOMS: **Accommodations Express** (☎ 800/444–7666). **Central Reservation Service (CRS)** (☎ 800/548–3311). **Hotel Reservations Network** (☎ 800/964–6835). **Players Express Vacations** (☎ 800/458–6161). **Quickbook** (☎ 800/789–9887). **Room Finders USA** (☎ 800/473–7829). **RMC Travel** (☎ 800/245–5738). **Steigenberger Reservation Service** (☎ 800/223–5652).

PACKAGE DEALS

Don't confuse packages and guided tours. When you buy a package, you travel on your own, just as though you had planned the trip yourself.

Fly/drive packages, which combine airfare and car rental, are often a good deal. In cities, ask the local visitor's bureau about hotel packages that include tickets to major museum exhibits or other special events.

GAY & LESBIAN TRAVEL

➤ LOCAL PUBLICATIONS: *Seattle Gay News* (☎ 206/324–4297). *Xtra West* (☎ 604/684–9696) for Vancouver.

➤ GAY- AND LESBIAN-FRIENDLY TRAVEL AGENCIES: **Different Roads Travel** (✉ 8383 Wilshire Blvd., Suite 902, Beverly Hills, CA 90211, ☎ 323/651–5557 or 800/429–8747, FAX 323/651–3678). **Kennedy Travel** (✉ 314 Jericho Turnpike, Floral Park, NY 11001, ☎ 516/352–4888 or 800/237–7433, FAX 516/354–8849). **Now Voyager** (✉ 4406 18th St., San Francisco, CA 94114, ☎ 415/626–1169 or 800/255–6951, FAX 415/626–8626). **Yellowbrick Road** (✉ 1500 W. Balmoral Ave., Chicago, IL 60640, ☎ 773/561–1800 or 800/642–2488, FAX 773/561–4497). **Skylink Travel and Tour** (✉ 1006 Mendocino Ave., Santa Rosa, CA 95401, ☎ 707/546–9888 or 800/225–5759, FAX 707/546–9891), serving lesbian travelers.

HOLIDAYS

Major national U.S. holidays include New Year's Day (Jan. 1); Martin Luther King, Jr., Day (3rd Mon. in Jan.); Presidents' Day (3rd Mon. in Feb.); Memorial Day (last Mon. in May); Independence Day (July 4); Labor Day (1st Mon. in Sept.); Thanksgiving Day (4th Thurs. in Nov.); Christmas Eve and Christmas Day (Dec. 24 and 25); and New Year's Eve (Dec. 31).

In Canada, the national holidays for 2000 are: New Year's Day, Good Friday (April 21), Easter Monday (April 24), Victoria Day (4th Mon. in May), Canada Day (July 1), Labour Day (1st Mon. in Sept.), Thanksgiving (2nd Mon. in Oct.), Remembrance Day (November 11), Christmas (December 25), and Boxing Day (December 26).

British Columbia Day (1st Mon. in Aug.) is a provincial holiday.

SMART TRAVEL TIPS A TO Z

INSURANCE

The most useful travel insurance plan is a comprehensive policy that includes coverage for trip cancellation and interruption, default, trip delay, and medical expenses (with a waiver for preexisting conditions).

Without insurance you will lose all or most of your money if you cancel your trip, regardless of the reason. Default insurance covers you if your tour operator, airline, or cruise line goes out of business. Trip-delay covers expenses that arise because of bad weather or mechanical delays. Study the fine print when comparing policies.

Always **buy travel policies directly from the insurance company**; if you buy it from a cruise line, airline, or tour operator that goes out of business you probably will not be covered for the agency or operator's default, a major risk. Before you make any purchase **review your existing health and home-owner's policies** to find what they cover away from home.

➤ TRAVEL INSURERS: In the U.S. Access America (✉ 6600 W. Broad St., Richmond, VA 23230, ☎ 804/285–3300 or 800/284–8300), **Travel Guard International** (✉ 1145 Clark St., Stevens Point, WI 54481, ☎ 715/345–0505 or 800/826–1300). In Canada **Voyager Insurance** (✉ 44 Peel Center Dr., Brampton, Ontario L6T 4M8, ☎ 905/791–8700; 800/668–4342 in Canada).

➤ INSURANCE INFORMATION: In the U.K. the **Association of British Insurers** (✉ 51–55 Gresham St., London EC2V 7HQ, ☎ 020/7600–3333, FAX 020/7696–8999). In Australia the **Insurance Council of Australia** (☎ 03/9614–1077, FAX 03/9614–7924).

LODGING

The lodgings we list are the cream of the crop in each price category. We always list the facilities that are available—but we don't specify whether they cost extra: when pricing accommodations, always ask what's included and what costs extra. Properties indicated by an ✕🏠 are lodging establishments whose restaurant warrants a special trip.

Assume that hotels operate on the European Plan (EP, with no meals) unless we specify that they use the Continental Plan (CP, with a Continental breakfast daily), Modified American Plan (MAP, with breakfast and dinner daily), or the Full American Plan (FAP, with all meals).

APARTMENT RENTALS

If you want a home base that's roomy enough for a family and comes with cooking facilities, **consider a furnished rental.** These can save you money, especially if you're traveling with a group. Home-exchange directories sometimes list rentals as well as exchanges.

➤ INTERNATIONAL AGENTS: **Europa-Let/Tropical Inn-Let** (✉ 92 N. Main St., Ashland, OR 97520, ☎ 541/482–5806 or 800/462–4486, FAX 541/482–0660). **Hometours International** (✉ Box 11503, Knoxville, TN 37939, ☎ 423/690–8484 or 800/367–4668). **Interhome** (✉ 1990 N.E. 163rd St., Suite 110, Miami Beach, FL 33162, ☎ 305/940–2299 or 800/882–6864, FAX 305/940–2911). **Rent-a-Home International** (✉ 7200 34th Ave. NW, Seattle, WA 98117, ☎ 206/789–9377, FAX 206/789–9379). **Vacation Home Rentals Worldwide** (✉ 235 Kensington Ave., Norwood, NJ 07648, ☎ 201/767–9393 or 800/633–3284, FAX 201/767–5510). **Hideaways International** (✉ 767 Islington St., Portsmouth, NH 03801, ☎ 603/430–4433 or 800/843–4433, FAX 603/430–4444; membership $99).

B&BS

➤ RESERVATION SERVICES: **Bed & Breakfast Association of Seattle** (☎ 206/547–1020). **Best Canadian Bed & Breakfast Network** (✉ 1064 Balfour Ave., Vancouver, BC V6H 1X1, ☎ 604/738–7207). **Northwest Bed & Breakfast Reservation Service** (✉ 610 S.W. Broadway, Portland, OR 97205, ☎ 503/243–7616). **Traveller's Bed & Breakfast** (✉ Box 492, Mercer Island, WA 98040, ☎ 206/232–2345). In the United Kingdom: **American Bed & Breakfast, Inter-Bed Network** (✉ 31 Ernest Rd., Colchester, Essex CO7 9LQ, ☎ 0206/223162).

HOME EXCHANGES

If you would like to exchange your home for someone else's, **join a home-exchange organization,** which will send you its updated listings of available exchanges for a year and will include your own listing in at least one of them. It's up to you to make specific arrangements.

➤ EXCHANGE CLUBS: **HomeLink International** (✉ Box 650, Key West, FL 33041, ☎ 305/294–7766 or 800/638–3841, FAX 305/294–1448; $88 per year). **Intervac U.S.** (✉ Box 590504, San Francisco, CA 94159, ☎ 800/756–4663, FAX 415/435–7440; $83 per year).

HOSTELS

No matter what your age you can **save on lodging costs by staying at hostels.** In some 5,000 locations in more than 70 countries around the world, Hostelling International (HI), the umbrella group for a number of national youth-hostel associations, offers single-sex, dorm-style beds and, at many hostels, couples rooms and family accommodations. Membership in any HI national hostel association, open to travelers of all ages, allows you to stay in HI-affiliated hostels at member rates (one-year membership is about $25 for adults; hostels run about $10–$25 per night). Members also have priority if the hostel is full; they're eligible for discounts around the world, even on rail and bus travel in some countries.

➤ ORGANIZATIONS: **Australian Youth Hostel Association** (✉ 10 Mallett St., Camperdown, NSW 2050, ☎ 02/9565–1699, FAX 02/9565–1325). **Hostelling International—American Youth Hostels** (✉ 733 15th St. NW, Suite 840, Washington, DC 20005, ☎ 202/783–6161, FAX 202/783–6171). **Hostelling International—Canada** (✉ 400–205 Catherine St., Ottawa, Ontario K2P 1C3, ☎ 613/237–7884, FAX 613/237–7868). **Youth Hostel Association of England and Wales** (✉ Trevelyan House, 8 St. Stephen's Hill, St. Albans, Hertfordshire AL1 2DY, ☎ 01727/855215 or 01727/845047, FAX 01727/844126). **Youth Hostels Association of New Zealand** (✉ Box 436, Christchurch, New Zealand, ☎ 03/379–9970, FAX 03/365–4476).

Membership in the U.S. $25, in Canada C$26.75, in the U.K. £9.30, in Australia $44, in New Zealand $24.

HOTELS

Many big-city hotels offer special weekend rates, sometimes up to 50% off regular prices. However, these deals are usually not extended during peak summer months, when hotels are normally full. In Canada, rates can drop by as much as 50% in the winter. All hotels listed have private bath unless otherwise noted.

➤ TOLL-FREE NUMBERS: **Best Western** (☎ 800/528–1234). **Choice** (☎ 800/221–2222). **Clarion** (☎ 800/252–7466). **Colony** (☎ 800/777–1700). **Comfort** (☎ 800/228–5150). **Days Inn** (☎ 800/325–2525). **Doubletree and Red Lion Hotels** (☎ 800/222–8733). **Embassy Suites** (☎ 800/362–2779). **Four Seasons** (☎ 800/332–3442). **Hilton** (☎ 800/445–8667). **Holiday Inn** (☎ 800/465–4329). **Howard Johnson** (☎ 800/654–4656). **Hyatt Hotels & Resorts** (☎ 800/233–1234). **Inter-Continental** (☎ 800/327–0200). **Marriott** (☎ 800/228–9290). **Le Meridien** (☎ 800/543–4300). **Nikko Hotels International** (☎ 800/645–5687). **Omni** (☎ 800/843–6664). **Quality Inn** (☎ 800/228–5151). **Radisson** (☎ 800/333–3333). **Ramada** (☎ 800/228–2828). **Renaissance Hotels & Resorts** (☎ 800/468–3571). **Ritz-Carlton** (☎ 800/241–3333). **Sheraton** (☎ 800/325–3535). **Sleep Inn** (☎ 800/221–2222). **West Coast Hotels/Coast Hotels** (☎ 800/426–0670) **Westin Hotels & Resorts** (☎ 800/228–3000). **Wyndham Hotels & Resorts** (☎ 800/822–4200).

MOTELS/MOTOR INNS

Chain-run motels and motor inns can be found throughout the Pacific Northwest. Some of these establishments offer basic facilities; others provide restaurants, swimming pools, and other amenities.

➤ MAJOR CHAINS: **Days Inn** (☎ 800/325–2525). **La Quinta Inns** (☎ 800/531–5900). **Motel 6** (☎ 800/440–6000). **Quality Inns** (☎ 800/228–5151). **Shilo Inns** (☎ 800/222–2244). **Super 8 Motels** (☎ 800/848–8888). **Travelodge** (☎ 800/255–3050).

SMART TRAVEL TIPS A TO Z

➤ REGIONAL CHAINS: **Cavanaugh's** (☎ 800/843–4667). **Nendel's** (☎ 800/547–0106). **Sandman Inns** (☎ 800/726–3626).

MAIL & SHIPPING

POSTAL RATES

Postage rates vary for different classes of mail and destinations. Check with the local post office for rates before mailing a letter or parcel. At press time, it cost 33¢ to mail a standard letter anywhere within the United States. Mail to Canada costs 52¢ per first ounce and 12¢ for each additional half-ounce. Mail to Great Britain and other foreign countries costs 60¢ for the first half ounce, and 40¢ for each additional half ounce.

First-class rates in Canada are 46¢ for mail of up to 30 grams delivered within Canada in a standard-sized envelope, 55¢ for up to 30 grams delivered to the United States, 80¢ for 30 to 50 grams. International mail and postcards run 95¢ for up to 20 grams, $1.45 for 20–50 grams.

RECEIVING MAIL

Visitors can have letters or parcels sent to them while they are traveling by using the following address: Name of addressee, c/o General Delivery, Main Post Office, City and State/Province, U.S./Canada, Zip Code (U.S.) or Postal Code (Canada). Contact the nearest post office for further details. Any item mailed to "General Delivery" must be picked up by the addressee in person within 15 days or it will be returned to the sender.

MONEY MATTERS

Prices throughout this guide are given for adults. Substantially reduced fees are almost always available for children, students, and senior citizens. For information on taxes, *see* Taxes, *below*.

ATMS

Cirrus (☎ 800/424–7787). **Plus** (☎ 800/843–7587 for locations in the U.S. and Canada, or visit your local bank).

BANKS

In general, U.S. and Canadian banks will not cash a personal check for you unless you have an account at that bank (it doesn't have to be at that branch). Only in major cities are large bank branches equipped to exchange foreign currencies (though U.S. currency is widely accepted in Canada). Therefore, it's best to rely on credit cards, cash machines, and traveler's checks to handle expenses while you're traveling.

CREDIT CARDS

Throughout this guide, the following abbreviations are used: AE, American Express; D, Discover; DC, Diners Club; MC, Master Card; and V, Visa.

➤ REPORTING LOST CARDS: To report lost or stolen credit cards, call the following toll-free numbers: **American Express** (☎ 800/327–2177); **Discover Card** (☎ 800/347–2683); **Diners Club** (☎ 800/234–6377); **Master Card** (☎ 800/307–7309); and **Visa** (☎ 800/847–2911).

CURRENCY

The United States and Canada both use the same currency denominations—dollars and cents—although each currency has a different value on the world market. At press time, one Canadian dollar was worth U.S. 70¢. One U.S. dollar was worth $1.40 Canadian. In this book, prices in Canada are always quoted in Canadian dollars (C$). U.S. currency is widely accepted in Canadian cities and tourist resorts, but you'll get a better exchange rate at a bank. Canadian money is not accepted in the United States.

EXCHANGING MONEY

For the most favorable rates, **change money through banks.** Although fees charged for ATM transactions may be higher abroad than at home, Cirrus and Plus exchange rates are excellent because they are based on wholesale rates offered only by major banks. You won't do as well at exchange booths in airports or rail and bus stations, in hotels, in restaurants, or in stores, although you may find their hours more convenient. To avoid lines at airport exchange booths, **get a bit of local currency before you leave home.**

➤ EXCHANGE SERVICES: **Chase *Currency To Go*** (☎ 800/935–9935; 935–

9935 in NY, NJ, and CT). **International Currency Express** (☎ 888/842–0880 on the East Coast, 888/278–6628 on the West Coast). **Thomas Cook Currency Services** (☎ 800/287–7362 for telephone orders and retail locations).

TRAVELER'S CHECKS

Do you need traveler's checks? It depends on where you're headed. If you're going to rural areas and small towns, go with cash; traveler's checks are best used in cities. Lost or stolen checks can usually be replaced within 24 hours. To ensure a speedy refund, buy your own traveler's checks—don't let someone else pay for them: irregularities like this can cause delays. The person who bought the checks should make the call to request a refund.

NATIONAL PARKS

Look into discount passes to save money on park entrance fees. The Golden Eagle Pass ($50) gets you and your companions free admission to all parks for one year. (Camping and parking are extra). Both the Golden Age Passport ($10), for those 62 and older, and the Golden Access Passport (free), for travelers with disabilities, entitle holders to free entry to all national parks, plus 50% off fees for the use of many park facilities and services. You must show proof of age and of U.S. citizenship or permanent residency (such as a U.S. passport, driver's license, or birth certificate) and, if requesting Golden Access, proof of disability. All three passes are available at all national park entrances where entrance fees are charged. Golden Eagle and Golden Access passes are also available by mail.

If you plan to visit several parks in British Columbia, you may be able to **save money on park fees by buying a multipark pass,** including the Western Canada Annual Pass, available to Canadians and non-Canadians. Parks Canada is decentralized, so it's best to contact the park you plan to visit for information. You can buy passes at the parks covered by the pass.

➤ PASSES BY MAIL: **National Park Service** (⊠ National Capitol Area

Office, 1100 Ohio Dr. SW, Washington, DC 20242, ☎ 202/208–4747). **Parks Canada** (⊠ 220 4th Ave. SE, Room 552, Calgary T2G 4X3, ☎ 403/292–4401).

OUTDOOR ACTIVITIES & SPORTS

FISHING

➤ INFORMATION/LICENSES: **Department of Fisheries and Oceans** (⊠ Recreational Fisheries Division, 555 W. Hastings St., Suite 400, Vancouver, BC V6B 5G3, ☎ 604/666–2828) for saltwater fishing. **British Columbia Department of Environment and Lands** (⊠ 10470–152nd St., Surrey, BC V3R 0Y3, ☎ 604/582–5200) for freshwater fishing. **Washington Department of Fish and Wildlife** (⊠ 600 Capitol Way N, Olympia, WA 98501, ☎ 360/902–2200) for all types of fishing.

HIKING

National Parks and Forests Outdoor Recreation Information Center(⊠ 222 Yale Ave. N, Seattle, WA 98109, ☎ 206/470–4060) has maps of regional trails.

SCUBA DIVING

The crystal-clear waters of Puget Sound and coastal British Columbia present excellent opportunities for scuba diving and underwater photography.

➤ RENTALS & INFORMATION: **Underwater Sports** (⊠ 10545 Aurora St., Seattle, WA 98133, ☎ 206/362–3310). **The Diving Locker** (⊠ 2745 W. 4th. Ave., Vancouver, BC V6K 1P9, ☎ 604/736–2681) offers lessons, excursions, and rentals.

SKIING

In addition to a number of commercial downhill and cross-country ski areas in the Cascade range east of Seattle, Washington operates a system of more than 40 **SnoParks.** The cost to ski these groomed cross-country trails within state parks is $7 per day and $20 for a seasonal pass. British Columbia has more than 40 downhill and cross-country ski resorts, including the top-rated **Whistler** resort near Vancouver.

➤ PASSES & INFORMATION: **Office of Winter Recreation, Parks and Recre-**

SMART TRAVEL TIPS A TO Z

ation Commission (✉ 7150 Cleanwater La., Box 42650, Olympia, WA 98504, ☎ 360/902–8500).

PACKING

Summer days in the Pacific Northwest are warm but evenings can cool off substantially. Your best bet is to **dress in layers**—sweatshirts, sweaters, and jackets are removed or put on as the day progresses. Chances are **you'll need rain gear,** too, especially if you're visiting in the winter. If you plan to explore the region's cities on foot, or if you choose to hike along mountain trails or beaches, bring comfortable walking shoes. Dining out is usually an informal affair, although some restaurants prefer a jacket and tie for men and dresses for women.

If you plan on hiking or camping during the summer, insect repellent is a must.

In your carry-on luggage **bring an extra pair of eyeglasses or contact lenses** and **enough of any medication you take** to last the entire trip. You may also want your doctor to write a spare prescription using the drug's generic name, since brand names may vary from country to country. In luggage to be checked, **never pack prescription drugs or valuables.** To avoid customs delays, carry medications in their original packaging. And don't forget to copy down and carry addresses of offices that handle refunds of lost traveler's checks.

CHECKING LUGGAGE

How many carry-on bags you can bring with you is up to the airline. Most allow two, but not always, so make sure that everything you carry aboard will fit under your seat, and get to the gate early. Note that if you have a seat at the back of the plane, you'll probably board first, while the overhead bins are still empty.

If you are flying internationally, note that baggage allowances may be determined not by piece but by weight—generally 88 pounds (40 kilograms) in first class, 66 pounds (30 kilograms) in business class, and 44 pounds (20 kilograms) in economy.

Airline liability for baggage is limited to $1,250 per person on flights within the United States. On international flights it amounts to $9.07 per pound or $20 per kilogram for checked baggage (roughly $640 per 70-pound bag) and $400 per passenger for unchecked baggage. You can buy additional coverage at check-in for about $10 per $1,000 of coverage, but it excludes a rather extensive list of items, shown on your airline ticket.

Before departure **itemize your bags' contents** and their worth, and label the bags with your name, address, and phone number. (If you use your home address, cover it so that potential thieves can't see it readily.) Inside each bag **pack a copy of your itinerary.** At check-in **make sure that each bag is correctly tagged** with the destination airport's three-letter code. If your bags arrive damaged or fail to arrive at all, file a written report with the airline before leaving the airport.

PASSPORTS & VISAS

When traveling internationally, **carry a passport even if you don't need one** (it's always the best form of I.D.), and make **two photocopies of the data page** (one for someone at home and another for you, carried separately from your passport). If you lose your passport, promptly call the nearest embassy or consulate and the local police.

U.S. CITIZENS

Citizens and legal residents of the United States do not need a passport or a visa to enter Canada, but proof of citizenship (a birth certificate or valid passport) and photo identification may be requested. Naturalized U.S. residents should carry their naturalization certificate or "green card." U.S. residents entering Canada from a third country must have a valid passport, naturalization certificate, or "green card."

CANADIAN CITIZENS

A passport is not required for entry into the United States, but some proof of Canadian citizenship, such as a birth certificate, may be required.

U.K. CITIZENS

Citizens of the United Kingdom need only a valid passport to enter Canada for stays of up to 90 days.

British citizens need a valid passport to enter the United States. If you are staying for fewer than 90 days on vacation, with a return or onward ticket, you probably will not need a visa. However, you will need to fill out the Visa Waiver Form, 1-94W, supplied by the airline.

➤ U.K. CITIZENS: **U.S. Embassy Visa Information Line** (☎ 01891/200290; calls cost 49p per minute, 39p per minute cheap rate) for U.S. visa information. **U.S. Embassy Visa Branch** (✉ 5 Upper Grosvenor Sq., London W1A 1AE) for U.S. visa information; send a self-addressed, stamped envelope. Write the **U.S. Consulate General** (✉ Queen's House, Queen St., Belfast BTI 6EO) if you live in Northern Ireland. Write the **Office of Australia Affairs** (✉ 59th fl., MLC Centre, 19-29 Martin Pl., Sydney NSW 2000) if you live in Australia. Write the **Office of New Zealand Affairs** (✉ 29 Fitzherbert Terr., Thorndon, Wellington) if you live in New Zealand.

PASSPORT OFFICES

The best time to apply for a passport or to renew is during the fall and winter. Before any trip, check your passport's expiration date, and, if necessary, renew it as soon as possible.

➤ AUSTRALIAN CITIZENS: **Australian Passport Office** (☎ 131–232).

➤ NEW ZEALAND CITIZENS: **New Zealand Passport Office** (☎ 04/494–0700 for information on how to apply; 04/474–8000 or 0800/225–050 in New Zealand for information on applications already submitted).

➤ U.K. CITIZENS: **London Passport Office** (☎ 0990/210410) for fees and documentation requirements and to request an emergency passport.

SENIOR-CITIZEN TRAVEL

To qualify for age-related discounts **mention your senior-citizen status up front** when booking hotel reservations (not when checking out) and before you're seated in restaurants (not when

paying the bill). When renting a car ask about promotional car-rental discounts, which can be cheaper than senior-citizen rates.

➤ EDUCATIONAL PROGRAMS: **Elderhostel** (✉ 75 Federal St., 3rd fl., Boston, MA 02110, ☎ 877/426–8056, FAX 877/426–2166).

STUDENTS IN SEATTLE AND VANCOUVER

➤ STUDENT IDs & SERVICES: **Council on International Educational Exchange** (CIEE, ✉ 205 E. 42nd St., 14th fl., New York, NY 10017, ☎ 212/822–2600 or 888/268–6245, FAX 212/822–2699) for mail orders only, in the U.S. **Travel Cuts** (✉ 187 College St., Toronto, Ontario M5T 1P7, ☎ 416/979–2406 or 800/667–2887) in Canada.

TAXES

SALES TAX

The sales tax in Washington varies from 7% to 8.6%. Seattle adds 5% to the rate for hotel rooms. In British Columbia, consumers pay a 7% sales tax. The tax does not apply to food, ferries, or accommodations. Taxes of 10% are, however, levied on accommodations and alcoholic beverages sold in bars and restaurants.

GST

Canada's Goods and Services Tax (GST) is 7%, applicable on virtually every purchase except basic groceries and a small number of other items. Visitors to Canada may claim a full rebate of the GST on any goods taken out of the country as well as on short-term accommodations. Some duty-free shops will provide instant cash rebates up to $500 for U.S. residents only, and some vendors will not charge GST on goods shipped directly to the purchaser's home. Otherwise, rebates can be claimed by mail.

Always **save your original receipts** from stores and hotels, and **be sure the date and the name and address of the establishment are shown on the receipt.** Handwritten receipts must be marked paid, or be supported with a credit card slip. You must also have your receipts stamped with a **proof of export stamp** at the border crossing or airport as you leave the country. At press time the system was still being phased in, and overseas visitors may be asked to submit travel tickets until the system export stamps are more widely available.

Original receipts are not returned unless requested. The total value of each receipt before taxes must be at least $50, and the total value of receipts submitted with each application must be at least $200 before taxes (i.e. the GST claimed must add up to at least $14). Rebate forms can be obtained at airports and duty-free shops, by writing to Revenue Canada, or on Revenue Canada's web site at www.rc.gc.ca/visitors.

➤ INFORMATION: **Revenue Canada** (✉ Visitor Rebate Program, Summerside Tax Centre, Summerside, Prince Edward Island C1N 6C6, ☎ 800/ 668–4748 in Canada; 902/432–5608 from outside of Canada).

TELEPHONES

COUNTRY CODES

All U.S. and Canadian telephone numbers consist of 10 digits—the three-digit area code, followed by a seven-digit local number. If you're calling a number from another area code, dial "1" then all 10 digits. For many calls in Washington State and British Columbia, even within the same area code you need to dial "1" then all 10 digits (the exceptions include numbers within the 360 area code, for which you need only dial "1" plus the seven-digit number). A map of area codes is printed in the front of most local telephone directories; throughout this book, we have listed each phone number in full, including its area code.

Four special prefixes, "800," "888," "877," and "900," are not area codes but indicators of particular kinds of service. "800," "888," and "877" numbers can be dialed free from anywhere in the country—usually they are prepaid commercial lines that make it easier for consumers to obtain information, products, or services. The "900" numbers charge you for making the call and generally offer some kind of entertainment, such as horoscope readings, sports scores, or sexually suggestive conver-

sations. These services can be very expensive, so **know what you're getting into before you dial a "900" number.**

CREDIT-CARD CALLS

U.S. and Canadian telephone credit cards are not like the magnetic cards used in some European countries, which pay for calls in advance; they simply represent an account that lets you charge a call to your home or business phone. On any phone, you can make a credit-card call by punching in your individual account number or by telling the operator that number. Certain specially marked pay phones (usually found in airports, hotel lobbies, and so on) can be used only for credit-card calls. To get a credit card, contact your long-distance telephone carrier, such as AT&T, MCI, or Sprint.

DIRECTORY & OPERATOR INFORMATION

For assistance from an operator, dial "0." To find out a telephone number, call directory assistance, 555–1212 in every locality. These calls are free even from a pay phone. In Canada, dial 1–area code–555–1212; there is a 95¢ charge for each number found. If you want to charge a long-distance call to the person you're calling, you can call collect by dialing "0" instead of "1" before the 10-digit number, and an operator or a computer will come on the line to assist you (the party you're calling, however, has the right to refuse the call).

INTERNATIONAL CALLS

International calls can be direct-dialed from most phones; dial "011," followed by the country code and then the local number (the front pages of many local telephone directories include a list of overseas country codes). To have an operator assist you, dial "0" and ask for the overseas operator. The country code for Australia is 61; New Zealand, 64; and the United Kingdom, 44.

LONG-DISTANCE CALLS

Competitive long-distance carriers make calling within the United States and Canada relatively convenient and let you avoid hotel surcharges. By dialing an 800 number, you can get connected to the long-distance company of your choice.

➤ LONG-DISTANCE CARRIERS: **AT&T** (☎ 800/225–5288). **MCI** (☎ 800/888–8000). **Sprint** (☎ 800/366–2255).

PUBLIC PHONES

Local calls from pay telephones in Washington State and Canada cost 25¢. Charge phones are also found in many locations, including airports and some shopping malls. These phones can be used to charge a call to a telephone-company credit card, your home phone, or the party you are calling: you do not need to deposit 25¢.

TIPPING

Tips and service charges are usually not automatically added to a bill in the United States or Canada. If service is satisfactory, customers generally give waiters, waitresses, taxi drivers, barbers, hairdressers, and so forth, a tip of from 15% to 20% of the total bill. Bellhops, doormen, and porters at airports and railway stations are generally tipped $1 for each item of luggage.

TOURS & PACKAGES

On a prepackaged tour or independent vacation everything is prearranged so you'll spend less time planning—and often get it all at a good price.

BOOKING WITH AN AGENT

Travel agents are excellent resources. But it's a good idea to collect brochures from several agencies because some agents' suggestions may be influenced by relationships with tour and package firms that reward them for volume sales. If you have a special interest **find an agent with expertise in that area**; ASTA (☞ Travel Agencies, *below*) has a database of specialists worldwide.

Make sure your travel agent knows the accommodations and other services of the place they're recommending. Ask about the hotel's location, room size, beds, and whether it has a pool, room service, or programs for children, if you care about these. Has your agent been there in person or sent others whom you can contact?

Do some homework on your own, too: local tourism boards can provide information about lesser-known and small-niche operators, some of which may sell only direct.

BUYER BEWARE

Each year consumers are stranded or lose their money when tour operators—even large ones with excellent reputations—go out of business. So **check out the operator.** Ask several travel agents about its reputation, and try to **book with a company that has a consumer-protection program.** (Look for information in the company's brochure.) In the United States, members of the National Tour Association and United States Tour Operators Association are required to set aside funds to cover your payments and travel arrangements in case the company defaults. It's also a good idea to choose a company that participates in the American Society of Travel Agent's Tour Operator Program (TOP); ASTA will act as mediator in any disputes between you and your tour operator.

Remember that the more your package or tour includes the better you can predict the ultimate cost of your vacation. Make sure you know exactly what is covered, and **beware of hidden costs.** Are taxes, tips, and transfers included? Entertainment and excursions? These can add up.

➤ TOUR-OPERATOR RECOMMENDATIONS: **American Society of Travel Agents** (☞ Travel Agencies, *below*). **National Tour Association** (NTA, ✉ 546 E. Main St., Lexington, KY 40508, ☎ 606/226–4444 or 800/682–8886). **United States Tour Operators Association** (USTOA, ✉ 342 Madison Ave., Suite 1522, New York, NY 10173, ☎ 212/599–6599 or 800/468–7862, FAX 212/599–6744).

THEME TRIPS

The companies listed below provide multiday tours in Seattle and Vancouver. Additional local or regionally based companies that have different-length trips with these themes are listed in each chapter, either with information about the town or in the A to Z section that concludes the chapter.

SMART TRAVEL TIPS A TO Z

➤ ADVENTURE: **American Wilderness Experience** (☎ 303/444–2622 or 800/444–0099). **Canadian Adventure Tours** (☎ 604/938–0727). **Wells Gray Adventures** (☎ 250/587–6444 or 888/754–8735).

➤ FISHING: **Fishing International** (✉ Box 2132, Santa Rosa, CA 95405, ☎ 800/950–4242). **Oak Bay Marine Group** (☎ 250/598–3366 or 800/663–7090).

➤ WALKING/HIKING: **Country Walkers** (☎ 802/244–1387 or 800/464–9255).

TRAIN TRAVEL

Amtrak, the U.S. passenger rail system, has daily service to Seattle from the Midwest and California. The *Empire Builder* takes a northern route from Chicago to Seattle. The *Coast Starlight* begins in southern California, makes stops throughout western Oregon and Washington, and terminates its route in Seattle. The once-daily *Mt. Baker International* takes a highly scenic coastal route from Seattle to Vancouver. High-speed train service between Eugene, Oregon, and Vancouver, with stops in Portland, Seattle, and elsewhere, is tentatively scheduled to begin in late 1999 or early 2000.

Canada's passenger service, **VIA Rail Canada,** operates transcontinental routes on the *Canadian* three times weekly in each direction between eastern Canada and Vancouver.

➤ TRAIN INFORMATION: **Amtrak** (☎ 800/872–7245). **VIA Rail Canada** (☎ 800/561–3949 in the U.S.; 800/561–8630 in Canada).

WITHIN THE PACIFIC NORTHWEST

The Pacific Northwest has a number of scenic train routes in addition to those operated by Amtrak and VIA Rail Canada. The **Rocky Mountaineer** is a two-day all-daylight rail cruise that runs from May through October between Vancouver and the Canadian Rockies. There are two routes—one to Banff/Calgary and the other to Jasper—through landscapes considered to be the most spectacular in the world. An overnight hotel stop is made in Kamloops.

On Vancouver Island, **VIA Rail** runs the *E&N Railway* daily in summer and six times a week in winter from Victoria north to Courtenay. **BC Rail** operates daily service from its North Vancouver terminal to Whistler and thrice-weekly service to the town of Prince George. At Prince George it is possible to connect with VIA Rail's *Skeena* service east to Jasper and Alberta or west to Prince Rupert. BC Rail also operates two summertime (May–October) excursion trains along scenic Howe Sound: the *Royal Hudson* steam train and the *Pacific Starlight Dinner Train.*

➤ RAIL COMPANIES: **Rocky Mountaineer** (✉ Great Canadian Railtour Co., Ltd., 1150 Station St., 1st floor, Vancouver, BC V6A 2X7, ☎ 604/606–7245 in Vancouver; 800/665–7245 in the U.S. and elsewhere in Canada). **BC Rail** (✉ 1311 W. 1st St., North Vancouver, BC V7P 1A6, ☎ 604/984–5500 in Vancouver; 800/663–8238 in the U.S. and elsewhere in Canada). **VIA Rail** (☎ 800/561–3949 in the U.S.; 800/561–8630 in Canada).

DISCOUNT PASSES

VIA Rail Canada offers a **Canrailpass** that is good for 12 days of travel within 30 days. System-wide passes cost C$379 (from mid-October through May) and C$589 (from June to mid-October). Tickets can be purchased in the United States from a travel agent or upon arrival in Canada.

➤ INFORMATION: **VIA Rail** (☎ 800/561–3949 in the U.S.; 800/561–8630 in Canada).

TRAVEL AGENCIES

A good travel agent puts your needs first. Look for an agency that has been in business at least five years, emphasizes customer service, and has someone on staff who specializes in your destination. In addition **make sure the agency belongs to a professional trade organization.** The American Society of Travel Agents (ASTA), with 27,000 agents in some 170 countries, is the largest and most influential in the field. Operating under the motto "Integrity in Travel," it maintains and enforces a strict code of ethics and will step in to help mediate any agent-client disputes if necessary. ASTA also maintains a Web site that includes a directory of agents. (Note that if a travel agency is also acting as your tour operator *see* Buyer Beware *in* Tours & Packages, *above.*

➤ LOCAL AGENT REFERRALS: American Society of Travel Agents (ASTA, ☎ 800/965–2782 24-hr hot line, FAX 703/684–8319). Association of British Travel Agents (✉ 55–57 Newman St., London W1P 4AH, ☎ 020/7637–2444, FAX 020/7637–0713). Association of Canadian Travel Agents (✉ 1729 Bank St., Suite 201, Ottawa, Ontario K1V 7Z5, ☎ 613/521–0474, FAX 613/521–0805). Australian Federation of Travel Agents (✉ Level 3, 309 Pitt St., Sydney 2000, ☎ 02/9264–3299, FAX 02/9264–1085). Travel Agents' Association of New Zealand (✉ Box 1888, Wellington 10033, ☎ 04/499–0104, FAX 04/499–0786).

VISITOR INFORMATION

Also see Visitor Information *in* the A to Z sections at the end of the Seattle and Vancouver chapters, and the Essentials sections throughout the Side Trips from Seattle and Side Trips from Vancouver chapters.

➤ SEATTLE: **Visitors Information Center** (✉ Washington State Convention Center, 8th Ave. and Pike St., Seattle, WA 98104, ☎ 206/461–5840).

➤ VANCOUVER: **Vancouver Tourist Info Center** (✉ 200 Burrard St., Vancouver, BC V6C 3L6, ☎ 604/683–2000).

WEB SITES

Do **check out the World Wide Web** when you're planning. You'll find everything from up-to-date weather forecasts to virtual tours of famous cities. Fodor's Web site, www.fodors.com, is a great place to start your on-line travels. For more information specifically on Seattle and Vancouver, visit the following sites.

➤ BC FERRIES: This constantly updated site is invaluable if you're planning side trips to Vancouver Island or the Gulf Islands: www.bc-ferries.bc.ca

➤ DISCOVER VANCOUVER: The very useful Discover Vancouver site is a one-stop source for up-to-date events listings and dining, nightlife, and lodging options: www.discovervancouver.com

➤ GREATER VANCOUVER CONVENTION AND VISITORS BUREAU: The official site of the **Greater Vancouver Convention and Visitors Bureau** has useful trip planning information, information about side trips, and a searchable database of hotels, restaurants and tour operators: www.tourism-vancouver.org

➤ SEATTLE TIMES: The Web page of the *Seattle Times,* the city's biggest daily newspaper, carries news and features, plus dining and nightlife listings and reviews: www.seattle-times.com

➤ SEATTLE WEEKLY: The Web page of the *Seattle Weekly,* the city's leading alternative weekly, carries news and features, plus events information: www.seattleweekly.com

➤ SEATTLE CONVENTION AND VISITORS BUREAU: The official site of the **Seattle Convention and Visitors Bureau** carries events and other listings; you can type in your address and they'll mail you a visitor information packet: www.seeseattle.org

➤ VANCOUVER MAGAZINE: The site of the breathlessly enthusiastic *Vancouver Magazine* has up-to-date shopping, dining, arts and entertainment reviews, and a city guide aimed at newcomers. www.vanmag.com

➤ VICTORIA & VANCOUVER VISITORS' GUIDE: The **Victoria & Vancouver Visitors' Guide** site has much information about the city and southern Vancouver Island but no events listings: www.vits.bc.ca

WHEN TO GO

The Pacific Northwest's climate is the most enjoyable from June through September. Spring and fall are also excellent times to visit. The weather usually remains quite good, and the prices for accommodations, transportation, and tours can be lower (and the crowds much smaller) in the

SMART TRAVEL TIPS A TO Z

most popular destinations. In winter, the coastal rain turns to snow in the nearby mountains, making the region a skier's dream.

CLIMATE

Tempered by a warm Japan current and protected by the mountains from the extreme weather conditions found inland, the coastal regions of Washington and British Columbia experience a uniformly mild climate.

Average daytime summer highs are in the 70s; winter temperatures are generally in the 40s. Snow is uncommon in the lowland areas. If it does snow (usually in December or January), everything grinds to a halt.

The area's reputation for rain is somewhat misleading, as the amount of rainfall in the Pacific Northwest varies greatly from one locale to another. On the coast, 160 inches of rain falls annually, creating temperate rain forests. In some parts of central Washington and British Columbia, near-desert conditions prevail, with rainfall as low as 6 inches per year.

Seattle has an average of only 36 inches of rainfall a year—less than New York, Chicago, or Miami. The wetness, however, is concentrated during the winter months, when cloudy skies and drizzly weather persist. More than 75% of Seattle's annual precipitation occurs from October through March.

➤ FORECASTS: **Weather Channel Connection** (☎ 900/932–8437), 95¢ per minute from a Touch-Tone phone.

The following are average daily maximum and minimum temperatures for Seattle and Vancouver.

SEATTLE

Jan.	45F	7C	May	66F	19C	Sept.	69F	20C
	35	2		47	8		52	11
Feb.	50F	10C	June	70F	21C	Oct.	62F	16C
	37	3		52	11		47	8
Mar.	53F	12C	July	76F	24C	Nov.	51F	10C
	38	3		56	13		40	4
Apr.	59F	13C	Aug.	75F	24C	Dec.	47F	8C
	42	5		55	13		37	3

VANCOUVER

Jan.	41F	5C	May	63F	17C	Sept.	64F	18C
	32	0		46	8		50	10
Feb.	46F	8C	June	66F	19C	Oct.	57F	14C
	34	1		52	11		43	6
Mar.	48F	9C	July	72F	22C	Nov.	48F	9C
	36	2		55	13		37	3
Apr.	55F	13C	Aug.	72F	22C	Dec.	45F	7C
	41	5		55	13		34	1

1 DESTINATION: SEATTLE AND VANCOUVER

THE METROPOLITAN PACIFIC NORTHWEST

YOUR PLANE ARRIVED after dark, and you fought the ubiquitous traffic jam on your drive from the airport to your downtown hotel. But you had a good night's rest—interrupted only occasionally by a police or ambulance siren—and you wake to the happy trilling of birds. As you open your window, the sweet aroma of blossoms wafts into your room. At the foot of the hill, the golden morning sun skips over the rippling wavelets of a saltwater fjord. Above the homes of the far shore, the tall trees of an evergreen forest cover the slopes. Snowcapped peaks tower in the distance. A bald eagle soars by on stiff wings. Welcome to the metropolitan cities of the Pacific Northwest.

Both Vancouver and Seattle are bordered by water and ringed by forests and mountains. Even though their urban environs are home to several million people, wild nature is never far. It's as close as the shore, as near as an urban creek where salmon spawn in season, or a wooded ravine where coyotes or deer may hide. The shore side alders and wild blackberry tangles along Seattle's Lake Union (which is about as urban as a lake can get, with boatyards, restaurants, condos, and houseboats) provide shelter for sparrows, goldfinches, wrens, and sharpshinned hawks. Beavers gnaw on shade trees, river otters frolic in the water. Great blue herons, ducks, wild swans, and raccoons hang out in Vancouver's Stanley Park. (Vancouver is the only city where you can get panhandled by a raccoon.) Cougars and black bears occasionally show up on North shore trails.

Hardly any locals take note of bald eagles, beavers, or otters anymore, but you might want to call a local TV station if you meet a bear or mountain lion. You'll probably see it on the evening news. Orcas, too, still create a stir whenever a pod cruises past the Seattle waterfront. Even though this happens several times a year, expect traffic jams near waterfront vista points.

Residents in these two cities are very friendly, but they fudge at times, especially when it comes to the weather. It's rarely as cold and rainy as the natives claim in a ruse designed to discourage outsiders from moving here. Due to the maritime influence, the climate is surprisingly benign for such northerly cities. Some flowers are in bloom during every season: plum, cherry, magnolia, and daffodils in early spring, followed by tulips, rhododendrons, and peonies; summer is brightened by roses and lilies; pink and red camellia blossoms add a warm glow to chilly autumn days; winter is fragrant with sweet-scented heather.

While both cities are beautiful in all seasons, Vancouver does have the more spectacular setting. The mountains rise closer to the city, from the northern shore of Burrard Inlet. Seattle's mountains are a bit farther away, but you see a greater variety of them: Mount Baker and the craggy North Cascades to the north and east, Mount Rainier to the south, and the jagged crest of the Olympics across the sound to the west. Some of the mountains (Erie, Constitution, Lummi) are on islands. Seattle residents cherish those clear days when they can see Mount Rainier loom on the horizon and joyously tell each other "the Mountain is out."

Vancouver gets more rain than Seattle because it is closer to the coastal mountains but—curiously, even though this city is farther north—it can be quite a bit warmer than Seattle in winter. Those same mountains shield it from the frigid northeasters. Vancouver is almost always cooler in summer. Temperatures here rarely soar to the 80s, while they may exceed the 90s in Seattle. Seattle's mild climate allows palm trees to flourish. You may see a few stately specimens at the Ballard Locks, in the Arboretum, and in other places around town but Seattleites aren't much into palms. They violate the "northwest" or "evergreen" spirit of the city and smack of Southern California (a region generally loathed but much visited by locals). Vancouver, on the other hand, like Victoria and the southern Okanagan Valley, likes to think of itself as part of Canada's southern "Riviera." It encourages sidewalk and rooftop cafés as well as palm trees. One notable cluster grows just north of the English Bay beach.

Both cities started out as mill towns—Seattle in 1851 and Vancouver in 1867. Forests of tall trees were cut into lumber and shipped by steamer, bark, or schooner to Asia and the South Pacific. Seattle soon grew into the region's premier city. Vancouver didn't get a boost until the Canadian Pacific railway built the western terminal of its transcontinental rail line above the budding town's muddy waterfront in 1887. Today, of course, the railroad is no longer omnipresent, and the waterfront is no longer muddy.

Seattle missed out on the railroad at first. When the monopolistic Northern Pacific railroad chose Tacoma as its western terminal (because real estate came more cheaply), Seattleites began to build a railroad of their own in 1874, forcing the monopoly to relent. By the end of the 19th century both Seattle and Vancouver had developed the lucrative trade with Asia that they still maintain.

By World War II, Seattle's Boeing company was well on its way to becoming the world's most prolific producer of commercial aircraft. The company has dominated the local economy for more than 50 years. One could argue that Seattle is a Boeing company town despite the tumid presence of Microsoft in suburban Redmond. This became ominously clear in the early 1970s, when a major Boeing slump almost shut down the city. A local billboard illuminated the plight by asking, "Will the last person to leave Seattle please turn off the lights?"

Some economists now claim that Seattle is no longer that dependent on Boeing. But listen to the hysterical outburst on the evening news whenever Boeing announces layoffs, and you're bound to agree that the company is still perceived as the dominant local employer.

Vancouver is quite definitely not a company town. There's so little visible industry here that visitors may wonder how exactly all of these people make a living. But as vast warehouse complexes, office towers, and luxury hotels prove, Vancouver thrives on trade and tourism. Even so, Vancouver was a somewhat sleepy little metropolis until the mid-1980s, when an influx of immigrants from Hong Kong flooded the city and bolstered the local economy. Unlike earlier immigrants, this latest wave was flush with cash—lots of it. Real estate prices skyrocketed and, for a while, Vancouver had a boomtown atmosphere.

Things were moving so fast at times, you could leave for a month or two and come back to a changed city. Familiar corners where a strip mall or restaurant or car dealership once resided were replaced by office or condominium towers. Exciting new restaurants sprung up all over town and in the suburbs, more than even the most ardent connoisseur could possibly visit in a lifetime of happy eating. Because the wealthy new immigrants know good food and can afford the best, the import of specialty foods has soared. Suckling pig is now served in the fast food courts of shopping malls. You can even find such delicacies as snake soup or durian ice cream. Seattle, too, has experienced a restaurant revolution of sorts. But here much of it is dominated by upscale local or national chains (Wolfgang Puck, Jeremiah Towers, et al).

Both cities have large ethnic populations, but Seattle's tends to be confined to neighborhoods on the southern edge of downtown, in the Central District and in West Seattle. Vancouver's has burst the boundaries of Chinatown and "Little Punjab" and can be found all over the city. Chinese shops and restaurants can be found all over Vancouver and its suburbs (there are several ultramodern, all-Chinese shopping malls), and Sikh temples rise above many neighborhoods, from east Vancouver south to Surrey. In Seattle you have to head to the International District south of downtown to buy the ingredients for an authentic Asian dinner. In Vancouver, you're not surprised to discover a Chinese grocery wedged between a hallal butcher and German bakery.

Vancouver, founded by staid British empire builders, is perhaps a bit more sedate than Seattle, which was founded by Yankee adventurers. Seattle is more high-spirited, with a good (occasionally wacky) sense of humor. Look for the Fremont Troll, a giant concrete sculpture of that mythical creature, under the northern end of the Aurora Bridge, where it munches on a real VW Beetle. You might also want to check out the amusing statue of a Neanderthal-like family ardently watching TV outside the King TV studios on Dexter Avenue.

The countryside surrounding both Seattle and Vancouver is beautifully varied and invites travelers to explore. To the west, beyond the waters of the Salish Sea, the islands of Puget Sound, the San Juans, and the Gulf Islands beckon. Farther west lie the Olympic Peninsula and Vancouver Island with their mountains, surf-swept coastline, fjords, rain forests, and First Nations villages. To the east loom the Cascades with their rugged peaks, wildflower meadows, lakes, waterfalls, and ski runs. Best of all, even though much of this countryside is very rugged, it is traversed by modern highways. Nor is it unmitigated wilderness, for most regions have comfortable inns to lodge and feed visitors, and enough natural and historical attractions to keep curious minds occupied.

There's lots more to see and do in Seattle and Vancouver and the surrounding islands, coast, and countryside. But don't take anyone's word for it. Come and see for yourself. Every morning may be as special as that first one.

–John Doerper

WHAT'S WHERE

Seattle Area

Seattle, justly celebrated for its laid-back lifestyle, is the metropolitan hub of **Puget Sound,** a fast-growing region of more than 3 million residents. The city's natural splendors at times make one forget its standing as a center of industry and an economic and cultural portal to the Pacific Rim. But most visitors can't help noticing that for all its dynamism, the city still seems to have one speed: slow. Seattle residents live on and among lakes and hills. Getting from place to place sometimes takes a while because the geography demands it. Few cities are as defined by and identified with their environment as Seattle. This harmony, which has an incalculable effect on the city's quality of life, is also the key to its appeal.

One of the great attractions of Seattle is how quickly you can leave it all behind. In a minute, the gray mist that commonly enshrouds the city can evaporate, revealing "The Mountain," as locals call **Mount Rainier,** or a ferry gliding gently across **Elliott Bay.** For a true escape from the (relative) bustle of city life take the 35-minute drive east to the town of **Snoqualmie,** gateway to the Cascades. Merely stepping on a ferry at Coleman Dock seems to take you light years away from the city, but within 30 minutes you're standing on **Bainbridge Island,** a perfect launching pad to **Port Townsend** and the **Olympic Peninsula.** In the summer months many residents board boats bound for the **San Juan Islands.** In a very real sense, you haven't seen Seattle until you leave Seattle, so consider at least one excursion to the other side of the mist.

Vancouver Area

The spectacular setting of cosmopolitan Vancouver has inspired people from around the world to settle here. The Pacific Ocean and the mountains of the **North Shore** form a dramatic backdrop to the gleaming towers of commerce downtown and make it easy to pursue outdoor pleasures. You can trace the city's history in **Gastown** and **Chinatown,** savor the wilderness only blocks from the city center in **Stanley Park,** or dine on superb ethnic or Pacific Northwest cuisine before you sample the city's nightlife. People from every corner of the world create a vibrant atmosphere.

Museums and buildings of architectural and historical significance are the primary draw in **downtown Vancouver.** There's also plenty of fine shopping to provide breaks along the way. Vancouver is a new city, when compared to others, but one that's rich in culture and diversity.

As with Seattle, you can steal away from the hubbub of the city in minutes to the Pacific beaches, rugged mountains, and forested islands of **British Columbia.** There are plenty of opportunities for whale- and nature-watching, as well as year-round skiing and superb fishing and kayaking. Whether your visit takes you to the Anglophile city of **Victoria** or nearby coastal and island towns, you'll encounter the diversity of the area's residents.

FODOR'S CHOICE

Seattle

Magic Seattle Moments

★ **Coffee from a drive-through.** You'll certainly never forget your first double-tall nonfat latte, especially if it's from a drive-through espresso bar. If you're trying to lay off the caffeine, substitute a double shot of wheat grass from a juice bar.

★ **Floatplane flight from Lake Union to Friday Harbor.** Hop on the plane that lands on the sea for unforgettable views of Puget Sound and the San Juan Islands.

★ **Pike Place Market on a Saturday afternoon.** It's fun here anytime, but there's no place in the world quite like Pike Place Market in full swing on a Saturday afternoon. "If we get separated, I'll meet you by the pig in an hour." But watch for low-flying fish!

★ **Sunset over Elliott Bay from a westbound ferry.** Catch a late-afternoon ferry heading west. You'll get an unobstructed view of the snowcapped Olympics silhouetted against the setting sun, with a return trip toward a twinkling Seattle skyline.

Parks

★ **Washington Park Arboretum.** The Arboretum is a true Seattle gem, a 200-acre park that's perfect for a picnic, a stroll through the greenhouse, or a quiet afternoon in the immaculate Japanese garden.

★ **Woodland Park Zoo.** Many of the animals in this award-winning facility roam free in climate-specific habitats. The African savanna, the elephant forest, and the Northern Trail (housing brown bears, wolves, mountain goats, and otters) are of particular interest.

Sights and Attractions

★ **Ballard Locks.** Follow the fascinating progress of fishing boats and pleasure craft through the locks, part of the Lake Washington Ship Canal, then watch as salmon and trout make the same journey via a "fish ladder" from salt water to fresh water.

★ **Museum of Flight.** Exhibits on the history of human flight and more than 20 classic airplanes, dating from the Wright brothers to the jet era, are among the attractions at this splendid museum at Boeing Field.

★ **Pike Place Market.** Read the hundreds of names etched into the floor tiles as you wander among stalls selling fresh seafood, produce, cheese, Northwest wines, bulk spices, tea, coffee, and arts and crafts.

★ **Space Needle.** There's nothing like the view of the city at night from the observation deck of this Seattle landmark.

Flavors

★ **El Gaucho.** Some of the city's most traditional, most satisfying fare is served up at this swanky retro steak house. Dress to see and be seen. For the complete show, order the items prepared table-side. $$$$

★ **Lampreia.** The subtle beige-and-gold interior of this Belltown restaurant is the perfect backdrop for owner and chef Scott Carsberg's clean, sophisticated cuisine. $$$$

★ **Rover's.** An intimate escape from the energy of downtown, Rover's offers exceptional French cooking with a daily-changing menu founded on fresh, locally available ingredients. Chef-owner Thierry Rautureau is a James Beard Award winner. $$$$

★ **Dahlia Lounge.** The easygoing ambience of the Dahlia Lounge suits chef Tom Douglas's penchant for simple, if uncommon, preparations. His signature Dungeness crab cakes lead an ever-evolving menu focused on regional ingredients. $$$

★ **Metropolitan Grill.** This clubby downtown spot serves custom-aged, mesquite-broiled steaks—the best in Seattle—in a classic steak-house atmosphere. $$$

★ **Ray's Boathouse.** The view of Puget Sound may be the drawing card, but the seafood is impeccably fresh, well prepared, and complemented by one of the area's finest wine lists. $$$

★ **Marco's Supperclub.** This casual, lively bistro is a favorite with locals. Multiregional cuisine and friendly service is the specialty here. $$–$$$

★ **Saigon Gourmet.** This small café in the International District is about as plain as they get, but the Vietnamese food is super and the prices are incredibly low. $

⭐ **Four Seasons Olympic Hotel.** Seattle's most elegant hotel has a 1920s Renaissance Revival–style grandeur. Public rooms are appointed with marble, wood paneling, potted plants, and thick rugs. *$$$$*

⭐ **Inn at the Harbor Steps.** This B&B in the heart of the city offers all of the amenities of home in a modern luxury high-rise. The spacious rooms have gas fireplaces, and a full breakfast is served each morning. *$$$–$$$$*

⭐ **Inn at the Market.** This sophisticated but unpretentious hotel, right up the street from the Pike Place Market, combines the best aspects of a small French country inn with the informality of the Pacific Northwest. *$$$–$$$$*

⭐ **Gaslight Inn.** Rooms at this Capitol Hill–area B&B range from a cozy crow's nest to suites with antique carved beds and gas fireplaces. *$$–$$$*

Vancouver

⭐ **Dr. Sun Yat-Sen Classical Chinese Garden.** The first authentic Ming Dynasty–style garden outside of China, this garden was built in 1986 by 52 artisans from Suzhou, the Garden City of the People's Republic.

⭐ **Granville Island.** This small sandbar was a derelict factory district, but its industrial buildings and tin sheds, painted in upbeat primary colors, now house restaurants, a public market, marine activities, and artists' studios.

⭐ **Museum of Anthropology.** Vancouver's most spectacular museum displays aboriginal art from the Pacific Northwest and around the world—dramatic totem poles and canoes; exquisite carvings of gold, silver, and argillite; and masks, tools, and textiles from many cultures.

⭐ **Stanley Park.** An afternoon in this 1,000-acre wilderness park, only blocks from downtown, can include beaches, the ocean, the harbor, Douglas fir and cedar forests, and a good look at the North Shore mountains.

⭐ **C.** A marina-side location overlooking False Creek makes a perfect setting for this innovative seafood restaurant. *$$$–$$$$*

⭐ **Bacchus.** Low lighting, velvet drapes, and Venetian glass lamps create a mildly decadent feel at this seriously sensuous Italian restaurant inside the Wedgewood Hotel. *$$–$$$$*

⭐ **Il Giardino di Umberto.** Tuscan favorites are served in this little yellow house at the end of Hornby Street. The vine-draped courtyard with a wood-burning oven is especially romantic. *$$–$$$$*

⭐ **Liliget Feast House.** This intimate downstairs longhouse near English Bay is one of the few places in the world serving original Northwest Coast native cuisine. *$$–$$$$*

⭐ **Tojo's.** Hidekazu Tojo is a sushi-making legend, with more than 2,000 preparations tucked away in his creative mind. *$$$*

⭐ **Imperial Chinese Seafood.** This Cantonese restaurant in the Art Deco Marine Building has two-story floor-to-ceiling windows with stupendous views of Stanley Park and the North Shore mountains across Burrard Inlet. *$$–$$$*

⭐ **Vij's.** Vikram Vij, who calls his elegant South Granville restaurant a "curry art gallery," brings together the best of the subcontinent and the Pacific Northwest for exciting new interpretations of Indian cuisine. *$$*

⭐ **Hotel Vancouver.** The copper roof of this grand château-style hotel dominates Vancouver's skyline. The hotel itself, opened in 1939 by the Canadian National Railway, commands a regal position in the center of town. *$$$$*

⭐ **Pan Pacific Hotel.** A centerpiece of Vancouver's Trade and Convention Centre and a cruise-ship terminal, the luxurious Pan Pacific has a dramatic three-story atrium lobby and expansive views of the harbor and mountains. *$$$$*

⭐ **Listel Vancouver.** This Robson Street hotel doubles as an art gallery, with about half of its guest rooms displaying the works of well-known contemporary artists. *$$$–$$$$*

⭐ **Sutton Place.** This property feels more like an exclusive European guest house than a large modern hotel. Guest rooms are furnished with rich, dark woods reminiscent of 19th-century France, and the service is gracious and attentive. $$$–$$$$

⭐ **English Bay Inn.** In this renovated 1930s Tudor house a block from the ocean and Stanley Park, the guest rooms have wonderful sleigh beds with matching armoires. $$–$$$

⭐ **West End Guest House.** This lovely Victorian house built in 1906 is a true "painted lady," from its gracious front parlor, cozy fireplace, and early 1900s furniture to its bright-pink exterior. $$–$$$

⭐ **River Run.** This unique bed-and-breakfast is part of a small houseboat community in Ladner, 30 minutes south of Vancouver. The accommodations include a floating house, a net loft, and two river's-edge cottages. $$

BOOKS AND VIDEOS

Seattle

Above Seattle, with photos by Robert Cameron and text by Emmett Watson, provides, literally, an overview of the city, via historical and contemporary aerial photographs.

The late Bill Speidel, one of Seattle's most colorful characters, wrote about the early history of the city in books replete with lively anecdotes and legends. *Sons of the Profits* and *Doc Maynard* are two of his best. David Buerge's *Seattle in the Eighteen Eighties* is difficult to find but worth the effort; it documents a period of great growth and turmoil. Buerge also compiled the history and photographs in *Chief Seattle,* part of a series about the Northwest. Quintard Taylor's scholarly *The Forging of a Black Community: Seattle's Central District, From 1870 Through the Civil Rights Era* studies race relations in the city through anecdotal and other research.

John T. Gaertner's *North Bank Road: The Spokane, Portland and Seattle Railway* outlines the impact that railroads had on the Northwest. The book is one of several titles on the subject published by Washington State University Press, whose other titles include *The Way We Ate:*

Pacific Northwest Cooking 1843–1900 and *Raise Hell and Sell Newspapers: Alden J. Blethen and The Seattle Times.*

In her memoir *Nisei Daughter,* Monica Itoi Sone recalls her time in Seattle before World War II, the social and other struggles of her family and other Japanese-Americans during the war, and life in the postwar era. The treatment of Japanese-Americans during World War II is one of the subjects of David Guterson's *Snow Falling on Cedars.* The novel, which takes place in the 1950s on an island north of Puget Sound, won the PEN/Faulkner award for fiction.

Screaming Music: A Chronicle of the Seattle Music Scene, by Charles Peterson and Michael Azerrad, delivers the dish on the grunge and other musical eras. Rock music reporter Clark Humphrey covers the city's music scene from the 1960s into the 1990s in *Loser: The Real Seattle Music.*

Seattle has the largest municipal gardening program in the United States. You'll get a minitour of the city and some great recipe ideas from *The City Gardener's Cookbook: Totally Fresh, Mostly Vegetarian, Decidedly Delicious Recipes from Seattle's P-Patches.*

In John Saul's best-selling *Black Lightning,* a Seattle journalist spends years tracking a serial killer. The journalist finds herself facing new horrors when similar murders begin occurring after the killer's execution.

One of the first talking pictures with scenes shot in Seattle was the 1930s comedy *Tugboat Annie,* starring Marie Dressler (as the title character) and Wallace Beery. (Dressler's famous line: "And I didn't get the name pushin' toy boats around the bathtub either.") Lizabeth Scott, a star of the late 1940s and early 1950s, debuted in the sentimental *You Came Along* (gal on warbond tour falls in love with a GI), parts of which were filmed in Seattle. Elvis Presley flew into town—literally. He played a crop-dusting pilot for *It Happened at the World's Fair,* shot in 1962. The film is no great shakes, but has some fine views of the fair and the city.

Stars continued to pass through Seattle in the 1970s as film production in and around the city increased. All or part of the James Caan sailor-on-leave vehicle *Cinderella Liberty,* John Wayne's *McQ* (he plays a Seattle police detective), and Warren

Beatty's paranoid political thriller *The Parallax View* take place in the city.

Car thief Stockard Channing drove through Seattle in *Dandy the All-American Girl* (a.k.a. *Sweet Revenge*). Michael Sarrazin, James Coburn, and Walter Pidgeon picked pockets in Seattle and Salt Lake City in the peculiar *Harry in Your Pocket*, now more memorable for Pidgeon's performance and the location shots in the two cities (and also Vancouver) than the plot. The San Juan Islands were among the places through which Jack Nicholson drifted in director Bob Rafelson's *Five Easy Pieces*, which also includes scenes in British Columbia.

Scenes from *Eleanor and Franklin* and other made-for-TV movies were shot in Seattle in the 1970s, but the pace of television production picked up in the 1980s with the feature-length *The Divorce Wars* (in which Tom Selleck and Jane Curtin spar) and *Jacqueline Bouvier Kennedy*. Parts of the pilot for David Lynch's idiosyncratic *Twin Peaks* series were shot in North Bend, Snoqualmie, and Everett. Major theatrical films shot during the 1980s in the area included *An Officer and a Gentleman*, *War Games*, *Trouble in Mind*, *Starman*, and *The Fabulous Baker Boys*.

The hits continued in the 1990s with *Singles*, director Cameron Crowe's tale of Seattle twentysomethings; *The Hand That Rocks the Cradle*, in which nanny from hell Rebecca de Mornay terrorizes a yuppie couple; *Disclosure*, in which corporate boss Demi Moore terrorizes employee Michael Douglas; and *Sleepless in Seattle*, in which the town provides a backdrop for love to conquer all for the characters played by Tom Hanks and Meg Ryan. Most of the American footage in *Little Buddha*, Bernardo Bertolucci's tale of an American lama, was shot in the Seattle area. Scenes from *Free Willy* and *Free Willy II* were shot in the San Juan Islands. The contemporary Seattle skyline is seen to great effect in the television show *Frasier*.

Seattle became a haven for independent producers in the 1990s. Jeff Bridges starred in the major studio release *The Vanishing*, parts of which were shot here, but received better notices for his performance in the independently financed *American Heart*, also shot in the area, in which he plays a convict whose 12-year-old son re-

joins him upon his release from prison. A grim view of the city can be seen in *Black Circle Boys*, in which a southern California swimmer moves to Seattle and gets caught up in satanic rituals, drugs, and the underground music scene. For a cheerier portrait, see *Steaming Milk*. Its lead character, a struggling screenwriter, encounters a cross-section of Seattleites at his day job at a Queen Anne espresso café. The 1997 documentary *Hype* is an alternately enlightening and creepy glimpse at the rise and fall of the grunge music scene.

Vancouver

Photographer Morton Beebe's beautiful *Cascadia: A Tale of Two Cities, Seattle and Vancouver, B.C.* explores the cultural and natural wonders of Seattle, Vancouver, and the regions surrounding each city. Chuck Davis's *Greater Vancouver Book* is a comprehensive look at Vancouver's past and present.

Pauline Johnson's *Legends of Vancouver* is a colorful compilation of regional native myths. Longtime Vancouver resident George Bowering wrote the lively *British Columbia: A Swashbuckling History of the Province*. Lois Simmie's children's book *Mister Got-to-Go* takes place in the Sylvia Hotel. Annette, the protagonist of Margaret A. Robinson's *A Woman of Her Tribe*, leaves her village to study in Victoria but feels alienated upon her return.

Denise Chong's *The Concubine's Children*, and Wayson Joy's *The Jade Peony* are novels about immigrant life in Vancouver's Chinatown.

Michael Kluckner's *Heritage Walks Around Vancouver*, Robin Ward's *Vancouver*, and Rhodri Windsor Liscombe's *The New Spirit: Modern Architecture in Vancouver 1938–1963* explore the city's architectural heritage. Gerald B. Straley's *Trees of Vancouver* is a good survey of the major and less-common varieties. Straley's book is one of many titles published by the press of University of British Columbia about Canada's far west.

Film and television production is a big business in British Columbia—C$808 million was spent in 1998 making it the third largest production area in North America, after Los Angeles and New York.

Vancouver often stands in for other urban areas—including New York City in *Rum-*

ble in the Bronx (1994) and Friday the 13th: Jason Takes Manhattan (1989)—but occasionally plays itself. The 1995 Canadian feature The War Between Us re-creates 1940s Vancouver as it explores the fate of a well-to-do family of Japanese descent whose members are interned in a camp in interior British Columbia following the outbreak of World War II. Once in a Blue Moon (1995), another period piece shot in British Columbia, concerns a 10-year-old boy who comes of age in the suburbs of Vancouver in the late 1960s. For a peek at Vancouver's 1990s slacker culture, check out Live Bait, a 1995 homage to Woody Allen. The sometimes goofy sci-fi flick Cyberjack (1995) conjures up a Vancouver of the 21st century, complete with flying SeaBuses.

The last decade has been the heyday of British Columbia film production, but the area's cinematic roots go back more than a half century. Estelle Taylor, Thomas Meighan, and Anna May Wong starred in The Alaskan, a 1924 Paramount drama about a man who rescues Alaska from the clutches of corrupt robber barons. The 1945 Son of Lassie is not one of the lovable collie's best pictures, but does contain scenes shot in British Columbia. Rugged Sterling Hayden starred in Timberjack, a 1954 offering from Republic Pictures. Oliver Reed starred in the 1966 film The Trap, about a 19th-century trapper and his wife in British Columbia.

Robert Altman shot scenes in British Columbia for two of his early films, That Cold Day in the Park and McCabe and Mrs. Miller. The 1976 remake of the Orson Welles thriller Journey Into Fear, starring Vincent Price, Shelley Winters, and Sam Waterston, was shot in and around Vancouver, as was the 1980 The Grey Fox, based on the life of an early 1900s stagecoach bandit. Klondike Fever, a 1979 picture starring Rod Steiger, concerns the 1897–98 gold rush.

Among the productions filmed wholly or partly in British Columbia in the past decade or so are Roxanne, Stakeout, The Accused, the Look Who's Talking movies, the Jean Claude Van Damme action picture Time Cop, The Crush, Cousins, This Boy's Life, Stay Tuned, Jennifer Eight, the Robin Williams fantasy Jumanji, the Adam Sandler comedy Happy Gilmore, the remake of Little Women, Cyberteens in Love (check your local video store for this curious Canadian production), Bounty Hunters II, Mr. Magoo, Deep Rising, Seven Years in Tibet, and Kundun.

The TV series 21 Jump Street, which made Johnny Depp a star, was one of several 1980s television series filmed in Vancouver. Since then, production has increased greatly. Other small-screen shows shot here include Poltergeist, Highlanders, Millennium, and The X-Files. Neon Rider, Northwood, The Odyssey, and Mom P.I. are among the Canadian series produced in Vancouver or elsewhere in British Columbia in the 1990s.

FESTIVALS AND SEASONAL EVENTS

WINTER

➤ JAN.: The **Polar Bear Swims** on New Year's Day in Vancouver and Victoria are said to bring good luck all year. **Skiing competitions** take place at most alpine ski resorts throughout British Columbia (through Feb.).

➤ MAR.: The **Pacific Rim Whale Festival** on Vancouver Island's west coast celebrates the spring migration of gray whales with tours by whale experts and accompanying music and dancing.

SPRING

➤ LATE MAR.–MID-APR.: The **Skagit Valley Tulip Festival** enchants visitors with more than 1,000 acres of tulips in full bloom, as well as with music, crafts, and parades in nearby Mount Vernon, Washington, midway between Seattle and Vancouver. Sip the world's best vintages at the **Vancouver International Wine Festival.**

➤ MAY: The **Seattle International Children's Festival** brings international music, dance, and theater to young audiences. The **Seattle International Film Festival** presents more than 200 features in three weeks at various locations around Seattle. Highlights include the New Directors Show-

case, the Children's Film Fest, and the Secret Festival. **Swiftsure International** draws more than 300 competitors to Victoria's harbor for an international yachting event. The **Vancouver International Children's Festival,** said to be the largest event of its kind in the world, presents dozens of performances in mime, puppetry, music, and theater.

➤ LATE MAY: **Northwest Folklife Festival** lures musicians and artists to Seattle for one of the largest folk fests in the United States. The **Pike Place Market Festival** celebrates the enduring contribution of the market to the life and character of Seattle, with entertainment, food booths, and an even higher than usual concentration of crafts artisans and vendors. **Victoria Day,** on the second to last weekend in May, is a holiday throughout Canada, but Victoria, B.C., celebrates in earnest, with picnics and a parade.

SUMMER

➤ JUNE: The **Fremont Street Fair** is the best of Seattle's summer neighborhood street fairs (others are held in Capitol Hill and the University District). Vancouver's **Canadian International Dragon Boat Festival** in late June features races between long, slender boats decorated with huge dragon heads, an event

based on a Chinese "awakening the dragons" ritual. The festival also includes community and children's activities, dance performances, and arts exhibits. The **Du Maurier International Jazz Festival,** also in late June, celebrates a broad spectrum of jazz, blues, and related improvised music, with more than 200 performances in venues around Vancouver.

➤ JUNE–SEPT.: **Bard on the Beach** is a series of Shakespearean plays performed under a huge seaside tent at Vanier Park in Vancouver.

➤ JULY 1: **Canada Day** inspires celebrations around the country in honor of Canada's birthday. In Vancouver, **Canada Place** hosts an entire day of free outdoor concerts followed by a fireworks display in the harbor. Victoria hosts the daylong **Great Canadian Family Picnic** in Beacon Hill Park. The event usually includes children's games, bands, food booths, and fireworks.

➤ JULY 4: **Independence Day** in Seattle means two spectacular celebrations. Gasworks Park is the site of a day of entertainment, culminating in orchestral music (usually provided by the Seattle Symphony) and a fireworks display over Lake Union. A full slate of cultural and other activities unwinds on the other side of Queen Anne Hill at the Fourth of Jul-Ivar Celebration before the skies light up over Elliott Bay.

➤ JULY: **Bite of Seattle** serves up sumptuous specialties from the city's finest restaurants. People travel from all over Canada to attend Vancouver's **Folk Music Festival.** Seattle's **King County Fair** serves up loads of traditional old-fashioned fun with with carnival rides, agricultural displays, country music, and kid-oriented activities.

➤ MID-JULY–EARLY AUG.: **Seafair,** Seattle's biggest festival of the year (really a collection of smaller regional events), kicks off with a torchlight parade through downtown and culminates in hydroplane races on Lake Washington. **The Benson & Hedges Symphony of Fire,** the world's largest musical fireworks competition,

lights up Vancouver's English Bay for four evenings. The **Vancouver International Comedy Festival** presents all manner of silliness (much of it free) on Granville Island.

➤ LATE AUG.–EARLY SEPT.: **Bumbershoot,** a Seattle festival of the arts, presents more than 400 performers in music, dance, theater, comedy, and the visual and literary arts.

AUTUMN

➤ SEPT.: The **Vancouver Fringe Festival** attracts

cutting-edge theater to Vancouver's smaller stages.

➤ LATE SEPT.–EARLY OCT.: The **Vancouver International Film Festival** brings top Canadian and international films and film directors to the city. Nearly 100 local, national, and international theater companies perform at the 10-day **Seattle Fringe Festival.**

➤ OCT.: Pop and highbrow authors read, sign books, and speak at the **Vancouver International Writers Festival.**

2 SEATTLE

Coffeehouses, brew pubs, independent music, and lots of rain—these are what many people associate with the hippest city in the U.S. Northwest. But Seattle has more to offer than steaming lattes and garage bands. You can wander historic neighborhoods, browse amid the sights and smells of the Pike Place Market, explore lakes and islands, or just eat, eat, eat. Seattle restaurants are among the nation's most innovative and diverse.

By Wier
Harman

Updated by
Julie Fay

EATTLE IS DEFINED BY WATER. There's no use denying the city's damp weather, or the fact that its skies are cloudy for much of the year. Seattleites don't tan, goes the joke, they rust. But Seattle is also defined by the rivers, lakes, and canals that bisect its steep green hills, creating a series of distinctive areas along the water's edge. Funky fishing boats, floating homes, swank yacht clubs, and waterfront restaurants exist side by side.

A city is defined by its people as well as by its geography, and the people of Seattle—a half million within the city proper, another 2.5 million in the surrounding Puget Sound region—are a diversified bunch. Seattle has long had a vibrant Asian and Asian-American population, and well-established communities of Scandinavians, African-Americans, Jews, Native Americans, and Latinos live here, too. It's impossible to generalize about such a varied group, but the prototypical Seattleite was once pithily summed up by a *New Yorker* cartoon in which one arch-eyebrowed East Coast matron says to another, "They're backpacky, but nice."

Seattle's climate fosters an easygoing indoor lifestyle. Overcast days and long winter nights have made the city a haven for moviegoers and book readers. Hollywood often tests new films here, and residents' per-capita book purchases are among North America's highest. Seattle has all the trappings of a metropolitan hub—two daily newspapers, a state-of-the-art convention center, professional sports teams, a diverse music-club scene, and top-notch ballet, opera, symphony, and theater companies. A major seaport, the city is a vital link in Pacific Rim trade.

Seattle's expansion has led to the usual big-city problems—increases in crime, drug abuse, homelessness, poverty, and traffic congestion, along with a decline in the quality of the public schools. Many residents have fled to the nearby suburb of Bellevue, which has swollen from a quiet farming community to become Washington's fifth-largest city. But despite the growing pains they've endured, Seattleites have a great love for their city and a firm commitment to maintaining its reputation as one of the most livable areas in the country.

Pleasures and Pastimes

Dining

The best Seattle restaurants build their menus around local ingredients. The city has an invaluable resource in the Pike Place Market, which warehouses bountiful supplies of seafood and produce. A quick scan of the stalls will tell you what to expect on restaurant plates in any given season: strawberries in June; Walla Walla sweets—a mild softball-size onion—in July; wild blackberries in August; and Washington's renowned apples during autumn. All year long you'll find Washington wines and beer at Seattle restaurants. The locally produced ingredients and the synthesis of European and Asian cooking techniques (with a touch of irreverence) are the basis for what has come to be known as Pacific Northwest cuisine.

Nightlife and the Arts

A mid-1990s restaurant boom in Seattle has resulted in a livelier nightlife that lasts later into the evening than before. Seattle achieved fleeting notoriety in the early 1990s as the birthplace of grunge rock. Nirvana, Pearl Jam, and Soundgarden were among the bands to emerge from the local music scene. But jazz, blues, and R&B have been perennial favorites, and you'll find clubs that showcase everything from tinny garage bands to subtle stylists. Beyond music, you can catch a comedian or a movie—or have a drink while watching the lights flicker on the water. On any given night there are usually several worthwhile dance or theater offerings. Seattle's galleries support an active community of painters, sculptors, woodworkers, and glass artists. The annual Northwest Folklife Festival on Memorial Day weekend celebrates their creativity.

Parks and Gardens

"Seattle possesses extraordinary landscape advantages. . . . In designing a system of parks and parkways the primary aim should be to secure and preserve for the use of the people as much as possible of these advantages of water and mountain views and of woodlands . . . as well as some fairly level land for field sports and the enjoyment of scenery." These words appeared in a surveyors report prepared in 1903 for Seattle's fledgling parks commission and established the foundation for an ambitious master plan, the spirit of which has been maintained to this day. Seattle's extensive parks system retains that delicate balance between the fanciful and functional—the primeval growth of Schmitz Park, the manicured ball fields around Green Lake, the sprawl of the Washington Park Arboretum, and Parson's Garden, a prim urban oasis.

EXPLORING SEATTLE

Seattle, like Rome, is built on seven hills. As a visitor, you're likely to spend much of your time on only two of them (Capitol Hill and Queen Anne Hill), but the seven knobs are indeed the most definitive element of the city's natural and spiritual landscape. Years of largely thoughtful zoning practices have kept tall buildings from obscuring the lines of sight, maintaining vistas in most directions and around most every turn. The hills are lofty, privileged perches from which residents are constantly reminded of the beauty of the forests, mountains, and water lying just beyond the city. That is, when it stops misting long enough to see your hand in front of your face.

To know Seattle is to know its distinctive neighborhoods. Because of the hills, comfortable walking shoes are a must.

Ballard, home to Seattle's fishing industry and fun-to-tour locks, is at the mouth of Salmon Bay, northwest of downtown.

Capitol Hill, northeast of downtown on Pine Street, east of Interstate 5 (I–5), is the center of youth culture in this very young city.

Downtown is bounded on the west by **Elliott Bay,** on the south by **Pioneer Square** (the city's oldest neighborhood) and the **International District,** on the north by the attractive residences lining the slopes of **Queen Anne Hill,** and by I–5 to the east. You can reach most points of interest by foot, bus, trolley, or the monorail that runs between the Seattle and Westlake centers.

Fremont, Seattle's eccentric and artsy hamlet, is north of **Lake Union** and the **Lake Washington Ship Canal,** east of Ballard, west of **Wallingford,** and south of **Woodland Park.**

Magnolia, dotted with expensive (and precariously perched) homes, is at the northwestern edge of Elliott Bay, west of Queen Anne Hill.

University District, the area around the University of Washington, is north of Capitol Hill and Union Bay.

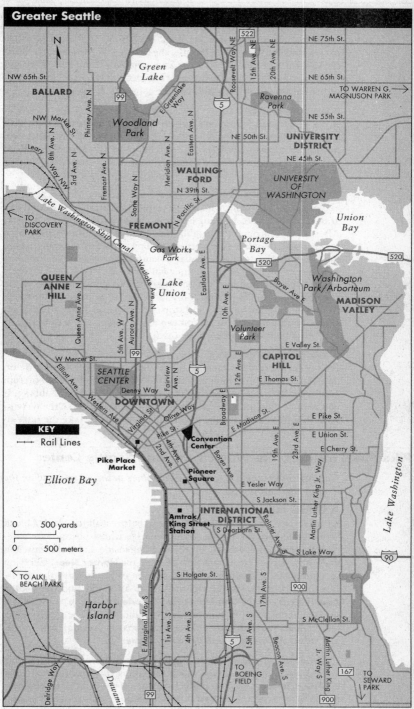

Greater Seattle

N

NE 75th St.

NE 65th St.

TO WARREN G.
MAGNUSON PARK →

NW 65th St.

BALLARD

*Green
Lake*

NE 55th St.

Roosevelt Way NE

15th Ave. NE

20th Ave. NE

Ravenna
Park

99

5

NW Market St.

NW 8th Ave. N

Leary

Phinney Ave. N

*Woodland
Park*

NE 50th St.

E Greenlake Way

Eastern Ave. N

**UNIVERSITY
DISTRICT**

NE 45th St.

3rd Ave. N

Fremont Ave. N

Stone Way N

Meridian Ave. N

**WALLING-
FORD**

N 39th St.

N Pacific St.

**UNIVERSITY
OF
WASHINGTON**

Lake Washington Ship Canal

FREMONT

*Gas Works
Park*

*Portage
Bay*

*Union
Bay*

← TO
DISCOVERY
PARK

520

520

*Lake
Union*

*Washington
Park/Arboretum*

Eastlake Ave. E

Boyer Ave. E

**QUEEN
ANNE
HILL**

Queen Anne Ave. N

5th Ave. W

Aurora Ave. N

10th Ave. E

*Volunteer
Park*

**MADISON
VALLEY**

99

5

W Mercer St.

E Valley St.

Fairview Ave. N

**CAPITOL
HILL**

Elliott Ave.

**SEATTLE
CENTER**

Denny Way

DOWNTOWN

Virginia St.

Olive Way

Broadway E

12th Ave. E

E Thomas St.

E Madison St.

Western Ave.

Pike St.

**Convention
Center**

E Pike St.

19th Ave. E

23rd Ave. E

2nd Ave.

4th Ave.

Boren Ave.

E Union St.

E Cherry St.

KEY

— Rail Lines

**Pike Place
Market**

**Pioneer
Square**

E Yesler Way

Martin Luther King Jr. Way

Elliott Bay

S Jackson St.

**Amtrak/
King Street
Station**

**INTERNATIONAL
DISTRICT**

S Dearborn St.

Rainier Ave. S

0   500 yards

0   500 meters

S Lake Way

90

← TO ALKI
BEACH PARK

S Holgate St.

17th Ave. S

900

*Harbor
Island*

1st Ave. S

4th Ave. S

15th Ave. S

S McClellan St.

E Marginal Way S

Defridge Way

Duwamish

Beacon Ave. S

Martin Luther King Jr. Way S

167

TO
SEWARD
PARK

5

TO
BOEING
FIELD

99

900

Lake Washington

Great Itineraries

If you're planning to visit all or most of Seattle's top tourist destinations, pick up a **Citypass** ticket book for $26.50 and you'll get 50% off admission to the Space Needle, the Seattle Art Museum, the Seattle Aquarium, the Pacific Science Center, the Woodland Park Zoo, and the Museum of Flight. The Citypass booklet, which is available at any of the six attractions, is valid for nine consecutive days.

IF YOU HAVE 1 DAY

If you've come to Seattle on business or for another reason only have a day for sightseeing, focus your energy on downtown. Weather permitting, an after-dinner ferry ride to Bainbridge Island (☞ Chapter 3) and back is a perfect way to conclude your day.

IF YOU HAVE 3 DAYS

Get a feel for what makes Seattle special at Pike Place Market and then explore more of downtown and the waterfront. Start your second day at the Ballard Locks, heading east to Fremont in time for lunch there. After a stroll through the neighborhood's galleries and shops, grab a beer at the Redhook Brewery before heading to the Space Needle, where the views are the most spectacular as sunset approaches. Venture outside the city on I–90 to Snoqualmie Falls (☞ Chapter 3) on day three. Hike to the falls and lunch at Salish Lodge. To get a true sense of the pace of life in the Northwest, on your return to Seattle, detour north from I–90 on Highway 203 and stop in tiny Duvall, home to antiques shops, boutiques, and cafés. You can easily make it back to Seattle in time for dinner or a night on the town.

IF YOU HAVE 5 TO 7 DAYS

Follow the three-day itinerary above. Take a morning bay cruise on day four and spend the afternoon at the Washington Park Arboretum before heading to Capitol Hill for dinner and some nightclubbing. If you're only staying in the Seattle area one more day, take the ferry to Port Townsend on day five. If you have a few days, take the ferry to one or more of the San Juan Islands.

Pike Place Market, the Waterfront, and Seattle Center

Numbers in the text correspond to numbers in the margin and on the Downtown Seattle map.

A Good Tour

Spend some time at **Pike Place Market** ① before walking south a block on 1st Avenue to the **Seattle Art Museum** ②, whose postmodern exterior is worth a look even if you're not going inside. From the museum, walk west across 1st Avenue and descend the **Harbor Steps.** Carry on straight ahead one block from the bottom of the steps to the waterfront. Head north (to the right). At Pier 59 you'll find the **Seattle Aquarium** ③ and the **Omnidome Film Experience** ④. You can walk out on Piers 62 and 63 for a good view of Elliott Bay. The newly refurbished **Bell Street Pier** (Pier 66) contains a marina, several restaurants, and **Odyssey: The Maritime Discovery Center** ⑤.

Continue up the waterfront to **Myrtle Edwards Park,** past Pier 70. It's a good place to rest a moment before making the several-block walk up **Broad Street** through the northern part of the Belltown neighborhood (be forewarned: the first three blocks are a tad steep) to the **Seattle Center** and the **Space Needle** ⑥. Especially if you've got kids in tow, you'll want to arrive here before the **Pacific Science Center** ⑦ and **Seattle Children's Museum** ⑧ close. Music fans won't want to miss the **Experience Music Project** ⑨, an interactive museum celebrating American Popular Music slated to open in mid-2000. Take the **Seattle Center Mono-**

rail to return to downtown. The monorail stops at **Westlake Center** ⑩, at 5th Avenue and Pine Street. To get to the **Washington State Convention and Trade Center** ⑪, walk one block southeast to Pike Street and east to 8th Avenue. Seattle's main **Visitor Information Center** is inside the street-level mall at Convention Place.

TIMING

It would take about half the day to complete the above route stopping only a little, but you'll need to devote the whole day or more to fully appreciate the various sights. A visit to Pike Place Market can easily fill two hours. Plan on an hour for the art museum. The aquarium is a two-hour stop at most. You could spend half a day or more in Seattle Center. Most sights listed below are open daily; the Frye Art Museum and the Seattle Art Museum are closed on Monday and open until 9 PM on Thursday.

Sights to See

⑨ **Experience Music Project.** This 140,000-square-ft interactive museum celebrating American popular music is slated to open in mid-2000. The nonprofit EMP is funded by Microsoft cofounder Paul Allen and designed by Frank Gehry. The exhibits will include a Jimi Hendrix gallery containing the world's largest collection of Hendrix artifacts. There will also be a gallery featuring guitars owned by Bob Dylan, Hank Williams, Kurt Cobain, and the bands Pearl Jam, Soundgarden, and the Kingsmen. An interactive Sound Lab will let visitors experiment with various instruments and recording equipment. At press time, admission fees and opening hours had not been announced. ⊠ *5th Ave., between Broad St. and Thomas St.,* ☎ *425/990–0575.*

Frye Art Museum. Among the pivotal late-19th- and early 20th-century American and European realist works at this gallery east of downtown are German artist Franz von Stuck's *Sin,* a painting with Impressionist leanings that predates the movement, and Alexander Koester's *Ducks,* an example of the Academy school of German painting. The Frye, which opened in 1952, has an outdoor garden courtyard and a reflecting pool. ⊠ *704 Terry Ave.,* ☎ *206/622–9250.* ☜ *Free.* ☉ *Tues.–Sat. 10–5 (Thurs. until 9), Sun. noon–5.*

Myrtle Edwards Park. Sandwiched between the Burlington Northern Railroad to the east and the gently lapping waters of Elliott Bay to the west, this sliver of a park north of Pier 70 is popular for jogging, walking, and picnicking. As a place to catch the sunset, it's rivaled only by the deck of a westbound Bainbridge Island ferry. ⊠ *Alaskan Way between W. Bay and W. Thomas Sts.*

⑤ **Odyssey: The Maritime Discovery Center.** Cultural and educational maritime exhibits on Puget Sound and ocean trade are the focus of this new waterfront attraction. Also here are a conference center, a short-stay boat basin, fish-processing terminals, a fish market, and a restaurant. ⊠ *Pier 66 off Alaskan Way,* ☎ *206/374–4001.* ☜ *$6.50.* ☉ *Daily 10–5, extended hrs in July and Aug.*

④ **Omnidome Film Experience.** The theater next to the aquarium shows 30–45-minute films on a large, curved screen. Recent topics have included Alaska and whales; the eruption of Mount St. Helens is a mainstay. ⊠ *Pier 59 off Alaskan Way,* ☎ *206/622–1868.* ☜ *$6.95; combination tickets including aquarium admission $13.50.* ☉ *Daily 10–5.*

⑦ **Pacific Science Center.** An excellent stop for children and adults, the Pacific Science Center has 200 hands-on exhibits. The large, brightly colored machines of Body Works amusingly analyze human physiol-

18

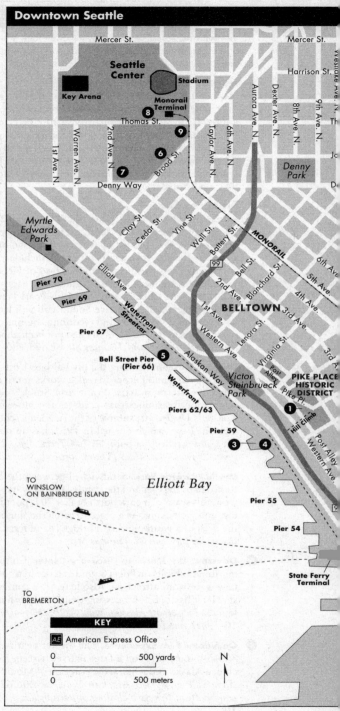

Downtown Seattle

ogy, while Tech Zones has robots and virtual-reality diversions that participants can control. The dinosaurs exhibit is wildly popular. IMAX screenings and laser light shows take place daily. A *Jetsons*-style outdoor plaza, with fountains and concrete towers, dates from the 1962 World's Fair. ⊠ *200 2nd Ave. N,* ☎ *206/443–2001.* ☑ *$7.50.* ⊙ *Weekdays 10–5, weekends 10–6.*

★ ❶ **Pike Place Market.** The heart of the Pike Place Historical District, this Seattle institution began in 1907 when the city issued permits to farmers allowing them to sell produce from their wagons parked at Pike Place. Later the city built stalls for the farmers. At one time the market was a madhouse of vendors hawking their produce and haggling with customers over prices. Some of the fishmongers still carry on this kind of frenzied banter, but chances are you won't get them to waver on their prices.

Urban renewal almost killed the market, but city voters, led by the late architect Victor Steinbrueck, rallied and voted it an historical asset in 1973. Many buildings have been restored, and the project is connected to the waterfront by stairs and elevators. Besides a number of restaurants, you'll find booths selling fresh seafood—which can be packed in dry ice for your flight home—produce, cheese, Northwest wines, bulk spices, tea, coffee, and arts and crafts.

If the weather is nice, gather a picnic—fresh fruit and smoked salmon, of course, but soups, sandwiches, pastries, and various ethnic snacks are also available in the market or from the small shops facing it along Pike Place. Carry your bounty north, past the market buildings, to **Victor Steinbrueck Park**, a small green gem named for Pike Place's savior. ⊠ *Pike Pl. at Pike St., west of 1st Ave.,* ☎ *206/682–7453.* ⊙ *Mon.–Sat. 9–6, Sun. 11–5.*

NEED A
BREAK?
Three Girls Bakery (⊠ Pike Pl. Market, 1514 Pike Pl., ☎ 206/622–1045), a 13-seat glassed-in lunch counter that's tucked behind a bakery outlet, serves sandwiches, soups, and pastries. Go for the chili and a hunk of Sicilian sourdough, or buy a loaf at the take-out counter, pick up some smoked salmon at the fish place next door, and head for a picnic table in Steinbrueck Park.

 ❸ **Seattle Aquarium.** Pacific Northwest marine life is the emphasis at this waterfront facility. At the Discovery Lab you'll see baby barnacles, minute jellyfish, and other "invisible" creatures through high-resolution video microscopes. The Tide Pool exhibit re-creates Washington's rocky coast and sandy beaches at low tide. There's even a 6,000-gallon wave that sweeps in over the underwater life. Sea otters and seals swim and dive in their pools, and the "State of the Sound" exhibit shows the aquatic life and ecology of Puget Sound. ⊠ *Pier 59 off Alaskan Way,* ☎ *206/386–4320.* ☑ *$8.* ⊙ *Memorial Day–Labor Day, daily 10–8, Labor Day–Memorial Day, daily 10–6.*

❷ **Seattle Art Museum.** Postmodern architect Robert Venturi designed this five-story museum, which is a work of art in itself. The 1991 building has a limestone exterior with large-scale vertical fluting accented by terra-cotta, cut granite, and marble. Sculptor Jonathan Borofsky's several-stories-high *Hammering Man* pounds away outside the front door. The extensive collection inside surveys Asian, Native American, African, Oceanic, and pre-Columbian art. Among the highlights are the anonymous 14th-century Buddhist masterwork *Monk at the Moment of Enlightenment* and Jackson Pollock's *Sea Change.* A ticket to the museum is valid for admission to the Seattle Asian Art Museum (☞ *below*) in Volunteer Park if used within one week. ⊠ *100 University St.,* ☎ *206/*

654–3100. 🍽 *$7; free 1st Thurs. of month.* 🕙 *Tues.–Sun. 10–5 (Thurs. until 9).*

Seattle Center. The 74-acre Seattle Center complex was built for the 1962 World's Fair. A rolling green campus organized around the massive International Fountain, the center includes an amusement park, theaters, exhibition halls, museums, shops, restaurants, a skateboard park, Key Arena, the Pacific Science Center (☞ *above*), and the Space Needle (☞ *below*). Among the arts groups headquartered here are the Seattle Repertory Theatre, Intiman Theatre, the Seattle Opera, and the Pacific Northwest Ballet. The center hosts several professional sports teams: the Seattle Supersonics (NBA basketball), Sounders (soccer), Seadogs (indoor soccer), and Thunderbirds (hockey). It's a bit cramped, and parking can be a nightmare, but the Seattle Center is the undisputed hub of the city's leisure life. It's also the site of three of the area's largest summer festivals: the Northwest Folklife Festival, Bite of Seattle, and Bumbershoot. *See* Festivals and Seasonal Events *in* Chapter 1 for details about these. The **Seattle Center Monorail** (☞ Getting Around *in* Seattle A to Z, *below*) travels between the center and Westlake Center. ✉ *Between 1st and 5th Aves. N and Denny Way and Mercer St.,* ☎ *206/684–8582.*

🐾 ⑧ **Seattle Children's Museum.** The global village at this colorful and spacious facility introduces children to everyday life in Ghana, the Philippines, and other lands. A mountain wilderness area (including a slide and waterfall) educates kids about climbing, camping, and the Northwest environment. Cog City is a giant maze of pipes and pulleys. A pretend neighborhood contains a post office, café, fire station, and grocery store. An area for infants and toddlers is well padded for climbing and sliding. Arts-and-crafts activities, special exhibits, and workshops are also offered. ✉ *Seattle Center House, fountain level, 305 Harrison St.,* ☎ *206/441–1768.* 🍽 *$5.50 children, $4 adults.* 🕙 *Weekdays 10–5, weekends 10–6.*

★ ⑥ **Space Needle.** The distinctive exterior of the 520-ft-high Space Needle can be seen from almost any spot in the downtown area. The view (especially at sunset) from the inside out is even better. The observation deck, a 42-second elevator ride from street level, yields vistas of the entire region. Have a drink at the Space Needle Lounge or a latte at the adjacent coffee bar and take in Elliott Bay, Queen Anne Hill, and on a clear day the peaks of the Cascade Range. (If it's stormy, have no fear: 25 lightning rods protect the tower.) The needle's rotating restaurants, one family style and the other more formal, are not known for innovative cuisine. ✉ *5th Ave. and Broad St.,* ☎ *206/443–2111.* 🍽 *Observation deck $9.* 🕙 *Daily 8 AM–11 PM.*

⑪ **Washington State Convention and Trade Center.** Seattle's vine-covered exhibition hall straddles I–5. The design of verdant **Freeway Park** south of here is intended to convey the spirit and flavor of the Pacific Northwest, which it does fairly well, considering the urban location. The street-level **Visitor Information Center** has maps, brochures, and event listings. ✉ *Visitor center: 800 Convention Pl., at 8th Ave. and Pike St.,* ☎ *206/461–5840.* 🕙 *Memorial Day–Labor Day, daily 10–4; Labor Day–Memorial Day, weekdays 8:30–5, Sat. 10–4.*

⑩ **Westlake Center.** This three-story mall (☞ Shopping, *below*) is also a major terminus for buses and the Seattle Center Monorail, which was built for the 1962 World's Fair and connects downtown to Seattle Center. The ground-level Made in Washington store showcases the state's products. ✉ *1601 5th Ave.,* ☎ *206/467–1600.* 🕙 *Mon.–Sat. 9:30–8, Sun. 11–6.*

Pioneer Square and the International District

A walk through Seattle's Pioneer Square and International District provides a glimpse into the city's days as a logging and shipping center and a haven for immigrants from Asia and the Pacific Islands.

Numbers in the text correspond to numbers in the margin and on the Downtown Seattle map.

A Good Walk

Begin at **Pioneer Place,** at 1st Avenue and Yesler Way in the **Pioneer Square District.** Explore the shops and historic buildings along 1st Avenue before heading to the **Klondike Gold Rush National Historical Park** ⑫, on Main Street two blocks south and one block east of Pioneer Place. A restful stop along Main Street heading east to the **International District** is **Waterfall Garden** park, designed by Masao Kinoshita on the site where the messenger service that became United Parcel Service began operations.

Head south (right) on 2nd Avenue South and east (left) at South Jackson Street. You'll see the **Kingdome** sports stadium and Amtrak's **King Street Station** on your right as you head up South Jackson to 7th Avenue, where the **Wing Luke Museum** ⑬ surveys the past and present of immigrants from Asia and the Pacific Islands and their descendants. The museum has walking-tour maps of historic buildings and businesses. One intriguing stop is the **Uwajimaya** store at 6th Avenue South and South King Street (head south one block on 7th Avenue South and turn right on South King Street). You can return to the harbor in one of the vintage **Waterfront Streetcar** trolleys—the southern terminus is at 5th Avenue South and Jackson Street. You can also catch a bus to downtown at the same corner.

TIMING

You can explore Pioneer Square and the International District in one to two hours unless you stop for lunch or like to shop. The Wing Luke Museum is closed on Monday.

Sights to See

International District. The 40-block "I.D.," as the International District is locally known, began as a haven for Chinese workers who came to the United States to work on the transcontinental railroad. The community has remained largely intact despite anti-Chinese riots and the forcible eviction of Chinese residents during the 1880s, and the internment of Japanese-Americans during World War II. About one third of the I.D.'s residents are Chinese, one third are Filipino, and another third come from elsewhere in Asia or the Pacific Islands. The district, which includes many Chinese, Japanese, and Korean restaurants, also contains herbalists, acupuncturists, antiques shops, and private clubs for gambling and socializing. Among the many great markets is the huge **Uwajimaya** Japanese supermarket and department store (☞ Shopping, *below*). ⊠ *Between Main and S. Lane Sts. and 4th and 8th Aves.*

⑫ **Klondike Gold Rush National Historical Park.** Film presentations, exhibits, and gold-panning demonstrations are among the ways this indoor center illustrates Seattle's role in the 1897–98 gold rush in northwestern Canada's Klondike region. ⊠ *117 S. Main St.,* ☎ *206/553-7220.* ⊡ *Free.* ☉ *Daily 9–5; closed major holidays.*

Pioneer Square District. The ornate iron-and-glass pergola at **Pioneer Place,** at 1st Avenue and Yesler Way, marks the site of the pier and sawmill owned by Henry Yesler, one of Seattle's first businessmen. Timber logged off the hills was sent to the sawmill on a "skid road"—now Yesler Way—made of small logs laid crossways and greased so that the freshly cut trees would slide down to the mill. The area grew into Seattle's first business center; in 1889 a fire destroyed many of the district's wood-frame buildings, but the industrious residents and businesspeople rebuilt them with brick and mortar.

With the 1897 Klondike gold rush, however, this area became populated with saloons and brothels. Businesses gradually moved north, and the old pioneering area deteriorated. Eventually, only drunks and bums hung out in the neighborhood that had become known as Skid Row, and the name became synonymous with "down and out." The Pioneer Square District encompasses about 18 blocks and includes restaurants, bars, shops, and the city's largest concentration of art galleries. It is once again a hangout for those down on their luck. Incidents of crime in the neighborhood have increased lately, especially after dark, but few find it intimidating during the day.

⑬ Wing Luke Museum. The small but well-organized museum named for the first Asian-American elected official in the Northwest surveys the history and cultures of people from Asia and the Pacific Islands who have settled in the Pacific Northwest. The emphasis is on how immigrants and their descendants have transformed and been transformed by American culture. The permanent collection includes costumes, fabrics, crafts, basketry, photographs, and Chinese traditional medicines. ✉ *407 7th Ave. S,* ☎ *206/623–5124.* 🎫 *$2.50.* ☉ *Tues.–Fri. 11–4:30, weekends noon–4.*

Capitol Hill Area

With its mix of theaters and churches, coffeehouses and nightclubs, stately homes and student apartments, Capitol Hill demonstrates Seattle's diversity better than any other neighborhood. There aren't many sights in the traditional sense, but you can while away an enjoyable day here and perhaps an even more pleasurable evening.

Numbers in the text correspond to numbers in the margin and on the Downtown Seattle and North Seattle maps.

A Good Walk

If you're prepared for some hills, this walk will give you a great overview of the area. From downtown, walk up Pine Street to Melrose Avenue, where you can fortify yourself with a jolt of java at the **Bauhaus** coffeehouse. This section of the hill is called the **Pike–Pine corridor** ⑭. Continue east on Pine Street to Broadway and turn left (but don't miss the Art Deco Egyptian Theater to the right). Passing Seattle Central Community College you'll cross Denny Way, the unofficial threshold of the **Broadway shopping district** ⑮. After six blocks, the road bears to the right, becoming 10th Avenue East.

You'll notice many beautiful homes on the side streets off 10th Avenue East in either direction as you continue north to Prospect Street. Turn right at Prospect and gird yourself for another hill. Continue on to 14th Avenue East and turn left (north) to enter **Volunteer Park** ⑯. After walking around a picturesque water tower (with a good view from the top), you'll see the **Volunteer Park Conservatory** straight ahead, the **reservoir** to your left, and the **Seattle Asian Art Museum** to your right. Leave the park to the east via Galer Street. At 15th Avenue East, you can turn left (north) to visit **Lakeview Cemetery** (where Bruce Lee lies in repose), or turn right (south) and walk four blocks to shops and cafés. To return to downtown, continue walking south on 15th Avenue East and west on Pine Street (if you've had enough walking, catch Metro Bus 10 at this intersection; it heads toward Pike Place Market). At Broadway, cut one block south to Pike Street for the rest of the walk. The

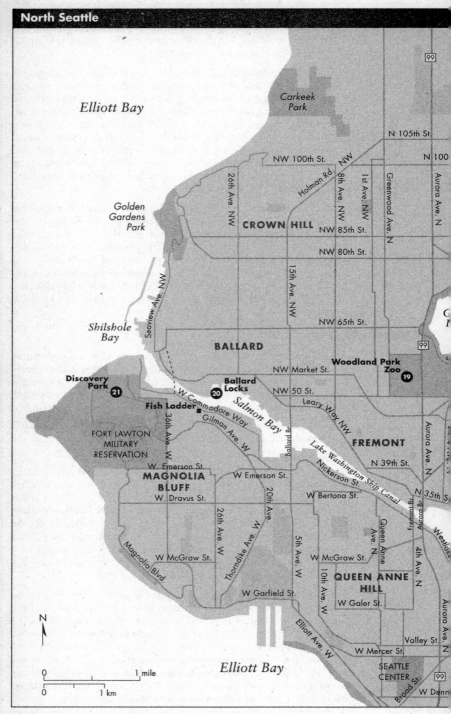

Elliott Bay

Carkeek Park

N 105th St.

NW 100th St.

N 100

Golden Gardens Park

26th Ave. NW

Holman Rd. NW

8th Ave. NW

1st Ave. NW

Greenwood Ave. N

Aurora Ave. N

CROWN HILL

NW 85th St.

NW 80th St.

15th Ave. NW

Seaview Ave. NW

Shilshole Bay

NW 65th St.

BALLARD

Woodland Park Zoo

99

NW Market St.

19

Discovery Park

21

Ballard Locks

20

NW 50 St.

Leary Way NW

Fish Ladder

W Commodore Way

Salmon Bay

36th Ave. W

Gilman Ave. W

Ballard Br.

Lake Washington Ship Canal

FREMONT

FORT LAWTON MILITARY RESERVATION

N 39th St.

Aurora Ave. N

MAGNOLIA BLUFF

W. Emerson St.

W Emerson St.

20th Ave.

Nickerson St.

N 35th St.

W. Dravus St.

W Bertona St.

Fremont Br.

Aurora Br.

Westlake

26th Ave. W

Thorndike Ave. W

5th Ave. W

Queen Anne Ave. N

4th Ave. N

Magnolia Blvd

W McGraw St.

W McGraw St.

10th Ave. W

QUEEN ANNE HILL

W Garfield St.

W Galer St.

N

Elliott Ave. W

Valley St.

Aurora Ave. N

0   1 mile

0   1 km

Elliott Bay

W Mercer St.

SEATTLE CENTER

99

Broad St.

W Denn

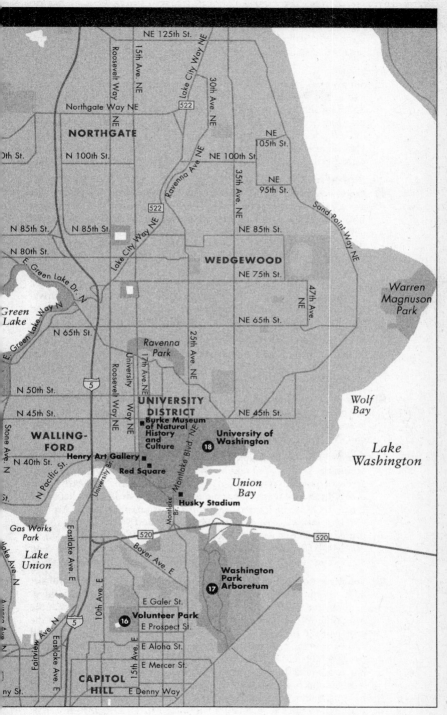

above tour is a good survey of Capitol Hill, but it's by no means complete. The area's best attraction, the **Washington Park Arboretum** ⑰, is too far to walk. You'll need to take the bus (catch Metro Bus 11 heading northeast along East Madison Street) or drive.

TIMING

Simply walking this tour requires about four hours—two if you start and end in the Broadway shopping district. Allow at least one to two hours for shopping the Pike–Pine corridor and Broadway, an hour for the Asian Art Museum, and a half hour for the conservatory. The amount of time you spend at Bruce Lee's grave is between you and Mr. Lee. Plan on at least two hours for a visit to the arboretum, where losing track of time, and yourself, is pretty much the point.

Sights to See

⓯ **Broadway shopping district.** Seattle's youth-culture, old-money, and gay scenes all converge on the lively stretch of Broadway East between East Denny Way and East Roy Street. A great place to stroll and sip coffee or have a brew, the strip contains the obligatory art-house movie theater (☞ Harvard Exit *in* Nightlife and the Arts, *below*), record shops and new and vintage clothing stores, and plenty of cafés. The three-story **Broadway Market** (⊠ 401 Broadway E) has the Gap, Urban Outfitters, and other slick merchandisers, along with some smaller boutiques. You won't be able to miss the glaring sign for the open-air **Dick's Drive-In** (⊠ 115 Broadway E). Dropping in for a Dick's Deluxe Burger and a shake at 1 AM is a quintessential Seattle experience.

Lakeview Cemetery. Kung-fu star **Bruce Lee's grave** is the most-visited site at this cemetery directly north of Volunteer Park. Inquire at the office for a map. ⊠ *1554 15th Ave. E,* ☎ *206/322–1582.* ▨ *Free.* ⊙ *Weekdays 9–4:30.*

⓮ **Pike–Pine corridor.** A hip center of activity, this strip between downtown and the south end of the Broadway shopping district holds galleries, thrift shops, music stores, restaurants, and rock clubs. ⊠ *Pike and Pine Sts. between 6th Ave. and Broadway.*

Seattle Asian Art Museum. This facility holds thousands of paintings, sculptures, pottery, and textiles from China, Japan, India, Korea, and several southeast Asian countries. You can sip any of nearly three dozen distinctive teas at the tranquil **Kado Tea Garden.** A ticket to the Asian Art Museum is good for $3 off admission to the Seattle Art Museum (☞ Pike Place Market, the Waterfront, and Seattle Center, *above*) if used within one week. ⊠ *Volunteer Park, 1400 E. Prospect St.,* ☎ *206/654–3100.* ▨ *$3; free 1st Thurs. and Sat. of month.* ⊙ *Tues.–Sun. 10–5 (Thurs. until 9) and some Mon. holidays; call for tour schedule.*

⓰ **Volunteer Park.** High above the mansions of North Capitol Hill sits 45-acre Volunteer Park, a grassy affair perfect for picnicking, sunbathing, reading, and strolling. It's a mere 108 steps to some great views at the top of the water tower near the main entrance. Beside the lake in the center of the park is the **Seattle Asian Art Museum** (☞ *above*), and across from the museum is the romantic **Volunteer Park Conservatory** (☎ 206/684–4743). The greenhouse, which was completed in 1912, has accumulated its inhabitants largely by donation, including an extensive collection of orchids begun in 1919. Rooms here are dedicated to ferns, palms, cacti, and exotic flowers. Admission is free; hours are seasonal, so call ahead. ⊠ *Park entrance: 14th Ave. E, at Prospect St.*

⓱ **Washington Park Arboretum.** The 200-acre arboretum's Rhododendron Glen and Azalea Way are in full bloom from March through June. During the rest of the year other plants and wildlife flourish. From March

TIME TO RELAX

BECAUSE THERE'S SO MUCH TO explore in Seattle, trying to take it all in can be overwhelming. So let yourself off the hook. The city is best visited at the pace it's lived—relaxed.

Lose your cares at prim, perfectly manicured **Parsons Garden** (⌂ 650 W. Highland Dr.) or the 50 acres of rugged old-growth forest at West Seattle's **Schmitz Park** (⌂ 5551 SW Admiral Way), steps from Alki Beach. **Volunteer Park Conservatory** (☞ Capitol Hill area) has an exquisite collection of exotic flowers and trees, and the **Japanese Garden** (☞ Capitol Hill Area) at the Washington Park Arboretum is the essence of tranquillity.

Two striking pieces of public art create entirely new landscapes. In **Warren Magnuson Park** (☞ University District) the windmill-like structures of Douglas Hollis's **Soundgarden** overlook Lake Washington. Closer to downtown, Masao Kinishita's **Waterfall Garden** (⌂ S. Main St. and 2nd Ave. S) is a 22-ft rush of water, stone, trees, and flowering plants designed to keep the bustle of Pioneer Square at bay.

Fly a kite atop the hill at **Gasworks Park** at the north shore of Lake Union or rent a vintage sailboat at the **Center for Wooden Boats** (☞ Fremont Area for both). Bike the **Burke/Gilman Trail,** a 12-mi path following an old railroad line along Seattle's lakefront, or hit a bucket of balls at the **Interbay Family Golf Center** (☞ Participant Sports for both). The mood is almost meditative at **211 Club** (☞ Participant Sports), a no-nonsense billiards hall where talking is discouraged (a mere display of enthusiasm can get you kicked out).

Treat yourself to a day at the **Ummelina International Day Spa** (⌂ 1525 4th Ave., ☎ 206/624–1370) or longer at the **Salish Lodge** (☞ Snoqualmie *in* Chapter 3), a hotel and spa atop a bluff overlooking Snoqualmie Falls. Take a leisurely hike to the base of the falls, where you can perch on the rocks at the base of the rushing water. Your worries will melt away.

Seattle is infatuated with coffee, but a cup of tea at **Teahouse Kuan Yin** (⌂ 1911 N. 45th St., ☎ 206/632–2055 for hours) or the **Kado Tea Garden** (☞ Capitol Hill Area) can soothe mind and body after an active day. If you prefer a taste of the grape, the **Bungalow** (⌂ 2412 N. 45th St., ☎ 206/632–0254) wine bar is perfect for a quiet encounter with a friend or a volume of poetry from Open Books, Seattle's poetry bookshop, right downstairs.

For a low-tech getaway take a ride on the **Bainbridge Island ferry** (Bainbridge Island *in* Chapter 3) at sunset. A local newspaper poll rated the upper deck as one of Seattle's most romantic places to kiss. Even without that special someone, the view is spectacular.

Finally, when Seattleites say "the mountain's out," drop what you're doing and look south. The mist has lifted and you're rewarded with a glimpse of Mount Rainier, suspended weightlessly beyond the city's edge. If you're lucky enough to catch this magnificent sight during your visit to Seattle, consider yourself truly blessed.

through October visit the peaceful **Japanese Garden,** a compressed world of mountains, forests, rivers, lakes, and tablelands. The **Graham Visitors Center** at the north end provides explanations of the arboretum's flora and fauna and has brochures with self-guided walking tours. Or you can dispense with maps and follow your bliss. ✉ *2300 Arboretum Dr. E,* ☎ *206/325–4510.* ✆ *Free.* ☉ *Park daily 7* AM–*sunset, visitor center daily 10–4.*

University District

The U District, as the University District is called locally, is bounded by Ravenna Boulevard to the north, the Montlake Cut waterway (connecting Lake Union and Lake Washington) to the south, 25th Avenue Northeast to the east, and I–5 to the west. A stroll through the University of Washington campus can include stops at its museums and other cultural attractions. To get a whiff of the slightly anarchic energy that fuels this part of town, head off campus to "The Ave," the student-oriented shopping area along University Way Northeast.

Numbers in the text correspond to numbers in the margin and on the North Seattle map.

A Good Walk

Start at Northeast 45th Street and University Way Northeast. Proceed south on University Way ("The Ave") through the heart of the district's many shopping and dining options. Turn left at Northeast Campus Parkway, stopping by the visitor center at the **University of Washington** ⑱. Straight ahead at the end of the block is the **Henry Art Gallery.** Continue east to Central Plaza, better known as **Red Square.** On clear days you'll be rewarded with views of Mount Rainier to the southeast. Walk down Rainier Vista (past the Frosh Pond and fountain) to Stevens Way, turning left into **Sylvan Grove,** a gorgeous outdoor theater. Return via Rainier Vista to Red Square and strike out due north. A walk along shady Memorial Way past the commuter lot deposits you at the **Burke Museum of Natural History.** From the Burke step out onto Northeast 45th Street, walking two longish blocks to the left to return to University Way Northeast.

TIMING

The route above should only take about two hours, but factor in an hour or so each for the Henry gallery and Burke museum and an additional hour if you want to shop along The Ave.

Sights to See

The Ave. University Way Northeast, the hub of University of Washington social life, has all the activities (and the grungy edge) one expects in a student-oriented district—great coffeehouses, cinemas (☞ the Grand Illusion and Varsity theaters *in* Nightlife and the Arts, *below*), clothing stores, and cheap restaurants, along with panhandlers and pockets of grime. The major action along The Ave is between 42nd and 50th streets, though there are more shops and restaurants as University Way continues north to 58th Street and the entrance to Ravenna Park. Stop in the **Big Time Brewery** (☞ Brew Pubs *in* Nightlife and the Arts, *below*) for a pint of ale and a gallon of local color.

Burke Museum of Natural History and Culture. Exhibits at this facility on the northwest edge of the University of Washington campus survey the cultures of the Pacific Northwest and Washington State's 35 Native American tribes. The museum's permanent collection focuses on anthropological, geological, and zoological specimens. ✉ *17th Ave. NE and N.E. 45th St.,* ☎ *206/543–5590* ✆ *$5.50.* ☉ *Daily 10–5 (Thurs. until 8).*

Henry Art Gallery. The many works by Northwest artists at this gallery on the west side of the University of Washington campus include photography, 19th- and 20th-century paintings, and textiles; the facility often presents important touring exhibitions. ⊠ *15th Ave. NE and N.E. 41st St.,* ☎ *206/543–2280.* 🖾 *$5.* ☉ *Tues.–Sun. 11–5 (Thurs. until 8).*

Ⓒ **Museum of History and Industry.** An 1880s-era room and a Seattle time line at this museum depict the city's earlier days. Other displays from the permanent collection are shown on a rotating basis—a recent one surveyed Pacific Coast League baseball teams—along with traveling exhibits. ⊠ *2700 24th Ave. E,* ☎ *206/324–1125.* 🖾 *$5.50.* ☉ *Week-days 11–5, weekends 10–5.*

⓲ **University of Washington.** Locals know this university with 35,000 students as "U-Dub." Founded in 1861 downtown, the university moved in 1895 to Denny Hall, the first building on the present campus. The Alaska-Yukon-Pacific Exposition, which the school hosted in 1909, brought the Northwest national attention. The University of Washington is respected for its research and graduate programs in medicine, nursing, oceanography, drama, physiology, and social work, among many others. Its athletic teams—particularly football and women's basketball—have strong regional followings, and the **Henry Art Gallery** and **Burke Museum of Natural History and Culture** (☞ *above*) are both worth a look. **Red Square** is the nerve center for student activity and politics. The "red" refers to its brick paving, not students' political inclinations. This is a decidedly nonactivist campus, though it's in the square that you'll see animal-rights, environmental, and other advocates attempting to rouse the masses. On sunny days the steps are filled with students sunbathing, studying, or hanging out. ⊠ *Visitor Information Center, 4014 University Way NE,* ☎ *206/543–9198.* ☉ *Daily 8–5.*

OFF THE
BEATEN PATH

WARREN MAGNUSON PARK – Jutting into Lake Washington northeast of the University District, "Sand Point" (as it's called by locals) is one of the best beaches in the city for quiet sunbathing. The Soundgarden, a grassy area filled with metal sculptures that emit tones when the wind blows, is in the northern part of the park, through the turnstile and across *Moby Dick* Bridge (embedded with quotes from Melville's novel). ⊠ *Park entrance: Sand Point Way NE at 65th St.*

Fremont and Environs

Around Seattle, the word "Fremont" is invariably preceded by the words "funky," "artsy," or "eclectic." And why not? The neighborhood's residents—largely artists—do little to challenge the image. "The Artists' Republic of Fremont," as many prefer to call it, brims with sass and self-confidence. Signs on the outskirts proclaim it THE CENTER OF THE UNIVERSE and instruct visitors to set their watches back five minutes, or to throw them away entirely. Given the area's many assets—galleries, restaurants, coffeehouses, brew pubs, antiques shops, and the like—dispensing with time can be a very good idea. To the east of Fremont is Wallingford, an inviting neighborhood of bungalow homes and boutique shopping. You'll find Phinney Ridge and the Woodland Park Zoo to the north of Fremont. Ballard, a neighborhood with a strong Scandinavian flavor, and the center of Seattle's fishing industry, lies to the west.

Numbers in the text correspond to numbers in the margin and on the North Seattle map.

A Good Tour

Coming from downtown, you'll probably enter Fremont via the **Fremont Bridge,** one of the busiest drawbridges in the world. Central Fremont is tiny and can easily be explored by intuition. Here's one strategy: proceed north on Fremont Avenue North, turning right at North 35th Street. Walk two blocks to the **Aurora Bridge** (you'll be standing underneath it). Turn left and walk one block, but approach with care. The "Fremont troll"—a whimsical concrete monster that lurks beneath the bridge—jealously guards his Volkswagen Beetle. Head back along North 36th Street, making a hard left at the **statue of Lenin** (seriously) at Fremont Place, the first street after you cross Fremont Avenue North. Walk a half block southeast, go right at the crosswalk, and then make a right on North 35th Street. At the end of the block is the 53-ft **Fremont Rocket,** officially designating the center of the universe. Walk straight ahead one long block to Phinney Avenue to **Redhook Brewery** (tours are conducted daily) and the **Trolleyman** (☞ Brew Pubs *in* Nightlife and the Arts, *below*). Turn left and continue one block to the **Ship Canal.** On the right is **Canal Park.** Linger there, or turn left on North 34th Street and return to the Fremont Bridge. On the way you'll pass a parking lot that hosts two important Fremont traditions—the Sunday Flea and Crafts Market (from spring to fall, weather permitting) and the Outdoor Cinema (bring a chair on Saturday after dusk in the summer).

The major Fremont-area attractions are best reached by car, bus, or bike. The **Woodland Park Zoo** ⑲ is due north of Fremont via Fremont Avenue North (catch Bus 5 heading north from the northeast corner of Fremont Avenue North and North 39th Street). The **Ballard Locks** ⑳ are west of Fremont (take Bus 28 from Fremont Avenue North and North 35th Street to Northwest Market Street and 8th Avenue North and transfer to Bus 44 or, on weekdays only, Bus 46, heading west). **Discovery Park** ㉑ is a walk of less than a mile from the south entrance to the Ballard Locks. Head west (right) on Commodore Way and south (left) on 40th Street.

TIMING

The walk around Fremont takes an hour at most, but the neighborhood is meant for strolling, browsing, sipping, and shopping. Plan to spend a full morning or a good part of an afternoon. You could easily spend two hours at the Ballard Locks and several hours at Discovery Park or the zoo.

Sights to See

★ ⊛ ⑳ **Ballard Locks.** Officially the Hiram M. Chittenden Locks, this part of the 8-mi Lake Washington Ship Canal connects Lake Washington and Lake Union with the salt water of Shilshole Bay and Puget Sound. The locks, which were completed in 1917, service 100,000 boats yearly by raising and lowering water levels anywhere from 6 to 26 ft. On the north side of the locks is a 7-acre **ornamental garden** of native and exotic plants, shrubs, and trees. Also on the north side are a staffed visitor center with displays on the history and operation of the locks as well as several fanciful sculptures by local artists. Along the south side is a 1,200-ft promenade with a footbridge, a fishing pier, and an observation deck.

Take some time to watch the progress of fishing boats and pleasure craft passing through the locks. Observe how the marine population makes the same journey from saltwater to fresh on the **fish ladder,** whose 21 levels form a gradual incline that allows an estimated half-million salmon and trout each year to swim upstream. Several windows at the waterline afford views of the fish struggling against the current as they migrate to their spawning grounds. Most of the migration takes place between June and October. (The fish ladder, by the way, is where various attempts are being carried out to prevent sea lions, including the locally notorious Herschel, from depleting the salmon population.) If you're coming via bus from downtown, take Bus 15 or 18 to the stop at Northwest Market Street and 15th Avenue Northwest and transfer to Bus 44 or (weekdays only) 46 heading west on Market. ✉ *3015 N.W. 54th St.; from Fremont, head north on Leary Way NW, west on N.W. Market St., and south on 54th St.,* ☎ *206/783–7059.* ✆ *Free.* ☉ *Locks daily 7 AM–9 PM, visitor center June–Sept., daily 10–7; Oct.– May, Thurs.–Mon. 11–5; call for tour information.*

Center for Wooden Boats. Though slightly off the main drag at the south end of Lake Union, the center is a great place to launch your expedition if you're interested in exploring the water (or just the waterfront). You can check out the 1897 schooner *Wawona* and the other historic vessels on display, watch the staff at work on a restoration, rent a boat at the Oarhouse for a sail around the lake, or have a picnic. ✉ *1010 Valley St.,* ☎ *206/382–2628.* ✆ *Free.* ☉ *Memorial Day–Labor Day, daily 11–6 (boat rentals until 7); Labor Day–Memorial Day, daily 11– 5 (museum and rentals); closed Tues.*

㉑ **Discovery Park.** At Seattle's largest park (520 acres), a former military base converted into a wildlife sanctuary, you can hike through cool forests, explore saltwater beaches, or take in views of Puget Sound and Mount Rainier. A 2.8-mi trail traverses this urban wilderness. From Fremont, take Leary Way Northwest to 15th Avenue Northwest, turn left, and head south on 15th Avenue over the Ballard Bridge. Turn right on West Emerson Street, right on Gilman Avenue West, left on West Fort Street, and right on East Government Way. From downtown, take Elliott Avenue north until it becomes 15th Avenue Northwest, turn left on West Emerson, and follow the previous directions the rest of the way. ✉ *3801 E. Government Way,* ☎ *206/386–4236.* ✆ *Free.* ☉ *Park daily 6 AM–11 PM, visitor center daily 8:30–5.*

Fremont Center. The self-styled Republic of Fremont is one of Seattle's most distinctive neighborhoods. The center is an eclectic strip of Fremont Avenue stretching from the Ship Canal at the south end to North 36th Street, with shops and cafés two blocks to either side. The area also contains many lighthearted attractions, including a statue of Lenin, a 53-ft rocket, and the Fremont troll.

Gasworks Park. Colorful kites soar in the air and bright-hued spinnakers bob offshore in Lake Union on summer days at this park. Get a glimpse of your future (and downtown Seattle) from the zodiac sculpture at the top of the hill, or feed the ducks on the lake. Outdoor concerts take place at Gasworks in summer. On Independence Day there's a fireworks display and a performance by the Seattle Symphony. ✉ *North end of Lake Union, N. Northlake Way and Meridian Ave. N.*

Green Lake. Across Highway 99 (Aurora Avenue North) from the Woodland Park Zoo (☞ *below*), Green Lake is the recreational hub of the city's park system. A 3-mi jogging and bicycling trail rings the lake, and there are facilities for basketball, tennis, baseball, and soccer. The park is generally packed (and the facilities overbooked) on weekday evenings, which has made this the best time for active Seattleites to see and be seen (it's something of a young-singles' scene). ✉ *E. Green Lake Dr. N and W. Green Lake Dr. N.*

☝ ⑲ **Woodland Park Zoo.** Many of the 300 species of animals in this 92-acre botanical garden roam freely in habitat areas that have won several design awards. The African Savanna, the Asian Elephant Forest, and the Northern Trail, which shelters brown bears, wolves, mountain goats, and otters, are of particular interest. Wheelchairs and strollers can be rented. A memorial to musician Jimi Hendrix, a Seattle native, overlooks the African Savanna exhibit; appropriately, it's a big rock. ⊠ *5500 Phinney Ave. N,* ☎ *206/684–4800.* ⌸ *$8.50.* ☉ *Mid-Mar.–mid-Oct., daily 9:30–6; mid-Oct.–mid-Mar., daily 9:30–4.*

On Seattle's Outskirts and Beyond

Chateau Ste. Michelle Winery. One of the oldest wineries in the state is 15 mi northeast of Seattle on 87 wooded acres that were once part of the estate of lumber baron Fred Stimson. Trout ponds, a carriage house, a caretaker's cottage, formal gardens, and the 1912 family manor house—which is on the National Register of Historic Places—are part of the original estate. Visitors are invited to picnic and explore the grounds; the wine shop sells delicatessen items. During the summer Chateau Ste. Michelle hosts nationally known performers and arts events in its amphitheater. ⊠ *14111 N.E. 145th St., Woodinville,* ☎ *425/488–1133. From downtown Seattle take I–90 east to north I–405. Take Exit 23 east (S.R. 522) to the Woodinville exit.* ☉ *Complimentary wine tastings and cellar tours daily 10–4:30, except holidays.*

Columbia Winery. Founded in 1962 by a group of University of Washington professors, this is the oldest winery in the state. Using only European vinifera-style grapes grown in Eastern Washington, the founders' aim was to take advantage of the fact that the vineyards share the same latitude as the best wine-producing areas of France. The gift shop is open year-round and offers the wines themselves and a variety of wine-related merchandise. Columbia hosts special events throughout the year that focus on food and wine pairings, and is the final destination of the Spirit of Washington Dinner Train (see Guided Tours, *below*). ⊠ *14030 N.E. 145th St., Woodinville,* ☎ *425/488–2776 or 800/488–2347. From downtown Seattle take I–90 east to north I–405. Take Exit 23 east (S.R. 522) to the Woodinville exit, go right. Go right again on 175th St., and left on Hwy. 202.* ☉ *Complimentary wine tastings daily 10–7, cellar tours available on weekends.*

Jimi Hendrix Grave Site. The famed guitarist's grave is in Greenwood Cemetery in Renton. From Seattle take I–5 south to the Renton exit, then I–405 past Southcenter to Exit 4B. Bear right under the freeway. Take a right on Sunset Boulevard and another right one block later at 3rd Street. Continue 1 mi, turning right at the third light. ⊠ *3rd and Monroe Sts.,* ☎ *425/255–1511.* ☉ *Daily until dusk. Inquire at the office; a counselor will direct you to the site.*

★ ☾ **Museum of Flight.** Boeing, the world's largest builder of aircraft, is based in Seattle, so it's not surprising that this facility at Boeing Field is one of the city's best museums. The Red Barn, Boeing's original airplane factory, houses an exhibit on the history of human flight. The Great Gallery, a dramatic structure designed by Ibsen Nelson, contains more than 20 vintage airplanes. ⊠ *9404 E. Marginal Way S (take I–5 south to Exit 158; turn right on Marginal),* ☎ *206/764–5720.* ⌸ *$8.* ☉ *Daily 10–5 (Thurs. until 9).*

DINING

See the Downtown Seattle and Capitol Hill Dining map to locate restaurants in those areas and the North of Downtown Seattle Dining map for all other establishments.

CATEGORY	COST*
$$$$	over $35
$$$	$25–$35
$$	$15–$25
$	under $15

*per person for a three-course meal, excluding drinks, service, and sales tax (about 9.1%, varies slightly by community)

Downtown Seattle and Capitol Hill

Chinese

$$–$$$ ✗ **Chef Wang.** Striving for a balance between the hipness of its Belltown neighbors and the unintentional kitsch of the "classic" American Chinese restaurant, Chef Wang is generally on target. The decor benefits from clean lines, rich colors, and low-voltage lighting, but suffers from a feeling of incompleteness, as if the budget ran out sooner than expected. Ingredients are above-average in quality and freshness and cooked with a more delicate touch and presentation than one might expect from the typical Chinese restaurant. The menu contains familiar dishes, such as Peking duck and mu shu pork, executed with a welcome piquancy, depth, and textural subtlety. You can also create your own combination dish from the 22-item list of meats, vegetables, and sauces. ⊠ 2230 First Ave., ☎ 206/448–5407. MC, V. No lunch weekends.

Contemporary

$$$$ ✗ **Hunt Club.** Dark wood and plush seating provide a traditional setting for chef Brian Scheehser's interpretations of Pacific Northwest meat and seafood. The house-made squash ravioli or saffron mussel bisque are excellent starters. Entrées on the seasonal menu include succulent jumbo prawns, pan-roasted sea scallops served with truffle risotto, and steak with garlic mashed potatoes and paper-thin onion rings. ⊠ Sorrento, 900 E. Madison St., ☎ 206/622–6400. AE, DC, MC, V.

$$$–$$$$ ✗ **El Gaucho.** Dress to impress here—you don't want to be outclassed
★ by the waistcoated wait staff coolly navigating the packed floor of this retro steak house. El Gaucho serves up some of the city's most basic, most satisfying fare in a swanky, expansive room. For the complete show, order the items prepared table-side. From the flaming lamb shish kebab to the cool Caesar salad (the best in the city), everything tastes better—or at least it seems that way—with the virtuosic presentation. ⊠ 2505 1st Ave., ☎ 206/728–1337. Reservations essential. AE, MC, V. No lunch.

$$$–$$$$ ✗ **Fullers.** Consistently ranked at or near the top of Seattle's restaurants in local and national publications, Fullers delivers a rare commodity: a dining experience of exceptional poise and restraint born of unconventional risk-taking. Chef Tom Black, who trained as a line cook under Monique Barbeau, shows his unique sensibilities in menu offerings such as pan-seared king salmon with braised fennel ravioli, haricot verts, and caviar–dill beurre blanc; five-spice duck with savory bread pudding; artichoke and baby Italian onion salad with port reduction; and New York strip steak with potato cake and escarole. Works by Northwest artists adorn an otherwise austere dining room. ⊠ Seattle Sheraton Hotel and Towers, 1400 6th Ave., ☎ 206/447–5544. Reservations essential. AE, D, DC, MC, V. Closed Sun. No lunch Sat.

$$$–$$$$ ✗ **Lampreia.** The beige-and-gold interior of this Belltown restaurant
★ is the perfect backdrop for chef-owner Scott Carsberg's sophisticated cuisine. After an appetizer of cream of polenta with shiitake mushrooms, try one of the seasonal menu's intermezzo or light main courses—perhaps squid and cannelloni filled with salmon—or a full entrée such as pheasant with apple-champagne sauerkraut or lamb with pesto and

whipped potatoes. The clear flavors of desserts like lemon mousse with strawberry sauce bring a soothing conclusion to an exciting experience. ⊠ *2400 1st Ave.,* ☎ *206/443–3301. Reservations essential. AE, MC, V. Closed Sun.–Mon. No lunch.*

$$$–$$$$ ✕ **Metropolitan Grill.** Meals at this favorite lunching spot of the white-
★ collar crowd are not for timid eaters: custom-aged mesquite-broiled steaks—the best in Seattle—are huge and come with baked potatoes or pasta. Even the veal chop is extra thick. Lamb, chicken, and seafood entrées are also on the menu. Among the accompaniments, the onion rings and the sautéed mushrooms are tops. ⊠ *818 2nd Ave.,* ☎ *206/ 624–3287. AE, D, DC, MC, V. No lunch weekends.*

$$$–$$$$ ✕ **Painted Table.** Chef Tim Kelly selects the freshest regional ingredients for dishes that are served on hand-painted plates. His seasonal menu might include spicy rock-shrimp linguine, wild-mushroom risotto, or herb-crusted lamb with grilled Japanese eggplant, fennel, and polenta. Desserts include a frozen-banana soufflé and a jasmine-rice custard made with coconut milk. ⊠ *Alexis Hotel, 1007 1st Ave.,* ☎ *206/624–3646. Reservations essential. AE, D, DC, MC, V. No lunch weekends.*

$$$–$$$$ ✕ **Place Pigalle.** Large windows look out on Elliott Bay from this restaurant tucked behind a meat vendor in Pike Place Market's main arcade; in nice weather, they're left ajar to admit the fresh salt breeze. Bright flowers lighten up the café tables, and the friendly staff makes you feel right at home. Despite its French name, this is a very American restaurant. Go for the rich oyster stew, the Dungeness crab (available only when it is truly fresh), or the fish of the day baked in hazelnuts. ⊠ *81 Pike Pl. Market,* ☎ *206/624–1756. AE, MC, V. Closed Sun.*

$$$–$$$$ ✕ **Stars.** After a bumpy start, San Francisco chef Jeremiah Tower seems to have worked out the kinks at this Seattle location opened in 1998. He has transplanted some of the menu items, along with adding new creations featuring local ingredients, such as grilled spiced duck with pear, Washington apple, and fresh fig compote. The space is dramatic and fun, with 25-ft-high ceilings, equally tall windows, an enormous circular fireplace in the bar with a grand stainless-steel flue, and a smart seating arrangement from which to view the proceedings. There is an ever-so-slight tendency toward style over substance, but the staff helps to keep things from getting too pretentious. ⊠ *600 Pine St.,* ☎ *206/264–1112. AE, DC, MC, V.*

$$–$$$$ ✕ **Dahlia Lounge.** Romantic Dahlia worked its magic on Tom Hanks
★ and Meg Ryan in *Sleepless in Seattle.* With valentine-red walls lighted so dimly you can't see much farther than your dinner companion's eyes, this place is cozy and then some. But the food plays its part, too. Crab cakes, served as an entrée or an appetizer, lead an ever-changing regionally oriented menu. Other standouts are seared ahi tuna, near-perfect gnocchi, and desserts like coconut-cream pie and fresh fruit cobblers. Chef-owner Tom Douglas is Seattle's most energetic restaurateur. He also owns Etta's Seafood in Pike Place Market, and the excellent Palace Kitchen on 5th Avenue, but Dahlia is the one to make your heart go pitter-pat. ⊠ *1904 4th Ave.,* ☎ *206/682–4142. Reservations essential. AE, D, DC, MC, V. No lunch weekends.*

$$–$$$$ ✕ **Sazerac.** The spunky restaurant at the Hotel Monaco gleefully thumbs its nose at the traveler's fallback, the hotel dining room. "Big dawg" Jan Birnbaum presides over a whimsical (if not downright goofy) patchwork of Northwest and American favorites with a quirky Southern accent. The cedar-plank smoked salmon sits comfortably alongside collard greens, the braised pork shoulder hosts "apple-cider luv sauce" and "soft sexy grits." A great bar (with late-night service) and an indulgent dessert list round out the fun. ⊠ *1101 4th Ave.,* ☎ *206/624–7755. AE, D, DC, MC, V.*

$$-$$$$ ✗ **Wolfgang Puck Café.** A laid-back staff serves postmodern comfort food—barbecued-duck quesadillas, jerk-chicken Caesar salads, linguine with seared jumbo sea scallops—at this vivacious enterprise across 1st Avenue from the Seattle Art Museum. You can slurp down some oyster shooters or "sip" a jumbo gulf-shrimp "martini" at the seafood bar. This is one of the kid-friendliest of the downtown restaurants; children are given pieces of dough at their tables to make little pizzas. Their creations are cooked in the wood-fire ovens and returned for consumption by the junior chefs. ✉ *1225 1st Ave.,* ☎ *206/621–9653. AE, D, DC, MC, V.*

Delicatessen

$ ✗ **Bakeman's Restaurant.** Low on frills but high on atmosphere, this well-lighted lunchery attracts a steady stream of business suits with its signature turkey and meat-loaf sandwiches, served on fluffy white bread. Bakeman's, open weekdays from 10 to 3, is within easy striking distance of Pioneer Square, but the feel here is far from touristy. ✉ *122 Cherry St.,* ☎ *206/622–3375. Reservations not accepted. No credit cards. Closed weekends. No dinner.*

Eclectic

$$$-$$$$ ✗ **Andaluca.** A synthesis of fresh local ingredients and Mediterranean techniques, the food at this secluded spot downstairs at the Mayflower Park Hotel includes small plates that can act as starters or be combined to make a satisfying meal. A Dungeness crab tower with avocado, hearts of palm, and gazpacho salsa is cool and light, while the beef tenderloin with pears and blue cheese is a glorious trip to the opposite end of the sensory spectrum. ✉ *407 Olive Way,* ☎ *206/382–6999. AE, D, DC, MC, V.*

$$-$$$$ ✗ **Axis.** Restaurant as theater is the angle at this Belltown spot with a wood-fire grill. Diners can view the kitchen from almost every seat in the house. The food is worthy of the show, with appetizers like crispy eggplant wonton and an entrée of oven-roasted Dungeness crab with Cajun seasonings. ✉ *2214 1st Ave.,* ☎ *206/441–9600. Reservations essential. AE, DC, MC, V. No lunch.*

$$-$$$$ ✗ **Palace Kitchen.** The star of this chic yet convivial Tom Douglas eatery may be the 45-ft bar, but the real show takes place within the giant open kitchen at the back. Sausages, sweet-pea ravioli, salmon carpaccio, and a nightly selection of exotic cheeses vie for your attention on an ever-changing menu of small plates, a few entrées, and 10 fantastic desserts. There's always a rotisserie special from the apple-wood grill as well. ✉ *2030 5th Ave.,* ☎ *206/448–2001. AE, D, DC, MC, V. No lunch.*

$$-$$$ ✗ **Marco's Supper Club.** Multiregional cuisine is the specialty of this
★ casual restaurant with shrimp-color walls and mismatched flatware. Start with the fried sage-leaf appetizer with garlic aioli and salsa, then move on to sesame-crusted ahi tuna, Jamaican jerk chicken, or a pork porterhouse in an almond mole sauce. ✉ *2510 1st Ave.,* ☎ *206/441–7801. AE, MC, V. No lunch weekends.*

$ ✗ **Fare Start.** The homeless men and women who operate this café, a project of FareStart, a job-training program, prepare a simple lunch buffet during the week. On Thursday night a guest chef from a restaurant like Ray's Boathouse or the Metropolitan Grill runs the kitchen. You're assured a great meal for a great cause and a real taste of Seattle's community spirit. ✉ *1902 2nd Ave.,* ☎ *206/443–1233, ext. 28. Reservations essential for Thurs. dinner. D, MC, V. No lunch weekends, dinner Thurs. only.*

Downtown Seattle and Capitol Hill Dining

Volunteer Park

CAPITOL HILL

Broadway Playfield

Seattle Central Community College

E. Galer St.
E. Highland Dr.
E. Prospect St.
E. Aloha St.
E. Roy St.
E. Ward St.
E. Valley St.

20th Ave. E.
19th Ave. E.
18th Ave. E.
17th Ave. E.
16th Ave. E.
15th Ave. E.
14th Ave. E.
13th Ave. E.
12th Ave. E.

15th Ave. E.
Malden Ave. E.
14th Ave. E.
13th Ave. E.
12th Ave. E.
11th Ave. E.

E. John St.

Federal Ave. E.
10th Ave. E.
Broadway E.
Harvard Ave. E.
Boylston Ave. E.
Belmont Ave. E.

E. Denny Way

E. Mercer St.
E. Roy St.

Summit Ave. E.

Bellevue Ave. E.
Melrose Ave. E.
Seattle Freeway

Lakeview Blvd. E.

E. Republican St.
E. Harrison St.
E. Thomas St.

E. Olive Way

E. Howell St.
E. Olive St.
E. Pine St.

Eastlake Ave. E.
Yale Ave. N.
Pontius Ave. N.
Minor Ave. N.

Fairview Ave. N.
Eastlake Ave. E.

Fairview Ave. N.

Boren Ave. N.

Republican St.
Harrison St.

Mercer St.
Terry Ave. N.
Westlake Ave. N.
9th Ave. N.

Thomas St.
John St.

Denny Way

Boren Ave.
Terry Ave.
9th Ave.
8th Ave.

Howell St.

Lenora St.
Blanchard St.
7th Ave.
6th Ave.
5th Ave.

Lake Union

South Lake Union Park

Valley St.
Roy St.

Denny Park

8th Ave. N.

Dexter Ave. N.
Aurora Ave. N.

Dexter Ave. N.
Aurora Ave. N.

QUEEN ANNE HILL

Galer St.
Taylor Ave. N.
5th Ave. N.
6th Ave. N.

Highland Dr.
Prospect St.
Ward St.
Aloha St.
Valley St.
Roy St.

6th Ave. N.
Taylor Ave. N.

Monorail

Cedar St.
Vine St.
Wall St.
Battery St.
Bell St.
Blanchard St.

SEATTLE CENTER

Space Needle

Broad St.

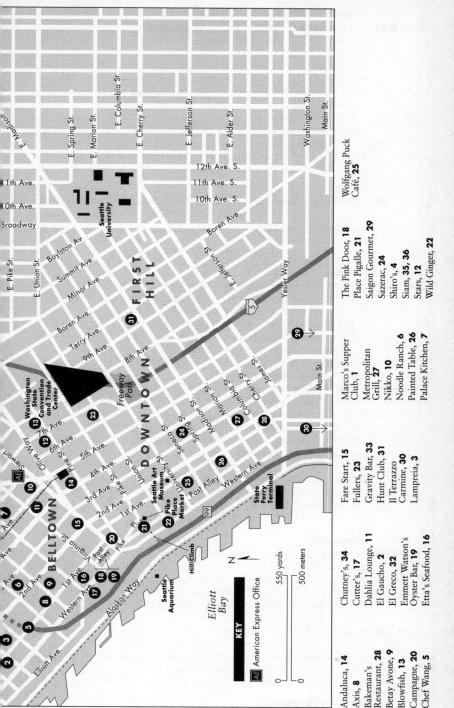

Andaluca, **14**
Axis, **8**
Bakeman's
Restaurant, **28**
Betay Avone, **9**
Blowfish, **13**
Campagne, **20**
Chef Wang, **5**

Chutney's, **34**
Cutter's, **17**
Dahlia Lounge, **11**
El Gaucho, **2**
El Greco, **32**
Emmett Watson's
Oyster Bar, **19**
Etta's Seafood, **16**

Fare Starr, **15**
Fullers, **23**
Gravity Bar, **33**
Hunt Club, **31**
Il Terrazzo
Carmine, **30**
Lampreia, **3**

Marco's Supper
Club, **1**
Metropolitan
Grill, **27**
Nikko, **10**
Noodle Ranch, **6**
Painted Table, **26**
Palace Kitchen, **7**

The Pink Door, **18**
Place Pigalle, **21**
Saigon Gourmet, **29**
Sazerac, **24**
Shiro's, **4**
Siam, **35, 36**
Stars, **12**
Wild Ginger, **22**

Wolfgang Puck
Café, **25**

French

$$$$ ✕ **Campagne.** The white walls, picture windows, snowy linens, candles, and fresh flowers at this urbane restaurant evoke Provence, as does the menu. French cuisine here means the robust flavors of the countryside, not the more polished tastes of Paris. To start, try the seafood sausage or the calamari fillets with ground almonds. Main plates include panfried scallops with a green-peppercorn and tarragon sauce, cinnamon-roasted quail served with carrot and orange essence, and Oregon rabbit accompanied by an apricot-cider and green-peppercorn sauce. Campagne, which overlooks Pike Place Market and Elliott Bay, is open only for dinner, but the adjacent Café Campagne serves breakfast, lunch, and dinner daily. ⊠ *Inn at the Market, 86 Pine St.,* ☎ *206/ 728–2800. Reservations essential. AE, DC, MC, V. No lunch.*

Indian

$$ ✕ **Chutney's.** The local chain (☞ Indian *in* North of Downtown Seattle Dining, *below*) has a Capitol Hill branch. The outstanding dishes include tandoori halibut and prawns, chicken kebabs, five curries, and rack of lamb. ⊠ *605 15th Ave. E,* ☎ *206/726–1000. AE, D, DC, MC, V.*

Italian

$$$–$$$$ ✕ **Il Terrazzo Carmine.** On the ground floor of a Pioneer Square office building, this restaurant owes its refined ambience to ceiling-to-floor draperies, genteel service, and quiet music. Chef-owner Carmine Smeraldo prepares flavorful chicken dishes with prosciutto and fontina, and his veal baked with spinach and scallops is excellent. The pasta dishes are superb. In the summer you can eat outdoors on a patio that faces a large fountain. ⊠ *411 1st Ave. S,* ☎ *206/467–7797. AE, D, DC, MC, V. Closed Sun. No lunch Sat.*

$$–$$$ ✕ **The Pink Door.** This restaurant with a "secret" entrance off Post Alley dishes up a generous portion of atmosphere along with solid Italian food. The roasted garlic and *tapenada* (a caper, anchovy, and black-olive spread) are eminently sharable appetizers; spaghetti *alla puttanesca* (with anchovies, capers, and tomatoes) and cioppino are the standout entrées. The quirky bar is often crowded with young people, and cabaret acts regularly perform on a small stage in the corner. But the real draw here is the outdoor deck, rimmed in flowers, topped with a canopy of colored lights, and perched perfectly over Pike Place Market, with a terrific view of the water beyond. ⊠ *1919 Post Alley,* ☎ *206/443–3241. AE, MC, V. Closed Sun.–Mon.*

Japanese

$$$–$$$$ ✕ **Nikko.** The ultrachic sushi bar is the architectural centerpiece at sophisticated Nikko, where the talented chefs prepare some of the best sushi and sashimi in Seattle. On the regular menu, the Kasu sake–marinated cod and teriyaki salmon are consistent winners. ⊠ *Westin Hotel, 1900 5th Ave.,* ☎ *206/322–4641. AE, D, DC, MC, V. Closed Sun. No lunch Sat.*

$$–$$$ ✕ **Shiro's.** Willfully unconcerned with atmosphere, this simple spot is a real curiosity amid Belltown's chic establishments. The focus is entirely on the exceptional menu of authentic Japanese fare. Indulge your curiosity in the more exotic offerings; a sure hand guides this sushi bar. ⊠ *2401 2nd Ave.,* ☎ *206/443–9844. AE, MC, V. Closed Sun.*

Mediterranean

$$–$$$ ✕ **Betay Avone.** The Mediterranean-inspired dishes at this restaurant inside an unassuming Belltown storefront are administered under rabbinical supervision. Moroccan *bysteeyas* (braised chicken with scallions, cinnamon, cayenne, and cumin wrapped in phyllo) are a fantastic starter, and the salmon fillet with caramelized onions and tahini over couscous is an imaginative spin on a Northwest staple. ✉ *113 Blanchard St.,* ☎ *206/448–5597. AE, MC, V. Closed Fri.–Sat. No lunch.*

$$–$$$ ✕ **El Greco.** Long on entertainment and shopping, the stretch of Broadway through Capitol Hill is curiously short on interesting dining options. El Greco's fresh, unadorned Mediterranean fare is your best bet. A Moroccan vegetable stew and rosemary grilled lamb are standouts on a sturdy menu, and there's a satisfying Sunday brunch. ✉ *219 Broadway E,* ☎ *206/328–4604. AE, MC, V. Closed Mon. No dinner Sun.*

Pan-Asian

$$–$$$ ✕ **Blowfish.** From the pachinko machines around the bar to the colorful origami and rattan fans on the ceiling, kid-friendly Blowfish is a festive, freewheeling place that takes advantage of the yen of Seattleites for Pan-Asian cuisine. The seafood and noodle specialties are worth investigating, but the small plates from the grill are the real stars on the flashy menu. Try the Korean *bulgogi* skirt steak (marinated in a tangy sauce of soy, mirin, and ginger) or the chicken wings in a caramel ginger sauce. Top it all off with a lime leaf and lemongrass "limontini." ✉ *722 Pine St.,* ☎ *206/467–7777. AE, D, DC, MC, V.*

$$–$$$ ✕ **Wild Ginger.** The seafood and Southeast Asian fare at this restaurant near Pike Place Market ranges from mild Cantonese to spicier Vietnamese, Thai, and Korean dishes. House specialties include *satay* (chunks of beef, chicken, or vegetables skewered and grilled, and usually served with a spicy peanut sauce), live crab cooked to order, sweetly flavored duck, wonderful soups, and some fine vegetarian options. The satay bar, where you can sip local brews and eat skewered tidbits until 2 AM, is a local hangout. The clubby, old-fashioned dining room has high ceilings and lots of mahogany and Asian art. ✉ *1400 Western Ave.,* ☎ *206/623–4450. AE, D, DC, MC, V. No lunch Sun.*

$–$$ ✕ **Noodle Ranch.** Tongue planted firmly in cheek, Noodle Ranch bills itself as Belltown's purveyor of "Pan-Asian vittles." Standouts on chef Nga Bui's inexpensive menu include sugar-cane shrimp, Japanese eggplant in ginger, and a spicy basil stir-fry. The gentle sense of humor evident in the name is borne out in the dressed-down decor. ✉ *2228 2nd Ave.,* ☎ *206/728–0463. AE, MC, V. Closed Sun.*

Seafood

$$–$$$$ ✕ **Cutter's.** Enthusiastic service and a harbor view go a long way to recommend Cutter's, but its allure doesn't stop there. Fresh fish is prepared on an apple-wood grill in a variety of creative ways. Fish and chips receive traditional treatment, but Asian accents can be discerned in a dish like the Penn Cove mussels in a coconut-curry broth, and European and South American influences are at work as well. ✉ *2001 Western Ave.,* ☎ *206/448–4884. AE, D, DC, MC, V.*

$$–$$$$ ✕ **Etta's Seafood.** Tom Douglas's restaurant near Pike Place Market has a sleek and slightly whimsical design and views of Victor Steinbrueck Park. In season try the Dungeness crab cakes or the various Washington oysters on the half shell. Brunch, served on weekends, always includes zesty seafood omelets, but the chef also does justice to French toast, eggs and bacon, and Mexican-influenced breakfast dishes. ✉ *2020 Western Ave.,* ☎ *206/443–6000. AE, D, DC, MC, V.*

$ ✕ **Emmett Watson's Oyster Bar.** This unpretentious spot can be hard to find—it's in the back of the Pike Place Market's Soames-Dunn Building, facing a small flower-bedecked courtyard—but for Seattleites and visitors who know their oysters, it's worth the special effort. Not only are the oysters very fresh and the beer icy cold, but both are inexpensive and available in any number of varieties. If you don't like oysters, try the salmon soup or the fish-and-chips—flaky pieces of fish with very little grease. ✉ *1916 Pike Pl.,* ☎ *206/448–7721. Reservations not accepted. No credit cards. No dinner Sun.*

Thai

$–$$ ✕ **Siam.** Thai cooking is ubiquitous in Seattle—it can almost be considered a mainstream cuisine. Start your meal at popular Siam with a satay skewer or the city's best *tom kah gai,* a soup of coconut, lemongrass, chicken, and mushrooms. Entrées include curries, noodle dishes, and many prawn, chicken, and fish preparations. You can specify one to five stars according to your tolerance for heat. The location on Fairview Avenue near Lake Union has a more relaxed atmosphere than the energetic Capitol Hill original on Broadway. ⊠ *616 Broadway,* ☎ *206/ 324–0892;* ⊠ *1880 Fairview Ave. E,* ☎ *206/323–8101. AE, MC, V. No lunch weekends.*

Vegetarian

$ ✕ **Gravity Bar.** Sprouty sandwiches and other "modern food," all healthful and then some, are dished up at this congenial juice bar with a sci-fi–industrial ambience. The juices—from any number of fruits and vegetables, solo or in combo—are often zippier than the solid food. ⊠ *415 Broadway E,* ☎ *206/325–7186. No credit cards.*

Vietnamese

$ ✕ **Saigon Gourmet.** This small café in the International District is ★ about as plain as they get, but the food is superb and incredibly inexpensive. Aficionados make special trips for the Cambodian soup and the shrimp rolls, but also consider the unusual papaya with beef jerky. Parking can be a problem, but the food rewards your patience. ⊠ *502 S. King St.,* ☎ *206/624–2611. Reservations not accepted. MC, V. Closed Mon.*

North of Downtown Seattle

American

$$$$ ✕ **Canlis.** Little has changed at this Seattle institution since the '50s, when steak served by kimono-clad waitresses represented the pinnacle of high living. Renovations in the mid-'90s made for a less old-boy clubby feel than before, but the restaurant is still very expensive and very popular. The view across Lake Union is almost as good as ever, though it now includes a forest of high-rises. Besides the famous steaks, there are equally famous oysters from Quilcene Bay and fresh fish in season. In 1998, *Wine Spectator* magazine bestowed a Grand Award on Canlis for its wine list and service. ⊠ *2576 Aurora Ave. N,* ☎ *206/ 283–3313. Reservations essential. AE, DC, MC, V. Closed Sun. No lunch.*

$$$ ✕ **Kaspar's.** A decidedly unglamorous atmosphere and its location amid lower Queen Anne Hill's low-rise office buildings and light-industrial warehouses focus the attention at this restaurant where it belongs— on chef-owner Kaspar Donier's finely wrought contemporary cuisine. Seafood, steak, and poultry options abound. The Muscovy duck with bosc pears and Hanoi-style sea bass with fennel and green onions are especially striking. The five-course Northwest seafood dinner is a lifeline for the indecisive. Its proximity to Seattle Center makes Kaspar's a natural destination before or after your evening's entertainment, but the food insists that you take your time. ⊠ *19 W. Harrison St., west of Queen Anne Ave. N,* ☎ *206/298–0123. AE, MC, V. Closed Sun.– Mon. No lunch.*

$$–$$$ ✕ **Five Spot.** Up the hill from Seattle Center, the unpretentious Five Spot has a regional American menu that makes a new stop every four months or so—Little Italy, New Orleans, and Florida have been previous ones. The Five Spot is also popular for Sunday brunch. At the restaurant's kitchen cousins, Jitterbug in Wallingford and the Coastal Kitchen in Capitol Hill, the same rotating menu strategy, with more

North of Downtown Seattle Dining

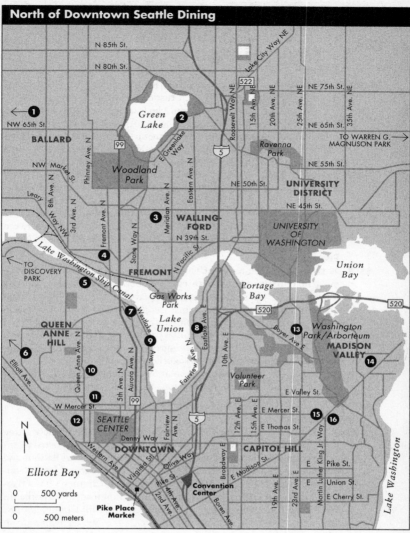

international flavor but equally satisfying results, applies. ✉ *1502 Queen Anne Ave. N,* ☎ *206/285–7768. MC, V. Jitterbug:* ✉ *2114 N. 45th St.,* ☎ *206/547–6313. MC, V. Coastal Kitchen:* ✉ *429 15th Ave. E,* ☎ *206/322–1145. MC, V.*

Eclectic

$$–$$$ ✕ **Bandoleone.** Here's a place that leads a double life. The dining room is simple and austere, even rustic, but the deck out back is festive and fun, decorated with colorful Mexican paper cutouts. Both spaces are perfect for a romantic dinner. The atmosphere here is decidedly unpretentious, and the sophisticated menu of large and small plates roams Spain, the Caribbean, and Central and South America. A sweet and clean grilled ahi tuna entrée comes with papaya black-bean salsa; the eggplant *relleno* is a swampy blend of squash, summer corn, sweet onions, and goat cheese. Tequila-cured salmon gravlax and a banana-macadamia empanada with a tamarind dipping sauce are two of several outstanding tapas. The gravlax also appears on the imaginative and inexpensive menu for Saturday and Sunday brunch (served between 9 and 2). ✉ *2241 Eastlake Ave. E,* ☎ *206/329–7559. MC, V. No lunch.*

French

$$$$ ✕ **Rover's.** The restaurant of Thierry Rautereau, one of the Northwest's
★ most imaginative chefs, is an essential destination on any culinary tour of Seattle. Sea scallops, venison, squab, lobster, and rabbit are frequent offerings (vegetarian items are also available) on the restaurant's prix-fixe menu. The incomparable sauce work and reliance on delicacies such as foie gras and truffles pay homage to Rautereau's French roots, but bold combinations of ingredients are evidence of his wanderlust. The service at Rover's is excellent—friendly but unobtrusive— the setting romantic, and the presentation stunning. ✉ *2808 E. Madison St.,* ☎ *206/325–7442. Reservations essential. AE, MC, V. Closed Sun.–Mon. No lunch.*

Indian

$$ ✕ **Chutney's.** The aromas of cardamom, cumin, and jasmine wafting through the air may make you feel like you've been transported to another continent. The outstanding dishes include tandoori halibut and prawns, chicken kebabs, five different curries, and rack of lamb. Consistently rated as one of Seattle's top restaurants, Chutney's has a flagship location in Queen Anne, a branch in Wallingford, and another in Capitol Hill (☞ Downtown Seattle and Capitol Hill Dining, *above*). ✉ *Queen Anne: 519 1st Ave. N,* ☎ *206/284–6799.* ✉ *Wallingford: 1815 N. 45th St.,* ☎ *206/634–1000. AE, D, DC, MC, V.*

Italian

$$$ ✕ **Saleh Al Lago.** Some of the best Italian and Mediterranean food in the city can be found north of downtown. The well-lighted dining room here is done in soft colors and, with its view of Green Lake, invites slow-paced dining. The traditional dishes are excellent, as are more exotic offerings like beet ravioli with Dungeness crab and caviar, and pan-seared tenderloin in a balsamic vinegar and peppercorn glaze. ✉ *6804 E. Greenlake Way N,* ☎ *206/522–7943. AE, DC, MC, V. Closed Sun.–Mon. No lunch Sat.*

$$–$$$$ ✕ **Cafe Lago.** Hugely popular with locals, Cafe Lago specializes in wood-fired pizzas and light handmade pastas. The lasagna—ricotta, béchamel, and cherry-tomato sauce amid paper-thin pasta sheets—perfectly represents the menu's inclination toward the simply satisfying. Spare table settings, high ceilings, and a friendly atmosphere make the restaurant suitable for a night out with friends or a romantic getaway. ✉ *2305 24th Ave. E,* ☎ *206/329–8005. D, DC, MC, V. Closed Mon. No lunch.*

Mediterranean

$$$–$$$$ ✕ **Adriatica.** The dining room and upstairs bar in this hillside Crafts-man-style house have terrific views of Lake Union. The food could best be described as Pacific Northwest–influenced Greek and Italian cuisine. Regular offerings include fresh fish, pastas, risotto, and seafood souvlaki. ⊠ *1107 Dexter Ave. N,* ☏ *206/285–5000. Reservations essential. AE, DC, MC, V. No lunch.*

Mexican

$$–$$$ ✕ **El Camino.** The atmosphere at this loose, loud, and funky Fremont storefront perfectly mirrors El Camino's irreverent Northwest interpretation of Mexican cuisine. Rock-shrimp quesadillas, chipotle-pepper and garlic sea bass, and duck with a spicy green sauce are typical of the kitchen's gentle spin. Even a green salad becomes transformed with toasted pumpkin seeds on crispy romaine with a cool dressing of garlic, lime juice, and cilantro. As for cool, there's no better place to chill on a summer afternoon than El Camino's deck. A tart margarita, served in a pint glass, makes the perfect accessory. ⊠ *607 N. 35th St.,* ☏ *206/632–7303. AE, DC, MC, V. No lunch weekdays.*

Seafood

$$$–$$$$ ✕ **Palisade.** The short ride to the Magnolia neighborhood yields a stunning view back across Elliott Bay to the lights of downtown. And there's no better place to take in the vista than this restaurant at the Elliott Bay Marina. Palisade scores points for its playfully exotic ambience—complete with a gurgling indoor stream. As for the food, the simpler preparations, especially the signature plank-broiled salmon, are most satisfying. Maggie Bluffs, an informal café downstairs, is a great spot for lunch on a breezy summer afternoon. ⊠ *2601 W. Marina Pl.; from downtown, take Elliott Ave. northwest across Magnolia Bridge to Elliott Bay Marina exit,* ☏ *206/285–1000. AE, D, DC, MC, V.*

$$$–$$$$ ✕ **Ray's Boathouse.** The view of Puget Sound may be the big draw here,
★ but the seafood is impeccably fresh and well prepared. Perennial favorites include broiled salmon, Kasu sake–marinated cod, Dungeness crab, and regional oysters on the half shell. Ray's has a split personality: there's a fancy dining room downstairs and a casual café and bar upstairs. In warm weather you can sit on the deck outside the café and watch the parade of fishing boats, tugs, and pleasure craft floating past, almost right below your table. ⊠ *6049 Seaview Ave. NW,* ☏ *206/789–3770. Reservations essential for dining room; reservations not accepted for café. AE, DC, MC, V.*

$$–$$$$ ✕ **Ponti.** Working in a placid canal-side villa-like location a stone's throw from the Fremont and Aurora Bridges, chef Alvin Binuya builds culinary bridges between Northwest ingredients and Mediterranean and Asian techniques. Alaskan king crab legs with a chardonnay butter and herb mayonnaise manifest the kitchen's classic restraint; the grilled mahimahi with satsuma potato gratin and shallot jus walks on the wilder side. ⊠ *3014 3rd Ave. N,* ☏ *206/284–3000. AE, DC, MC, V.*

Southwestern

$$ ✕ **Cactus.** It's worth the drive to Madison Park to experience the rich flavors and colorful atmosphere of Cactus. The food, which displays Native American, Spanish, and Mexican influences, will satisfy wide-ranging palates, from the vegetarian to the carnivorous. From the tapas bar, sample the marinated eggplant, the garlic shrimp, or the tuna *escabeche* (spicy cold marinade). Larger plates include the vegetarian chili relleno, the grilled pork with orange and chipotle peppers, and a flavorful ancho-chili and cinnamon roasted chicken. ⊠ *4220 E. Madison St.,* ☏ *206/324–4140. D, DC, MC, V.*

Vegetarian

$$–$$$　✕ **Cafe Flora.** This sophisticated Madison Valley café attracts vegetarians and meat eaters for artistically presented full-flavored meals. An adventurous menu includes Portobello mushroom Wellington, fajitas, and polenta topped with onion, rosemary, and mushrooms. Sunday brunch draws a crowd. ✉ *2901 E. Madison St.,* ☎ *206/325–9100. MC, V. Closed Mon. No dinner Sun.*

LODGING

Seattle has lodgings to suit most budgets. Though the city has many rooms, you need to book as far in advance as possible if you're coming between May and September. The most elegant properties are downtown; less expensive but still tasteful options, usually smaller in size (and with more of a Seattle feel), can be found in the University District. Many of the lower-price motels along Aurora Avenue North (Highway 99) were built for the 1962 World's Fair. Air travelers often stay along Pacific Highway South (also Highway 99), near Seattle-Tacoma International Airport. Always inquire about special rates based on occupancy or weekend stays.

CATEGORY	COST*
$$$$	over $170
$$$	$110–$170
$$	$60–$110
$	under $60

All prices are for a standard double room, excluding 15.6% combined hotel and state sales tax.

Downtown

$$$$　🏨 **Alexis Hotel.** The European-style Alexis occupies two restored buildings near the waterfront. Complimentary sherry awaits you in the lobby bar upon your arrival, a prelude to the attentive service you'll receive during your stay. Rooms are decorated in subdued colors and with imported Italian and French fabrics, with at least one piece of antique furniture. Some suites have whirlpool tubs or wood-burning fireplaces, and some have marble fixtures. Unfortunately, views are limited and rooms facing 1st Avenue can be noisy. Amenities include shoe shines, the morning newspaper, and access to workout facilities. Pets are welcome. ✉ *1007 1st Ave., 98104,* ☎ *206/624–4844 or 800/426–7033,* 𝔽𝔸𝕏 *206/621–9009. 65 rooms, 44 suites. Restaurant, bar, in-room data ports, minibars, room service, spa, steam room, exercise room, laundry service, meeting rooms, parking (fee). Continental breakfast. AE, D, DC, MC, V.*

$$$$　🏨 **Four Seasons Olympic Hotel.** The 1920s Renaissance Revival–style Olympic is the grande dame of Seattle hotels. Marble, wood paneling, potted plants, thick rugs, and plush armchairs adorn the public spaces. Palms and skylights in the Garden Court provide a relaxing background for lunch, afternoon tea, or dancing to a live swing band on the weekends. The Georgian Room, the hotel's premier dining room, exudes Italian Renaissance elegance. The Shuckers oyster bar is more casual. Guest rooms, decorated with period reproductions and floral print fabrics, are less luxurious than the public areas but have a homey feel. All have sofas, comfortable reading chairs, and desks. Amenities include valet parking, chocolates on your pillow, complimentary shoe shines, the morning newspaper, and a bathrobe. ✉ *411 University St., 98101,* ☎ *206/621–1700 or 800/223–8772,* 𝔽𝔸𝕏 *206/682–9633. 450 rooms. 3 restaurants, lounge, in-room data ports, in-room safes, minibars, room*

service, indoor pool, health club, children's programs, laundry service, concierge, meeting rooms, parking (fee). AE, D, DC, MC, V.

$$$$ ★ 🏨 **Hotel Monaco.** Goldfish in your room are among the fun touches at this luxury hotel inside a former office building in the heart of the Financial District. The light and whimsical lobby has high ceilings and hand-painted nautical murals inspired by the fresco at the Palace of Knossos in Crete. A pleasing blend of bold and bright colors and patterns graces the spacious guest rooms. The in-room amenities include voice mail, fax machines, irons, hair dryers, coffeemakers, and stereos with compact-disc players. The hotel welcomes pets. ⊠ *1101 4th Ave., 98101,* ☎ *206/621–1770 or 800/945–2240,* FAX *206/621–7779. 144 rooms, 45 suites. Restaurant, bar, in-room data ports, no-smoking rooms, room service, exercise room, dry cleaning, laundry service, concierge, business services, meeting rooms, airport shuttle, parking (fee). AE, D, DC, MC, V.*

$$$$ 🏨 **Hotel Vintage Park.** As a tribute to the state's growing wine industry, each accommodation in this small hotel is named for a Washington winery or vineyard. The theme is extended to complimentary servings of local wines each evening in the lobby, where patrons can relax on richly upholstered sofas and chairs arranged around a marble fireplace. The rooms, which are decorated in color schemes of dark green, plum, deep red, taupe, and gold, are furnished with custom-made cherry-wood pieces and original works by San Francisco artist Chris Kidd. For literary-minded guests, hotel staff will check out and deliver your choice of titles from the nearby Seattle Public Library. The more athletically inclined can have exercise equipment brought to their rooms. ⊠ *1100 5th Ave., 98101,* ☎ *206/624–8000 or 800/624–4433,* FAX *206/623–0568. 126 rooms. Restaurant, in-room data ports, minibars, no-smoking floors, refrigerators, room service, spa, laundry service, concierge, meeting rooms, parking (fee). AE, D, DC, MC, V.*

$$$$ 🏨 **Mayflower Park Hotel.** The brass fixtures and antiques at this older property near the Westlake Center lend its public and private spaces a muted Asian feel. The service here is unobtrusive and smooth. Rooms are on the small side, but the Mayflower Park is so sturdily constructed that it is much quieter than many modern downtown hotels. Guests have privileges at a nearby health club. ⊠ *405 Olive Way, 98101,* ☎ *206/623–8700 or 800/426–5100,* FAX *206/382–6997. 159 rooms, 13 suites. Restaurant, bar, no-smoking rooms, room service, exercise room, laundry service, business services, meeting rooms, parking (fee). AE, D, DC, MC, V.*

$$$$ 🏨 **Seattle Hilton.** This hotel west of I–5 hosts many conventions and meetings. The tastefully nondescript rooms have soothing color schemes. The Top of the Hilton serves well-prepared salmon dishes and other local specialties and has excellent views of the city. An underground passage connects the Hilton with the Rainier Square shopping concourse, the 5th Avenue Theater, and the convention center. ⊠ *1301 6th Ave., 98101,* ☎ *206/624–0500, 800/542–7700, or 800/426–0535,* FAX *206/ 682–9029. 237 rooms, 3 suites. 2 restaurants, piano bar, in-room data ports, minibars, no-smoking floors, room service, exercise room, laundry service, concierge, business services, meeting rooms, parking (fee). AE, D, DC, MC, V.*

$$$$ 🏨 **Sorrento.** The Sorrento, built in 1909, was designed to look like an Italian villa. The dramatic entrance is along a circular driveway around a fountain ringed with palms. Sitting high on First Hill, the hotel has views overlooking downtown and Elliott Bay. The rooms, some of them quite small, are quiet and comfortable. The largest are the corner suites, which have some antiques and spacious baths. The Hunt Club (☞ *Dining, above*) serves Pacific Northwest dishes. The dark-paneled Fireside Lounge in the lobby is an inviting spot for coffee, tea, or cock-

46

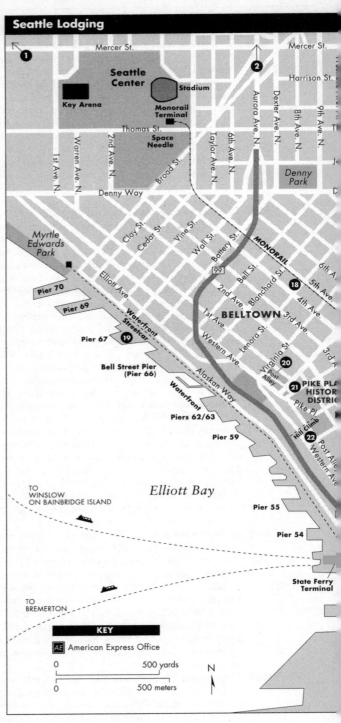

Seattle Lodging

Mercer St. — Mercer St.

Harrison St.

Seattle Center

Stadium

Key Arena

Monorail Terminal

Thomas St.

Space Needle

Aurora Ave. N.

Dexter Ave. N.

8th Ave. N.

9th Ave. N.

1st Ave. N.

Warren Ave. N.

2nd Ave. N.

Taylor Ave. N.

6th Ave. N.

Denny Park

Denny Way

Myrtle Edwards Park

Clay St. Cedar St. Vine St. Wall St. Battery St.

MONORAIL

99

Bell St.

Blanchard St.

6th A

5th Ave.

4th Ave.

18

Elliott Ave.

Pier 70

Pier 69

Waterfront Streetcar

Pier 67

19

2nd Ave.

1st Ave.

Western Ave.

Lenora St.

3rd Ave.

BELLTOWN

3rd A

Bell Street Pier (Pier 66)

Alaskan Way

Waterfront

Virginia St.

Post Alley

20

21 PIKE PLA HISTOR DISTRIC

Piers 62/63

Pike Pl.

Hill Climb

22

Post Alle

Western Av

Pier 59

Elliott Bay

TO WINSLOW ON BAINBRIDGE ISLAND

Pier 55

Pier 54

TO BREMERTON

State Ferry Terminal

KEY

AE American Express Office

0 — 500 yards

0 — 500 meters

N

Republican St.

E. Mercer St.

CAPITOL HILL

E. Republican St.

③ ④ ⑦ ⑧ ⑫

E. Harrison St.

Wa____ Ave. N.

Terry Ave. N.

omas St.

Boren Ave. N.

Fairview Ave. N.

Minor Ave. N.

Pontius Ave. N.

Yale Ave. N.

Eastlake Ave. E.

Seattle Freeway

Melrose Ave. E.

Bellevue Ave. E.

Summit Ave. E.

Belmont Ave. E.

Harvard Ave. E.

Boylston Ave. E.

Broadway E.

10th Ave. E.

11th Ave. E.

Federal Ave. E.

E. John St.

ohn St.

E. Thomas St.

⑬

enny Way

E. Olive Way

E. Denny Way

Boren Ave.

Terry Ave.

9th Ave.

Howell St.

8th Ave.

7th Ave.

Stewart St.

E. Howell St.

Seattle Central Community College

E. Olive St.

Broadway

10th Ave.

11th Ave.

12th Ave.

Broadway Playfield

⑭

E. Pine St.

E. Pike St.

Olive Way

⑮

⑯

E. Union St.

13th Ave.

14th Ave.

15th Ave.

AE

⑰

Pine St.

⑳④

⑦th Ave.

Washington State Convention and Trade Center

Boylston Ave.

Summit Ave.

Minor Ave.

Boren Ave.

Terry Ave.

Seattle University

⑳③

Monorail Terminal

4th Ave.

5th Ave.

6th Ave.

⑳⑤

Union St.

⑳⑥

Freeway Park

8th Ave.

9th Ave.

CE

T

Pike St.

OWNTOWN

⑳⑨

University St.

2nd Ave.

⑳⑧ ③①

Seneca St.

③③ ③②

⑳⑥

Spring St.

⑳⑦

FIRST HILL

Cherry St.

11th Ave.

10th Ave.

③⑩

③④

Madison St.

Marion St.

Frye Museum of Art ■

Boren Ave.

⑨

③⑤

1st Ave.

Columbia St.

Cherry St.

James St.

E. Jefferson St.

Pioneer Place ■

Yesler Way

Washington St.

⑳⑥ **PIONEER SQUARE**

Waterfall Garden ■

Main St.

S. Jackson

S. King

2nd Ave. S.

INTERNATIONAL DISTRICT

Uwajimaya ■

Maynard Ave. S.

7th Ave. S.

8th Ave. S.

S. King St.

10th Ave. S.

12th Ave.

S. Weller St.

S. Lane

Kingdome

1st Ave. S.

Occidental Ave. S.

4th Ave. S.

Airport Way S.

S. Dearborn St.

③⑦ ⑳③

9

tails. Other amenities include complimentary limousine service within the downtown area and privileges at a nearby athletic club. ⊠ *900 Madison St., 98104,* ☎ *206/622–6400 or 800/426–1265,* FAX *206/343–6155. 76 rooms, 42 suites. Restaurant, bar, in-room data ports, minibars, room service, laundry service, concierge, meeting rooms, parking (fee). AE, D, DC, MC, V.*

$$$$ 🏨 **Warwick Hotel.** Despite its size, the Warwick has an intimate feel. Service is friendly and leisurely (but not slow), and the rooms are understated without being bland. Most have small balconies with views of downtown. There is live entertainment in the Liaison restaurant and lounge, and 24-hour courtesy transportation within downtown. ⊠ *401 Lenora St., 98121,* ☎ *206/443–4300 or 800/426–9280,* FAX *206/448–1662. 225 rooms, 4 suites. Restaurant, bar, in-room data ports, no-smoking rooms, room service, indoor pool, hot tub, sauna, exercise room, concierge, parking (fee). AE, D, DC, MC, V.*

$$$$ 🏨 **WestCoast Roosevelt Hotel.** An older hotel near the convention center and the shopping district, the Roosevelt has an elegant lobby with a grand piano, a fireplace, a Chinese lacquered screen, and walls of windows—a great place to relax and watch the foot traffic outside. Smallish rooms are furnished with period reproduction furniture upholstered in mellow pinks and greens. Thanks to the insulated windows you can enjoy city views without hearing street noise. Some bathrooms have their original tile work, though there isn't much counter space. ⊠ *1531 7th Ave.,* ☎ *206/621–1200 or 800/426–0670,* FAX *206/233–0335. 138 rooms, 13 suites. Restaurant, bar, in-room data ports, no-smoking rooms, room service, exercise room, laundry service, meeting rooms, parking (fee). AE, D, DC, MC, V.*

$$$$ 🏨 **Westin Hotel.** The flagship of the Westin chain often hosts visiting dignitaries, including U.S. presidents. Northeast of Pike Place Market, the hotel is easily recognizable by its twin cylindrical towers. With this design, all rooms have terrific views of Puget Sound, Lake Union, the Space Needle, or the city. Airy rooms are furnished in a plain but high-quality style. A number have been turned into guest office rooms equipped with fax machines, speakerphones, and modem hookups. ⊠ *1900 5th Ave., 98101,* ☎ *206/728–1000 or 800/228–3000,* FAX *206/727–5896. 822 rooms, 43 suites. 3 restaurants, 2 bars, in-room data ports, in-room safes, minibars, no-smoking floors, room service, indoor pool, beauty salon, massage, exercise room, children's programs, laundry service, concierge, business services, convention center, car rental, parking (fee). AE, D, DC, MC, V.*

$$$–$$$$ 🏨 **Edgewater.** The spacious accommodations on the waterfront side of the only hotel on Elliott Bay have views of ferries, barges, and the Olympic Mountains. Rooms are decorated in rustic plaids and pale unfinished wood furniture. From the lobby's comfortable sofas and chairs, you can sometimes see sea lions frolicking in the bay. A courtesy van shuttles patrons to the downtown area on a first-come, first-served basis. ⊠ *Pier 67, 2411 Alaskan Way, 98121,* ☎ *206/728–7000 or 800/624–0670,* FAX *206/441–4119. 237 rooms. Restaurant, bar, in-room data ports, minibars, no-smoking rooms, room service, exercise room, bicycles, laundry service, concierge, meeting rooms, parking (fee). AE, D, DC, MC, V.*

$$$–$$$$ 🏨 **Inn at Harbor Steps.** On the lower floors of a high-rise residential
★   building, this lodging is a departure for Four Sisters Inns, whose collection of small hotels focuses on country getaways. Although the entrance and corridors have something of a yuppie-dormitory feel to them, the rooms are commodious, with high ceilings, gas fireplaces, and tidy kitchenettes. The bathrooms accommodate large tubs (some of them whirlpools) and oversize glass-enclosed shower stalls. A tempting breakfast buffet is served in the dining room; afternoon tea, poured in

the library, provides a welcome respite from the bustle of the city outside. ✉ *1221 First Ave., 98101,* ☎ *206/748–0973 or 888/728–8910,* ℻ *206/682–6045. 20 rooms. In-room data ports, refrigerators, indoor pool, sauna, basketball court, exercise room, coin laundry, laundry service, concierge, meeting room, parking (fee). Full breakfast. AE, MC, V.*

$$$–$$$$ 🏨 **Inn at the Market.** This sophisticated yet unpretentious property up
★ the street from Pike Place Market is perfect for travelers who prefer originality, personality, and coziness. The good-size rooms are decorated with comfortable modern furniture and small touches such as fresh flowers and ceramic sculptures. Ask for a room with views of the market and Elliott Bay. Coffee and the morning newspaper are complimentary each morning. An added plus is the fifth-floor deck, furnished with Adirondack chairs and overlooking the water and market. Guests have access to a health club and spa. The restaurants here include Campagne (☞ Dining, *above*), its less formal yet equally romantic café spin-off, and Bacco, which serves tasty variations on breakfast classics. ✉ *86 Pine St., 98101,* ☎ *206/443–3600 or 800/446–4484,* ℻ *206/448–0631. 60 rooms, 10 suites. 3 restaurants, in-room data ports, no-smoking rooms, refrigerators, room service, laundry service, concierge, meeting room, parking (fee). AE, D, DC, MC, V.*

$$$–$$$$ 🏨 **Madison.** Rooms at this high-rise between downtown and I–5 are decorated in deep green, burgundy, and brown, with metal accents and dark-wood furniture. Good views of downtown, Elliott Bay, and the Cascades can be had from above the 10th floor—above the 20th they're excellent. Guests on club-level floors (25, 26, and 27) receive complimentary Continental breakfast and have their own concierge. Amenities on other floors include complimentary coffee, the morning newspaper, and shoe shines. The health club has a 40-ft rooftop pool and a hot tub. ✉ *515 Madison St., 98104,* ☎ *206/583–0300 or 800/ 278–4159,* ℻ *206/622–8635. 466 rooms, 88 suites. 2 restaurants, bar, in-room data ports, minibars, room service, laundry service, concierge, meeting rooms, parking (fee). AE, D, DC, MC, V.*

$$$–$$$$ 🏨 **Marqueen Hotel.** This elegant 1918 brick apartment building at the foot of Queen Anne Hill was converted into a hotel in 1998. Just blocks away from the Seattle Center, this location is ideal for patrons of the opera, ballet, theater, or events at the Key Arena. The dark lobby has marble floors, original wainscoting, box beam ceilings, overstuffed furniture, Asian-style lacquered screens and a grand staircase looking out at a garden mural painted on the facing building. All of the guest rooms are spacious with kitchens and sitting areas. The beds have down comforter covers in green, gold, pink, and burgundy that coordinate with the window coverings. The rooms are furnished with antique replicas. A complimentary paper is left outside the door each morning. ✉ *600 Queen Ave. N., 98109,* ☎ *206/282–7407,* ℻ *206/283–1499. 47 rooms, 4 suites. Kitchens, in-room data ports, room service, laundry service, valet parking (fee). AE, D, DC, MC, V.*

$$$–$$$$ 🏨 **Paramount Hotel.** The château-style Paramount opened in 1996 as a companion to the high-tech entertainment sites one block away, including Planet Hollywood, GameWorks, NikeTown, and a 16-screen Cineplex Odeon multiplex. Neither the Paramount nor these facilities has a particularly Seattle feel, but the hotel's comfortable lobby has a fireplace, bookshelves, and period reproductions lending it the feel of a country gentleman's smoking parlor. Rooms, quiet but small, are decorated in hunter green and beige with gray accents. All have work areas, lounge chairs, large bathrooms, and movie and game systems. ✉ *724 Pine St., 98101,* ☎ *206/292–9500 or 800/426–0670,* ℻ *206/292–8610. 146 rooms, 2 suites. Restaurant, in-room data ports, no-smoking rooms, room service, exercise room, laundry service, concierge, meeting rooms, parking (fee). AE, D, DC, MC, V.*

$$$–$$$$ ▦ **Pioneer Square Hotel.** A mid-1990s renovation trimmed this 1914 workmen's hotel down to 75 generously sized rooms and three suites. Furnishings are standard issue; the color scheme is predominantly pink. Rooms at the back of the hotel face an air shaft, creating a dark but peaceful refuge. Guests have access to a nearby health club. ⊠ 77 *Yesler Way, 98104,* ☎ *206/340–1234,* FAX *206/467–0707. 75 rooms, 3 suites. Coffee shop, pub, in-room data ports, no-smoking rooms, room service, laundry service, concierge, business services, meeting rooms, parking (fee). Continental breakfast. AE, D, DC, MC, V.*

$$$–$$$$ ▦ **Seattle Sheraton Hotel and Towers.** Business travelers are the primary patrons of this large hotel near the convention center. Rooms on the top five floors, larger and more elegant than those on lower floors, include concierge service and complimentary Continental breakfast. Dining options within the complex include Fullers (☞ Dining, *above*), one of Seattle's best restaurants. The Pike Street Cafe serves all-American cuisine in a casual atmosphere. The lobby features an art-glass collection by well-known Northwest artist Dale Chihuly. ⊠ *1400 6th Ave., 98101,* ☎ *206/621–9000 or 800/325–3535,* FAX *206/621–8441. 800 rooms, 40 suites. 4 restaurants, 2 bars, in-room data ports, in-room safes, minibars, room service, indoor pool, health club, laundry service, concierge, meeting rooms, parking (fee). AE, D, DC, MC, V.*

$$$ ▦ **Crowne Plaza.** This favorite of business travelers is directly off I–5, midway between First Hill and the Financial District. The lobby is small and plainly appointed in teal and cream with brass accents and houseplants. Rooms are quiet and spacious, with views of the Kingdome and Harbor Island to the south and Elliott Bay and the Space Needle to the north; all have lounge chairs and work areas. The relaxed and friendly staff is very attentive. ⊠ *1113 6th Ave., 98101,* ☎ *206/464–1980 or 800/521–2762,* FAX *206/340–1617. 415 rooms, 28 suites. Restaurant, bar, in-room data ports, no-smoking rooms, room service, sauna, health club, laundry service, concierge, business services, meeting rooms, parking (fee). AE, D, DC, MC, V.*

$$–$$$ ▦ **Pacific Plaza.** This 1929 property that retains a '20s–'30s feel is a good bargain for singles or couples; families may find the nondescript rooms too small to accommodate them. ⊠ *400 Spring St., 98104,* ☎ *206/623–3900 or 800/426–1165,* FAX *206/623–2059. 159 rooms. Restaurant, coffee shop, pizzeria, no-smoking rooms, concierge, parking (fee). Continental breakfast. AE, D, DC, MC, V.*

$$–$$$ ▦ **WestCoast Camlin Hotel.** The lobby of this 1926 apartment-hotel on the edge of downtown but near the convention center has Oriental carpets, large mirrors, and lots of marble. Rooms ending with the number 10 are the best; they have windows on three sides. All rooms have work spaces with a chair and a table, and a cushioned chair to relax in. One drawback here is the noisy heating, air-conditioning, and ventilation system, but these (along with the rest of the hotel) are slated to be upgraded in 2000. ⊠ *1619 9th Ave., 98101,* ☎ *206/682–0100 or 800/426–0670,* FAX *206/682–7415. 132 rooms, 4 suites. Restaurant, bar, in-room data ports, room service, pool, dry cleaning, concierge, meeting rooms. AE, D, DC, MC, V.*

$$ ▦ **Pensione Nichols.** One block from Pike Place Market, the location of this B&B can't be beat. Suites on the second floor have enclosed balconies, full-size kitchens, private baths, separate bedrooms, and large open living rooms. Most rooms on the third floor have skylights rather than windows and are decorated in light colors with antique and contemporary furnishings. ⊠ *1923 1st Ave., 98101,* ☎ *206/441–7125 or 800/440–7125. 10 rooms share 4 baths, 2 suites. Continental breakfast. AE, D, DC, MC, V.*

$ ⊡ **Youth Hostel: Seattle International.** You can bed down in dormitory style for about $20 a night at this hostel near Pike Place Market. Guests have kitchen and dining-room access. ⊠ *84 Union St., 98101,* ☎ *206/622–5443. 3 rooms, 191 dormitory beds share baths. Library, coin laundry. AE, MC, V.*

Capitol Hill

$$–$$$ ⊡ **Gaslight Inn.** The rooms at this B&B range from a crow's nest with
★ peeled-log furniture and Navajo-print fabrics to suites with gas fireplaces and antique carved beds. There's also an apartment with a blown-glass chandelier and views of downtown and Elliott Bay. The large common areas have a masculine feel, with oak wainscoting, animal statuary, high ceilings, and hunter-green carpeting. One owner's past career as a professional painter is evident in the impeccable custom-mixed finishes throughout the inn. All patrons have the use of a laundry room; those staying in the suites receive free off-street parking. ⊠ *1727 15th Ave., 98122,* ☎ *206/325–3654,* FAX *206/328–4803. 9 rooms, 7 suites. No-smoking rooms, pool. Continental breakfast. AE, MC, V.*

$$–$$$ ⊡ **Hill House.** Inside an impeccably restored 1903 Victorian, this B&B contains richly colored rooms with a mix of antique and contemporary furnishings. Two suites have phones and televisions. That the rates here include a filling breakfast and free off-street parking makes this one of the city's best bargains. Book well in advance for summer weekends. ⊠ *1113 E. John St.,* ☎ *206/720–7161 or 800/720–7161,* FAX *206/ 323–0772. 7 rooms, 5 with private bath. Free parking. Full breakfast. AE, D, DC, MC, V.*

Lake Union and Fremont

$$$$ ⊡ **Marriott Residence Inn.** An extended-stay hotel on scenic Lake Union, the Marriott is a perfect choice for families. All rooms are either one- or two-bedroom suites, each with a living room and a fully equipped kitchen. Decorated in greens and blues, the comfortable suites get plenty of natural light. The lobby is within a seven-story atrium with a waterfall and many areas to relax, watch TV, play games, or look up recipes in cookbooks displayed on bookshelves. Room rates include complimentary shuttle service within a 2½-mi radius of the hotel. ⊠ *800 Fairview Ave. N, 98109,* ☎ *206/624–6000; 800/331–3131 (central reservations),* FAX *206/223–8160. 234 suites. Room service, no-smoking rooms, indoor pool, sauna, spa, exercise room, children's programs, parking (fee). Continental breakfast. AE, D, DC, MC, V.*

$$–$$$ ⊡ **Chelsea Station.** The feel is very Seattle at this B&B across the street from the Woodland Park Zoo. The parlor and breakfast rooms are decorated in sage green with mission-oak furniture, brocade upholstery, lace curtains, and works by local artists. Spacious guest rooms, each with a phone and a writing desk, have antique and contemporary furnishings. The accommodations in front have views of the Cascades. One suite has a piano, another a kitchen. Several rooms have adjoining doors, useful for families or larger groups. Breakfast will be tailored to your special dietary needs upon request. ⊠ *4915 Linden Ave. N, 98103,* ☎ *206/547–6077 or 800/400–6077,* FAX *206/632– 5107. 2 rooms, 7 suites. In-room data ports. Full breakfast. AE, D, DC, MC, V.*

University District

$$$$ ⊞ **Edmond Meany Tower Hotel.** This 1931 property within blocks of the University of Washington contains rooms bathed in soothing shades of white, with bright-red lounge chairs providing a bold contrast. The rooms, whose amenities include hair dryers and irons with boards, have unparalleled views of the university, Mount Rainier, Green Lake, or Lake Union. ⊠ *4507 Brooklyn Ave. NE, 98105,* ☎ *206/634–2000 or 800/899–0251,* ℻ *206/547–6029. 155 rooms. Restaurant, bar, in-room data ports, no-smoking rooms, room service, exercise room, laundry service, concierge, meeting rooms, free parking. AE, DC, MC, V.*

$$–$$$$ ⊞ **University Plaza Hotel.** Families and business travelers like this full-service motor hotel across I–5 from the University of Washington. The mock-Tudor decor gives the place a dated feel, but the service is cheerful and the rooms are spacious and pleasantly decorated in teak furniture. Ask for a room away from the freeway. ⊠ *400 N.E. 45th St., 98105,* ☎ *206/634–0100 or 800/343–7040,* ℻ *206/633–2743. 135 rooms. Restaurant, bar, no-smoking rooms, room service, pool, beauty salon, exercise room, meeting rooms, free parking. AE, D, DC, MC, V.*

$$$ ⊞ **University Inn.** The no-nonsense accommodations at this modern hotel have writing desks and are decorated in light wood and floral patterns. Some rooms have decks. Units in back are quieter. Enjoy the hot tub year-round and the outdoor pool in season. ⊠ *4140 Roosevelt Way NE, 98105,* ☎ *206/632–5055 or 800/733–3855,* ℻ *206/547–4937. 102 rooms. Restaurant, in-room data ports, in-room safes, no-smoking floors, outdoor pool, hot tub, exercise room, coin laundry, dry cleaning, meeting rooms, free parking. Continental breakfast. AE, D, DC, MC, V.*

$$–$$$ ⊞ **Chambered Nautilus.** A resident teddy bear will keep you company at this Georgian Colonial B&B that was built in 1915 by a professor of Oriental studies at the University of Washington. Rooms all have private baths, some with antique dressers converted to serve as sinks and counters. Most rooms have private porches, one has a fireplace, and all come with robes and well-stocked bookshelves. Breakfast might include French toast with orange syrup or a breakfast pie made with salmon, dill, and Swiss cheese. ⊠ *5005 22nd Ave. NE, 98105,* ☎ *206/522–2536,* ℻ *206/528–0898. 6 rooms. Full breakfast. AE, MC, V.*

Seattle-Tacoma International Airport

$$$–$$$$ ⊞ **Doubletree Inn, Doubletree Suites.** These two hotels across the street from each other are adjacent to the Southcenter shopping mall and convenient to business-park offices. The Inn is a classic Pacific Northwest–style lodge; its rooms are smaller and less lavish than those at the Suites, but they're perfectly fine and cost at least $25 less. Accommodations at the Suites all have sofas, tables and chairs, and wet bars. ⊠ *Doubletree Inn, 205 Strander Blvd., 98188,* ☎ *206/575–8220 or 800/325–8733,* ℻ *206/575–4743. 193 rooms, 5 suites. Bar, coffee shop, dining room, indoor pool, outdoor pool, meeting rooms, airport shuttle, free parking. Doubletree Suites, ⊠ 16500 Southcenter Pkwy., 98188,* ☎ *206/575–8220 or 800/325–8733,* ℻ *206/575–4743. 221 suites. Restaurant, bar, refrigerators, indoor pool, hot tub, sauna, health club, racquetball, meeting rooms, airport shuttle, free parking. AE, D, DC, MC, V.*

$$$–$$$$ ⊞ **Marriott Sea-Tac.** The luxurious Marriott has a five-story, 21,000-
★   square-ft tropical atrium that's complete with a waterfall, a dining area, an indoor pool, and a lounge. Rooms are decorated in greens and mauve with dark-wood and brass furnishings. ⊠ *3201 S. 176th St., 98188,* ☎ *206/241–2000 or 800/643–5479,* ℻ *206/248–0789. 459 rooms.*

Restaurant, lobby lounge, in-room data ports, no-smoking rooms, room service, indoor pool, hot tubs, sauna, health club, video games, laundry service, concierge, meeting rooms, airport shuttle, free parking. AE, D, DC, MC, V.

$$$-$$$$ 🏨 **Wyndham Garden Hotel.** This hotel has convenient airport access. The elegant lobby has a fireplace, a marble floor, and comfortable furniture. Rooms have large desks, overstuffed chairs, irons and boards, coffeemakers, and hair dryers. ⊠ *18118 Pacific Hwy. S, 98188,* ☎ *206/ 244–6666,* FAX *206/244–6679. 180 rooms, 24 suites. Restaurant, lobby lounge, in-room data ports, no-smoking floors, room service, indoor pool, exercise room, coin laundry, laundry service, meeting rooms, airport shuttle, free parking. AE, D, DC, MC, V.*

$$$ 🏨 **Doubletree Hotel Seattle Airport.** The Doubletree is a full-service convention hotel. The large and bright rooms all have balconies—corner "king rooms" have wraparound ones with great views. Furnishings include comfortable chairs, a dining table, and a desk. ⊠ *18740 Pacific Hwy. S, 98188,* ☎ *206/246–8600,* FAX *206/431–8687. 837 rooms, 13 suites. 3 restaurants, 2 bars, in-room data ports, room service, pool, beauty salon, exercise room, laundry service, meeting rooms, airport shuttle, parking (fee). AE, D, DC, MC, V.*

$$$ 🏨 **Seattle Airport Hilton.** With its lobby fireplace and paintings of Northwest scenery, this hotel, only a half-hour drive from downtown, has a surprisingly cozy feel. Large rooms are bright and decorated in pastel colors. ⊠ *17620 Pacific Hwy. S, 98188,* ☎ *206/244–4800,* FAX *206/ 248–4499. 175 rooms, 3 suites. Restaurant, bar, in-room data ports, pool, exercise room, coin laundry, laundry service, concierge, business services, meeting rooms, airport shuttle, free parking. AE, D, DC, MC, V.*

$$-$$$ 🏨 **WestCoast Gateway Hotel.** Perfect for the traveler catching an early flight, this hotel contains quiet rooms in shades of burgundy and gray. All have coffeemakers. ⊠ *18415 Pacific Hwy. S, 98188,* ☎ *206/248– 8200 or 800/426–0670,* FAX *206/244–1198. 145 rooms. Breakfast room, in-room data ports, no-smoking floors, room service, exercise room, dry cleaning, meeting room, airport shuttle, free parking. Continental breakfast. AE, D, DC, MC, V.*

$$-$$$ 🏨 **WestCoast Sea-Tac Hotel.** The enthusiastic and helpful staff at this conveniently located property make it attractive to the business or leisure traveler. Guests are welcome to play the baby grand piano in the small but comfortable lobby. All rooms come equipped with Nintendo systems. Rooms in the rear have views of Bow Lake. ⊠ *18220 International Blvd., 98188,* ☎ *206/246–5535 or 800/426–0670,* FAX *206/ 246–9733. 146 rooms. Restaurant, bar, room service, pool, hot tub, sauna, exercise room, business services, meeting rooms, airport shuttle, free parking. AE, D, DC, MC, V.*

Bellevue/Kirkland

$$$$ 🏨 **Bellevue Club Hotel.** The locally produced fine, decorative, and ap-
★ plied artwork that adorns its public and private spaces are among the standout features of this boutique hotel that has won numerous awards for its design. The warm earth tones incorporated into the decidedly modern setting, coupled with the clever use of lighting, create an illusion of sunlight even when it's raining outside. Original oil paintings by Northwest artist Mark Rediske hang in each room. Pillows made from African Kuba textiles, Turkish area rugs, and raku pottery offset cherry-wood furniture. All the rooms have sumptuous armchairs and large spa-inspired, limestone-tiled bathrooms with separate tubs and glass-enclosed showers. ⊠ *11200 S.E. 6th St., Bellevue 98004,* ☎ *425/454–4424 or 800/579–1110,* FAX *425/688–3101. 64 rooms, 3*

suites. 2 restaurants, lounge, in-room data ports, in-room safes, mini-bars, refrigerators, room service, pool, spa, tennis, basketball, health club, laundry service, concierge, business services, meeting rooms, parking (fee). AE, DC, MC, V.

$$$$ ⊞ **Doubletree Hotel Bellevue.** The 10-story Doubletree has an airy atrium filled with trees, shrubs, and flowering plants. The property also has a formal dining room, a lounge with two dance floors, and oversize guest rooms decorated in hunter green, burgundy, and beige. Rooms have either king- or queen-size beds. Two-room suites contain wet bars and whirlpool tubs. ⊠ *300 112th Ave. SE, Bellevue 98004,* ☎ *425/455–1300 or 800/733–5466,* FAX *425/455–0466. 348 rooms, 5 suites. 2 restaurants, bar, in-room data ports, room service, pool, exercise room, laundry service, concierge, business services, meeting rooms, free parking. AE, D, DC, MC, V.*

$$$$ ⊞ **Hyatt Regency Bellevue.** Near Bellevue Square and other downtown shopping centers, the Hyatt has an exterior much like any other sleek high-rise, but its interior has Asian touches like antique Japanese chests and huge displays of fresh flowers. The rooms are decorated in similarly understated ways, with dark wood and earth tones predominating. Deluxe suites include two bedrooms, bar facilities, and meeting rooms with desks and full-length tables; business-plan rooms have modem lines. Guests have access to a health club and pool. The restaurant serves excellent and reasonably priced breakfast, lunch, and dinner; an English-style pub and sports bar serves lunch and dinner. ⊠ *900 Bellevue Way NE, 98004,* ☎ *425/462–2626,* FAX *425/646–7567. 353 rooms, 29 suites. Restaurant, sports bar, no-smoking rooms, room service, concierge, meeting rooms, parking (fee). AE, D, DC, MC, V.*

$$$$ ⊞ **Woodmark Hotel.** Only steps away from downtown Kirkland, 7 mi
★ east of Seattle, this hotel is the only one on the shores of Lake Washington. Its contemporary-style rooms, which face the water, a courtyard, or the street, are done in exquisite shades of café au lait, taupe, and ecru. The numerous amenities include terry-cloth bathrobes, coffeemakers, irons, hair dryers, complimentary shoe shines, and the morning paper. Guests have privileges at the health club in the hotel complex. A circular staircase descends from the lobby to the Library Lounge, passing a huge bay window with a vast view of Lake Washington. Waters Bistro serves Pacific Rim cuisine, with dishes such as lemongrass steamed clams or grilled halibut with roasted onion-ginger relish. ⊠ *1200 Carillon Pt., Kirkland 98033,* ☎ *425/822–3700 or 800/822–3700,* FAX *425/822–3699. 79 rooms, 21 suites. Restaurant, bar, in-room data ports, in-room safes, minibars, refrigerators, room service, exercise room, laundry service, concierge, business services, meeting rooms, parking (fee). AE, DC, MC, V.*

$$ ⊞ **WestCoast Bellevue Hotel.** This hotel–motor inn has a number of town-house suites, suitable for two to four people, with sleeping lofts and wood-burning fireplaces. Rooms are clean. Those facing the courtyard are larger and quieter than the others. The hotel is a 20-minute walk from Bellevue Square. A substantial, complimentary appetizer buffet, served in the lounge weekdays between 5 and 7, includes seafood and roast beef. ⊠ *625 116th Ave. NE, Bellevue 98004,* ☎ *425/455–9444,* FAX *425/455–2154. 160 rooms, 16 suites. Restaurant, bar, room service, pool, exercise room, laundry service, business services, meeting rooms, free parking. AE, D, DC, MC, V.*

NIGHTLIFE AND THE ARTS

The Thursday edition of the *Seattle Times* and the Friday *Seattle Post-Intelligencer* include pullout weekend sections that detail upcoming arts and entertainment events. *Seattle Weekly,* which hits most newsstands on Wednesday, has even more detailed coverage and reviews. *The Stranger,* a provocative free weekly, provides broad, though not necessarily deep, coverage of the city's cultural activities and is the unofficial bible of the music and club scenes.

Ticketmaster (☎ 206/628–0888) sells tickets to most arts, entertainment, and sports events in the Seattle area; for a steep fee, you can charge by phone. The two locations of **Ticket/Ticket** (⊠ Broadway Market, 401 Broadway E, 2nd floor, ☎ 206/324–2744; ⊠ Pike Pl. Market Information Booth, 1st Ave. and Pike St., ☎ 206/682–7453, ext. 226) sell half-price tickets to many events on the day of the performance (or previous day for matinees). Sales are cash and in-person only.

Nightlife

Neighborhoods with high concentrations of clubs and bars include **Ballard, Pioneer Square, Capitol Hill, and Belltown** (also known as the Denny Regrade, north of Pike Place Market).

Amusement Centers/Theme Entertainment

The amusements at **GameWorks** (⊠ 7th Ave. and Pike St., ☎ 206/521–0952) a Steven Spielberg–Sega collaboration, run the gamut from old-style arcade games to high-tech road-racing and other electronic games. In the same block with Gameworks is **NikeTown** (⊠ 6th Ave. and Pike St., ☎ 206/447–6453), where the line between shopping and entertainment has been all but blurred. The Seattle edition of **Planet Hollywood** (⊠ 6th Ave. and Pike St., ☎ 206/287–0001) is the same scene it is elsewhere around the world.

For a uniquely Seattle entertainment experience, venture out to South Lake Union, where **Entros** (⊠ 823 Yale Ave. N, ☎ 206/624–0057) bills itself as "an intelligent amusement park." This hip spot is an adult playground of interactive games and installations set around a first-rate bar and restaurant, the World Grill. Some people come just to eat or to play, but those adventurous enough to try the Segovian prawns in cayenne-lime butter or the tamarind chicken with Thai chilies tend to stick around for Interface (a high-tech trust walk using closed-circuit TV and two-way radios) and Perfect Burger (a conveyor-belt game reminiscent of the famous candy-factory episode from *I Love Lucy*).

Bars and Lounges

Bars with waterfront views are plentiful—you just have to pick your body of water. **Anthony's Home Port** (⊠ 6135 Seaview Ave. NW, ☎ 206/783–0780) overlooks Shilshole Bay. **Arnie's** (⊠ 1900 N. Northlake Way, ☎ 206/547–3242) has a great view of downtown from north Lake Union. **Duke's at Chandler's Cove** (⊠ 901 Fairview Ave. N, 206/382–9963) surveys south Lake Union. **Ernie's Bar & Grill** (⊠ Edgewater, 2411 Alaskan Way, Pier 67, ☎ 206/728–7000) has great views of Elliott Bay and the Olympic Mountains. The deck at **Ponti** (⊠ 3014 3rd Ave. N, ☎ 206/284–3000) overlooks the Ship Canal.

If the view's not important, check out three of Seattle's hipper venues, all near Pike Place Market. The **Alibi Room** (⊠ 85 Post Alley, ☎ 206/623–3180) is the unofficial watering hole of the city's film community. The romantic **Il Bistro** (⊠ 93A Pike St., ☎ 206/682–3049) has low lights, low ceilings, and stiff drinks. Installations by local artists adorn the **Virginia Inn** (⊠ 1937 1st Ave., ☎ 206/728–1937).

The **Bungalow** (⊠ 2412 N. 45th St., ☎ 206/632–0254) is an intimate spot to sip fine wines from around the world. The **Garden Court** (⊠ Four Seasons Hotel, 411 University St., ☎ 206/621–1700) is downtown's most elegant lounge. **Palomino** (⊠ 1420 5th Ave., ☎ 206/623–1300) is a sophisticated spot patronized by the after-work crowd.

In Pioneer Square check out **F. X. McRory's** (⊠ 419 Occidental Ave. S, ☎ 206/623–4800), near the Kingdome; the bar is famous for its single-malt whiskeys and fresh oysters. **Pioneer Square Saloon** (⊠ 77 Yesler Way, ☎ 206/340–1234) is a great, easygoing, no-frills tavern.

Brew Pubs

Seattle brew pubs churn out many high-quality beers made for local distribution. All the pubs listed below serve food and nonalcoholic beverages. If live music is performed, a cover charge may be required; otherwise admission is free. Unless noted, the establishments listed below are open daily from at least noon to 11 PM; call ahead if you're planning a visit at other hours.

Big Time Brewery (⊠ 4133 University Way NE, ☎ 206/545–4509) caters to the U District crowd and resembles an archetypal college-town pub, with the obligatory moose head on the wall and vintage memorabilia scattered about. Pale ale, amber, and porter are always on tap; the imaginative specialty brews change monthly.

The taps at the **Elysian Brewing Company** (⊠ 1221 E. Pike St., ☎ 206/860–1920) flow with Golden Fleece Ale, Zephyrus Pilsner, the Immortal India Pale Ale, and other brews. If the cute mythological names don't appeal, the dependable pub fare and eccentric Capitol Hill clientele will win you over.

Hales Ales Brewery and Pub (⊠ 4301 Leary Way NW, ☎ 206/782–0737) serves up nine regular and seasonal offerings in a cheerful Fremont setting. The pub's signature brews are its Honey Wheat and Moss Bay Amber ales; order a taster's "flight" to test the rest as well.

Pike Pub and Brewery (⊠ 1415 1st Ave., ☎ 206/622–6044), a dandy downtown establishment, is operated by the brewers of the award-winning Pike Place Pale Ale. Proudly proclaiming itself Beer Central, the Pike also houses the Seattle Microbrewery Museum and an excellent shop with supplies for home brewing.

Pyramid Alehouse (⊠ 91 S. Royal Brougham Way, at 1st Ave. S, ☎ 206/682–3377), south of the Kingdome, brews the varied Pyramid Line—including a top-notch Hefeweizen and an Apricot Ale that tastes much better than it sounds—and Thomas Kemper Lagers. A loud, festive atmosphere makes Pyramid the perfect place to gather after a Mariners baseball game.

Redhook Brewery has an in-town location (☞ Trolleyman, *below*) and a larger complex—with a pub, a beer garden, and a gift shop in addition to brewing facilities ($1 tours available daily; call for hours and directions)—in Woodinville (⊠ 14300 N.E. 145th St., ☎ 425/483–3232).

Six Arms (⊠ 300 E. Pike St., ☎ 206/223–1698) features the same comfortably eccentric decor that has become the trademark of the chain of pubs operated by the McMenamin family of Portland, Oregon. The beer is equally memorable, especially the challenging Terminator Stout. The Six Arms displays considerably more charm than her Seattle cousins, **McMenamin's** (⊠ 200 Roy St., ☎ 206/285–4722) and **Dad Watson's** (⊠ 3601 Fremont Ave., ☎ 206/632–6505), though the beer at all three tastes the same.

The Trolleyman (⊠ 3400 Phinney Ave. N, ☎ 206/548–8000), near the north end of the Fremont Bridge, is the birthplace of local favorites Ballard Bitter and Redhook Ale. The pub mixes Northwest style (whitewashed walls and a no-smoking policy) with a relaxed atmosphere that includes a fireplace and ample armchairs. The original Redhook Brewery is right next door—take a 45-minute tour before you pop in for a pint. The pub opens at 11 AM except Sunday, when it opens at noon (and closes at 7). Call for tour times.

Coffeehouses

Unlike the city's brew pubs, Seattle's coffeehouses are defined as much by the people they serve as the beverages they pour. Most cafés serve the same drinks, but though some Seattleites will linger for hours over their latte, others prefer a cup to go from a drive-through espresso stand. Every neighborhood has its own distinctive coffee culture—usually three or four, actually. Below are a few of the options on Capitol Hill and downtown.

CAPITOL HILL

Local favorite **B&O Espresso** (⊠ 204 Belmont Ave. E, ☎ 206/322–5028) lures Capitol Hill hipsters and solitary types. The on-site bakery turns out gorgeous wedding cakes. A youngish crowd browses through the art and architecture books on the shelves of **Bauhaus** (⊠ 301 E. Pine St., ☎ 206/625–1600). Scribble and brood with the poetry set at **Café Vita** (⊠ 1005 E. Pike St., ☎ 206/325–2647). Take a trip to Paris when you enter **Septième** (⊠ 214 Broadway E, ☎ 206/860–8858), which, despite its white-linen tablecloths, has a calculatedly seedy feel. In back is an open patio, where during the summer you can listen to rhumba and salsa music and sip by the light of tiki torches. The friendly **Habitat Espresso** (⊠ 202 Broadway E, ☎ 206/329–3087) is a coffee collective that donates a significant portion of its profits to local and national charities. Exceptional, no-nonsense **Vivace Roasteria** (⊠ 901 E. Denny Way, ☎ 206/860–5869) roasts its own coffee and sells to other coffeehouses.

DOWNTOWN

The rich smell of the roaster as you step through the door of tiny **Caffé Vitta** (⊠ 2621 5th Ave., ☎ 206/441–4351) is intoxicating. **Lux** (⊠ 2226 1st Ave., ☎ 206/443–0962) has a thrift-store opulence that's right at home among the boutiques of 1st Avenue and the Belltown arts scene. The **Sit & Spin** (⊠ 2219 4th Ave., ☎ 206/441–9484) café has a full-service laundry on one side. Sit & Spin's rival for the award for the coffeehouse most likely to improve your time management is **Speakeasy** (⊠ 2304 2nd Ave., ☎ 206/728–9770), where you can download your E-mail along with your caffeine. Both cafés also double—or is it triple?—as performance spaces in the evening.

Comedy Clubs

Comedy Underground (⊠ 222 S. Main St., ☎ 206/628–0303), a Pioneer Square club that's literally underground, beneath Swannie's bar and restaurant, presents stand-up comedy nightly. **Giggles** (⊠ 5220 Roosevelt Way NE, ☎ 206/526–5653) in the University District books local and nationally known comedians from Thursday through Sunday, with late shows on Friday and Saturday.

Music

For $8 you can purchase the Pioneer Square joint cover charge, which will admit you to up to 10 area clubs; contact the New Orleans Restaurant (☞ Jazz, *below*) for details.

BLUES AND R&B

Ballard Firehouse (⊠ 5429 Russell St. NW, ☎ 206/784–3516), Ballard's music mecca, books local and national blues acts. **Larry's** (⊠ 209 1st Ave. S, ☎ 206/624–7665) presents live blues and rhythm and blues nightly in an unpretentious, friendly, and usually jam-packed tavern-restaurant in Pioneer Square. **Old Timer's Cafe** (✉ 620 1st Ave., ☎ 206/623–9800), a popular Pioneer Square restaurant and bar, has live music—mostly rhythm and blues—nightly. **Scarlet Tree** (✉ 6521 Roosevelt Way NE, ☎ 206/523–7153), a neighborhood institution north of the University District, serves up great burgers and live rhythm and blues most nights.

DANCE CLUBS

The local chapter of the **U.S. Amateur Ballroom Dancing Association** (☎ 425/822–6686) holds regular classes and dances throughout the year at the **Avalon Ballroom** (✉ 1017 Stewart St.). The **Century Ballroom** (✉ 915 E. Pine St., ☎ 206/324–7263) holds regular classes and dances throughout the year. The **Washington Dance Club** (✉ 1017 Stewart St., ☎ 206/628–8939) sponsors nightly workshops and dances in various styles.

Several Seattle clubs celebrate cocktail culture. **700 Club** (✉ 700 Virginia Ave., ☎ 206/343–1255) presents live and recorded swing music. The chic **Baltic Room** (✉ 1207 Pine St., ☎ 206/625–4444) hosts retro and contemporary dance nights and the occasional film screening. **Pampas Room** (✉ 90 Wall St., ☎ 206/728–1140) presents jazz on Friday and Saturday evenings.

For more contemporary sounds, **Downunder** (✉ 2407 1st Ave., ☎ 206/728–4053) is an old-school disco with a packed floor. The moody **Romper Room** (✉ 106 1st Ave. N, ☎ 206/284–5003) specializes in '70s soul. **Re-Bar** (✉ 1114 Howell St., ☎ 206/233–9873) presents an eclectic mix of music nightly, including acid jazz, rock, and soul. The **Vogue** (✉ 2018 1st Ave., ☎ 206/443–0673) hosts reggae, industrial, and gothic dance nights. Several rock clubs (☞ *below*) have dance floors.

FOLK

The cheerful **Hopvine Pub** (✉ 507 15th Ave. E, ☎ 206/328–3120) hosts local folk musicians. **Kells** (✉ 1916 Post Alley, ☎ 206/728–1916), a snug Irish-style pub near Pike Place Market, books Celtic-music artists from Wednesday through Saturday. **Murphy's Pub** (✉ 2110 45th St. NE, ☎ 206/634–2110), a neighborhood bar, has Irish and other folk music on Friday and Saturday.

JAZZ

Dimitriou's Jazz Alley (✉ 2037 6th Ave., ☎ 206/441–9729), a downtown club, books nationally known, consistently high-quality performers every night but Sunday. Excellent dinners are served before the first show. **Latona Pub** (✉ 6423 Latona Ave. NE, ☎ 206/525–2238) is a funky, friendly neighborhood bar at the south end of Green Lake that presents local folk, blues, or jazz musicians nightly. **New Orleans Restaurant** (✉ 114 1st Ave. S, ☎ 206/622–2563), a popular Pioneer Square restaurant, has good food and jazz nightly—mostly top local performers, with occasional national acts.

ROCK

The **Moore Theater** (✉ 1932 2nd Ave., ☎ 206/443–1744) and the **Paramount** (✉ 907 Pine St., ☎ 206/682–1414 or 206/628–0888 or ☎ 206/682–1414 or 206/628–0888) are elegant structures from the early 20th century that host visiting big-name acts.

Crocodile Café (✉ 2200 2nd Ave., ☎ 206/441–5611), one of Seattle's most successful rock clubs, books alternative music acts nightly except Monday. **The Fenix** (✉ 315 2nd Ave. S, ☎ 206/467–1111) is a crowded Pioneer Square venue with an ever-changing roster of local and national acts. **O.K. Hotel** (✉ 212 Alaskan Way S, ☎ 206/621–7903) hosts rock, folk, and jazz nightly in a small venue near Pioneer Square. **Showbox**

(✉ 1426 1st Ave., ☎ 206/628–3151) presents locally and nationally acclaimed artists near Pike Place Market.

The Arts

The Arts for Free

Seattle's summer concerts, the **Out to Lunch Series** (☎ 206/623–0340), happen every weekday at noon from mid-June to early September in various parks, plazas, and atriums downtown. Concerts showcase local and national musicians and dancers.

First Thursday Gallery Walk (☎ 206/587–0260), an open house hosted by Seattle's art galleries, visits new local exhibits on the first Thursday of every month from 6 to 9 PM.

Dance

Meany Hall for the Performing Arts (✉ University of Washington campus, ☎ 206/543–4880) hosts important national and international companies, from September through May, with an emphasis on modern and jazz dance.

On the Boards (✉ 100 W. Roy St., ☎ 206/217–9888) presents and produces contemporary dance performances and also theater, music, and multimedia events. The main subscription series runs from October through May, but events are scheduled nearly every weekend year-round.

Pacific Northwest Ballet (✉ Opera House at Seattle Center, Mercer St. at 3rd Ave., ☎ 206/441–2424) is a resident company and school. Attending its Christmastime production of *The Nutcracker,* with choreography by Kent Stowell and sets by Maurice Sendak, is a Seattle tradition.

Film

The strongest evidence of Seattle's passion for the movies is the wildly popular **Seattle International Film Festival** (☎ 206/324–9996), held each May and June. For show times and theater locations of current releases, call the **Seattle Times InfoLine** (☎ 206/464–2000, ext. 3456).

The **Egyptian Theater** (✉ 801 E. Pine St., at Broadway, ☎ 206/323–4978), an Art Deco movie palace that was formerly a Masonic temple, screens first-run films and is the prime venue of Seattle's film festival. **Grand Illusion Cinema** (✉ 1403 N.E. 50th St., at University Way, ☎ 206/523–3935), in the U District, was a tiny screening room for exhibitors in the '30s. A venue for independent and art films, it has a terrific espresso bar. **Harvard Exit** (✉ 807 E. Roy St., ☎ 206/323–8986), a first-run and art-film house, has Seattle's most inviting theater lobby—complete with couches and a piano. **Varsity Theater** (✉ 4329 University Way NE, ☎ 206/632–3131), in the U District, usually dedicates two of its three screens to classic films.

Music

Northwest Chamber Orchestra (✉ 1305 4th Ave., ☎ 206/343–0445) presents a full spectrum of music, from baroque to modern, at the University of Washington's Kane Hall. The subscription series, generally from September through May, includes a baroque-music festival every fall. **Seattle Symphony** (✉ Benaroya Hall, 1203 2nd Ave., at University St., ☎ 206/215–4747) performs under the direction of Gerard Schwartz from September through June in the Benaroya Hall.

Opera

Seattle Opera (✉ Opera House at Seattle Center, Mercer St. at 3rd Ave., ☎ 206/389–7676), considered among the top operas in the United States, presents five productions during its season, which runs from August through May.

Performance Venues

Broadway Performance Hall (✉ Seattle Central Community College, 1625 Broadway, ☎ 206/325–3113), small but acoustically outstanding, often hosts dance and music concerts.

Cornish College of the Arts (✉ 710 E. Roy St., ☎ 206/323–1400) serves as headquarters for distinguished jazz, dance, and other groups.

Fifth Avenue Theater (✉ 1308 5th Ave., ☎ 206/625–1900) is the home of the Fifth Avenue Musical Theater Company (☞ Theater Companies, *below*). When the company is on hiatus, this chinoiserie-style historic landmark, carefully restored to its original 1926 condition, hosts traveling musical and theatrical performances.

Moore Theater (✉ 1932 2nd Ave., ☎ 206/443–1744), a 1908 music hall, presents dance concerts and rock shows.

Paramount Theatre (✉ 907 Pine St., ☎ 206/682–1414), a 3,000-seat building from 1929 that has seen duty as a music hall and a movie palace, hosts Best of Broadway touring shows and national pop-music acts.

Seattle Center (✉ 305 Harrison St., ☎ 206/684–8582) contains several halls that present theater, opera, dance, music, and performance art.

Theater Companies

Annex Theatre (✉ 1916 4th Ave., ☎ 206/728–0933), run by a collective of artists, presents avant-garde works year-round. **A Contemporary Theater** (✉ Eagles Auditorium, 700 Union St., ☎ 206/292–7676) specializes in regional premieres of new works by established playwrights. Every December the theater revives its popular production of *A Christmas Carol*. **Crêpe de Paris** (✉ 1333 5th Ave., ☎ 206/623–4111), a restaurant in the Rainier Tower building downtown, books sidesplitting cabaret theater and musical revues.

Empty Space Theater (✉ 3509 Fremont Ave., ☎ 206/547–7500) has a reputation for introducing Seattle to new playwrights. Its season generally runs from November through June, with five or six main-stage productions and several smaller shows. **Fifth Avenue Musical Theater Company** (✉ Fifth Avenue Theater, 1308 5th Ave., ☎ 206/625–1900) is a resident professional troupe that mounts four lavish musicals from October to May. **Intiman Theater** (✉ Playhouse at Seattle Center, 2nd Ave. N and Mercer St., ☎ 206/269–1901) presents important contemporary works and classics of the world stage. The season generally runs from May through November.

New City Theater and Arts Center (✉ 1634 11th Ave., ☎ 206/323–6800) hosts experimental performances by local, national, and international artists. **Seattle Children's Theatre** (✉ Charlotte Martin Theatre at Seattle Center, 2nd Ave. N and Thomas St., ☎ 206/441–3322), the second-largest resident professional children's theater company in the United States, has commissioned several dozen new plays, adaptations, and musicals. The theater's six-play season runs from September through June. **Seattle Repertory Theater** (✉ Bagley Wright Theater at Seattle Center, 155 Mercer St., ☎ 206/443–2222) performs six new or classic plays on its main stage from October through May, along with three developmental shows at an adjoining smaller venue. **Village Theater** (✉ 303 Front St. N, Issaquah, ☎ 425/392–2202) produces high-quality family musicals, comedies, and dramas from September through May in Issaquah, a town east of Seattle. The main stage is at 303 Front

Street; the theater's original venue, at 120 Front Street, is known as First Stage.

OUTDOOR ACTIVITIES AND SPORTS

Beaches

If you happen to be in town on a sunny day, catch those precious rays at **Golden Gardens** (⊠ Seaview Ave. NW, ☎ 206/684–4075), a bit north of the Ballard Locks, or at **Alki Beach** (⊠ Alki Ave. SW; from downtown, take Hwy. 99 west, then head north on Harbor Ave. SW, ☎ 206/684–4075) in West Seattle. Another option is **Warren Magnuson Park** (☞ University District, *in* Exploring Seattle, *above*).

There are several public beaches on the western shores of Lake Washington. Where eastbound Madison Street runs into the lake you'll find **Madison Beach** (⊠ 2300 43rd Ave. E). This spot offers a playground, sandy beach, and easy access to the water. Heading south along Lake Washington Boulevard East is **Denny Blaine,** with a grassy park under towering shady trees and difficult access to the water. A mile farther south lies **Madrona Beach** (⊠ 853 Lake Washington Blvd.) which has a sculpted sand garden for the kids. **Mt. Baker Beach** (⊠ 2521 Lake Park Dr. S) has a dock and anchored raft with diving boards. **Seward Park** (⊠ 5898 Lake Washington Blvd. S), which offers a large playfield, has many covered picnic spots and a playground.

All of these locations are operated and maintained by the Seattle Parks Department (☎ 206/684–4075). With the exception of Denny Blaine, all of the beaches have lifeguards on duty during the summer months. The water stays pretty cold in Seattle year-round, with the best swimming temperatures in July and August.

Participant Sports

Seattle Parks and Recreation (☎ 206/684–4075) has information about participant sports and facilities.

Bicycling

The Burke-Gilman Trail and the trail that circles Green Lake are popular among recreational bicyclists and children, but at Green Lake joggers and walkers tend to impede fast travel. The city-maintained Burke-Gilman Trail extends 12.1 mi along Seattle's waterfront from Lake Washington nearly to Salmon Bay along an abandoned railroad line; it is a much less congested path. Myrtle Edwards Park, north of Pier 70, has a two-lane path for jogging and bicycling.

Gregg's Greenlake Cycle (⊠ 7007 Woodlawn Ave. NE, ☎ 206/523–1822) in North Seattle rents mountain bikes, standard touring or racing bikes, and equipment.

Billiards

Rack 'em up and run the table at the **211 Club** (⊠ 2304 2nd Ave., ☎ 206/443–1211). For billiards with a Vegas feel and a hibachi grill there's **Jillian's Billiard Cafe** (⊠ 731 Westlake Ave. N, ☎ 206/223–0300). **Temple Billiards** (⊠ 126 S. Jackson St., ☎ 206/682–3242), in Pioneer Square, caters to the hip crowd.

Boating and Sailboarding

Wind Works Rentals (⊠ 7001 Seaview Ave. NW, ☎ 206/784–9386), on Shilshole Bay, rents sailboats with or without skippers by the half day, day, or week. **Yarrow Bay Marina** (⊠ 5207 Lake Washington Blvd.

NE, ☎ 425/822–6066 or 800/336–3834), in Kirkland, rents 17 and 20 ft runabouts by the day or week.

Lake Union and Green Lake are Seattle's prime sailboarding spots. Sailboards can be rented year-round at **Urban Surf** (✉ 2100 N. Northlake Way, ☎ 206/545–9463) on Lake Union.

Fishing

There are plenty of good spots for fishing on Lake Washington, Green Lake, and Lake Union, and there are several fishing piers along the Elliott Bay waterfront. Companies operating from Shilshole Bay operate charter trips for catching salmon, rock cod, flounder, and sea bass. **Ballard Salmon Charter** (☎ 206/789–6202) is a recommended local firm. Like most companies, **Pier 54 Adventures** (☎ 206/623–6364) includes the cost of a two-day fishing license ($3.50) in its fee.

Golf

The city-run **Jackson Park** (✉ 1000 N.E. 135th St., ☎ 206/363–4747), **Jefferson Park** (✉ 4101 Beacon Ave. S, ☎ 206/762–4513), and **West Seattle Golf Course** (✉ 4470 35th Ave. SW, ☎ 206/935–5187) golf facilities each have an 18-hole course (greens fee: $18.50, plus $20 for optional cart) and a 9-hole executive course ($8, plus $13 for optional cart). Closer to downtown, the **Interbay Family Golf Center** (✉ 2501 15th Ave W, ☎ 206/285–2200) has a driving range and nine-hole executive and miniature golf courses.

Jogging, Skating, and Walking

Green Lake is far and away Seattle's most popular spot for jogging, and the 3-mi circumference of this picturesque lake is custom-made for it. Walking, bicycling, rollerblading, fishing, lounging on the grass, and feeding the plentiful waterfowl are other possibilities. Several outlets clustered along the east side of the lake have skate and cycle rentals. Seward Park has a much more secluded and less used 3-mi loop where the park juts out into Lake Washington in Southeast Seattle.

Other good jogging locales are along the Burke-Gilman Trail (☞ Bicycling, *above*), around the reservoir at Volunteer Park (☞ Capitol Hill Area *in* Exploring Seattle, *above*), and at Myrtle Edwards Park, north of Pier 70 downtown.

Kayaking

Kayaking—around the inner waterways (Lake Union, Lake Washington, the Ship Canal) and open water (Elliott Bay)—affords some singular views of Seattle. The **Northwest Outdoor Center** (✉ 2100 Westlake Ave. N, ☎ 206/281–9694), on the west side of Lake Union, rents one- or two-person kayaks and equipment by the hour or week and provides both basic and advanced instruction.

Skiing

There's fine downhill skiing in and around Snoqualmie (☞ Chapter 3). For Snoqualmie ski reports and news about conditions in the more distant White Pass, Crystal Mountain, and Stevens Pass, call 206/634–0200 or 206/634–2754. For recorded messages about road conditions in the passes, call 888/766–4636.

Tennis

There are public tennis courts in parks around the Seattle area. Many courts are in the U District, and several are near Capitol Hill. For information, contact the athletics office of the **King County Parks and Recreation Department** (☎ 206/684–7093).

Spectator Sports

Ticketmaster (☎ 206/622–4487) sells tickets to many local sporting events.

Baseball

The **Seattle Mariners** (☎ 206/346–4000) in the West Division of the American League play at a new retractable-roof stadium, opened in the summer of 1999, called **Safeco Field** (✉ 1st Ave. S. and Atlantic St.).

Basketball

The **Seattle SuperSonics** (☎ 206/283–3865) of the National Basketball Association play at **Key Arena** (✉ 1st Ave. N and Mercer St.) in the Seattle Center.

Boat Racing

The **unlimited hydroplane races** (☎ 206/628–0888) are a highlight of Seattle's Seafair festivities from mid-July to the first Sunday in August. The races are held on Lake Washington near Seward Park. Tickets cost from $10 to $20. Weekly sailing regattas are held in the summer on Lakes Union and Washington. Call the **Seattle Yacht Club** (☎ 206/325–1000) for schedules.

Football

Seattle Seahawks (☎ 425/827–9777) National Football League games take place in the **Kingdome** (✉ 201 S. King St.). The **University of Washington Huskies** (☎ 206/543–2200), every bit as popular as the Seahawks, play out their fall slate at Husky Stadium, off Montlake Boulevard Northeast on the UW campus.

Horse Racing

Take in Thoroughbred racing from April through September at **Emerald Downs** (✉ 2300 Emerald Downs Dr., Auburn, ☎ 253/288–7000), a 166-acre track about 15 mi south of downtown, east of I–5.

Soccer

For outdoor soccer, catch the A-League **Seattle Sounders** at Memorial Stadium (✉ Seattle Center, 5th Ave. N and Harrison St., ☎ 800/796–5425).

SHOPPING

Most Seattle stores are open daily. Mall hours are generally from 9:30 to 9 except Sunday, when stores usually stay open from 11 to 6. Some specialty shops keep shorter evening and Sunday hours.

Shopping Districts

Broadway in the Capitol Hill neighborhood is lined with clothing stores selling new and vintage threads and high-design housewares shops.

Fremont Avenue contains a funky mix of galleries, thrift stores, and boutiques around its intersection with North 35th Street, above the Fremont Bridge.

The **International District,** bordered roughly by South Main and South Lane streets and 4th and 8th avenues, contains many Asian herb shops and groceries. **Uwajimaya** (✉ 519 6th Ave. S, ☎ 206/624–6248), one of the largest Japanese stores on the West Coast, sells Asian foods and affordable china, gifts, fabrics, and housewares. Okazuya, the snack bar in Uwajimaya, prepares noodle dishes, sushi, tempura, and other Asian dishes to take out or to eat in.

University Way Northeast, in the University District between Northeast 41st and Northeast 50th streets, has a few upscale shops, many bookstores, and businesses that carry such student-oriented imports as ethnic jewelry and South American sweaters.

Shopping Centers and Malls

Bellevue Square (⊠ N.E. 8th St. and Bellevue Way, ☎ 425/454–8096), an upscale shopping center about 8 mi east of Seattle, is home to more than 200 shops and includes a children's play area, the Bellevue Art Museum, and covered parking.

Northgate Mall (⊠ I–5 and Northgate Way, ☎ 206/362–4777), 10 mi north of downtown, houses 118 stores, including Nordstrom, The Bon Marché, Lamonts, and J.C. Penney.

Pacific Place (⊠ 6th and Pine Sts.), a chichi glass-ceiling complex opened in 1998, has Tiffany & Co., J. Crew, Barnes & Noble, Restoration Hardware, Stars restaurant, and other mostly chain operations.

Southcenter Mall (⊠ I–5 and I–405 in Tukwila, ☎ 206/246–7400) contains 140 shops and department stores.

University Village (⊠ NE 45th St. and 25th Ave. NE, ☎ 206/523–0622) is an upscale open-air mall with more than 80 national and locally owned shops and restaurants, including the Pottery Barn, the Gap, Sundance, and Restoration Hardware.

Westlake Center (⊠ 1601 5th Ave., ☎ 206/467–1600), in downtown Seattle, has 80 upscale shops and covered walkways to Seattle's two major department stores, Nordstrom and The Bon Marché.

Specialty Shops

Antiques
Antique Importers (⊠ Alaskan Way between Columbia and Yesler, ☎ 206/628–8905), a large warehouselike structure, carries mostly English oak and Victorian pine antiques.

Art Galleries
Foster/White Gallery (⊠ 311 Occidental Ave. S, ☎ 206/622–2833) represents many Northwest painters and sculptors, as well as glass artists of the Pilchuck School, which is outside Seattle. **Frank & Dunya** (⊠ 3418 Fremont Ave. N, ☎ 206/547–6760) carries unique art pieces, from furniture to jewelry. **The Glass House** (⊠ 311 Occidental Ave. S, ☎ 206/682–9939) has one of the largest displays of glass artwork in the city. **Stonington Gallery** (⊠ 2030 1st Ave., ☎ 206/405–4040) specializes in contemporary Native American and other Northwest works.

Books and Maps
Bailey/Coy Books (⊠ 414 Broadway, ☎ 206/323–8842), on Capitol Hill, stocks contemporary and classic fiction and nonfiction, and has a magazine section. **Elliott Bay Book Company** (⊠ 101 S. Main St., ☎ 206/624–6600), a mammoth general independent bookstore in Pioneer Square, hosts lectures and readings by local and international authors, and a children's story hour at 11 AM on the first Saturday of the month. **M. Coy Books** (⊠ 117 Pine St., ☎ 206/623–5354), in the heart of downtown, carries a large selection of contemporary literature and has a small espresso bar.

Metsker Maps (⊠ 702 1st Ave., ☎ 206/623–8747), on the edge of Pioneer Square, stocks many regional maps. **University of Washington Bookstore** (⊠ 4326 University Way NE, ☎ 206/634–3403), which carries textbooks and general-interest titles, is one of Seattle's best bookshops. **Wide World Books and Maps** (✉ 1911 N. 45th St., ☎ 206/634–3453), north of downtown in the Wallingford neighborhood, carries travel books and maps.

Barnes & Noble (✉ 2700 Northeast University Village, ☎ 206/517–4107; ✉ 626 106th Ave. NE, Bellevue, ☎ 425/451–8463) has 11 stores in Seattle and environs. **Borders Books & Music** (✉ 1501 4th Ave., ☎ 206/622–4599; ✉ 16549 Northeast 74th St., Redmond, ☎ 425/869–1907; ✉ 17501 Southcenter Pkwy., Suite 200, Tukwila, ☎ 206/575–4506) is also conveniently located throughout the area.

Clothing
Baby and Co. (✉ 1936 1st Ave., ☎ 206/448–4077) sells contemporary fashions and accessories for women. **Butch Blum** (✉ 1408 5th Ave., ☎ 206/622–5760) carries contemporary menswear. **C. C. Filson** (✉ 2700 4th Ave. S, ☎ 206/622–3147) is a renowned outdoor outfitter. **Ebbets Field Flannels** (✉ 406 Occidental Ave. S, ☎ 206/623–0724) specializes in replicas of vintage athletic apparel. **Helen's Of Course** (✉ 1302 5th Ave., ☎ 206/624–4000) stocks classic fashions for women.

Isadora's Antique Clothing (✉ 1915 1st Ave., ☎ 206/441–7711) specializes in women's antique clothing and jewelry. **Local Brilliance** (✉ 1535 1st Ave., ☎ 206/343–5864) is a showcase for fashions from local designers. **Opus 204** (✉ 2004 1st Ave., ☎ 206/728–7707) carries its own private label of clothing constructed from fabrics chosen for their longevity and ease of care, as well as their unique look. **Passport** (✉ 112 Pine St., ☎ 206/628–9799) specializes in natural fiber clothing. **Rudy's Vintage Clothing** (✉ 1424 1st Ave., ☎ 206/682–6586) stocks vintage men's and women's clothing and antiques.

Crafts
Dusty Strings (✉ 3406 Fremont Ave. N, ☎ 206/634–1656) is the place to pick up hammered dulcimers. **Hands of the World** (✉ 1501 Pike Pl., ☎ 206/622–1696) carries textiles, jewelry, and art from around the world. **Ragazzi's Flying Shuttle** (✉ 607 1st Ave., ☎ 206/343–9762) displays handcrafted jewelry, whimsical folk art, and hand-knit items.

Gifts
At **Armadillo & Co.** (✉ 3510 Fremont Pl. N, ☎ 206/633–4241), you'll find jewelry, T-shirts, and other armadillo-theme accessories and gifts. **Ruby Montana's Pinto Pony** (✉ 1623 2nd Ave., ☎ 206/443–9363) is kitsch heaven. You'll find furniture, housewares, T-shirts, books, and other postmodern accessories here.

Jewelry
Fireworks Gallery (✉ 210 1st Ave. S, ☎ 206/682–8707; ✉ 400 Pine St., ☎ 206/682–6462) sells handmade gifts.

Newspapers and Magazines
Read All About It (✉ 93 Pike Pl., ☎ 206/624–0140) serves downtown. **Steve's Broadway News** (✉ 204 Broadway E, ☎ 206/324–7323) covers Capitol Hill. **Steve's Fremont News** (✉ 3416 Fremont Ave. N, ☎ 206/633–0731) is north of the bridge in Fremont Center.

Outdoor Wear and Equipment
Recreational Equipment, Inc. (✉ 222 Yale Ave. N, ☎ 206/223–1944)—which everybody calls REI—has Seattle's most comprehensive selection of gear for the great outdoors at its state-of-the-art downtown facility. The nearly 80,000-square-ft store contains a mountain-bike test trail, a simulated rain booth for testing outerwear, and the REI Pinnacle, an enormous freestanding indoor climbing structure. It's unbelievable, but there's room left over for a wildlife art gallery, a café, and a 250-seat meeting room for how-to clinics.

BOOK-LOVERS' PARADISE

WITH ITS DIVERSE, literate population, Seattle is a book-lover's paradise. New and used, antiquarian and specialty bookshops are tucked away in nearly every neighborhood. You don't have to spend your whole vacation reading, but there's no harm in browsing, right? Make sure you pack an extra suitcase.

The national chains, **Borders** (✉ 1501 4th Ave., ☎ 206/622–4599), **Tower Books** (✉ 20 Mercer St., ☎ 206/283–6333), and **Barnes and Noble** (✉ 2700 N.E. University Village, ☎ 206/517–4107 and other locations), stock huge selections and host frequent author appearances, many of them by well-known talents. **Elliott Bay Book Co.** (✉ 101 S. Main St., ☎ 206/624–6600), has long been the area's lifeline to the literary arts. Readings and talks by local, national, and international figures occur almost every night. The children's-book section is extensive, and monthly meetings of the Elliott Bay Young Writers Group take place at the store. Other interesting specialty outlets are **Bowie and Company** (✉ 314 1st Ave. S, ☎ 206/624–4100) for antiquarian books, **David Ishii Books** (✉ 212 1st Ave. S, ☎ 206/622–4719) for books on baseball and fly-fishing, and **Flora and Fauna Books** (✉ 121 1st Ave. S, ☎ 206/623–4727) for nature-oriented titles.

Seattle Mystery Bookshop (✉ 117 Cherry St., ☎ 206/587–5737) straddles downtown and Pioneer Square. **Arundel Books** (✉ 944 3rd Ave., ☎ 206/624–4442), across from the Seattle Art Museum, carries used art and architecture titles. **Peter Miller** (✉ 1930 1st Ave., ☎ 206/441–4114) stocks excellent new architecture and design books. **The Moun-** taineers Bookstore (✉ 300 3rd Ave. W, ☎ 206/284–6310) sells expert guides to the great outdoors. The specialties at **Left Bank Books** (✉ 92 Pike St., ☎ 206/622–0195) and **Pistil Books and News** (✉ 1013 E. Pike St., ☎ 206/325–5401) include progressive politics, gender issues, and poetry. **Fillipi Books and Records** (✉ 1351 E. Olive Way, ☎ 206/682–4266) stocks old sheet music and 78 rpm recordings and has a sizable general-interest collection. The large Capitol Hill location of **Twice Sold Tales** (✉ 905 E. John St., ☎ 206/324–2421) is open 24 hours on Friday and Saturday for restless sleepers.

The University District is home to a large concentration of general-interest stores, including **Brooklyn Avenue Books** (✉ 5049 Brooklyn Ave. NE, ☎ 206/525–4559), **Magus Books** (✉ 1408 Northeast 42nd St., ☎ 206/633–1800), and **Recollection Books** (✉ 4519 University Way NE, ☎ 206/548–1346). **Zenith Supplies** (✉ 6300 Roosevelt Way N.E., ☎ 206/525–7997) is a New Age store specializing in books on health, nutrition, and massage. The excellent **Cinema Books** (✉ 4753 Roosevelt Way NE, ☎ 206/547–7667) wears its specialties on, well, its spines. No used-book tour of Seattle would be complete without a trip to the new and expanded **Shorey's Books** (✉ 1109 N. 36th St., ☎ 206/633–2990). This supermarket of used books, maps, and ephemera relocated from its downtown site to a vast space in Fremont. Take a watch or an easily bored browse-o-phobe to make sure you don't while away an entire morning or afternoon.

For more bookstore listings, *see* Shopping *above.*

Toys

Archie McPhee (✉ 3510 Stone Way N, ☎ 206/545–8344), Seattle's self-proclaimed "outfitters of popular culture," specializes in bizarre toys and novelties. **Magic Mouse Toys** (✉ 603 1st Ave., ☎ 206/682–8097) has two floors of toys, from small windups to giant stuffed animals.

Wine

Delaurenti Wine Shop (✉ 1435 1st Ave., ☎ 206/622–0141) has a knowledgeable staff and a large selection of Northwest Italian–style wines. **Pike & Western Wine Merchants** (✉ Pike Pl. and Virginia St., ☎ 206/441–1307 or 206/441–1308) carries Northwest wines from small wineries.

SEATTLE A TO Z

Arriving and Departing

By Bus

Greyhound Lines (☎ 800/231–2222 or 206/628–5526) serves Seattle at 8th Avenue and Stewart Street.

By Car

Seattle is accessible by I–5 and Highway 99 from Vancouver (three hours north) and Portland (three hours south), and by I–90 from Spokane (six hours east).

By Plane

Among the carriers serving **Seattle–Tacoma International Airport** (☎ 206/431–4444), also known as Sea-Tac, are Air Canada, Alaska, America West, American, British Airways, Continental, Delta, EVA Airways, Hawaiian, Horizon, Japan, Northwest, Southwest, Thai, TWA, United, United Express, and US Airways. *See* Air Travel *in* Smart Travel Tips A to Z for airline phone numbers.

Between the Airport and the City: Sea-Tac is about 15 mi south of downtown on I–5; a taxi costs about $30. **Gray Line Airport Express** (☎ 206/626–6088) service to downtown hotels costs $7.50. **Shuttle Express** (☎ 206/622–1424; 800/487–7433 in WA only) has 24-hour door-to-door service from $18 to $25, depending on the location of your pickup. **Metro Transit** (☎ 206/553–3000) city buses (Express Tunnel Bus 194 and regular Buses 174 and 184) pick up passengers outside the baggage claim areas.

By Train

Amtrak (☎ 800/872–7245) trains serve Seattle from the north, south, and east. The *Mt. Baker International* operates between Seattle and Vancouver, there is daily service between Portland and Seattle, the *Empire Builder* comes into Seattle from Chicago, and the *Coast Starlight* heads north from Los Angeles. All the trains stop at **King Street Station** (✉ 303 S. Jackson St., ☎ 206/382–4125). In 1999, Amtrak began its *Cascades* high-speed train service between Vancouver, British Columbia, and Eugene, Oregon, with stops in Seattle.

Getting Around

By Bus and Streetcar

Metropolitan Transit (✉ 821 2nd Ave., ☎ 206/553–3000) is convenient, inexpensive, and fairly comprehensive. For questions about specific destinations, call the Automated Schedule Line (206/287–8463). Most buses run until around midnight or 1 AM; some run all night. Most buses are wheelchair accessible. The visitor center at the Washington State Convention and Trade Center has maps and schedules.

Between 6 AM and 7 PM, all public transportation is free within the **Metro Bus Ride Free Area,** bounded by Battery Street to the north, 6th Avenue to the east (and over to 9th Avenue near the convention center), South Jackson Street to the south, and the waterfront to the west; you'll pay as you disembark if you ride out of this area. At other times (or in other places), fares range from $1 to $1.75, depending on how far you travel and at what time of day. Onboard fare collection boxes have prices posted on them. On weekends and holidays you can purchase a **Day Pass** from bus drivers for $1.70, a bargain if you're doing a lot of touring.

The **Waterfront Streetcar** line of vintage 1920s-era Australian trolleys runs south along Alaska Way from Pier 70, past the Washington State Ferries terminal at Piers 50 and 52, turning inland on Main Street, and passing through Pioneer Square before ending in the International District. It runs at about 20-minute intervals daily from 7 AM to 9 or 10 PM (less often and for fewer hours in the winter). The fare is $1. The stations and streetcars are wheelchair accessible.

By Car
Parking downtown is scarce and expensive. Metered parking is free after 6 PM and on Sunday. Be vigilant during the day. Parking enforcement officers are notoriously efficient.

If you plan to be downtown longer than two hours (the maximum time allowed on the street), you may find parking in a garage easier. The Bon Marché garage (entrance on 3rd Avenue between Stewart and Pine streets) is centrally located. Many downtown retailers participate in the Easy Streets discount parking program. Tokens are good for $1 off parking in selected locations, and you receive more substantial reductions at the Shopper's Quick Park garages at 2nd Avenue and Union Street and at Rainier Square on Union Street between 4th and 5th avenues.

Right turns are allowed on most red lights after you've come to a full stop, and left turns are allowed on adjoining one-way streets.

By Ferry
Washington State Ferries (☎ 206/464–6400; 800/843–3779 in WA only) serves the Puget Sound and San Juan Islands area. For more information about the ferry system, *see* Ferry Travel *in* Smart Travel Tips A to Z.

By Monorail
The **Seattle Center Monorail** (☎ 206/441–6038), built for the 1962 World's Fair, shuttles between its terminals in Westlake Center and the Seattle Center daily weekdays from 7:30 AM to 11 PM, and weekends from 9 AM to 11 PM; the trip takes less than three minutes. The adult fare is $1.25.

By Taxi
It's difficult but not impossible to flag a taxi on the street, though it's usually easier to call for a ride. **Orange Cab** (☎ 206/522–8800) is Seattle's friendliest company. **Graytop Cab** (☎ 206/282–8222) is the oldest. Taxis are readily available at most downtown hotels, and the stand at the **Westin Hotel** (⊠ 1900 5th Ave., ☎ 206/728–1000) is generally attended all night.

Contacts and Resources

B&B Reservation Agencies
Bed & Breakfast Association of Seattle (☎ 206/547–1020).

Car Rental

Most major rental agencies have offices downtown as well as at Sea-Tac Airport, including **Avis** (⊠ 1919 5th Ave., ☎ 800/831–2847), **Enterprise** (⊠ 2116 Westlake Ave., ☎ 800/736–8222), **Hertz** (⊠ 722 Pike St., ☎ 800/654–3131), and **National** (⊠ 1942 Westlake Ave. N, ☎ 206/448–7368).

Consulates

Canadian Consulate (⊠ Plaza 600 Bldg., 6th Ave. and Stewart St., 4th floor, ☎ 206/443–1777). **U.K. Consulate** (⊠ First Interstate Center, 999 3rd Ave., Suite 820, ☎ 206/622–9255).

Emergencies

Ambulance (☎ 911). **Fire** (☎ 911). **Police** (☎ 911).

Doctors, Inc. (⊠ 1215 4th Ave., ☎ 206/622–9933) gives referrals of physicians and dentists in the Seattle area.

Guided Tours

Three companies offer orientation tours of Seattle. The price of most tours is between $18 and $29, depending on the tour's length and mode of transportation. Custom packages cost more.

Gray Line of Seattle (☎ 206/626–5208 or 800/426–7505) operates bus and boat tours, including a six-hour Grand City Tour ($33) that includes many sights, lunch in Pike Place Market, and admission to the Space Needle observation deck. **Show Me Seattle** (☎ 206/633–2489) surveys the major Seattle sights and also operates a tour that takes in the *Sleepless in Seattle* floating home, the Fremont Troll, and other offbeat stops. **Seattle Tours** (☎ 206/768–1234) conducts tours in customized vans. The tours cover about 50 mi with stops for picture-taking.

BALLOON

Over the Rainbow (☎ 206/364–0995) operates balloon tours in Woodinville in the spring and summer, weather permitting. They cost between $135 and $165.

BICYCLING

Terrene Tours (☎ 206/325–5569) operates day and overnight bicycling and other tours of Seattle, the wine country surrounding the city, and points farther afield. The prices vary, depending on the destination and length of the tour.

BOAT

Argosy Cruises (☎ 206/623–4252) sail around Elliott Bay (one hour, from Pier 55, $13.40), the Ballard Locks (2½ hours, from Pier 57, $21.70), and other area waterways. **Pier 54 Adventures** (☎ 206/623–6364) arranges speedboat rides, and sailboat excursions on Elliott Bay. Salmon-fishing packages are also available; rates vary.

CARRIAGE

Sealth Horse Carriages (☎ 425/277–8282) narrated tours ($60 per hour) trot away from the waterfront and Westlake Center.

PLANE

Galvin Flying Service (☎ 206/763–9706) departs from Boeing Field in southern Seattle on excursions over downtown, Vashon and Bainbridge Islands, and Snoqualmie Falls. Prices begin at $89 ($10 for a second person). **Seattle Seaplanes** (☎ 800/637–5553) operates a 20-minute scenic flight that takes in views of the Woodland Park Zoo, downtown Seattle, and the Microsoft "campus." Custom tours are also available. Prices begin at $42.50. **Sound Flight** (☎ 425/255–6500) runs a 30-minute scenic flight for $79, custom sightseeing packages, and flights to secluded fishing spots.

SAILING

Let's Go Sailing (☎ 206/624–3931) permits passengers to take the helm, trim the sails, or simply enjoy the ride aboard the *Obsession,* a 70-ft ocean racer. Three 1½-hour excursions ($22) depart daily from Pier 56. A 2½-hour sunset cruise ($38) is also available. Passengers can bring their own food on board. Private charters can also be arranged.

TRAIN

The **Spirit of Washington Dinner Train** (☎ 800/876–7245) departs from Renton for a 3-hour trip ($47–$69) along the Eastern shores of Lake Washington up to the Columbia Winery in Woodinville. Sights include the Boeing Renton Plant, the Wilburton Trestle, and the Sammamish River Valley.

WALKING

Chinatown Discovery Tours (☎ 206/236–0657) include four culinary excursions—from a light sampler to an eight-course banquet. The rates run between $9.95 and $34.95, based on a minimum of four participants.

Seattle Walking Tours (☎ 425/885–3173) through the city's historic areas, which give special attention to Pioneer Square, cost $15.

Underground Seattle (☎ 206/682–4646) tours ($6.50) of the now-buried original storefronts and sidewalks of Pioneer Square are extremely popular. They offer an effective primer on early Seattle history, and it may be a good place to take cover if your aboveground tour starts to get soggy.

Late-Night Pharmacies

Bartell Drugs (✉ 600 1st Ave. N, at Mercer St., ☎ 206/284–1353) is a 24-hour pharmacy.

Travel Agencies

AAA Travel (✉ 330 6th Ave. N, ☎ 206/448–5353). **American Express Travel Office** (✉ 600 Stewart St., ☎ 206/441–8622). **Doug Fox Travel** (✉ 1321 4th Ave., ☎ 206/628–6171).

Visitor Information

Seattle/King County Convention and Visitors Bureau (✉ 520 Pike St., Suite 1300, 98101, ☎ 206/461–5800). **Seattle Visitor Center** (✉ 800 Convention Pl., ☎ 206/461–5840). **Washington State Convention & Trade Center** (✉ 800 Convention Pl., ☎ 206/447–5000). **Washington Tourism Development Division** (✉ Box 42500, Olympia, WA 98504, ☎ 360/753–5600).

3 SIDE TRIPS FROM SEATTLE

Excursions from Seattle are usually into the mountains or out on the water. A trip of less than an hour by car or ferry will take you places that seem worlds away from the hubbub of the city. Islands and mountains surround Seattle. Seek out your own personal Eden.

THE WATERS OF PUGET SOUND SURROUND PEACEFUL, rural Whidbey Island, a one-hour ferry ride from Seattle. Port Townsend, across from Whidbey on the Olympic Peninsula, holds cultural and historical attractions enhanced by a beautiful setting. Plan on more than a day trip to fully appreciate the remote San Juan Islands. If you head east toward the Cascade Range to Snoqualmie, home to a towering waterfall, you can hike, bike, or take an historic train through forests and meadows. Farther east is alpine Leavenworth. Two hours southeast of Seattle is majestic Mount Rainier, the fifth-highest mountain in the continental United States. Mount Rainier National Park offers 400 square mi of wilderness.

Revised by Julie Fay

Pleasures and Pastimes

Dining

Spicy yet subtle flavorings testify to the strong Asian influence on the cuisine in the region surrounding Seattle. On the Olympic Peninsula, sweet, meaty Dungeness crab is the local specialty. Oysters, mussels, and clams are plentiful as well. Many of the finer coastal restaurants serve flavorful Ellensburg (in eastern Washington) beef and lamb.

CATEGORY	COST*
$$$$	over $35
$$$	$25–$35
$$	$15–$25
$	under $15

per person for a three-course meal, excluding drinks, service, and sales tax (about 7.9%, varies slightly by community)

Ferries

The vessels of the Washington State Ferries system range from the *Hiyu*, which holds 40 cars, to jumbo craft capable of carrying more than 200 cars and 2,000 passengers each. A diversion in and of themselves, the boats, which connect points all around Puget Sound, the San Juan Islands, and beyond, are the *only* way to reach some areas of western Washington. For information about ferry routes to the regions covered in this chapter, *see* Arriving and Departing *in* Essentials, at the end of the following sections: Bainbridge Island; Whidbey Island, Fidalgo Island, Port Townsend, and La Conner; and the San Juan Islands. For general information about the Washington State Ferries, *see* Ferry Travel *in* Smart Travel Tips A to Z.

Lodging

Spend the night in one of Puget Sound's waterfront or bed-and-breakfast inns and you'll quickly understand the attraction the water holds for residents. Most of the Northwest's smaller accommodations may lack the old-fashioned charm and historical ties of their counterparts in New England or the South, but they're often equipped with hot tubs and in-room fireplaces that take the edge off crisp coastal air. Prices generally run lower than those in Seattle, so you needn't break the bank to stay overnight, even in popular Leavenworth.

CATEGORY	COST*
$$$$	over $170
$$$	$110–$170
$$	$60–$110
$	under $60

All prices are for a standard double room, excluding taxes (generally 7.9%; slightly higher in some areas).

Outdoor Activities and Sports

The combination of flat and hilly terrain surrounding Seattle satisfies hikers and bikers of varying skills. Kayaking is a popular way to get close to otters, seals, whales, and other sea creatures; ample rental facilities are available at each of the destinations covered. Whale-watching tours are among the region's more passive outdoor options.

BAINBRIDGE ISLAND

Take the half-hour ride on the **Bainbridge Island ferry** (☞ *below*) for great views of the city skyline and the surrounding hills. The ferry trip itself lures most of the island's visitors—this is the least expensive way to cruise Puget Sound—along with Bainbridge's small-town atmosphere and scenic countryside. From the Bainbridge Island terminal, continue north up a short hill on Olympic Drive to Winslow Way. If you turn west (left), you'll find yourself in **Winslow,** where there are several blocks of antiques shops, clothing boutiques, galleries, bookstores, and restaurants.

The **Bainbridge Island Vineyard and Winery,** a family farm–estate winery, grows, produces, and bottles vintages that include pinot gris, pinot noir, and Sylvaner Riesling. It is open for tours and tastings. ✉ *682 Hwy. 305 (from ferry exit, continue on Olympic Dr. ¼ mi past the Winslow Way turnoff),* ☎ *206/842–9463.* ☞ *Free.* ☉ *Wed.–Sun., noon–5.*

You'll need a car to get to the **Bloedel Reserve,** whose grounds, the 150-acre estate of Prentice and Virginia Bloedel, contain a Japanese garden, a Bird Refuge, a moss garden, and number of other "garden rooms" designed to blend man-made gardens into the natural, untamed look of the island's native (second-growth) vegetation. Within the park are 2 mi of trails, ponds with ducks and trumpeter swans, and Bloedel's grand mansion, designed in the country-French château style by J. Lister Holmes and completed in 1930. Dazzling displays of rhododendrons and azaleas bloom in spring, and the leaves of Japanese maples and other trees colorfully signal the arrival of autumn. There is no food service and picnicking is not permitted. No pets are allowed. ✉ *7571 N.E. Dolphin Dr. (from ferry follow signs on Hwy. 305),* ☎ *206/842–7631.* ☞ *$6.* ☉ *Wed.–Sun. 10–4 (reservations essential).*

Bainbridge Island Essentials

Arriving and Departing

The **Bainbridge Island ferry** (☎ 206/464–6400), which takes cars and walk-on passengers, leaves Seattle once an hour during the day from Pier 52 (Coleman dock), south of the Pike Place Market, and stops at Winslow. Highway 305 is the main road through the island. The round-trip fare for walk-on passengers is $3.70. The fare is $6.50 each way for a car, and reservations are not accepted. The lines are long during rush hour, which is before 9 AM eastbound, and between 3 PM and 6:30 PM westbound. The last ferry from Bainbridge Island to Seattle leaves at 1:30 AM.

Visitor Information

The **Bainbridge Island Chamber of Commerce and Visitor Center** (✉ 590 Winslow Way, 98110, ☎ 206/842–3700), two blocks from the ferry dock, has maps and tourist information.

WHIDBEY ISLAND, FIDALGO ISLAND, PORT TOWNSEND, AND LA CONNER

Numbers in the margin correspond to points of interest on the Puget Sound map.

❶ On a nice day there's no better short excursion from Seattle than a ferry trip across Puget Sound to **Whidbey Island.** It's a great way to watch the seagulls, sailboats, and massive container vessels in the sound—not to mention the surrounding scenery, which takes in the Kitsap Peninsula and Olympic Mountains, Mount Rainier, the Cascade Range, and the Seattle skyline. Even when the weather isn't terrific, you can stay snug inside the ferry, have a snack, and listen to folk musicians.

The island, 30 mi northwest of Seattle, is a blend of bucolic hills, forests, meadows, sandy beaches, and dramatic cliffs. The best beaches, which you can explore by foot, boat, or kayak, are on the west side, where the sand stretches out to the sea and the view takes in the shipping lanes and the Olympic Mountains. **Maxwelton Beach** (⊠ Maxwelton Beach Rd.) is popular with the locals. **Possession Point** (⊠ off Coltas Bay Rd.) includes a park, a beach, and a boat launch. Fort Ebey in Coupeville has a sandy spread, and West Beach is a stormy patch north of the fort with mounds of driftwood.

Whidbey, which is 60 mi long and 8 mi wide, is easily accessible via a Washington State Ferries vessel from Mukilteo (pronounced muck-ill-*tee*-oh) to Clinton on the southern part of the island. Or you can drive across from the mainland on Highway 20 at the northern end of the island. The tour below begins at the island's southern tip, which has a mostly rural landscape of undulating hills, gentle beaches, and little coves.

Langley

From Seattle, take I–5 north 21 mi to Exit 189 (Whidbey Island–Mukilteo Ferry) and follow signs 7 mi to ferry landing. From Clinton (Whidbey Island ferry terminal), take Hwy. 525 north 2 mi to Langley Rd., turn right, and follow road 5 mi.

The village of Langley rises above a 50-ft-high bluff overlooking Saratoga Passage, which separates Whidbey from Camano Island. A grassy terrace just above the beach is a great place for viewing birds on the water or in the air. On a clear day, you can see Mt. Baker loom in the distance. It's a great vantage point for viewing wildlife on land and sea. Upscale boutiques selling art, glass, jewelry, and clothing line 1st and 2nd streets in the heart of town.

The **South Whidbey Historical Museum,** in a one-room schoolhouse built in 1900, focuses on the history of the small agricultural and fishing communities that developed on the south end of Whidbey during the second half of the 19th century. A kitchen and bathroom are decorated in period style, and there are displays of old Victrolas, farm tools, kitchen utensils, and antique toys. ⊠ *312 2nd St.,* ☎ *360/579–4696.* ☞ *Free.* ☉ *Weekends 1–4.*

Dining and Lodging

$$$$ ✕ **Country Kitchen.** Tables for two line the walls of this intimate restaurant. On the other side of the fireplace is the "great table," which seats 10. The prix-fixe five-course dinners might include locally gathered mussels in a black-bean sauce, breast of duck in a loganberry sauce, or rich Columbia River salmon. ⊠ *Inn at Langley, 400 1st St.,* ☎ *360/221–3033. Reservations essential. AE, MC, V.*

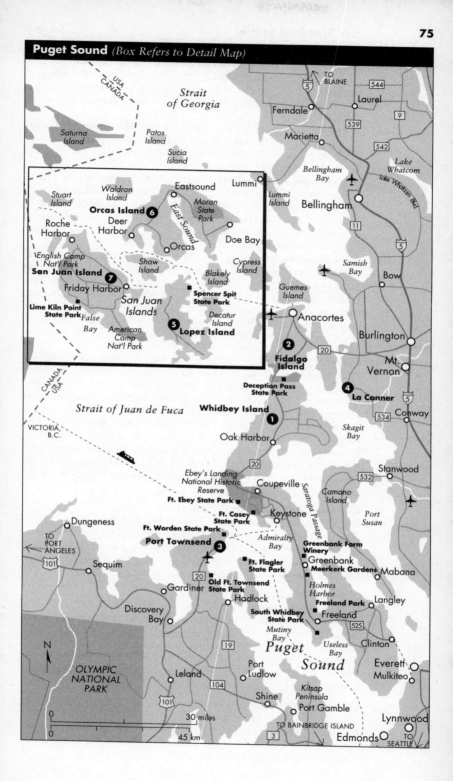

Puget Sound (Box Refers to Detail Map)

Strait of Georgia

USA / CANADA

TO BLAINE
5
544
Laurel
Ferndale
539
9
Marietta
542
Saturna Island
Patos Island
Sucia Island
Lake Whatcom
Bellingham Bay
Waldron Island
Eastsound
Lummi
Lummi Island
Bellingham
11
5
Orcas Island 6
Moran State Park
Deer Harbor
East Sound
Roche Harbor
Doe Bay
Orcas
Samish Bay
Bow
English Camp Nat'l Park
Shaw Island
Cypress Island
San Juan Island 7
Blakely Island
Guemes Island
Friday Harbor
Lime Kiln Point State Park
False Bay
San Juan Islands
Spencer Spit State Park
Decatur Island
Anacortes
2
Fidalgo Island
20
Burlington
Mt. Vernon
American Camp Nat'l Park
5 **Lopez Island**
4 **La Conner**
5
Deception Pass State Park
Conway
534
CANADA / USA
Strait of Juan de Fuca
Whidbey Island 1
Skagit Bay
VICTORIA, B.C.
Oak Harbor
20
Stanwood
532
Ebey's Landing National Historic Reserve
Coupeville
Saratoga Passage
Camano Island
Port Susan
Ft. Ebey State Park
Keystone
Dungeness
TO PORT ANGELES
101
Sequim
Ft. Casey State Park
Ft. Worden State Park
Port Townsend 3
Admiralty Bay
Greenbank Farm Winery
Greenbank
Meerkerk Gardens
Mabana
Ft. Flagler State Park
Holmes Harbor
Gardiner
20
Old Ft. Townsend State Park
Hadlock
Freeland Park
Freeland
Langley
Discovery Bay
South Whidbey State Park
525
N
Mutiny Bay
Useless Bay
Clinton
19
Port Ludlow
Puget
Everett
Mulkiteo
OLYMPIC NATIONAL PARK
Leland
104
Sound
Lynnwood
Shine
Kitsap Peninsula
Port Gamble
101
3
TO BAINBRIDGE ISLAND
Edmonds
TO SEATTLE

0 —— 30 miles
0 —— 45 km

$$–$$$ ✕ **Café Langley.** Terra-cotta tile floors, antique oak tables, and the aroma
★ of garlic, basil, and oregano set the mood at this Greek restaurant. The
menu includes eggplant moussaka, Dungeness crab cakes, Mediterranean
seafood stew, and lamb kebabs. Greek salads come with all entrées.
⊠ *113 1st St.,* ☎ *360/221–3090. MC, V. Closed Tues. in winter. No
lunch Tues.*

$$–$$$ ✕ **Star Bistro.** This slick bistro atop the Star Store serves up Caesar
salads, shrimp-and-scallop linguine, and gourmet burgers. Popular for
lunch, it remains crowded well into the late afternoon. ⊠ *201½ 1st
St.,* ☎ *360/221–2627. AE, MC, V. Closed Mon.*

$ ✕ **Dog House Backdoor Restaurant.** Collectibles that include a nick-
elodeon fill this laid-back waterfront tavern and family restaurant. Juicy
burgers, homemade chili, and vegetarian entrées are made from low-
salt recipes. The Dog House, which is on the National Register of Historic Places, has a fine view of Saratoga Passage. ⊠ *230 1st St.,* ☎ *360/
221–9825. Reservations not accepted. No credit cards.*

$$$$ 🛏 **Inn at Langley.** This Frank Lloyd Wright–inspired concrete-and-wood
★ structure perches on a bluff that descends to the beach. The Asian-style
guest rooms (for couples or singles only) have views of Saratoga Passage and the Cascades. All have whirlpool tubs, fireplaces, outdoor terraces, and TVs. Meals are served in the inn's restaurant, the Country
Kitchen (☞ *above*). Dinner starts promptly at 7 with a glass of sherry
and a tour of the wine cellar. ⊠ *400 1st St., 98269,* ☎ 🅵🅰🆇 *360/221–
3033. 24 rooms. Restaurant. AE, MC, V.*

$$$–$$$$ 🛏 **Saratoga Inn.** White rocking chairs dot the wraparound porch of
★ this Cape Cod–style inn overlooking the Saratoga Passage. On rainy
days you can cozy up with a book and a cookie on the overstuffed
couches and chairs around the living room fireplace. All the rooms at
this property, run by the Four Sisters Inns group, have gas fireplaces,
down comforters, and cable TV. Some rooms have water views. The
rooms in the main building have showers but no tubs. The carriage
house has its own entrance, sundeck, a kitchen, and an oversize bath-
room with an antique cast-iron tub. ⊠ *201 Cascade Ave., 98260,* ☎
*360/221–5801 or 800/698–2910. 15 rooms. Meeting room. Full break-
fast. AE, D, MC, V.*

Outdoor Activities and Sports

Langley's small **boat harbor** (☎ 360/221–4246) provides moorage for
35 boats, plus utilities and a 160-ft fishing pier, all protected by a tim-
ber-pile breakwater. You can fish for seaperch, lingcod, sculpin, and
perhaps a rockfish from the Langley pier. Supplies are available from
Offshore Marine (⊠ 202 Wharf St., ☎ 360/221–1771).

Shopping

Childers/Proctor Gallery (⊠ 302 1st St., ☎ 360/221–2978) exhibits
and sells paintings, jewelry, pottery, and sculpture. The **Cottage** (⊠ 210
1st St., ☎ 360/221–4747) stocks vintage and imported women's cloth-
ing. You can meet glass and jewelry artist Gwenn Knight at her shop,
the **Glass Knight** (⊠ 214 1st St., ☎ 360/221–6283). The **Museo** (⊠
215 1st St., ☎ 360/221–7737), a gallery and gift shop, carries con-
temporary art by recognized and emerging artists.

Outside Langley at the **Blackfish Studio** (⊠ 5075 S. Langley Rd., ☎
360/221–1274) you can view works-in-progress and finished pieces by
Kathleen Miller, who produces enamel jewelry and hand-painted cloth-
ing and accessories, and Donald Miller, whose photographs depict the
land and people of the Northwest.

Freeland

7 mi north of Langley on Hwy. 525.

Freeland Park (✉ Holmes Harbor, Washington Dr. off Freeland Ave., ☎ no phone) has picnic spots, a playground, a sandy beach, and a boat ramp. **South Whidbey State Park** (✉ S. Smugglers Cove Rd. off Hwy. 525, ☎ 360/331–4559; 800/452–5687 for campground reservations) has hiking trails and swimming facilities. The park's 54 campsites have fire rings, flush toilets, showers, and water; 2 sites have electric and water hookups. Campsites cost $10 a night ($15 for a hookup site), and reservations are essential from mid-May to mid-October.

Lodging

$$$–$$$$ 🏨 **Cliff House.** A winding drive through the woods leads to this secluded two-story house overlooking Admiralty Bay. The design is uncompromisingly modern; one side is nearly all glass and provides sweeping views. Rain and occasionally snow whisk through the open-air atrium in the middle of the house. An adjacent cottage also has sea views. Guests in both buildings are pampered with fresh flowers and every modern amenity. ✉ *727 Windmill Dr., 98249,* ☎ *360/331–1566. 2 rooms. No credit cards.*

Greenbank

11 mi north of Freeland on Hwy. 525.

About halfway up Whidbey is the town of Greenbank. Island County owns the 125-acre **Greenbank Farm Winery.** The vineyard here produces a small portion of the loganberries used for production of the island's unique spirit, Whidbey's Liqueur (available at the gift shop). Picnic tables are scattered throughout the farm. ✉ *765 E. Wonn Rd.,* ☎ *360/678–7700.* 🎫 *Free.* ☉ *Gift shop 10–5 (summer), 11–4 (winter).*

The 53-acre **Meerkerk Rhododendron Gardens** contain 1,500 native and hybrid species of rhododendrons, numerous walking trails, and ponds. The flowers are in full bloom in April and May. ✉ *Resort Rd.,* ☎ *360/678–1912.* 🎫 *$2.* ☉ *Daily 9–4.*

Lodging

$$$–$$$$ 🏨 **Guest House Cottages.** The very private log cabins here, surrounded
★ by 25 forested acres, have feather beds, VCRs, whirlpool tubs, country antiques, and fireplaces. Fresh flowers, robes, and a fine breakfast are among the other draws, along with an enormous two-story lodge filled with collectibles that include a working pump organ. ✉ *3366 Hwy. 525 S, 98253,* ☎ 🖷 *360/678–3115. 6 cabins. Pool, exercise room. Continental breakfast. AE, D, MC, V.*

Coupeville

17 mi north of Greenbank, Hwy. 525 to Hwy. 20.

Restored Victorian houses grace many of the streets in quiet Coupeville, which has one of the largest national historic districts in Washington and often serves to represent 19th-century New England villages in movies. Stores above the waterfront have maintained their second-story false fronts and old-fashioned character. Thomas Coupe, a sea captain, founded Coupeville in 1852. His house, built in 1853, is one of Washington's oldest.

The exhibits at the **Island County Historical Museum** survey the history of the island's fishing, timber, and agricultural industries. Docents lead walks around town and hour-long historical tours. The squared-timber blockhouse outside dates from the Puget Sound Indian War of 1855. ⊠ *908 N.W. Alexander St.,* ☎ *360/678–3310.* ☜ *$2.* ☉ *May–Oct., daily 10–5; Nov.–Apr., Fri.–Mon. 10–4.*

Ebey's Landing National Historic Reserve encompasses two state parks and some privately held farmland. The reserve holds nearly 100 nationally registered historical structures, most from the 19th century. A 22-acre beach area is the highlight of **Fort Ebey State Park.** The best view over Ebey's prairie can be had from the park's Sunnyside Cemetery. **Fort Casey State Park,** set on a bluff overlooking the Strait of Juan de Fuca, was one of three forts built in 1890 to protect Puget Sound. The park contains a small interpretive center, picnic sites, fishing spots, and a boat launch. ⊠ *Follow signs from Hwy. 20 to each park. Ft. Ebey State Park: 2 mi west of Hwy. 20,* ☎ *360/678–4636;* ⊠ *Ft. Casey State Park: 3 mi west of Hwy. 20,* ☎ *360/678–4519.* ☜ *Free (day use), $11–$16 (campsites).* ☉ *Daily 8 AM–sunset.*

Dining

$$$ ✕ **Rosi's.** Deceptively simple-looking Rosi's, inside the Victorian home
★   of its chef-owners, serves outstanding Italian and Northwest cuisine. Chicken mascarpone, osso buco, prime rib, and Penn Cove mussels are among the entrées. ⊠ *606 N. Main St.,* ☎ *360/678–3989. AE, MC, V. No lunch weekends.*

Oak Harbor

10 mi north of Coupeville on Hwy. 20.

Oak Harbor gets its name from the majestic Oregon oaks that grow above the bay. Dutch and Irish immigrants settled the town in the mid-1800s. Several windmills were recently built by the Dutch as symbols of their cultural tradition. Unfortunately, suburban sprawl has overtaken Whidbey Island's largest city in the form of multiple strips of fast-food restaurants and service stations.

★ **Deception Pass State Park** hosts more than 4 million visitors each year. With 19 mi of rocky shore and beaches, three freshwater lakes, and more than 38 mi of forest and meadow trails, it's easy to see why. The park is at the northernmost point of Whidbey Island, and on the southernmost tip of Fidalgo Island, to both sides of the Deception Pass Bridge. Park on Canoe Island and walk across the bridge for views of two dramatic saltwater gorges whose tidal whirlpools have been known to swallow large logs. ⊠ *Hwy. 20, 7 mi north of Oak Harbor,* ☎ *360/675–2417.* ☜ *Park free; campsite fees vary.* ☉ *Apr.–Sept., daily 6:30 AM–sunset; Oct.–Mar., daily 8 AM–sunset.*

Anacortes

15 mi north of Oak Harbor on Hwy. 20; 76 mi from Seattle, north on I–5 (to Exit 230) and west on Hwy. 20.

❷ Deception Pass Bridge links Whidbey to **Fidalgo Island.** From the bridge it's a short drive to Anacortes, Fidalgo's main town and the terminus for ferries going to the San Juan Islands. Anacortes consists mostly of strip malls and chain stores, but a small historical waterfront section contains some well-preserved redbrick buildings.

The frequently changing exhibits at the **Anacortes Museum** focus on the cultural heritage of Fidalgo and nearby Guemes Island. ⊠ *1305 8th St.,* ☎ *360/293–1915.* ☜ *$2 donation suggested.* ☉ *Thurs.–Mon. 1–5.*

Lodging

$$–$$$$ 🖭 **Majestic Hotel.** One of the finest small hotels in the Northwest
★   began life in 1889 as a mercantile building. From the Victorian-style
lobby you can enter the Rose & Crown pub or the Salmon Run Restau-
rant. A sweeping staircase ascends to an open mezzanine. An English-
style library nestles on one of the three guest floors. The marina,
Mount Baker, and the Cascades are among the views from the crow's-
nest gazebo on the top floor. Down comforters and European antiques
decorate the rooms, several of which contain whirlpool tubs. ⊠ *419
Commercial Ave., 98221,* ☎ *360/293-3355,* FAX *360/293-5214. 23
rooms. Restaurant, pub, library. Continental breakfast. MC, V.*

Port Townsend

★ ❸   *45 mi from Seattle; I–5 north to Edmonds Ferry to Kingston; from land-
ing drive northwest on Hwy. 307 to Rte. 3N, to Rte. 19. Port Townsend
can be accessed from Whidbey Island by ferry at Keystone.*

Many writers, musicians, painters, and other artists live in Port
Townsend, a Victorian city on the northern tip of the Olympic Penin-
sula. Handsome restored brick buildings from the 1888–1890 railroad
boom, with shops and restaurants inside, are lined up in two parallel
blocks near the waterfront. The many impressive yachts docked here
attest to the area's status as one of the Salish Sea's premier sailing spots.

The Genuine Bull Durham Smoking Tobacco ad on the **Lewis Build-
ing** (⊠ Madison and Water Sts.) is one of many charming relics of Port
Townsend's glory days as a customs port. The **bell tower** on Jefferson
Street, at the top of the Tyler Street stairs, is the last of its kind in the
country. Built in 1890, it was used to call volunteer firemen to duty.
The tower houses artifacts from the city museum, including a 19th-
century horse-drawn hearse that you can peek at through the windows.

The 1892 City Hall building—Jack London languished briefly in the
jail here on his way to the Klondike—contains the **Jefferson County
Historical Museum,** four floors of Native American artifacts, exhibits
on Port Townsend's past, and historic photographs of the Olympic Penin-
sula. ⊠ *210 Madison St.,* ☎ *360/385-1003.* ☜ *$2 donation sug-
gested.* ⊗ *Mon.–Sat. 11–4, Sun. 1–4.*

The neatly manicured grounds of 443-acre **Fort Worden State Park** in-
clude a row of restored Victorian officers' houses, a World War II bal-
loon hangar, and a sandy beach that leads to **Point Wilson Lighthouse,**
built in 1879. The fort, which was built on Point Wilson in 1896 to
defend Puget Sound, hosts art events sponsored by Centrum (☞
Nightlife and the Arts, *below*). The **Marine Science Center** has aquar-
iums and touch tanks where you can reach in and feel sea creatures
like crabs and anemones. ⊠ *200 Battery Way,* ☎ *360/385-4730.* ☜
Free (day use); $2 (science center). ⊗ *Park daily dawn–dusk, Marine
Science Center Tues.–Sun. noon–6.*

A 15- to 20-minute drive from town takes you to the tip of Marrow-
stone Island and **Fort Flagler State Park.** The turn-of-the-century gun
placements overlook beaches. The fort has campgrounds and 7 mi of
wooded and ocean-side hiking trails—the nameless remnants of old
army roads that radiated from the perimeter road. The inlets of the is-
land are great for paddling around, and you can rent canoes, kayaks,
and paddleboats from the **Nordland General Store** (☎ 360/385-0777),
near the park entrance. ⊠ *10341 Flagler Rd. (from Port Townsend
take Hwy. 20 and Hwy. 19 south to Hwy. 116 east), Nordland,* ☎ *360/
385-1259.* ☜ *Free (day use), $10–$16 (campsites).* ⊗ *Daily dawn–
dusk.*

Guided Historical Tours (✉ 820 Tyler St., ☎ 360/385–1967) conducts tours of Port Townsend, the most popular of which is a one-hour walking tour of the waterfront and downtown, focusing on the town's architecture and history.

Dining and Lodging

$$–$$$ ✕ **Fountain Café.** Old standbys at this funky art and knickknack-filled café include the house specialty, Oysters Dorado (pasta with oysters, mushrooms, and eggplant in a wine sauce), but you'll also find seafood and pasta entrées with imaginative twists—smoked salmon in a light cream sauce with a hint of Scotch, for example. Creative grilled sandwiches are served at lunch. Expect the occasional wait (call ahead to place your name on the list for tables) at this hot spot. ✉ *920 Washington St.,* ☎ *360/385–1364. Reservations not accepted. MC, V. Closed Tues. No lunch.*

$$–$$$ ✕ **Lanza's Ristorante.** A favorite with locals, Lanza's has been serving up old family recipes in this cozy neighborhood restaurant since 1985. With Lori Lanza at the helm, the kitchen combines past and current culinary trends. Try the spaghetti Lanza, with Grandma Gloria's famous meatballs made from a century-old recipe, or fettuccine with smoked salmon and a feta cream sauce. There's live piano music on weekends. ✉ *1020 Lawrence St.,* ☎ *360/379–1900. MC, V. Closed Sun.*

$$–$$$ ✕ **Lonny's.** Chef-owner Lonny Ritter aims to provide a sensual din-
★   ing experience. The handsome wooden furnishings and the texture of the ocher-color walls at his restaurant are as carefully selected as the professional staff and the extensive wine collection. Entrées on the seasonally changing menu might include a char-grilled Peking duck breast with Italian sausage stuffing or Lonny's signature Dungeness crab dish, prepared with basil butter, heavy cream, and sweet Gorgonzola cheese. The vegetarian entrées here are also thoughtfully conceived. ✉ *2330 Washington St.,* ☎ *360/385–0700. MC, V. Closed Tues. No lunch.*

$$–$$$$ 🏨 **James House.** Meticulously restored antiques fill this 1889 Queen Anne structure on the bluff overlooking downtown Port Townsend and the waterfront. Some rooms are spacious and have waterfront views, others are small and share baths. The hardwood floors, though exquisite, are creaky and the sounds of footsteps and conversations drift into the rooms. Breakfast is served in the formal dining room, as is complimentary sherry in the evening. The "Bungalow on the Bluff" next door has a wood-burning fireplace and a whirlpool tub. ✉ *1238 Washington St., 98368,* ☎ *360/385–1238 or 800/385–1238,* 𝔽𝔸𝕏 *360/379–5551. 12 rooms, 10 with bath. Dining room. Full breakfast. AE, MC, V.*

$$$ 🏨 **Tides Inn.** This waterfront inn was the setting for the steamy love scenes between Richard Gere and Debra Winger in the movie *An Officer and a Gentleman.* Comfortable and unfancy, the Tides has a briny smell and a seaside-motel atmosphere. Some rooms have small private decks that extend over the water's edge. All rooms have TVs and phones; some have kitchens, decks, hot tubs, or all three. ✉ *1807 Water St., 98368,* ☎ *360/385–0595 or 800/822–8696,* 𝔽𝔸𝕏 *360/385–7370. 21 rooms. Continental breakfast. AE, D, DC, MC, V.*

$$–$$$ 🏨 **Palace Hotel.** The decor of this hotel reflects the building's history as a bordello. One can easily imagine the exposed brick lobby filled with music and men waiting for the ladies whose names grace hallway plaques. The large rooms have 14-ft ceilings and worn antiques. The outstanding corner suite—Miss Marie's—has full views of the Bay and the original working fireplace from Marie's days as a madam. ✉ *1004 Water St., 98368,* ☎ *360/385–0773 or 800/962–0741,* 𝔽𝔸𝕏 *360/385–0780. 15 rooms, 12 with bath. AE, D, MC, V.*

Nightlife and the Arts

Centrum (☎ 800/733–3608), Port Townsend's well-respected performing-arts organization, presents performances, workshops, and conferences throughout the year at Fort Worden State Park. The **Centrum Summer Arts Festival** runs from June through September.

The Public House (⊠ 1038 Water St., ☎ 360/385–9706) hosts live jazz, folk, and acoustic rock on weekends. The old **Town Tavern** (⊠ 639 Water St., ☎ 360/385–4706) has live music—from jazz to blues to rock—on weekends.

Outdoor Activities and Sports

BICYCLING

P. T. Cyclery (⊠ 100 Taylor St., south of Water St., ☎ 360/385–6470) rents mountain bikes in July and August. The nearest place to go riding is Fort Worden, but you can range as far afield as Fort Flagler, the lower Dungeness trails (no bikes are allowed on the spit itself), or across the water to Whidbey Island.

BOAT CRUISE

P. S. Express (⊠ 431 Water St., ☎ 360/385–5288) operates narrated whale-watching tours to San Juan Island from April through October for $49 round-trip.

KAYAK TOURS

Kayak Port Townsend (⊠ 435 Water St., ☎ 360/385–6240) conducts guided kayak tours from April through October ($40 for about three hours or $70 for a full day with lunch).

Shopping

The best shopping in Port Townsend is near the waterfront, where boutiques and stores carry Northwest arts and crafts. **North by Northwest Gallery** (⊠ 18 Water St., ☎ 360/385–0955) specializes in Eskimo and Native American art, artifacts, jewelry, and clothing. **Russell Jaqua Gallery** (⊠ 21 Taylor St., ☎ 360/457–0482) exhibits blacksmith and other ironwork creations. **William James Bookseller** (⊠ 829 Water St., ☎ 360/385–7313) stocks used and out-of-print books in all fields, with an emphasis on nautical, regional-history, and theology titles.

Three dozen dealers at the two-story **Port Townsend Antique Mall** (⊠ 802 Washington St., ☎ 360/385–2590) flea market sell merchandise ranging from pricey Victorian collectors' items to cheap and funky junk.

More shops are uptown on **Lawrence Street** near an enclave of Victorian houses.

La Conner

❹ *65 mi from Seattle; I–5 north to exit 221. Follow Fir Island Rd. west.*

Morris Graves, Kenneth Callahan, Guy Anderson, Mark Tobey, and other painters set up shop in La Conner in the 1940s. The small fishing village at the mouth of the Skagit River has been a haven for artists ever since. The creation of the Skagit Valley Tulip Festival in the 1980s helped the town become a tourist destination. La Conner flirts with being too precious, but it is saved by the quality of its shops, restaurants, inns, and history. The town is a pleasant destination year-round.

Roozengaarde is one of the largest growers of tulips, daffodils, and irises in the nation with 200 varieties in all. The display gardens here are spectacular. ⊠ *1587 Beaver Marsh Rd.,* ☎ *360/424–8531.* ☞ *Free.* ☉ *Mar.–May, daily 9–5. Closed Sun.*

The **Museum of Northwest Art** presents the works of regional artists past and present. ⊠ *121 S. 1st St.*, ☎ *360/466–4446.* ⊠ *$3.* ⊙ *Tues.–Sun., 10–5.*

The **Skagit County Historical Museum** surveys domestic life in early Skagit County and Northwest coastal Native American history. ⊠ *501 4th St.*, ☎ *360/466–3365.* ⊠ *$2.* ⊙ *Tues.–Sun. 11–5.*

The **Tulip Festival** is held when the tulips are in bloom, usually late March to mid-April. Exact dates vary depending upon the growing conditions. Many of the growers have spectacular display gardens, and there's a salmon barbecue. ⊠ *P.O. Box 1784, Mt. Vernon 98273*, ☎ *360/428–5959.*

Dining and Lodging

$$$–$$$$ ✕ **Palmer's Restaurant and Pub.** There's a distinctly French influence to the seasonally changing menu at this restaurant a stone's throw from the water. The chef's signature dish is a braised lamb shank, but you'll also find inventive salads and an amazing oyster bisque on the menu. The adjacent pub serves bistro fare. ⊠ *205 E. Washington St.*, ☎ *360/ 466–4261. AE, MC, V. No lunch Mon.–Thurs., Sept.–Mar.*

$$$–$$$$ ☆ **La Conner Channel Lodge.** La Conner's only waterfront hotel is an
★ understated modern facility overlooking the narrow Swinomish Channel. Each room has a private balcony and a gas fireplace, and 12 rooms have whirlpool baths. ⊠ *205 N. 1st St., 98257*, ☎ *360/466–1500*, ℻ *360/466–5902. 29 rooms, 12 suites. Breakfast room, meeting room. Continental breakfast. AE, D, DC, MC, V.*

Whidbey Island, Fidalgo Island, Port Townsend, and La Conner Essentials

Arriving and Departing

BY CAR

Whidbey Island can be reached by heading north from Seattle on I–5, west on Highway 20 onto Fidalgo Island, and south across Deception Pass Bridge. The all-land route from Seattle to Port Townsend is a long one, south on I–5 to Olympia and north on U.S. 101 and Highway 20. To reach La Conner, take I–5 north to exit 221. Follow Fir Island Rd. west.

BY FERRY

Washington State Ferries (☎ 206/464–6400; 800/843–3779 in WA only) operates a ferry to Whidbey Island that leaves from Mukilteo, off I–5's Exit 189, 20 mi north of Seattle. Port Townsend can be reached by ferry from Whidbey Island at Keystone (in the middle of the island, where Highways 525 and 20 intersect). To get to Port Townsend from Seattle on the Edmonds Ferry, drive north 14 mi on I–5 to Exit 177 and board the ferry. From the Kingston landing, take Highway 104 to Route 19 and follow the signs. An alternative route is to take the Bainbridge Island Ferry from downtown Seattle to Bainbridge Island and then drive northwest on Highway 305 to Route 3 North to Highway 104 to Route 19 and follow the signs.

BY PLANE

Harbor Airlines (☎ 800/359–3220) flies to Whidbey Island from Friday Harbor and Sea-Tac Airport. **Kenmore Air** (☎ 425/486–1257 or 800/543–9595) can arrange charter floatplane flights to Whidbey Island. **Port Townsend Airways** (☎ 800/385–6554) flies charter planes between Sea-Tac airport and Port Townsend.

Visitor Information

Anacortes Chamber of Commerce (⊠ 819 Commercial Ave., Suite G, 98221, ☎ 360/293–7911). **Central Whidbey Chamber of Commerce**

(⊠ 5 S. Main St., Coupeville 98239, ☎ 360/678–5434). **La Conner Chamber of Commerce** (⊠ P.O. Box 1610, 98257, ☎ 360/466–4778). **Langley Chamber of Commerce** (⊠ 208 Anthes St., 98260, ☎ 360/221–6765). **Port Townsend Chamber of Commerce** (⊠ 2437 E. Sims Way, 98368, ☎ 360/385–2722).

THE SAN JUAN ISLANDS

Numbers in the margin correspond to points of interest on the Puget Sound map.

The San Juan Islands, which can be reached only by ferry or plane, beckon to souls longing for quiet, whether it be kayaking in a cove, walking a deserted beach, or sitting by the fire in an old farmhouse. Unfortunately, solitude becomes a precious commodity in the summer, when tourists descend on the islands. Not surprisingly, tourism and development are hotly contested issues among locals.

The San Juan archipelago comprises 743 islands at low tide and 428 at high tide. Sixty islands are populated and 10 are state marine parks. Ferries stop at the four largest islands: Lopez, Shaw, Orcas, and San Juan; other islands, many privately owned, must be reached by private plane or boat. Naturalists love the San Juans because they are home to three pods of orca and a few minke whales, plus seals, dolphins, otters, and more than 80 active pairs of breeding bald eagles. Because of their location in the rain shadow of the Olympics, the San Juans average more than 250 days of sunshine a year. Temperatures hover around 70°F in the summer and between 40°F and 60°F during the off-season.

San Juan's residents are a blend of highly educated sophisticates and '60s-era (or thusly inspired) folk who have sought alternative lifestyles in a rustic setting. Fishing, farming, and tourism are the only industries. Creative chefs operate small restaurants here, but though the food is as contemporary as anything in Seattle, other aspects of island life haven't changed substantially in 30 years. Each of the islands has a distinct character, yet all share basic features: serene farmland, mysteriously charmed light, the velvet-green waters of the Strait of Juan de Fuca, and vistas framed by either Mount Baker and the Cascade Range to the east or the Olympic Range to the south.

See San Juan Islands Essentials, *below,* for ferry information.

Lopez Island

❺ *45 mins by ferry from Anacortes.*

Quiet and relatively flat Lopez—the island closest to the mainland—is a favorite of bicyclists because of its gentle slopes. But Lopez has a lot to offer for anyone, from quiet beaches to peaceful walks through the woods. Of the three islands that accommodate visitors, Lopez has the smallest population (approximately 1,800), and with its old orchards, weathered barns, and pastures of sheep and cows, it's the most rustic, and in many ways the most serene. There is only one settlement, Lopez Village, which has a few shops, a good restaurant, galleries exhibiting local artists' works, and the post office.

The **Lopez Island Historical Museum,** across the street from the island's only bank, has some impressive ship and small-boat models. You can pick up maps of local landmarks here. ⊠ *Weeks Rd. at Washburn Rd.,* ☎ *360/468-2049.* ☞ *Free.* ☉ *July–Aug., Wed.–Sun. noon-4; May–June and Sept., Fri.–Sun. noon-4.*

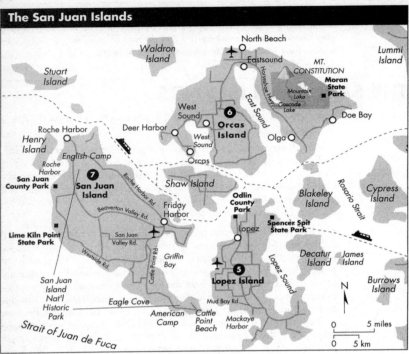

Beaches, trails, and wildlife are the draws at 130-acre **Spencer Spit State Park** (⊠ 521A Baker View Rd., ☎ 360/468–2251), on the northeast shore about 2 mi from Lopez Village. Popular **Odlin County Park** (⊠ Rte. 2, ☎ 360/468–2496) is 1 mi from the ferry landing. You'll probably spot marine life—sea anemones, bright orange sea cucumbers, purple sea stars, blue-green shore crabs, and small sculpins—in the tidepools, and perhaps seals and herons at the water's edge. You might even see river otters frolic among the sea lettuce and limpets at craggy, isolated **Shark Reef.** Park in the lot south of Lopez Village on Shark Reef Road and follow the unmarked trail (it begins next to the outhouse) for about 15 minutes through a thick forest to the water's edge.

The family-owned and -operated **Lopez Island Vineyard and Winery,** the only vineyard in the San Juans, grows, produces, and bottles organic Madeleine Angevine and Siegerrebe (native to Central Europe) and fruit wines. There's a picnic area, and tours and tastings take place. ⊠ *Fisherman Bay Rd. north of Cross Rd.,* ☎ *360/468–3644.* 🖾 *Free.* ☉ *Memorial Day–Labor Day, Wed.–Sun. noon–5 (call ahead for off-season hrs, which vary).*

Dining and Lodging

$$$ ✕ **Bay Café.** At this colorful restaurant you'll find everyone from locals and vacationers to movie stars. Many customers sail over and dock their boats at the restaurant's edge. Menu highlights include seafood tapas: prawns stuffed with basil and goat cheese, a ricotta corn cake with smoked salmon and blackberry ketchup, and sea scallops with sun-dried tomatoes. All entrées include soup and salad. Homemade sorbet and a fine crème caramel are among the desserts. ⊠ *Lopez Village,* ☎ *360/468–3700. MC, V. No lunch.*

$$$–$$$$ 🏠 **Edenwild.** A handsome Victorian-style farmhouse surrounded by gardens and framed by Fisherman's Bay looks as if it's been restored, but it dates from 1990, not 1890. Rooms are airy, each painted in a bold color. Some have fireplaces, and all are furnished with simple antiques. Well-selected contemporary art adorns the ocher-color hallways, bright lobby, and dining room. The inn welcomes children. ✉ *323 Eades Ln., 98261,* ☎ *360/468–3238,* FAX *360/468–4080. 8 rooms. Full breakfast. AE, D, MC, V.*

$$–$$$$ 🏠 **Inn at Swifts Bay.** Bay windows in the living and dining areas of this Tudor-style house overlook well-kept gardens, and a crackling fire warms the living room on winter evenings. Robes, sandals, and flashlights are available for your walk through the garden to a hot tub under the stars. The downstairs rooms have floral drapes and elaborate bed dressings, but are small and share baths. The downstairs suite has more space and a private entrance, but even better are the two upstairs suites, which are long and narrow, with high, sloping ceilings. Breakfasts include exotic creations such as pumpkin-eggnog muffins. ✉ *856 Port Stanley Rd., 98261,* ☎ *360/468–3636,* FAX *360/468–3637. 2 rooms with shared bath, 3 suites. Hot tub, sauna, exercise room, beach. Full breakfast. AE, D, MC, V.*

$$$ 🏠 **Lopez Farm Cottages.** Four cottages in a cedar grove offer unprecedented privacy for a B & B, and the innkeepers take every opportunity to protect guests from intrusions. Your breakfast basket (muffins, fruit, coffee, and tea) is discreetly delivered to your door every evening, and the rooms have no TVs or phones. Each cottage, equipped for two, has a fireplace, kitchenette, queen-size bed with down comforter, and Adirondack chairs on which you can sit and watch the sun set over an open field. ✉ *555 Fisherman Bay Rd., Box 610, 98261,* ☎ *360/468–3555 or 800/440–3556,* FAX *360/468–3966. 4 cottages. Hot tub. Continental breakfast. MC, V.*

$$–$$$ 🏠 **Mackaye Harbor Inn.** This two-story inn, a 1920s sea-captain's house with ½ mi of beach, is at the south end of Lopez Island. Rooms have golden-oak and brass details and wicker furniture; three have views of Mackaye Harbor. The carriage house has a two-bedroom suite with a steam room and full kitchen; a small studio also has a kitchen. Scandinavian specialties (Finnish pancakes on some mornings) are often served for breakfast, which is not included for guests in the carriage house. You can rent a kayak or use a mountain bike free of charge. ✉ *849 Mackaye Harbor Rd., 98261,* ☎ *360/468–2253,* FAX *360/468–2393. 5 rooms, 3 with bath; 2 suites. Beach, bicycles. Full breakfast. MC, V.*

Outdoor Activities and Sports

Islands Marine Center (✉ Fisherman Bay Rd. north of Hummel Lake Rd. near Lopez Village, ☎ 360/468–3377) has standard marina amenities, repair facilities, and transient moorage. **Lopez Bicycle Works and Lopez Island Kayaks** (✉ Fisherman Bay Rd., ☎ 360/468–2847) provides free bicycle delivery all year.

Shopping

The **Chimera Gallery** (✉ Lopez Village, ☎ 360/468–3265), an artists' cooperative, exhibits crafts, jewelry, and fine art. **Islehaven Books and Borzoi** (✉ Village Center Bldg., ☎ 360/468–2132) carries general interest and children's books, regional music, and prints by local artists.

Shaw Island

20 mins by ferry from Lopez; 65 mins from Anacortes.

At tiny Shaw Island, nuns wear their traditional habits while running the ferry dock. Few ferry passengers get off here, because there are no visitor facilities on this residential island. **King Salmon Charters** (☎ 360/ 468–2314) operates saltwater fishing excursions.

Orcas Island

❻ *10 mins from Shaw Island by ferry; 75 mins from Anacortes.*

The roads on saddlebag-shaped Orcas Island sweep through wide valleys and rise to marvelous hilltop views. Farmers, fishermen, and wealthy landowners on the largest island of the San Juans are balanced by a somewhat countercultural artists' community. Public access to the waterfront is limited to parks and public beaches.

Shops in **Eastsound Village,** the island's business and social center, at the top of East Sound, which almost cuts the island in half, sell jewelry, pottery, and other crafts of local artisans. Along Prune Alley are a handful of small shops and restaurants. Pick up free maps and brochures at the unstaffed **Travel Infocenter** (⊠ Main St., ☎ 360/376– 2273), next to the Orcas Island Museum (which is worth a stop if you're a history buff). Nearby is the simple yet stately **Emmanuel Church,** built in 1886 to resemble an English countryside chapel. The church's **Brown Bag Concerts** (☎ 360/376–2352)—anything from a piano sonata to a barbershop quartet—take place on summer Thursdays at noon.

Moran State Park has 151 campsites, 14 hiking trails, some sparkling lakes, 5,000 acres of old-growth forests, and **Mount Constitution,** the tallest peak in the San Juans. Drive to the mountain's 2,400-ft summit for exhilarating views of the San Juan Islands, the Cascades, the Olympics, and Vancouver Island. ⊠ *Star Rte. 22; from Eastsound, head northeast on Horseshoe Hwy. and follow signs,* ☎ *360/376–2326.* 🖾 *Camping: $11 fee, plus $6 per night.*

Dining and Lodging

$$$–$$$$ ✕ **Christina's.** The modern decor at the premier Orcas restaurant includes original artwork and copper-top tables. The seasonal menu changes daily but generally centers on local fish and seafood. You're almost certain to encounter a salmon entrée, delicately prepared and served with grilled vegetables. The extensive wine list highlights Pacific Northwest vintages. Expect a wait in-season at Christina's, which has fine views from its rooftop terrace and enclosed porch. ⊠ *310 Main St., Eastsound,* ☎ *360/376–4904. AE, D, DC, MC, V. Closed Tues.– Wed. Oct.–Apr. No lunch.*

$$–$$$ ✕ **Bilbo's Festivo.** Stucco walls, Mexican tiles, and weavings from New Mexico make clear this restaurant's culinary inclinations. Munch on burritos, enchiladas, and other Mexican favorites like orange-marinated chicken grilled over mesquite and served with fresh asparagus, potatoes, and salad. In warm weather it's pleasant to sip fresh margaritas in the courtyard. ⊠ *N. Beach Rd. and A St., Eastsound,* ☎ *360/ 376–4728. MC, V. No lunch Oct.–May.*

$$$$ 🖾 **Deer Harbor Resort.** This cluster of cottages, built in the 1930s to
★ house apple-pickers, sits on a hillside overlooking the serene Deer Harbor Marina. In 1998, eleven deluxe cottages were added to the existing collection of original cabins. While all of the cottages are a far cry from their humble roots, the deluxe cottages live up to their name with nearly 800 square ft of luxurious privacy. Each deluxe cottage has its own deck and private hot tub overlooking the harbor. In addition, the spacious bathrooms all have whirlpool tubs. The living areas have cathedral ceilings, king beds, gas fireplaces, stereo CD players, and kitchenettes equipped with refrigerators and microwaves. The remodeled vintage cottages have queen beds and are smaller, with many of the same amenities. ⊠ *Deer Harbor Rd., Box 200, Deer Harbor*

98243, ☎ 360/376–4420, FAX 360/376–5523. *26 cottages. Restaurant, in-room data ports, kitchenettes, pool, hot tubs. Continental breakfast. AE, D, MC, V.*

$$$$ 🏨 **Rosario Spa & Resort.** Shipbuilding magnate Robert Moran built this Mediterranean-style mansion on Cascade Bay in 1906. Told that he had six months to live, Moran pulled out all the stops on his last extravagance—then lived another 30 years. The original Mission-style furniture, displayed for the public, is worth a look even if you're not staying here. The house's centerpiece, an Aeolian pipe organ with 1,972 pipes, is used for summer concerts. The rooms have a motel-like feel; some have fireplaces and whirlpool tubs, and half have bay views. The spa offers everything from aerobic instruction to herbal wraps and massage. A shuttle meets every ferry and provides transportation into Eastsound. ⊠ *1 Rosario Way, off Horseshoe Hwy., Eastsound 98245, ☎ 360/376–2222 or 800/562–8820. 131 rooms. 2 restaurants, lounge, indoor pool, 2 outdoor pools, hot tub, sauna, spa, 2 tennis courts, hiking, dock, boating, fishing. AE, D, DC, MC, V.*

$$$$ 🏨 **Spring Bay Inn.** Sandy Playa and Carl Burger, former park rangers, ★ run this B&B on acres of woodland surrounding private Spring Bay. All rooms have bay views (this is the only Orcas B&B actually on the water), wood-burning fireplaces, feather beds, and private sitting areas; one room has an outdoor hot tub. Walking trails meander through the property. Mornings begin with coffee, fresh muffins, and croissants outside your door—fortification for a two-hour (optional) kayaking excursion. Expect to see bald eagles, herons, and other wildlife. While one of your hosts is out on the water, the other prepares a full breakfast that includes fresh-squeezed orange juice and smoothies. ⊠ *Obstruction Pass Trailhead Rd. off Obstruction Pass Rd., Olga 98279, ☎ 360/376–5531, FAX 360/376–2193. 5 rooms. Refrigerators, hot tub, kayaking. Full breakfast. D, MC, V.*

$$–$$$$ 🏨 **Orcas Hotel.** Construction began in 1900 on this three-story, red-roof Victorian hotel on a hill across from the Orcas ferry landing. A white picket fence and a wraparound porch are among the exterior details of the building. Feather beds, down comforters, and wicker, brass, and antique furnishings decorate the rooms, many of which have water views. All second-floor rooms share baths. Two suites have whirlpool tubs. The dining room—open from June through October to guests and nonguests—overlooks gardens and the ferry landing. You can grab an espresso or baked goods at the on-site café. ⊠ *Horseshoe Hwy., Box 155, Orcas 98280, ☎ 360/376–4300, FAX 360/376–4399. 12 rooms, 2 with bath, 3 with half bath, 7 rooms share 6 bathrooms. Restaurant, café. Full breakfast (in season). AE, D, MC, V.*

$$–$$$$ 🏨 **Turtleback Farm Inn.** Eighty acres of meadow, forest, and farmland in the shadow of Turtleback Mountain surround this forest-green inn that dates from the late 1800s. Guest rooms have easy chairs, good beds with woolen comforters made from the fleece of resident sheep, and views of meadows and forest. The Orchard House provides more privacy in four rooms with views of Mount Wollard. ⊠ *1981 Crow Valley Rd., Eastsound 98245, ☎ 360/376–4914 or 800/376–4914. 11 rooms. Full breakfast. D, MC, V.*

$–$$ 🏨 **Doe Bay Village Resort.** A haven for neohippies and outdoorsy families, this property at the eastern tip of Orcas morphed from a nudist colony into a commune, a youth hostel, and finally a resort. Prices for the patchwork of accommodations—campsites, yurts, a hostel, and cabins tucked between two forested hills—start as low as $12, and there's a mostly vegetarian café on site. The resort's small beach is perfect for kayak launches. Guests staying in the cabins may also use the resort's clothing-optional mineral baths and sauna for free ($3 fee for hostel guests and campers). ⊠ *Star Rte. 86 off Pt. Lawrence Rd. near*

Olga 98279, ☎ 360/376–2291, ⊠ 360/376–5809. *30 cabins and
structures, 30 campsites. Café, hot tubs, massage, mineral baths, sauna,
volleyball, beach. AE, D, MC, V.*

Outdoor Activities and Sports

BICYCLING

Dolphin Bay Bicycles (⊠ Killebrew Lake Rd., Orcas Village, ☎ 360/
376–4157) is at the ferry landing. **Wildlife Cycles** (⊠ N. Beach Rd.,
Eastsound, ☎ 360/376–4708) also has bikes for rent.

FISHING

Three lakes at **Moran State Park** (☞ *above*) are open for fishing from
late April through October.

MARINAS

Deer Harbor Resort & Marina (☎ 360/376–3037) and **West Sound Ma-
rina** (☎ 360/376–2314) have standard marina facilities. **Island Petroleum**
(⊠ Orcas, ☎ 360/376–3883) has gas and diesel at the ferry landing.
Rosario Resort (⊠ Eastsound, ☎ 360/376–2222) has boat slips.

Shopping

Darvill's Rare Print Shop (⊠ Eastsound, ☎ 360/376–2351) specializes
in maps and bird and floral prints difficult to find elsewhere. **Orcas Island Pottery** (⊠ 366 Old Pottery Rd., Eastsound, ☎ 360/376–2813),
the oldest pottery studio in the Northwest, carries works by more than
25 artists.

San Juan Island

❼ *45 mins by ferry from Orcas; 75 mins from Anacortes by express ferry.*

The story goes that **Friday Harbor** got its name when an explorer
rounding San Juan Island called from the boat "What bay is this?" A
man on shore heard "What day is this?" and called back "Friday." The
islands' county seat and the only incorporated town on San Juan Island is the most convenient destination for visitors traveling on foot.

Standing at the ferry dock facing the bluff and downtown, you'll recognize the modest **Whale Museum** by the whale mural painted on its
exterior. To reach the entrance, walk up Spring Street and turn right
on 1st Street. Models of whales and whale skeletons, recordings of whale
sounds, and videos of whales are the attractions. ⊠ *62 1st St. N, Friday Harbor,* ☎ *360/378–4710.* ☞ *$1.* ⊙ *June–Sept., daily 10–6; Oct.–
May, daily 11–4.*

San Juan County Park has 10 acres of beachfront on the west side of
San Juan Island. Orcas can be seen from the shore from May through
September; there's a boat launch and 25 year-round campsites with fire
rings, flush toilets, picnic areas, and water. ⊠ *380 Westside Rd. N, Fri-
day Harbor,* ☎ *360/378–2992.* ☞ *Free (day use), $16 (camping).* ⊙
Year-round daily 8 AM–dusk.

For an opportunity to see whales cavorting in Haro Strait, head to **Lime
Kiln Point State Park,** 6 mi from Friday Harbor on San Juan's west side.
The best time for sighting whales is from the end of April through Au-
gust. A resident pod of orcas regularly cruises past the point. ⊠ *6158
Lighthouse Rd.,* ☎ *360/378–2044.* ☞ *Free.* ⊙ *Daily 8 AM–10 PM.*

San Juan Island National Historic Park is a remnant of the "Pig War,"
a tempest that began in 1859 when a Yank killed a Brit's pig. American and British troops were called in, and though no gunfire was ex-
changed, troops from both countries remained on the island until
1872. The park encompasses two separate areas. British Camp, on the
northern end of the island (follow Roche Harbor Road north from Fri-

day Harbor), contains a blockhouse, a commissary, and barracks. At American Camp, on the island's southern end (follow Cattle Point Road south from Friday Harbor), are a laundry, fortifications, 6 mi of public beaches, and a visitor's center. From June through August the park conducts hikes and reenacts 1860s-era military life. ☎ *360/378–2240.* ◙ *Free.* ☉ *Dawn–11 PM.*

It seems hard to believe now that snazzy **Roche Harbor** at the northern end of San Juan was once the most important producer of builder's lime on the West Coast, shipping its product as far as Hawaii and South America. While the old limekilns of the 1882–1956 operation still stand below the bluff, the company town has undergone a major transformation into a resort. (Locals say it took two years for the limestone dust to wash off the trees around the harbor.) But even in its heyday as a limestone quarrying village, Roche Harbor was known for colorful flowers and comfortable accommodations. A former bunkhouse was transformed into a guest house (where such notables as Teddy Roosevelt stayed). It now serves as a hotel. The former owners' home is now a restaurant, and workers cottages have been transformed into comfortable visitors' lodgings. With its rose gardens, cobblestone waterfront, and well-manicured lawns, Roche Harbor retains the flavor of its days as a hangout for the world's elite—especially since the sheltered harbor is very popular with well-to-do pleasure boaters.

The historic **Hotel de Haro** (☞ Roche Harbor Resort, *below*) displays period photographs and artifacts in its lobby. If you're interested, ask the staff for a map that points out remnants of the quarrying industry and **The Mausoleum,** an eerie Greek-inspired memorial to former owner and Teddy Roosevelt confidant John S. McMillin.

Dining and Lodging

$$$–$$$$ ✕ **Duck Soup Inn.** Everything the Duck Soup Inn serves is made from scratch—bread, Mediterranean-inspired entrées, vegetarian dishes, and delicious ice cream. Start with Westcott Bay oysters smoked on an apple-wood grill, followed by pan-seared sea scallops in a red-curry–coconut sauce on a bed of cashews and greens. ✉ *3090 Roche Harbor Rd., near town of Roche Harbor,* ☎ *360/378–4878. D, MC, V. Closed Mon.–Tues. Apr.–Oct.; closed Nov.–Mar. No lunch.*

$$$ ✕ **Springtree Café.** Chef James Boyle designs his daily menu around fresh seafood and Waldron Island organic produce and herbs, creating savory dishes that you won't soon forget. Begin with the Caesar salad—made with tofu instead of eggs—and continue with the king salmon in pesto, the ginger shrimp with mango and dark rum, or other fish and meat entrées. Vegetarian options abound. There's a full bar and an extensive wine selection. ✉ *310 Spring St., Friday Harbor,* ☎ *360/378–4848. AE, MC, V. Closed Sun.–Mon. mid-Oct.–Apr.*

$–$$ ✕ **Front Street Ale House.** The English-style alehouse serves sandwiches, salads, and traditional pub dishes—lamb stew, meat pasties, steak-and-kidney pie. For vegetarians there's a vegetable patty lightly sautéed and stacked with cheese, mushrooms, lettuce, tomato, and onions. On-tap brews from the San Juan Brewing Company carry locally inspired names like Pig War Stout. ✉ *1 Front St., Friday Harbor,* ☎ *360/378–2337. Reservations not accepted. MC, V.*

$$$$ ✕▥ **Friday Harbor House.** The ceiling-to-floor windows of this con-
★ temporary bluff-top villa hotel were designed to take advantage of its views of the marina, ferry landing, and San Juan Channel, as was the placement of whirlpool tubs in the center of each room. Slate tiles, fireplaces, cable TV, and sleek modern wood wall units all contribute to the casually upscale atmosphere. Seafood is featured at dinner ($$–$$$; reservations essential). Guests take their elaborate breakfasts at the in-

timate harbor-view dining room. ✉ *130 West St., Friday Harbor 98250,* ☎ *360/378–8455,* FAX *360/378–8453. 20 rooms. Restaurant, refrigerators. Continental breakfast. AE, DC, MC, V.*

$$$–$$$$ ☷ **Mariella Inn & Cottages.** This impeccably maintained property sits on 8 acres along a cove outside Friday Harbor. Rooms in the 100-year-old country house have English antique furniture. Each room has a private bath and a view of either the water or the exquisite gardens, but some are small. Some of the private cottages and waterfront suites scattered throughout the grounds have modern amenities like VCRs and kitchenettes. Especially romantic are the contemporary solarium suites with private whirlpool tubs inside glass-enclosed atriums. ✉ *630 Turn Point Rd., Friday Harbor 98250,* ☎ *360/378–6868 or 800/700–7668,* FAX *360/378–6822. 8 rooms, 3 suites, 12 cottages. Bicycles. Continental breakfast. AE, MC, V.*

$$–$$$ ☷ **Hillside House.** Less than a mile from Friday Harbor, this split-level house has views of the waterfront and Mount Baker from a large deck. Rooms have either sophisticated or more whimsical decor. Some overlook the 10,000-square-ft full-flight aviary. Breakfast—made with resident hens' eggs, island jams, and fresh berries—is often served on the large deck that rings the house. ✉ *365 Carter Ave., Friday Harbor 98250,* ☎ *360/378–4730 or 800/232–4730,* FAX *360/378–4715. 6 rooms, 1 suite. Full breakfast. AE, D, MC, V.*

$$–$$$ ☷ **Roche Harbor Resort.** The choice here is between simple cottages and condominiums or rooms in the restored Hotel de Haro, which was built in 1886. The old hotel is better to look at than to stay in; its guest rooms are a tad shabby. On the other hand, the resort has extensive facilities, including slips for a few hundred boats, a full-service marina, and a 4,000-ft airstrip. ✉ *4950 Tarte Memorial Dr., 10 mi northwest of Friday Harbor off Roche Harbor Rd., Roche Harbor 98250,* ☎ *360/ 378–2155 or 800/451–8910,* FAX *360/378–6809. 59 rooms, 5 with bath. Restaurant, grocery, pool, tennis court, boating, motorbikes. AE, MC, V.*

$$ ☷ **San Juan Inn.** This site a half block from the ferry landing has been operated as an inn for more than 100 years. All rooms have brass, iron, or wicker beds, Queen Anne eyelet bedspreads, and some antiques. The garden suite behind the inn has a TV and VCR, a full kitchen, and a fireplace. ✉ *50 Spring St., Box 776, Friday Harbor 98250,* ☎ *360/ 378–2070 or 800/742–8210,* FAX *360/378–6437. 9 rooms, 4 with bath; 2 suites. Outdoor hot tub. Continental breakfast. AE, D, MC, V.*

Outdoor Activities and Sports

BICYCLING

San Juan Island Bicycles (✉ 380 Argyle St., Friday Harbor, ☎ 360/ 378–4941) has a reputation for good service and equipment. **Susie's Mopeds** (✉ Friday Harbor, ☎ 360/378–5244 or 800/532–0087), at the top of the hill behind the line to board the ferry, rents mopeds.

BOATING

Port of Friday Harbor (☎ 360/378–2688), **Roche Harbor Resort** (☎ 360/378–2155), and **Snug Harbor Resort Marina** (☎ 360/378–4762) have standard marina facilities.

FISHING

You can fish year-round for bass and trout at Egg and Sportsman lakes, both north of Friday Harbor off Roche Harbor Road. **Buffalo Works** (☎ 360/378–4612) arranges saltwater fishing trips. Licenses are required.

WHALE-WATCHING

San Juan Excursions (☎ 360/378–6636 or 800/809–4253) cruises the waters around the islands. **Western Prince Cruises** (☎ 360/378–5315 or 800/757–6722) operates a four-hour narrated tour.

Shopping

Boardwalk Bookstore (✉ 5 Spring St., Friday Harbor, ☎ 360/378–2787) is strong in the classics and has a good selection of popular literature. **Dan Levin Originals** (✉ 50 1st St., ☎ 360/378–2051) stocks handcrafted jewelry. **Napier Sculpture Gallery** (✉ 232 A St., ☎ 360/378–2221) exhibits bronze and steel sculptures. **Waterworks Gallery** (✉ 315 Argyle St., Friday Harbor, ☎ 360/378–3060) represents eclectic contemporary artists.

San Juan Islands Essentials

Arriving and Departing

BY CAR

To reach the San Juan Islands from Seattle, drive north on I–5 to Exit 230 (Mount Vernon), go west on Highway 20, and follow signs to Anacortes, where you can pick up one of the Washington State Ferries (☞ *below*). It is convenient to have a car in the San Juan Islands, but taking your car with you may mean waiting in long lines at the ferry terminals. With prior arrangement, most B&B owners will pick up guests without cars at the ferry terminals.

BY FERRY

Washington State Ferries (☎ 206/464–6400; 800/843–3779 in Washington only) vessels depart from Anacortes, about 76 mi north of Seattle, for the San Juan Islands. Departures vary during the year, starting between 5 and 7 in the morning and continuing regularly until 8 or 10 at night. Sunny weekends can be particularly crowded westbound on Friday evening and Saturday morning, and eastbound on Sunday evening. Some weekday ferries are crowded during commuter hours.

You pay for only westbound trips headed for the San Juans—prices vary depending on your point of departure and destination. Since no reservations are accepted on Washington State Ferries (except for the Sidney to Anacortes run during summer), arriving at least a half hour before a scheduled departure is always advised. Prior to boarding, lower your car's antenna. Only parking lights should be used at night, and it is considered bad form to start your engine before the ferry docks. Walk-on passengers and bicycles always load first unless otherwise instructed.

San Juan Islands Shuttle Express (✉ Alaska Ferry Terminal, 355 Harris Ave., No. 105, Bellingham 98225, ☎ 360/671–1137) takes passengers from Bellingham to Orcas Island and Friday Harbor.

BY PLANE

Harbor Airlines (☎ 800/359–3220) flies to Friday Harbor on San Juan Island from Sea-Tac. **Kenmore Air** (☎ 425/486–1257 or 800/543–9595) flies floatplanes from Lake Union in Seattle to the San Juan Islands. **West Isle Air** (☎ 360/293–4691 or 800/874–4434) flies to Friday Harbor from Sea-Tac and Bellingham airports.

Contacts and Resources

CAMPING

Marine State Parks (☎ 800/233–0321) are accessible only by private boat. No moorage or camping reservations are available, and fees are charged at some parks from May to Labor Day. Fresh water, where available, is limited. Island parks are Blind, Clark, Doe, James, Jones, Matia, Patos, Posey, Stuart, Sucia, and Turn. All have a few campsites; there are no docks at Blind, Clark, Patos, Posey, or Turn islands.

CHARTERS
Amante Sail Tours (☎ 360/376–4231). **Charters Northwest** (☎ 360/378–7196). **Harmony Sailing Charters** (☎ 360/468–3310). **Kismet Sailing Charters** (☎ 360/468–2435). **Nor'wester Sailing Charters** (☎ 360/378–5478).

KAYAKING
If you are kayaking on your own, beware of the ever-changing conditions, ferry and shipping landings, and strong tides and currents. Go ashore only on known public property. **Shearwater Sea Kayak Tours** (☎ 360/376–4699), **Doe Bay Resort** (☎ 360/376–2291), **San Juan Kayak Expeditions** (☎ 360/378–4436), and **Seaquest** (☎ 360/378–5767) conduct day trips and longer expeditions.

VISITOR INFORMATION
San Juan Island Chamber of Commerce (✉ Box 98, Friday Harbor 98250, ☎ 360/378–5240). **San Juan Islands Tourism Cooperative and Visitors Information Service** (✉ Lopez 98261, ☎ 360/468–3663).

SNOQUALMIE AND LEAVENWORTH

Interstate 90 heading east from Seattle winds through bucolic farmland with snowcapped mountains in the background. Nestled in the foothills is Snoqualmie Falls, one of the area's most popular destinations. Small mining towns dot the mountains, and to the north of the main I–90 route, you'll find Leavenworth, an alpine-style village with excellent sporting opportunities.

Snoqualmie

28 mi east of Seattle on I–90.

★ Spring and summer snowmelt turns the Snoqualmie River into the thundering torrent at **Snoqualmie Falls,** where the river pours over a 268-ft rock ledge (100 ft higher than Niagara Falls) to a 65-ft-deep pool below. The falls, which were considered sacred by the native people who lived along the riverbank, are Snoqualmie's biggest attraction, though some visitors come to see locations David Lynch used in his TV series *Twin Peaks.* A 2-acre park, including an observation platform 300 ft above the Snoqualmie River, affords a view of Snoqualmie Falls and the surrounding area. You can hike the **River Trail,** a 3-mi round-trip route through trees and open slopes that ends at the base of the falls. Be prepared for an uphill workout on the return to the trailhead.

The vintage cars of the **Snoqualmie Valley Railroad,** built in the mid-1910s for the Spokane, Portland, and Seattle Railroad, travel between the **Snoqualmie Depot** and a depot in North Bend. The 50-minute round-trip excursion passes through woods and farmland. The **Northwest Railway Museum** within Snoqualmie's depot displays memorabilia and has a bookstore. ✉ *Snoqualmie Depot: 38625 S.E. King St., at Hwy. 202,* ☎ *206/746–4025 (Seattle); 425/888–0373 (Snoqualmie).* 🎫 *$6.* ☉ *Trains: Apr.–Sept., weekends and holidays; Oct., Sun. only; on the hr 11–4 from Snoqualmie and on the 1/2 hr 11:30–3:30 from North Bend. Museum, depot, and bookstore: Thurs.–Mon. 10–5.*

Winding north through heavy forest from Snoqualmie, Highway 203 becomes Main Street when it reaches the unassuming town of **Duvall,** a good place to stop for a little antiquing or bookshop browsing, a glimpse of the Snoqualmie River, or a mid-afternoon latte. To return to Seattle you can backtrack to Snoqualmie or head west on Woodinville–Duvall Road.

Dining and Lodging

$$$$
★ ✕ **The Herbfarm.** The temple of Pacific Northwest cuisine serves a nine-course meal that includes five glasses of Northwest wine and takes between four and five hours. The delicacies served include goat-cheese biscuits, green pickled walnuts in the husk, salmon with a sauce of fresh garden herbs, and sorbet of rose geranium and lemon verbena. A devastating fire swept through the restaurant in early 1997, but reconstruction should be completed by mid-2000. Call for information on dinners being offered at an interim location. The gift shop sells food, herbs, medicinals, gardening supplies, and clothing. The Herbfarm also has a plant nursery and offers classes. ✉ *32804 Issaquah–Fall City Rd. (from I–90's Exit 22 head left, then take a right onto Preston–Fall City Rd.; follow this 3 mi to Y in road, then go left over bridge and another ½ mi), Fall City,* ☎ *206/784–2222. Reservations essential. MC, V.*

$$$$
★ ✕🏨 **Salish Lodge and Spa.** One of Seattleites' favorite weekend getaways, the Salish consistently rates high in polls conducted by *Condé Nast Traveler* and other publications of the country's best resorts. A few rooms look out over Snoqualmie Falls; others have views upriver. All the airy accommodations have wood furniture, whirlpool baths, and wood-burning fireplaces. Pampering treatments available at the on-site spa include massage, sea-algae wraps, and sea-salt cleansing scrubs. Dinners at the restaurant ($$$$; reservations essential) overlooking the falls incorporate local game, such as the herb-crusted fallow venison loin, or seafood (the Dungeness crab bisque is rich and flavorful). ✉ *6501 Railroad Ave. SE, 98065,* ☎ *425/888–2556 or 800/826–6124,* 𝖥𝖠𝖷 *425/888–2420. 91 rooms. Restaurant, bar, room service, spa, health club, laundry service, concierge, business services, meeting rooms. AE, D, DC, MC, V.*

Nightlife and the Arts

Snoqualmie Falls Forest Theater (☎ 425/222–7044) presents two or three plays, usually melodramas performed by acting students and community performers, in a 250-seat outdoor amphitheater near Fall City. From I–90 take Exit 22 and go 4 mi; take a right on David Powell Road, follow signs, and continue through the gate to the parking area. Tickets are $13. For another $12 you can enjoy a salmon or steak barbecue after the matinee or before the evening performance. Reservations are essential for dinner.

Outdoor Activities and Sports

Snoqualmie Pass has three downhill and cross-country ski areas—**Alpental, Ski Acres, and Snoqualmie Summit** (⊠ Mailing address for all three: 3010 77th St. SE, Mercer Island 98040, ☎ 206/232–8182). Each area rents equipment and has a full restaurant and lodge facilities.

Leavenworth

★ *128 mi from Seattle, I–5 north to U.S. 2 east.*

Leavenworth is a favorite weekend getaway for Seattle residents. And it's easy to see why: the charming (if occasionally *too* cute) Bavarian-style village, which teems with creative restaurants and attractive lodgings, is a hub for some of the Northwest's best skiing, hiking, rock climbing, rafting, canoeing, and snowshoeing.

Leavenworth was a railroad and mining center for many years, but by the 1960s had fallen on hard times. Civic leaders, looking for ways to capitalize on the town's setting in the heart of the Central Cascade Range, convinced shop owners and other businesspeople to maintain a gingerbread Bavarian style. Even the Safeway supermarket and the Chevron gas station carry out the theme. Restaurants prepare Bavarian-influenced dishes, candy shops sell gourmet Swiss-style chocolates, and stores and boutiques stock music boxes, dollhouses, and other Bavarian items.

The **Marlin Handbell Ringers** keep alive an 18th-century English tradition that evolved into a musical form. Twelve ringers play 107 bells covering 5½ chromatic octaves. The bells are rung as part of the town's Christmas festivities and also in early May.

The **Nutcracker Museum** displays more than 2,500 antique and present-day nutcrackers. ⊠ *735 Front St.,* ☎ *509/548–4708.* ⌛ *$2.50.* ☯ *May–Oct., daily 2–5.*

Dining and Lodging

$$$–$$$$ ✕ **Restaurant Österreich.** Chef Leopold Haas, who hails from Austria, prepares haute German cuisine such as marinated duck breast in a dumpling coating or elk stew. The menu changes daily. The walls of the main dining room, a large open space, are decorated with dried-flower arrangements and Bavarian paintings; the atmosphere is much more casual than the food. From May through October you can dine (dinner only) outside on the garden patio. ⊠ *Tyrolean Ritz Hotel, 633A Front St.,* ☎ *509/548–4031. MC, V. Closed Mon.*

$–$$$$ ✕ **Cougar Inn.** This family restaurant, established in 1890, is on the shores of Lake Wenatchee, about 25 mi from Leavenworth. Locals often come by boat and tie up at the restaurant's dock. Great views of the lake can be had, especially in summer from the big outdoor deck. Breakfast, lunch, and dinner are served daily; the hearty American-style Sunday brunch is popular. The dinner menu includes a sirloin steak for two, fried and baked fish, burgers, and standard pastas. ⊠ *23379 Hwy. 207, Lake Wenatchee,* ☎ *509/763–3354. AE, MC, V.*

\$\$–\$\$\$ ✕ **Lorraine's Edel House.** The candlelighted rooms at this modest restaurant, a rare Leavenworth eatery that doesn't emphasize German food, are quiet and cozy. From the appetizer of mussels sautéed in an orange cream sauce to exotic dessert wines and a homespun white- and dark-chocolate creation, you'll savor imaginatively mouthwatering combinations. The entrées include Asian-accented pastas, game and fish, and more obscure offerings like grilled wild boar or braised oxtail. ⊠ *320 9th St.,* ☎ *509/548–4412. D, DC, MC, V.*

\$–\$\$ ✕ **Andreas Keller.** Leavenworth's Bavarian theme is taken the extra mile at this fun, kid-friendly restaurant. The large portions of hearty German dishes like spaetzle, Wiener schnitzel, and red cabbage may leave you too full for the equally sturdy desserts. Several nights a week an accordion player entertains table side. ⊠ *829 Front St.,* ☎ *509/548– 6000. MC, V.*

\$–\$\$ ✕ **Leavenworth Brewery.** The only brewery in Leavenworth pours 8 to 10 fresh brews—the selection changes every two to three weeks. The highly trained brew masters provide detailed descriptions of their beers (daily brewery tours are given at 2 PM). Sandwiches and bar food are served. The slightly sweet brewery beer bread, made on the premises, is delicious. ⊠ *636 Front St.,* ☎ *509/548–4545. Reservations not accepted. MC, V.*

\$ ✕ **Danish Bakery.** Come to this small shop for tasty homemade pastries, strong espresso drinks, and friendly service. ⊠ *731 Front St.,* ☎ *509/548–7514. Reservations not accepted. No credit cards.*

\$\$\$\$
★ ▥ **Sleeping Lady.** No detail was overlooked in converting the youth camp that formerly occupied this property in Icicle Creek Canyon into an elegant, ecologically sensitive retreat. Salvaged or recycled materials were used to construct the clusters of free-standing buildings. Locally made log furniture and beds with down comforters decorate the rooms. The solar-heated swimming pool is made from cement poured into molds taken from real rocks in the surrounding mountains so as not to destroy existing animal habitats. The room rates include three meals, served cafeteria-style in a large alpine dining room. Don't let the method of service fool you, though; this is fine dining: roasted-pumpkin and ginger soup, orange roughy served with heart-of-palm salsa, beef tenderloin served with wild-mushroom sauce, and decadent desserts. ⊠ *7375 Icicle Rd., 98826,* ☎ *509/548–6344 or 800/574–2123,* FAX *509/ 548–6312. 58 rooms, 1 suite. Restaurant, bar, in-room data ports, pool, hot tub, massage, sauna, steam room, hiking, cross-country skiing, theater, library, business services, meeting rooms. American Plan. No smoking. AE, D, MC, V.*

\$\$–\$\$\$\$ ▥ **Pension Anna.** Rooms and suites at this family-run Austrian-style pension in the heart of the village are decorated with sturdy antique pine furniture. Two of the suites have whirlpool baths, and all except the ground-level rooms have small balconies. The two largest suites have fireplaces and handsome four-poster beds. A hearty European-style breakfast (cold cuts, meats, cheeses, soft-boiled eggs) is served in a room decorated with crisp linens, pine decor, and a cuckoo clock. ⊠ *926 Commercial St., 98826,* ☎ *509/548–6273 or 800/509–2662,* FAX *509/548–4656. 12 rooms, 3 suites. Full breakfast. AE, D, MC, V.*

\$\$–\$\$\$ ▥ **Pine River Ranch.** Mountains completely surround this B&B on 32 acres 16 mi outside Leavenworth. Two extremely private suites have kitchens, gas fireplaces, whirlpool tubs, stereos, televisions with VCRs, and decks. Four rooms in the farmhouse in front are significantly less spacious and private but still nice. ⊠ *19668 Hwy. 207, 98826,* ☎ *509/ 763–3959 or 800/669–3877,* FAX *509/763–2073. 6 rooms. Full breakfast. AE, D, MC, V.*

$$–$$$ ⊞ **Run of the River.** Bathrobes and private whirlpool tubs are among the amenities at this luxury accommodation. Each room is decorated with handmade willow furnishings and plush carpeting and is equipped with a TV. Innkeepers Monty and Karen Turner live next door and are readily at hand to meet your needs. ✉ *9308 E. Leavenworth Rd., 98826,* ☎ *509/548–7171 or 800/288–6491,* 𝔽𝔸𝕏 *509/548–7547. 6 rooms. Dining room, refrigerators. Full breakfast. D, MC, V.*

$$ ⊞ **Evergreen Motel.** Popular with hikers and skiers, the Evergreen was built in the 1930s. The property still has much of the charm of the downtown roadside inn it once was. Some of its two-bedroom suites have fireplaces or kitchens (though no utensils); others have multiple beds and can sleep up to six comfortably. ✉ *1117 Front St., 98826,* ☎ *509/ 548–5515 or 800/327–7212,* 𝔽𝔸𝕏 *509/548–6556. 39 rooms. Continental breakfast. AE, D, DC, MC, V.*

$$ ⊞ **Haus Lorelei.** On the high bank of the Wenatchee River, this B&B in a 1903 mansion built by a logging company is two blocks from the heart of Leavenworth. Two river-rock fireplaces are the focal points of the main floor. The large guest rooms, some of which contain four-poster or canopy beds, have views of the river and the Enchantment Mountains. Breakfasts that might include crepes or *ableskiver* (Swedish pancake balls) are served on antique china. ✉ *347 Division St., 98826,* ☎ *509/548–5726 or 800/514–8868,* 𝔽𝔸𝕏 *509/548–6548. 10 rooms. Hot tub, tennis, basketball, bicycles. Full breakfast. No smoking. 2-night minimum on weekends. No credit cards.*

$$ ⊞ **Linderhoff Motor Inn.** This non-Bavarian–style motel at the west end of Leavenworth is one of the nicest in town for the money. Rooms have contemporary decor, pine furnishings, and TVs and phones. Options include standard rooms, honeymoon suites with whirlpool tubs and fireplaces, and town-house units that sleep up to eight and have fully equipped kitchens and two bathrooms. You can have your breakfast—fresh fruit juice, muffins, and Danish pastries—in your room or outside on the inn's balcony. ✉ *690 Hwy. 2, 98826,* ☎ *509/548–5283 or 800/828–5680,* 𝔽𝔸𝕏 *509/548–6705. 34 rooms. Pool, hot tub. Continental breakfast. AE, D, DC, MC, V.*

$–$$ ⊞ **Mrs. Anderson's Lodging House.** Antique quilts and the vintage clothing that adorns the walls of this B&B create a funky Old West feel in the middle of pseudo-Bavaria. Most of the rooms, which are named after quilt designs, are small and rustic; some share decks overlooking the Wenatchee River. Buffet breakfasts include homemade granola, muffins, and fresh fruit. ✉ *917 Commercial St., 98826,* ☎ *509/548– 5311 or 800/829–5311,* 𝔽𝔸𝕏 *509/548–2104. 8 rooms, 6 with bath; 1 suite. Continental breakfast. D, MC, V.*

Outdoor Activities and Sports

FISHING

Trout and salmon are plentiful in many streams and lakes around Lake Wenatchee. **Leavenworth Ranger Station** (☎ 509/548–6977) issues permits for the Enchantment Lakes and Alpine Lake Wilderness area.

GOLF

Leavenworth Golf Club (✉ 9101 Icicle Rd., ☎ 509/548–7267) has an 18-hole, par-71 course. The greens fee is $25; an optional cart costs $22.

HIKING

The Leavenworth Ranger District has more than 320 mi of scenic trails, among them Hatchery Creek, Icicle Ridge, the Enchantments, Tumwater Canyon, Fourth of July Creek, Snow Lake, Stuart Lake, and Chatter Creek. Contact the **Leavenworth Ranger District** (✉ 600 Sherburne

St., 98826, ☎ 509/548–6977) or the **Lake Wenatchee Ranger Station** (✉ 22976 Hwy. 207, 98826, ☎ 509/763–3101) for more information.

HORSEBACK RIDING
Hourly and daily horseback rides and pack trips are available at **Eagle Creek Ranch** (✉ 7951 Eagle Creek Rd., ☎ 509/548–7798 or 800/221–7433) and **Red-Tail Canyon Farm** (✉ 11780 Freund Canyon Rd., ☎ 509/548–4512 or 800/678–4512).

SKIING
More than 20 mi of cross-country ski trails lace the Leavenworth area. **Mission Ridge** (☎ 800/374–1693) has 35 major downhill runs and night skiing from late December to early March. **Stevens Pass** (☎ 206/812–4510 or 360/634–1645) has 37 major downhill runs, and slopes and lifts for skiers of every level. Several shops in Leavenworth rent and sell ski equipment. For more information, contact the **Leavenworth Winter Sports Club** (☎ 509/548–5115, winter only).

SLEIGH RIDES
Horse-drawn sleigh rides take place daily during the winter months at **Eagle Creek Ranch** (✉ 7951 Eagle Creek Rd., ☎ 509/548–7798 or 800/221–7433) and **Red-Tail Canyon Farm** (✉ 11780 Freund Canyon Rd., ☎ 509/548–4512 or 800/678–4512).

WHITE-WATER RAFTING
Rafting is a popular sport from March through July. The prime high-country runoff occurs in May and June. The Wenatchee River, which runs through Leavenworth, is considered one of the best white-water rivers in the state—a Class 3 on the International Canoeing Association scale. Depending on the season and location, anything from a relatively calm scenic float to an invigorating white-water shoot is possible on the Wenatchee or on one of several other nearby rivers.

Rafting outfitters and guides in the area include **All Rivers Adventures/Wenatchee Whitewater** (☎ 509/782–2254 or 800/743–5628), **Alpine Adventures** (☎ 509/548–4159 or 800/926–7238), **Leavenworth Outfitters** (☎ 509/763–3733 or 800/347–7934).

Snoqualmie and Leavenworth Essentials

Arriving and Departing

BY BUS
Metro Bus 210 originates in downtown Seattle (☞ Seattle A to Z *in* Chapter 2) and travels to Snoqualmie and North Bend. The ride takes a little more than an hour. Call **Greyhound Lines** (☎ 800/231–2222) about buses from downtown Seattle to Snoqualmie and Leavenworth. The ride to Leavenworth takes three hours.

BY CAR
Snoqualmie is a 35-minute drive on I–90 east from Seattle. The quickest route from Seattle to Leavenworth is via I–5 north to U.S. 2 east; the drive usually takes a little more than two hours. Leavenworth is 54 mi north of I–90 on U.S. 97.

Visitor Information
Leavenworth Chamber of Commerce (✉ 894 U.S. 2, 98826, ☎ 509/548–5807). **Upper Snoqualmie Valley Chamber of Commerce** (✉ Box 356, North Bend 98045, ☎ 425/888–4440).

MOUNT RAINIER NATIONAL PARK

Magnificent 14,411-ft-high Mount Rainier is the centerpiece of Mount Rainier National Park. The local Native Americans called the mountain Tahoma, "the mountain that was God," and dared not ascend its icebound summit. In 1792 the first European to visit the region, British explorer George Vancouver, gazed in amazement at its majestic dome and named it after his friend Rear Admiral Peter Rainier.

Mount Rainier National Park encompasses nearly 400 square mi of wilderness. Three hundred miles of hiking trails crisscross the park, which contains lakes, rivers, glaciers, and ample camping facilities. Bears, mountain goats, deer, elk, eagles, beavers, and mountain lions live within the park. The dense vegetation includes old-growth Douglas fir, hemlock, cedar, ferns, and wildflowers.

Admission is $10 per vehicle, $5 for those who arrive by any other means, payable at the **Henry M. Jackson Visitor Center** (☎ 360/569–2211). It is possible to sample Rainier's main attractions in a single day by car, but you'll need to stay longer to stop more than just briefly elsewhere in the park or hike the forest, meadow, and high-mountain trails. A narrow and winding paved road links Rainier's main sights. During the peak months of July and August, traffic can be slow and heavy.

Finding a decent meal around Mount Rainier isn't difficult, but lodging can be a problem. Book in advance if possible. The park contains five drive-in campgrounds—Cougar Rock, Ipsut Creek, Ohanapecosh, Sunshine Point, and White River—which have almost 700 campsites for tents and RVs. All are first-come, first-served and have parking spaces, drinking water, garbage cans, fire grates, and picnic tables with benches. Most have flush or pit toilets, but none have hot water. In the winter, chains are often required to reach Paradise.

Ashford

84 mi southeast of Seattle; from I–5's Exit 127 follow Hwy. 512 east to Rte. 7 south to State Route 706 east.

Originally built to service loggers, Ashford now serves the 2 million annual visitors to Mount Rainier National Park. Stores, restaurants, and lodgings are along State Route 706.

Dining and Lodging

$$–$$$ ✕🏠 **Alexander's Country Inn.** The gingerbread facade and fairy-tale turret of this well-maintained 1912 inn are products of a later renovation. The rooms sparkle with fresh paint, carpeting, and antiques, but the walls in the main house are thin. Of the two adjacent ranch houses, the Chalet has more of the country-quaint qualities of the inn. The decor of the Forest House has little to recommend it, but moss covers its private backyard. A large hot tub outside the main house overlooks a trout pond. Room rates include a hearty breakfast and evening wine. The inn's cozy restaurant (closed on weekdays in winter), the best place in town for lunch or dinner, serves fresh fish and pasta dishes. ✉ 37515 S.R. 706 E (4 mi east of Ashford), Ashford 98304, ☎ 360/569–2300 or 800/654–7615, ℻ 360/569–2323. *12 rooms, 2 3-bedroom houses. Restaurant, hot tub. MC, V.*

$$–$$$ 🏠 **Wellspring.** The nine cabins at this spalike facility take advantage of the views of the woodlands. The romantic Nest room contains a hanging bed and a pillow-strewn floor. The Tatoosh, which has a huge stone fireplace and a whirlpool tub, can accommodate up to 10 people. Two structures shelter outdoor hot tubs, saunas, and massage rooms. Fees vary depending on how many of the spa amenities you use. A breakfast basket is delivered to the cabins in the morning. ✉ 54922 Kernehan Rd., off S.R. 706 E, 98304, ☎ 360/569–2514, ℻ 360/569–2285. *9 cabins. Hot tubs, massage, saunas, spa. MC, V.*

Finally, a travel companion that doesn't snore on the plane or eat all your peanuts.

123 456 7891 2345
J.D. SMITH

When traveling, your MCI WorldCom Card is the best way to keep in touch. Our operators speak your language, so they'll be able to connect you back home—no matter where your travels take you. Plus, your MCI WorldCom Card is easy to use, and even earns you frequent flyer miles every time you use it. When you add in our great rates, you get something even more valuable: peace-of-mind. So go ahead. Travel the world. MCI WorldCom just brought it a whole lot closer.

You can even sign up today at www.mci.com/worldphone or ask your operator to make a collect call to 1-410-314-2938.

EASY TO CALL WORLDWIDE

1 Just dial the WorldPhone access number of the country you're calling from.
2 Dial or give the operator your MCI WorldCom Card number.
3 Dial or give the number you're calling.

Australia ◆ To call using OPTUS To call using TELSTRA	**1-800-551-111** **1-800-881-100**
Bahamas/Bermuda	**1-800-888-8000**
British Virgin Islands	**1-800-888-8000**
Costa Rica ◆	**0-800-012-2222**
Denmark	**8001-0022**
Norway ◆	**800 -19912**
India For collect access	**000-127** **000-126**
United States/Canada	**1-800-888-8000**

For your complete WorldPhone calling guide, dial the WorldPhone access number for the country you're in and ask the operator for Customer Service. In the U.S. call 1-800-431-5402.

◆ Public phones may require deposit of coin or phone card for dial tone.

EARN FREQUENT FLYER MILES

AmericanAirlines
A'Advantage

Continental Airlines
OnePass

▲ Delta Air Lines
SkyMiles

MILEAGE PLUS.
United Airlines

U·S AIRWAYS
DIVIDEND MILES

MCI WorldCom, its logo and the names of the products referred to herein are proprietary marks of MCI WorldCom, Inc. All airline names and logos are proprietary marks of the respective airlines. All airline program rules and conditions apply.

MCI WORLDCOM

Distinctive guides packed with up-to-date expert advice
and smart choices for every type of traveler.

Fodor's. For the world of ways you travel.

$$ 🏠 **The Bunkhouse.** "The place to stop on the way to the top" was built in 1908 to house loggers and was originally located a few miles down the road, in the long-gone town of National. The rooms at this old-style motel range from inexpensive single bunks to private suites. ✉ *30205 S.R. 706 E, 98304,* ☎ *360/569–2439,* 𝐅𝐀𝐗 *360/569–2436. 19 rooms. Hot tub. MC, V.*

Longmire

12 mi east of Ashford on S.R. 706.

Glass cases at the **Longmire Museum** contain a few preserved plants and animals from Mount Rainier National Park, including a friendly-looking stuffed cougar. Photos and geographical displays provide an overview of the park's history. ✉ *S.R. 706, 6 mi east of Nisqually entrance,* ☎ *360/569–2211, ext. 3314.* ☉ *July–Labor Day, daily 9–5; Labor Day–June, daily 9–4.*

Dining and Lodging

$$–$$$ ✕🏠 **National Park Inn.** An early 1990s renovation robbed the only year-round lodging in the park of much of its charm—the old stone fireplaces are still here, but the public areas have a generic country-inn feel. The small rooms mix functionality with backwoods touches such as wrought-iron lamps and antique bentwood headboards. The food at the large restaurant sounds more exotic than it tastes: maple-coated chicken, panfried snapper with lemon butter and wine. ✉ *S.R. 706, 6 mi east of Nisqually entrance, 98304,* ☎ *360/569–2411 or 360/569–2275. 25 rooms, 18 with bath. Restaurant, shop. AE, D, DC, MC, V.*

Outdoor Activities and Sports

The Longmire Ski Touring Center (☎ 360/569–2411), adjacent to the National Park Inn, rents cross-country ski equipment and provides lessons from mid-December to early April. **Mount Rainier Guest Services** (✉ National Park Inn, S.R. 706, ☎ 360/569–2411) rents cross-country ski equipment, snowshoes, and hiking gear from mid-December to early April. **Ed Strauss** (☎ 360/569–2271), a ski instructor, is also a tour guide.

Paradise

9 mi east of Longmire on S.R. 706.

Fantastic mountain views, alpine meadows crisscrossed by trails, a welcoming lodge and restaurant, and an excellent visitor center make Paradise the primary goal of most visitors to Mount Rainier National Park. Exhibits at the **Henry M. Jackson Visitor Center** focus on geology, mountaineering, glaciology, winter storms, and alpine ecology. Two worthwhile 20-minute multimedia programs repeat at half-hour intervals. ✉ *S.R. 706, 20 mi east of Nisqually entrance,* ☎ *360/569–2211.* ☉ *Early May–mid-Oct., daily 9–6; mid-Oct.–Apr., weekends and holidays 10–5.*

Hiking trails to various points begin at the Visitor Center. One outstanding, if grueling, way to explore the high country is to hike the 5-mi Skyline Trail to Panorama Point, which has stunning 360° views.

Dining and Lodging

$$ ✕🏠 **Paradise Inn.** With its hand-carved cedar logs, burnished parquet floors, stone fireplaces, and glorious mountain views, this inn built in 1917 is loaded with atmosphere. Its smallish, sparsely furnished rooms, however, are not equipped with TVs or telephones and have thin walls and showers that tend to run cold during periods of peak use. The attraction here is the alpine setting. The full-service dining room serves leisurely Sunday brunches in summer. The lodge also has a small snack bar and a snug lounge. ⊠ *S.R. 706 (mailing address: c/o Mount Rainier Guest Services, Box 108, Star Rte., Ashford 98304),* ☎ *360/569–2275,* FAX *360/569–2770. 117 rooms, 96 with bath. AE, D, DC, MC, V. Closed Nov.–mid-May.*

Outdoor Activities and Sports

MOUNTAIN CLIMBING

Highly regarded **Rainier Mountaineering** (⊠ Paradise 98398, ☎ 253/627–6242 in winter, 360/569–2227 in summer) teaches the fundamentals of mountaineering at one-day classes held during the climbing season, which lasts from late May through early September.

SKIING

Mount Rainier is a major cross-country ski center. The ungroomed trails around Paradise are particularly popular.

SNOWSHOEING

Snowshoe rentals are available at the **Longmire Ski Touring Center** (☞ *above*). From December through April, park rangers lead free twice-daily snowshoe walks that start at the visitor center at Paradise and cover 1¼ mi in about two hours.

Eastern Side of Mount Rainier National Park

21 mi east of Paradise on S.R. 706.

★ The **Grove of the Patriarchs,** a small island of 1,000-year-old trees protected from the fires that afflicted surrounding areas, is one of the park's most stunning features. A 2-mi loop trail that begins just west of the Stevens Canyon entrance heads over a small bridge through lush old-growth forest of Douglas fir, cedar, and hemlock.

As you head north from the Grove of the Patriarchs are the White River and the **Sunrise Visitor Center,** from which you can watch the alpenglow fade from Mount Rainier's summit. The visitor center has exhibits on this region's alpine and subalpine ecology. ⊠ *70002 S.R. 410 E, Enumclaw,* ☎ *360/569–2211, ext. 2357.* ☉ *July 4–Oct. 1, daily 9–6.*

Outdoor Activities and Sports

SKIING

If you want to cross-country ski with fewer people, try the trails in and around the Ohanapecosh/Stevens Canyon area, which are just as beautiful as those at Paradise. Never ski on the plowed main roads. The snowplow operator can't see you.

SNOWMOBILING AND SNOWSHOEING

Snowmobiling is allowed on the east side of the park on sections of Highway 123 and Stevens Canyon Road—between the ranger station at Ohanapecosh Visitor Center and Box Canyon—and on Highway 410, which is accessible from the north entrance. Highway 410 is unplowed after its junction with the road to the Crystal Mountain Ski Area. A State of Washington Sno-Park permit, available at local stores and gas stations, is required to park in the area near the north park entrance arch. Highways 123 and 410 are good places to snowshoe.

Mount Rainier National Park Essentials

Getting Around

BY BUS

Gray Line of Seattle (☎ 206/624–5813) operates daily tours to Longmire and Paradise in the summer.

Most visitors arrive at the park's Nisqually entrance, the closest entrance to I–5, via **State Route 706. Highway 410** enters the park from the east. **Highway 123** enters from the southeast. Highways 410 and 123 are usually closed in winter. **Highway 165** leads to Ipsut Creek Campground through the Carbon River entrance to Mowich Lake, in the park's northwest corner.

Visitor Information

Superintendent, Mount Rainier National Park (⊠ Tahoma Woods, Star Rte., Ashford 98304, ☎ 360/569–2211).

4 VANCOUVER

The spectacular setting of cosmopolitan Vancouver has drawn people from around the world to settle here. The ocean and mountains form a dramatic backdrop to downtown's gleaming towers of commerce and make it easy to pursue all kinds of outdoor pleasures. You can trace the city's history in Gastown and Chinatown, savor the wilderness only blocks from the city center in Stanley Park, or dine on superb ethnic or Pacific Northwest cuisine before you sample the city's nightlife.

VANCOUVER IS A YOUNG CITY, even by North American standards. It was not yet a town when British Columbia became part of the Canadian confederation in 1871. The city's history, such as it is, remains visible to the naked eye: eras are stacked east to west along the waterfront, from cobblestone late-Victorian Gastown to shiny postmodern glass cathedrals of commerce.

By Sue Kernaghan

The Chinese, among the first to recognize the possibilities of Vancouver's setting, came to British Columbia during the 1850s seeking the gold that inspired them to name the province Gum-shan, or Gold Mountain. As laborers they built the Canadian Pacific Railway, giving Vancouver a purpose—one beyond the natural splendor that Royal Navy captain George Vancouver admired during his lunchtime cruise around its harbor on June 13, 1792. The Canadian transcontinental railway, along with the city's Great White Fleet of clipper ships, gave Vancouver a full week's edge over the California ports in shipping tea and silk to New York at the end of the 19th century.

For its original inhabitants, the Coast Salish peoples, Vancouver was the sacred spot where the mythical Thunderbird and Killer Whale flung wind and rain all about the heavens during their epic battles. How else to explain the coast's fits of meteorological temper? Devotees of a later religious tradition might worship in the groves of Stanley Park or in the fir and cedar interior of Christ Church Cathedral, the city's oldest church.

Vancouver, with a metropolitan-area population of 1.9 million, is booming. Many Asians have migrated here, mainly from Hong Kong, but other regions are represented as well. The mild climate, exquisite natural scenery, and relaxed, outdoor lifestyle is attracting new residents to British Columbia's business center, and the number of visitors is increasing for the same reasons. Many people get their first glimpse of Vancouver when catching an Alaskan cruise, and many return at some point to spend more time here.

Pleasures and Pastimes

Dining
Downtown bistros, creek-side seafood palaces, and upscale pan-Asian restaurants are among Vancouver's diverse gastronomical offerings. Several cutting-edge establishments are perfecting and defining Pacific Northwest fare, which incorporates regional salmon and oysters and locally grown produce, often accompanied by wines from British Columbia, Oregon, or Washington.

The Great Outdoors
Nature has truly blessed this city, surrounding it with verdant forests, towering mountains, coves, inlets, rivers, and the wide sea. Biking, hiking, skiing, snowboarding, and sailing are among the many outdoor activities possible in or near the city. Whether you prefer to relax on a beach by yourself or join a kayaking tour with an outfitter, Vancouver has plenty to offer.

Nightlife and the Arts
Vancouver residents support the arts enthusiastically, especially during the city's film, performing arts, and other cultural festivals, most of which take place between June and October. Year-round, there's a complete range of live music, from jazz and blues to heavy metal. The city's opera, ballet, and symphonic companies are thriving. Peculiar

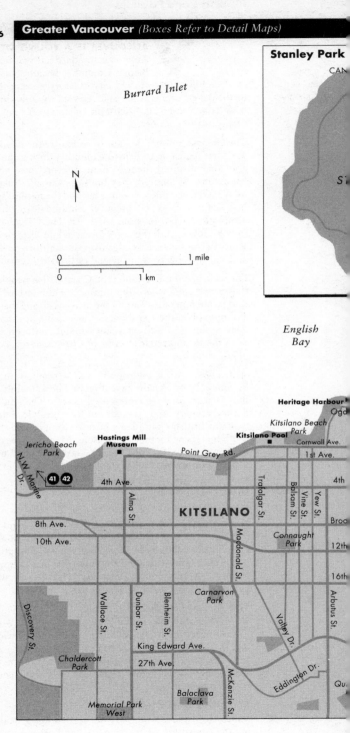

Greater Vancouver *(Boxes Refer to Detail Maps)*

Stanley Park

CAN

Burrard Inlet

N

0   1 mile

0   1 km

English Bay

Heritage Harbour

Oga

Kitsilano Beach Park

Kitsilano Pool

Cornwall Ave.

Hastings Mill Museum

Point Grey Rd.

1st Ave.

Jericho Beach Park

N.W. Marine Dr.

41 **42**

4th Ave.

4th

Trafalgar St.

Balsam St.

Vine St.

Yew St.

Alma St.

KITSILANO

Broa

8th Ave.

Connaught Park

10th Ave.

12th

Macdonald St.

16th

Carnarvon Park

Wallace St.

Dunbar St.

Blenheim St.

Arbutus St.

Valley Dr.

Discovery St.

King Edward Ave.

Eddington Dr.

Chaldercott Park

27th Ave.

McKenzie St.

Qu

Balaclava Park

Memorial Park West

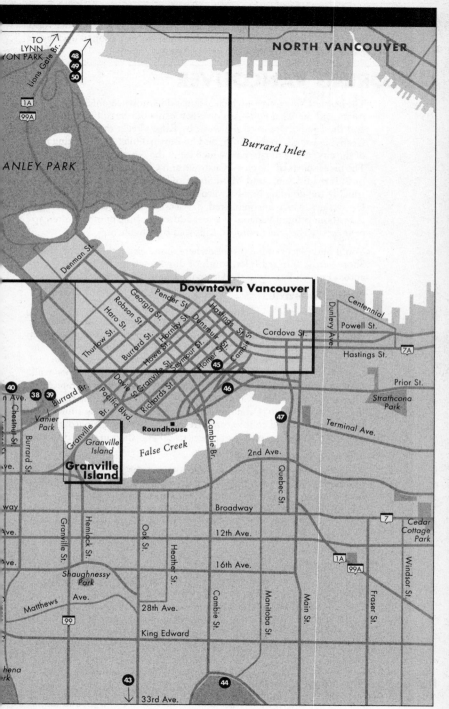

NORTH VANCOUVER

Burrard Inlet

48
49
50

TO
LYNN
YON PARK

Lions Gate Br.

1A
99A

ANLEY PARK

Denman St.

Downtown Vancouver

Georgia St.
Pender St.
Robson St.
Haro St.
Hastings St.
Dunsmuir St.
Thurlow St.
Burrard St.
Hornby St.
Howe St.
Seymour St.
Granville St.
Homer St.
Richards St.
Cambie St.

Cordova St.

Centennial

Dunlevy Ave.

Powell St.

Hastings St.

7A

45

46

Davie St.
Pacific Blvd.

47

Prior St.

Strathcona
Park

Terminal Ave.

40
38
39

Burrard Br.

n Ave.

Chestnut St.

Vanier
Park

Burrard St.

Granville

Granville
Island

**Granville
Island**

Roundhouse

False Creek

Cambie Br.

2nd Ave.

Quebec St.

Broadway

7

Cedar
Cottage
Park

way

Ave.

Granville St.

Hemlock St.

Oak St.

Heather St.

12th Ave.

16th Ave.

1A
99A

Windsor St.

Ave.

*Shaughnessy
Park*

Matthews
Ave.

99

28th Ave.

King Edward

Cambie St.

Manitoba St.

Main St.

Fraser St.

hena
ark

43

33rd Ave.

44

liquor laws have created a shortage of pubs and bars. Many pubs operate with a restaurant license, which requires patrons to order food with their drink. The situation may ease if the city council decides to allow a number of new pubs and cabarets to open.

EXPLORING VANCOUVER

The heart of Vancouver—which includes downtown, Stanley Park, Yaletown, and the West End—sits on a peninsula bordered by English Bay and the Pacific Ocean to the west; by False Creek, the inlet home to Granville Island, to the south; and by Burrard Inlet, the working port of the city, to the north, past which loom the North Shore mountains. The oldest parts of the city—Gastown and Chinatown—lie at the edge of Burrard Inlet, around Main Street, which runs north–south and is roughly the dividing line between the east side and the west side. All the avenues, which are numbered, have east and west designations. One note about printed Vancouver street addresses: suite numbers often appear *before* the street number, followed by a hyphen.

You'll find places of interest elsewhere in the city, either on the North Shore across Burrard Inlet, south of downtown in the Kitsilano area across English Bay, or in the Granville Island area across False Creek.

Great Itineraries

IF YOU HAVE 1 OR 2 DAYS

If you have only one day in Vancouver, start with an early morning walk, bike, or shuttle ride through Stanley Park to see the Vancouver Aquarium and Second Beach on English Bay. Head northeast from the park on Denman Street to Robson Street to lunch and meander on foot through the trendy shops between Denman and Burrard, and then walk northeast on Burrard Street to view the many buildings of architectural interest. Stop along the way at the Vancouver Art Gallery and the Canadian Craft Museum. On day two take a leisurely walking tour of the shops, eateries, and cobblestone streets of Gastown, Chinatown, and Yaletown. There are plenty of places to eat and shop in these districts.

IF YOU HAVE 3 OR 4 DAYS

If you have another day to tour Vancouver after you've followed the itinerary above, head to the south side of False Creek and English Bay on day three to delve into the many boutiques, dining outlets, theaters, and the public market of Granville Island. Buses and ferries provide easy transit. Parking is available, but traffic getting onto the island can be congested, especially on weekends. Touring Granville Island is best accomplished on foot.

On day four, tour the sights beyond downtown Vancouver. Make time for the Museum of Anthropology on the campus of the University of British Columbia. Also visit the Vancouver Museum, the Pacific Space Centre, and the Vancouver Maritime Museum, all south of downtown in the Kitsilano area. If you'd rather play outside, head to the North Shore Mountains, where you can swing high above the Capilano River on a suspension bridge and ride the Skyride to the top of Grouse Mountain.

Robson to the Waterfront

Numbers in the text correspond to numbers in the margin and on the Downtown Vancouver map.

Museums and buildings of architectural and historical significance are the primary draw in downtown Vancouver, but there's also plenty of fine shopping.

A Good Walk

Begin at the northwest end of **Robson Street** ①, at Bute or Thurlow street. Follow Robson southeast to Hornby to reach landscaped **Robson Square** ② and the **Vancouver Art Gallery** ③. On the north side of the gallery across Hornby Street sits the **Hotel Vancouver** ④, a city landmark. The **Cathedral Place** office tower stands across the street at Hornby Street and Georgia Street. The three large sculptures of nurses at the corners of the building are replicas of the statues that adorned the Georgia Medical-Dental Building, the Art Deco structure that previously occupied this site.

To the west of Cathedral Place is a walkway that leads to a peaceful green courtyard, off which is the **Canadian Craft Museum** ⑤. Farther to the west of Cathedral Place is the Gothic-style **Christ Church Cathedral** ⑥. North down Burrard Street, toward the water on the opposite side of the street, is the Art Deco **Marine Building** ⑦.

Cross Burrard and follow Hastings Street to the east for a look at the outside of the exclusive **Vancouver Club** ⑧. The club marks the start of the old financial district, which runs southeast along Hastings. The district's older temple-style banks, investment houses, and businesspeople's clubs are the surviving legacy of the city's sophisticated pre–World War I architecture. **Sinclair Centre** ⑨, at Hastings and Howe streets, is a magnificently restored complex of government buildings that houses offices and retail shops. Near Granville Street at 698 West Hastings, a jewelry store now occupies the Roman-influenced former headquarters of the **Canadian Imperial Bank of Commerce.** The equally striking **Royal Bank** building stands directly across the street. Southeast of here at Hastings and Seymour streets is the elevator to the **Lookout at Harbour Centre** ⑩.

Head northeast up Seymour toward Burrard Inlet to the **Waterfront Station** ⑪. Take a peek at the murals inside the 19th-century structure, then take the west staircase (to your left) up to Granville Square Plaza. Wander across the plaza to the SkyTrain station, and you'll face the soaring canopies of **Canada Place** ⑫, where you can stop for a snack in one of the dining outlets on the water or catch a film at the Imax theater. Across Canada Place Way (next door to the Waterfront Centre Hotel) is the **Vancouver Tourist Info Centre.**

TIMING

This tour takes about an hour to walk, not counting stops along the way. The Canadian Craft Museum and the Vancouver Art Gallery each warrant an hour or more, depending on the exhibits.

Sights to See

⑫ Canada Place. When Vancouver hosted the Expo '86 world's fair, a former cargo pier was transformed into the off-site Canadian pavilion. Following the fair, Canada Place was transformed yet again, into Vancouver's trade and convention center, below which cruise ships dock. The roof, shaped like 10 sails, that covers the convention space has become a landmark of Vancouver's skyline. The luxurious **Pan Pacific Hotel** (☞ Lodging, *below*) dominates the shoreline edge of Canada Place. At the north end are an Imax theater, a restaurant, and an outdoor performance space. A promenade around the pier affords views of Burrard Inlet and Stanley Park. ⊠ *999 Canada Pl.,* ☎ *604/775–8687.*

⑤ Canadian Craft Museum. One of Vancouver's most interesting cultural facilities, the craft museum displays functional and decorative modern and historical crafts. Exhibits change throughout the year, so there's always something new to see. The courtyard is a quiet place to

Downtown Vancouver

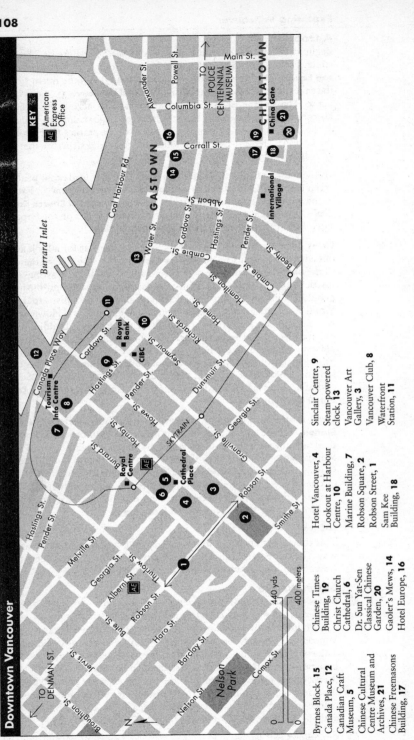

KEY

AE American Express Office

Burrard Inlet

TO DENMAN ST.

TO POLICE CENTENNIAL MUSEUM

GASTOWN

CHINATOWN

Nelson Park

Jervis St.
Bute St.
Haro St.
Barclay St.
Nelson St.
Comox St.
Broughton St.

Melville St.
Georgia St.
Robson St.
Smithe St.

Thurlow St.
Alberni St.
Burrard St.
Hornby St.
Howe St.
Granville St.
Seymour St.
Richards St.
Homer St.
Hamilton St.
Cambie St.
Beatty St.

Hastings St.
Pender St.
Dunsmuir St.
Georgia St.

Canada Place Way
Cordova St.
Water St.
Cordova St.
Hastings St.
Pender St.
Abbott St.
Coal Harbour Rd.

Alexander St.
Powell St.
Columbia St.
Carrall St.
Main St.

China Gate

International Village

Tourism Info Centre
Royal Centre
Cathedral Place
Royal Bank
CIBC
SKYTRAIN

N

0   440 yds
0   400 meters

Byrnes Block, **15**
Canada Place, **12**
Canadian Craft Museum, **5**
Chinese Cultural Centre Museum and Archives, **21**
Chinese Freemasons Building, **17**

Chinese Times Building, **19**
Christ Church Cathedral, **6**
Dr. Sun Yat-Sen Classical Chinese Garden, **20**
Gaoler's Mews, **14**
Hotel Europe, **16**

Hotel Vancouver, **4**
Lookout at Harbour Centre, **10**
Marine Building, **7**
Robson Square, **2**
Robson Street, **1**
Sam Kee Building, **18**

Sinclair Centre, **9**
Steam-powered clock, **13**
Vancouver Art Gallery, **3**
Vancouver Club, **8**
Waterfront Station, **11**

take a break. ⊠ *Cathedral Place Courtyard, 639 Hornby St. (also accessible from 925 W. Georgia St.),* ☎ *604/687–8266.* 🖾 *$5; Thurs. 5 PM–9 PM by donation.* ⊙ *May–Aug., Mon.–Wed. and Fri.–Sat. 10–5, Thurs. 10–9, Sun. noon–5; Sept.–Apr., Mon. and Wed. 10–5, Thurs. 10–9, Fri–Sat. 10–5, Sun. noon–5.*

❻ Christ Church Cathedral. The oldest church in Vancouver was built in 1889. Constructed in the Gothic style with buttresses and pointed-arch windows, the tiny cathedral looks like the parish church of an English village from the outside, but the Douglas fir and cedar interior is thoroughly Canadian. The stained glass windows show Vancouver landmarks (one shows Saint Christopher presiding over the Lions Gate Bridge), and the building's excellent acoustics enhance the choral evensong, carols, and Gregorian chants frequently sung here. ⊠ *690 Burrard St.,* ☎ *604/682–3848.* ⊙ *Weekdays 10–4.*

❹ Hotel Vancouver. One of the last railway-built hotels in Canada, the Hotel Vancouver was designed in the château style, its architectural details reminiscent of a medieval French castle. Construction began in 1928. The hotel was barely finished in time for the visit of King George VI of England in 1939. The exterior of the building, one of the most recognizable on Vancouver's skyline, has carvings of malevolent-looking gargoyles at the corners, native chiefs on the Hornby Street side, and an assortment of grotesque mythological figures. ⊠ *900 W. Georgia St.,* ☎ *604/684–3131.*

❿ Lookout at Harbour Centre. The lookout looks like a flying saucer stuck on top of a high-rise. At 167 m (553 ft) high, it affords one of the best views of Vancouver. A glass elevator whizzes you up 50 stories to the circular observation deck, where knowledgeable guides point out the sights. On a clear day you can see Vancouver Island. Tickets are good all day, so you can come during daylight hours and return for another peek after dark. The top-floor restaurant makes one complete revolution per hour; the ride up in the elevator is free for diners. ⊠ *555 W. Hastings St.,* ☎ *604/689–0421.* 🖾 *$8.* ⊙ *May–Aug., daily 8:30–10:30; Sept.–Apr., daily 9–9.*

❼ Marine Building. Terra-cotta bas-reliefs depicting the history of transportation—airships, steamships, locomotives, and submarines—adorn this Art Deco structure erected in 1930. Because most architects still applied classical or Gothic ornamentation, these motifs were considered radical at the time. From the east, the Marine Building is reflected in bronze by 999 West Hastings, and from the southeast it is mirrored in silver by the Canadian Imperial Bank of Commerce. Step inside for a look at the beautifully restored interior, and then walk to the corner of Hastings and Hornby streets for the best view of the building. ⊠ *355 Burrard St.*

❷ Robson Square. Architect Arthur Erickson designed this plaza, which was completed in 1979, to be *the* gathering place of downtown Vancouver. Landscaped walkways connect the **Vancouver Art Gallery** (☞ *below*), government offices, a convention center, and law courts. An ice-skating rink (that's used for ballroom dancing in summer) and restaurants occupy the level below the street. Political protests and impromptu rants take place on the gallery stairs, a tradition that dates from the days when the building that houses the gallery was a courthouse. ⊠ *Bordered by Howe, Hornby, Robson, and Smithe Sts.*

❶ Robson Street. Ultrachic Robson Street is often called Vancouver's Rodeo Drive because of the many see-and-be-seen sidewalk cafés and high-end boutiques. The street, which links downtown and the West End, is particularly lively between Jervis and Burrard streets. The shops (☞ Shopping, *below*) are like those you'll find anywhere. It's the people-watching, café-lounging, and window-shopping scene that draw the crowds day and night.

❾ Sinclair Centre. The outstanding Vancouver architect Richard Henriquez knitted four government office buildings into Sinclair Centre, an office-retail complex. The two Hastings Street buildings—the 1905 **Post Office,** which has an elegant clock tower, and the 1911 **Winch Building**—are linked with the **Post Office Extension** and **Customs Examining Warehouse** to the north. Painstaking and costly restoration involved finding master masons and uncovering and refurbishing the pressed-metal ceilings. ⊠ *757 W. Hastings St.*

❸ Vancouver Art Gallery. Painter Emily Carr's haunting evocations of the British Columbian hinterland are the biggest attraction at the city's main art gallery. Carr, who lived from 1871 to 1945, was a grocer's daughter from Victoria. She fell in love with the wilderness around her and shocked middle-class society by running off to paint it. Her work accentuates the mysticism and the danger of B.C.'s wilderness—no pretty landscapes here—and records the passing of native cultures. The gallery, which also hosts touring exhibits of varying quality, is inside a 1911 courthouse that Arthur Erickson redesigned in the early-1980s. Lions guard the majestic front steps, and columns and domes are among the original Classical architectural elements. The Gallery Café has a fine terrace, and the gallery's shop has a noteworthy selection of prints and cards. You can visit the café and the shop without an admission ticket. ⊠ *750 Hornby St.,* ☎ *604/662–4719.* ☜ *June–Sept. $10; Oct.–May $8; Thurs. 5–9 by donation.* ☉ *June–Sept., Mon.–Wed. and Fri. 10–6, Thurs. 10–9, Sat. 10–5, Sun. noon–5; Oct.–May, Tues., Wed., and Fri.–Sun. 10–5:30, Thurs. 10–9.*

❽ Vancouver Club. George Lister, Thornton Sharp, and Charles Joseph Thompson, the brains behind many city landmarks including the galleries of the Burrard Bridge and the original University of British Columbia, built this elite private club between 1912 and 1914. Its architecture evokes that of private clubs in England inspired by Italian Renaissance palaces. The Vancouver Club is still the private haunt of city businesspeople, so it's not possible to view the interior. ⊠ *915 W. Hastings St.*

Vancouver Tourist Info Centre. Here you'll find brochures and personnel to answer questions—and a nice view to boot. ⊠ *200 Burrard St.,* ☎ *604/683–2000.* ☉ *Sept.–late May, weekdays 8:30–5, Sat. 9–5; Late May–Aug., daily 8–6.*

⓫ Waterfront Station. This former Canadian Pacific Railway passenger terminal was built between 1912 and 1914 as the western terminus for Canada's transcontinental railway. After Canada's railways merged, the station became obsolete, but a 1978 renovation turned it into an office-retail complex and depot for SkyTrain, SeaBus, and West Coast Express passengers. Murals in the waiting rooms show the scenery travelers once saw on journeys across Canada. Here you can catch a 13-minute SeaBus trip across the harbor to the waterfront public market at Lonsdale Quay in North Vancouver. During 2000, SeaBuses may leave from a temporary station just to the east while a new waterfront development is under construction. ⊠ *601 W. Cordova St.,* ☎ *604/521–0400 for SeaBus and SkyTrain; 604/683–7245 for West Coast Express.*

Gastown and Chinatown

Gastown is where Vancouver originated after "Gassy" Jack Deighton arrived at Burrard Inlet in 1867 with his wife, some whiskey, and a few amenities. The smooth-talking Deighton convinced local loggers and trappers into building him a saloon for a barrel of whiskey. (It didn't take much convincing. His saloon was on the edge of lumber company land, where alcohol was forbidden.) When the transcontinental train arrived in 1887, Gastown became the transfer point for trade with the Far East and was soon crowded with hotels and warehouses. The Klondike gold rush encouraged further development that lasted until 1912, when the so-called Golden Years ended. From the 1930s to the 1950s hotels were converted into rooming houses, and the warehouse district shifted elsewhere. The neglected area gradually became run down. Gastown and Chinatown were declared historic districts in the late 1970s, though, and have been revitalized. Gastown contains boutiques, cafés, loft apartments, and souvenir shops.

Some of the oldest buildings in the city are in Chinatown, the third-largest such area in North America. There was already a sizable Chinese community here because of the 1858 Cariboo gold rush in central British Columbia, but the greatest influx from China came in the 1880s during construction of the Canadian Pacific Railway when more than 10,000 laborers were recruited. Though they were performing the valuable and hazardous task of blasting the rail bed through the Rocky Mountains, the Chinese were discriminated against. The Anti-Asiatic Riots of 1907 stopped growth in Chinatown for 50 years, and immigration from China was discouraged by increasingly restrictive policies that climaxed in a $500-per-head tax during the 1920s. In the 1960s the city council planned bulldozer urban renewal for Strathcona, the residential part of Chinatown, as well as freeway connections through the most historic blocks of the district. Fortunately, the project was halted, and today Chinatown is an expanding, vital neighborhood fueled by the investments of immigrants from Hong Kong and elsewhere. The style of architecture in Vancouver's Chinatown is patterned on that of Guangzhou (Canton).

Numbers in the text correspond to numbers in the margin and on the Downtown Vancouver map.

A Good Walk

Pick up Water Street at Richards Street in downtown Vancouver and head east into Gastown. At the corner of Water and Cambie streets you can see and hear the world's first **steam-powered clock** ⑬. About a block east on the other side of the street, tucked behind 12 Water Street, is **Gaoler's Mews** ⑭. Two buildings of historical and architectural note are the **Byrnes Block** ⑮, on the corner of Water and Carrall streets, and the **Hotel Europe** ⑯, at Powell and Alexander streets. A statue of Gassy Jack Deighton stands on the west side of Maple Tree Square, at the intersection of Water, Powell, Alexander, and Carrall streets, where he built his first saloon.

From Maple Tree Square it's only three blocks south on Carrall Street to Pender Street, where Chinatown begins. This route passes through a rough part of town. It's safer to backtrack two blocks on Water Street through Gastown to Cambie Street, then head south to Pender and east to Carrall.

If you come along Pender Street, you'll pass **International Village**, a new Asian-oriented shopping and cinema development. Old Chinatown starts at the corner of Carrall and Pender streets. The **Chinese Freemasons Building** ⑰ and the **Sam Kee Building** ⑱ are here, and directly across Carrall Street is the **Chinese Times Building** ⑲. About a half block east and across Pender, tucked into a courtyard behind the brightly painted China Gate is the **Dr. Sun Yat-Sen Classical Chinese Garden** ⑳. Next to the garden is the free, public **Dr. Sun Yat-Sen Park**. A short path through the park will take you out to Columbia Street, where, to your left, you'll find the entrance to the **Chinese Cultural Centre Museum and Archives** ㉑ (not to be confused with the Chinese Cultural Centre that fronts Pender Street). Finish up your tour of Chinatown by poking around in the open-front markets and import shops that line several blocks of Pender and Keefer running east. **Ten Ren Tea and Ginseng Company,** at 550 Main, and **Ten Lee Hong Tea and Ginseng,** at 500 Main, carry every kind of tea imaginable. For art, ceramics, and rosewood furniture have a look at **Yeu Hua Handicraft Ltd.,** at 173 East Pender. If you're in the area in summer on a Friday, Saturday, or Sunday, check out the bustling **Night Market,** for which the 200 blocks of Keefer and East Pender are closed to traffic from 6:30 to 11.

TIMING

The walk described above takes about an hour. Allow extra time for the guided tour of the Dr. Sun Yat-Sen Classical Chinese Garden. This tour is best done by day, though shops and restaurants are open into the night in both areas.

Sights to See

⓯ **Byrnes Block.** This building was constructed on the site of Gassy Jack Deighton's second saloon after the 1886 Great Fire, which wiped out most of the fledgling settlement of Vancouver. The date is visible at the top of the building above the door where it says "Herman Block," which was its name for a short time. The site of Deighton's original saloon, just east of the Byrnes block where his statue now stands, is the zero point from which all Vancouver street addresses start. ⊠ *2 Water St.*

㉑ **Chinese Cultural Centre Museum and Archives.** The first museum in Canada dedicated to preserving and promoting Chinese-Canadian history and culture opened in 1998. The art gallery on the main floor exhibits the works of Chinese and Chinese-Canadian artists. The museum on the second floor has an intriguing collection of historical photos. ⊠ *555 Columbia St.,* ☎ *604/687–0282.* ⊠ *$3.* ☼ *Tues.–Sun. 11–5.*

⓱ **Chinese Freemasons Building.** Two completely different facades distinguish this structure on the northwest corner of Pender and Carrall streets. The side facing Pender represents a fine example of Cantonese recessed balconies. The Carrall Street side displays the standard Victorian style common throughout the British Empire. Dr. Sun Yat-Sen hid for months in this building from agents of the Manchu dynasty while he raised funds for its overthrow, which he accomplished in 1911. ⊠ *3 W. Pender St.*

⓳ **Chinese Times Building.** Police officers during the early 20th century could hear the clicking sounds of clandestine mah-jongg games played after sunset on the hidden mezzanine floor of this 1902 structure. But attempts by vice squads to enforce restrictive policies against the Chinese gamblers proved fruitless because police were unable to find the players. ⊠ *1 E. Pender St.*

★ ⓴ **Dr. Sun Yat-Sen Classical Chinese Garden.** The first authentic Ming Dynasty–style garden outside of China, this garden was built in 1986 by 52 artisans from Suzhou, the Garden City of the People's Republic. It incorporates design elements and traditional materials from several of that city's centuries-old private gardens. No power tools, screws, or nails were used in the construction. Forty-five-minute guided tours, included in the ticket price, are offered throughout the day. Call ahead for times. On Friday evenings between mid-June and September, musicians perform traditional Chinese music in the garden. The free public park next door is also designed as a traditional Chinese garden. ⊠

578 Carrall St., ☎ 604/689–7133. ☞ $6.50. ☼ Mid-June–mid-Sept., daily 9:30–7:30; call for winter hrs.

⑭ **Gaoler's Mews.** Once the site of the city's first civic buildings—the constable's cabin and customs house, and a two-cell log jail—today this atmospheric cobblestone courtyard is home to cafés and architectural offices. ⊠ *Behind 12 Water St.*

⑯ **Hotel Europe.** Once billed as the best hotel in the city, this 1908 flat-iron building is one of the world's best examples of this style of tri-angular architecture. Now used for government-subsidized housing and not open to the public, the hotel still has its original Italian tile work and leaded glass windows. The glass tiles in the sidewalk on Alexander Street once provided light for an underground saloon. ⊠ *43 Powell St.*

⑱ **Sam Kee Building.** *Ripley's Believe It or Not!* recognizes this structure as the narrowest office building in the world. In 1913, when the city confiscated most of Chang Toy's land to widen Pender Street, he built on what he had left—just 6 ft—in protest. These days the building houses an insurance agency, whose employees make do within the 4 ft-10-inch–wide interior. ⊠ *8 W. Pender St.*

⑬ **Steam-powered clock.** An underground steam system, which also heats many local buildings, powers the world's first steam clock. Every quarter hour the whistle blows, and on the hour a huge cloud of steam spews from the apparatus, which was built by Ray Saunders of Landmark Clocks (⊠ 123 Cambie St.). ⊠ *Water and Cambie Sts.*

Stanley Park

A 1,000-acre wilderness park only blocks from the downtown section of a major city is both a rarity and a treasure. In the 1860s, because of a threat of American invasion, the area that is now Stanley Park was designated a military reserve—though it was never needed. When the city of Vancouver was incorporated in 1886, the council's first act was to request that the land be set aside as a park. In 1888 permission was granted and the grounds were named Stanley Park after Lord Stanley, then governor general of Canada.

If you're driving to Stanley Park, head northwest on Georgia Street from downtown and stay in the right lane or you'll end up going over the Lions Gate bridge. If you're taking public transit, catch any bus labeled Stanley Park at the corner of Hastings and Granville streets downtown. You can also catch North Vancouver buses 240 or 246 from anywhere on West Georgia Street to the park entrance at Georgia and Chilco streets, or a Robson bus 5 to Robson and Denman Streets, where you'll find a number of bicycle rental outlets.

To reach Stanley Park's main attractions, you can bike, walk, drive, or take the park shuttle. The seawall path, a 9 km (5½ mi) paved shoreline route popular with walkers, cyclists, and rollerbladers, is one of several car-free zones within the park. If you have the time (about a half day) and the energy, strolling the entire seawall is an exhilarating experience. Cyclists (☞ Biking, *below,* for information about rentals) must ride in a counterclockwise direction and stay on their side of the path.

The **Stanley Park Shuttle** (☎ 604/257–8400) operates between mid-May and mid-September, providing frequent (15 minute intervals) transportation between 14 major park sites. You can pick it up on Pipeline Road, near the Georgia Street park entrance, or at any of the stops in the park. At press time the shuttle was expected to remain free

Stanley Park

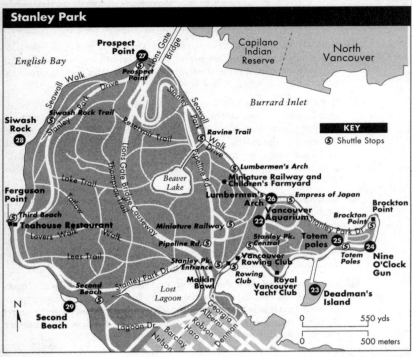

English Bay

Prospect Point

Capilano Indian Reserve

North Vancouver

Burrard Inlet

Siwash Rock

Ferguson Point

Third Beach

Teahouse Restaurant

Beaver Lake

Ravine Trail

Lumbermen's Arch

Miniature Railway and Children's Farmyard

Lumbermen's Arch

Empress of Japan

Vancouver Aquarium

Brockton Point

Totem poles

Totem Poles

Nine O'Clock Gun

Stanley Pk. Central

Vancouver Rowing Club

Stanley Pk. Entrance

Malkin Bowl

Rowing Club

Royal Vancouver Yacht Club

Deadman's Island

Second Beach

Lost Lagoon

KEY

Ⓢ Shuttle Stops

N

0 ___ 550 yds

0 ___ 500 meters

of charge and run 9:30 to 6 daily, though a small fare may be introduced.

Between mid-September and mid-May the traffic in Stanley Park is lighter and there's little competition for parking. There are lots at or near all the major attractions. A $5 ticket allows you to park all day, and to move between lots. Another way to see the park is on one of the **Stanley Park Horse Drawn Tours** (☞ Guided Tours *in* Vancouver A to Z, *below*).

Numbers in the text correspond to numbers in the margin and on the Stanley Park map.

A Good Tour

If you're walking or cycling, start at the foot of Alberni Street beside Lost Lagoon. Go through the underpass and veer right, following the cycle path markings, to the seawall. If you're driving, enter the park at the foot of Georgia Street. Keep to your right, and you'll go beneath an underpass. This will put you on scenic Stanley Park Drive, which circles the park.

Whether you're on the seawall or Stanley Park Drive, the old wooden structure that you pass on your right is home of the Vancouver Rowing Club, a private athletic club established in 1903. On your left are an **Information Booth** (staffed daily from April through October) and the turnoff to the **Vancouver Aquarium** ㉒ and the **Miniature Railway and Children's Farmyard**.

Continuing on Stanley Park Drive or the seawall, you'll next pass the Royal Vancouver Yacht Club. About ½ km (⅓ mi) farther is the causeway to **Deadman's Island** ㉓. The **totem poles** ㉕, which are a bit farther down Stanley Park Drive and slightly inland on your left, are a popular photo stop. Ahead at the water's edge is the **Nine O'Clock Gun** ㉔.

To the north is Brockton Point and its small lighthouse and foghorn. At kilometer 3 (mile 2) of the drive is **Lumbermen's Arch** ㉖, a log archway. The **Children's Water Park** across the road is well attended throughout the summer. Cyclists and walkers can turn off here for a shortcut back to the Aquarium, the Miniature Railway and the Children's Farmyard, and the park entrance.

About 2 km (1 mi) farther along the seawall or Stanley Park Drive is the Lions Gate Bridge. Here drivers and cyclists part company. Cyclists ride under the bridge and past the cormorants' nests tucked beneath **Prospect Point** ㉗. Drivers pass over the bridge and reach a viewpoint and café at the top of Prospect Point. Both routes then continue around to the English Bay side of the park and the beginning of sandy beaches. The imposing monolith offshore is **Siwash Rock** ㉘, the focus of a native legend.

The next attraction along the seawall is the large heated pool at **Second Beach** ㉙. If you're walking or cycling, you can take a shortcut from here back to Lost Lagoon by walking along the perpendicular pathway behind the pool, which cuts into the park. The wood footbridge that's ahead will lead you to a path along the south side of the lagoon to your starting point at the foot of Alberni or Georgia streets. If you continue along the seawall, you will emerge from the park into a high-rise residential neighborhood, the West End. You can walk back to Alberni Street along Denman Street, where there are places to stop for coffee, a drink, or ice cream. **Mum's Gelato,** at 855 Denman Street, serves delicious ice cream.

TIMING

The driving tour takes about an hour. You'll find parking near most of the sights in the park. Your biking time will depend on your speed, but with stops to see the sights, expect the ride to take several hours. It takes at least two hours to see the aquarium thoroughly. If you're going to walk the park and take in most of the sights, plan on spending the day. The seawall can get crowded on summer weekends, but inside the park is a network of peaceful, usually deserted, walking and cycling paths through old growth forest. Take a map—they're available at park concession stands—and don't go into the woods alone or after dusk.

Sights to See

㉓ **Deadman's Island.** This former burial ground for the local Salish people and the early settlers is a small naval training base called HMCS *Discovery.* The island is not open to the public.

㉖ **Lumbermen's Arch.** Made of logs, this archway, erected in 1947, is dedicated to the workers in Vancouver's first industry. Beside the arch is an asphalt path that leads back to Lost Lagoon and the Vancouver Aquarium.

↻ **Miniature Railway and Children's Farmyard.** A child-size steam train takes kids and adults on a ride through the woods. Next door there's a whole farmyard full of critters, including goats, rabbits, and guinea pigs. ✉ *Off Pipeline Rd.,* ☎ *604/257–8531.* ☞ *$2.50 for each.* ☉ *June–Sept., daily 11–4; Oct.–Dec. 4 and Jan. 4–Apr. 1, weekends 11–4 (weather permitting); Dec. 5–Dec. 12, daily 5–9; Dec. 13–Jan. 3, daily 2–9.*

㉔ **Nine O'Clock Gun.** This cannonlike apparatus by the water was installed in 1890 to alert fishermen to a curfew ending weekend fishing. Now it signals 9 o'clock every night.

㉗ **Prospect Point.** Cormorants build their seaweed nests along the cliff ledges here. The large black diving birds are distinguished by their long necks and beaks. When not nesting, they often perch atop floating logs or boulders. Another remarkable bird found along the park's shore is the beautiful great blue heron. Herons prey on fish. The oldest heron rookery in British Columbia is in the trees near the aquarium, where the birds like to horn in during feeding time for the whales.

Second Beach. In summer a draw is the 50-m pool, which has lifeguards and water slides. The shallow end fills up on hot days, but the lap-swimming end of the pool is usually deserted. Nearby is a sandy beach, a playground, and covered picnic sites.

Siwash Rock. Legend tells of a young Native American who, about to become a father, bathed persistently to wash his sins away so that his son could be born pure. For his devotion he was blessed by the gods and immortalized in the shape of Siwash Rock, just offshore. Two small rocks, said to be his wife and child, are on the cliff above the site.

Totem poles. Totem poles were not made in the Vancouver area. These, carved of cedar by the Kwakiutl and Haida peoples late in the 19th century, were brought to the park from the north coast of British Columbia. The carvings of animals, fish, birds, and mythological creatures are like family coats-of-arms or crests.

★ **Vancouver Aquarium Marine Science Centre.** The humid Amazon rainforest gallery here holds piranhas, tropical birds, and jungle vegetation. Other displays show the underwater life of coastal British Columbia, the Canadian arctic, and the tropics. Huge tanks (populated with orca and beluga whales, and playful sea otters) have large windows for underwater viewing. There are whale shows several times a day. A Pacific Canada Pavilion, built in 1999, looks at the aquatic life in the waters near Vancouver, and a demonstration salmon stream flows through Stanley Park from Burrard Inlet to the aquarium. ⊠ ☎ *604/ 659–3474.* 🖼 *$12.* ☉ *July–Labor Day, daily 9:30–7; Labor Day–June, daily 10–5:30.*

Granville Island

Granville Island was a sandbar until World War I, when the federal government dredged False Creek to provide access to the sawmills that lined the shore. The sludge from the creek was heaped onto the sandbar to create the island and to house much-needed industrial and logging-equipment plants. By the late 1960s many of the businesses that had once flourished on Granville Island had deteriorated. Buildings were rotted, rat-infested, and dangerous. In 1971 the government bought up leases from businesses that wanted to leave and developed an imaginative plan to refurbish the island with a public market, marine activities, and artisans' studios.

The small island's few residents live on houseboats. Most of the former industrial buildings and tin sheds have been retained but are painted in upbeat reds, yellows, and blues. Through a committee of community representatives, the government regulates the types of businesses on Granville Island. Most of the businesses permitted involve food, crafts, marine activities, and the arts.

Numbers in the text correspond to numbers in the margin and on the Granville Island map.

A Good Walk

To reach Granville Island on foot, make the 15-minute walk from downtown Vancouver to the south end of Hornby Street. Aquabuses (☎ *604/ 689–5858*) depart here and deliver passengers across False Creek to the Granville Island Public Market. False Creek Ferries (☎ *604/684– 7781*), which leave every five minutes from a dock behind the Van-

URBAN SAFARI

DURING WORLD WAR II the Canadian military set up watchtowers along Vancouver's Point Grey so soldiers could detect signs of a Japanese invasion. The lookouts called the alarm once, when they spotted a large, submerged object making its way into Burrard Inlet. Tension mounted, but Japanese subs rarely sport blow holes, so the innocent whale was left alone. You won't see many whales in Vancouver's harbor these days—they're across the way, off Vancouver Island—but in and near this city on the edge of a rain forest you do have a better chance of spotting wildlife than in almost any other urban area.

A good place to start is **Stanley Park** (☞ above), a 1,000-acre forest abutting the downtown core. Here cormorants nest in the cliffs under Prospect Point, blue herons stroll the public beaches, and outgoing (though hardly tame) raccoons and squirrels pose for tourist photos. Skunks and coyotes are more withdrawn but they also live here and, like the others, sometimes amble into the West End, a high-rise residential neighborhood bordering the park.

The 850-acre **George C. Reifel Migratory Bird Sanctuary** (✉ 5191 Robertson Rd., Delta, ☎ 604/946–6980 for directions), on Westham Island about an hour's drive south of Vancouver, is a stopping-off point for at least 270 species of migratory birds traveling along North America's Pacific Flyway. The sanctuary and the marshlands of nearby **Boundary Bay** host Canada geese, snow geese, and one of the largest populations of waterfowl to winter anywhere in Canada. Bird lovers won't want to miss these spots.

One species is the focus of the **Brackendale Eagle Reserve** (✉ Off Hwy. 99). About an hour's drive north of Vancouver, the reserve is 7 km (4 mi) north of Squamish in the town of Brackendale (follow signs from Highway 99). Every January since time immemorial, eagles (more than 1,800 in 1999) from all over North America have gathered here to feed on spawning salmon. Each January eagle-watchers attend the **Brackendale Eagle Festival,** sponsored by the Brackendale Art Gallery (✉ 41950 Government Rd., ☎ 604/898–3333), which started as simply a bird count and has since blossomed into a monthlong music, arts, and social event.

Less common, but all the more heart-stopping should you run into one on a trail, are the big mammals—the cougars, black bears, and other animals that once had the run of this territory. Most of the 3,000 or so cougars and 140,000 black bears in British Columbia avoid humans, but sightings have increased in recent years as urban development encroaches on their habitats. Cougars have been spotted in suburban North Vancouver, and in downtown Victoria (one, famously, at the Empress hotel and another in a basement suite near the Parliament buildings). From May through October in Whistler (☞ Chapter 5) it's not unusual to see bears near, or even in, the village, so it's important to follow a few rules. Don't leave food or garbage lying about. If you see a bear, don't approach it; back away slowly and speak in a calm voice. For more information about the bears of British Columbia contact the **Jennifer Jones Whistler Bear Foundation** (☎ 604/938–3570).

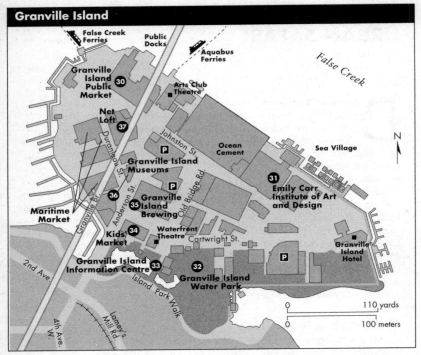

Granville Island

False Creek Ferries
Public Docks
Aquabus Ferries
False Creek
Granville Island Public Market ㉚
Arts Club Theatre
Net Loft ㊲
Durnleau St.
Johnston St.
Ocean Cement
Sea Village
Granville Island Museums
Emily Carr Institute of Art and Design ㉛
Granville Br.
Anderson St.
Old Bridge Rd.
Granville Island Brewing ㉟
㊱
Maritime Market
Waterfront Theatre
Cartwright St.
Kids' Market ㉞
Granville Island Hotel
Granville Island Information Centre ㉝
㉜
Granville Island Water Park
2nd Ave.
Island Park Walk
Lamey's Mill Rd.
4th Ave. W.
N

0 — 110 yards
0 — 100 meters

couver Aquatic Centre, are another option. Still another way to reach the island is to take a 20-minute ride on a Buslink (☎ 604/521–0400) bus. From Waterfront Station or stops on Granville Street take a False Creek South bus (No. 50) to the edge of the island. Or, from Granville and Broadway, catch Granville Island Bus 51 for direct service to Granville Island. Parking is free for one to three hours; paid parking is available in garages on the island.

Another way to travel is to hop the **Downtown Historic Railway** (604/665–3903) at Leg-in-Boot Square, near Sixth Avenue and Moberly Street (where pay parking is available) and ride the 1½-km (1-mi) line to the island. Part of an experiment to revive streetcar service around False Creek, the 1905 electric tram ran, at press time, only on summer weekend and holiday afternoons, but service is expected to expand, and possibly extend to Science World (☞ Yaletown and False Creek, *below*) by 2000.

A short walk from the bus, ferry, or tram stop is the **Granville Island Public Market** ㉚.

Walk south on Johnston Street to begin a clockwise loop tour of the island. Ocean Cement is one of the last of the island's industries; its lease does not expire until the year 2004. Next door is the **Emily Carr Institute of Art and Design** ㉛. Follow a walkway along the south side of the art school to Sea Village, one of the only houseboat communities in Vancouver. Take the boardwalk that starts at the houseboats and continues partway around the island.

Walk around the Granville Island Hotel, then turn right into Cartwright Street. This end of the island, home to an eclectic mix of craft galleries, studios, and workshops, is a fascinating place to watch artisans at work. You can see wooden boats being built at the Alder Bay Boat Company and watch printmakers in action at New Leaf Editions. The Federation of Canadian Artists Gallery and the Gallery of BC Ceramics both showcase local works. Also on Cartwright are the **Granville Island Water Park** ㉜ and the **Granville Island Information Centre** ㉝. A bit farther down the street is the **Kids' Market** ㉞. Adults can head for the microbrewery tour at **Granville Island Brewing** ㉟, across the street.

Cross Anderson Street and walk down Duranleau Street. On your left are the sea-oriented shops of the Maritime Market, and the fishing, train, and model boat displays at the **Granville Island Museums** ㊱. The last place to explore on Granville Island is the upscale **Net Loft** ㊲ shopping arcade. Once you have come full circle, you can either take the ferry back to downtown Vancouver or stay for dinner and catch a play at the Arts Club or the Waterfront Theatre (☞ Nightlife and the Arts, *below*).

TIMING

If your schedule is tight, you can tour Granville Island in three to four hours. If you're a shopping fanatic, you'll likely need a full day.

Sights to See

31 **Emily Carr Institute of Art and Design.** The institute's three main buildings—wooden structures formerly used for industrial purposes—were renovated in the 1970s. The **Charles H. Scott Gallery,** inside the front door to the right, hosts contemporary exhibitions in various media. ✉ *1399 Johnston St.,* ☎ *604/844–3811.* 🎫 *Free.* ⏲ *Weekdays noon–5, weekends 10–5.*

35 **Granville Island Brewing.** Tours of Canada's first modern microbrewery last about a half hour and include a souvenir glass and a taste of four different brews, including some that aren't on the market yet. Kids are welcome—they get a taste of root beer. ✉ *1441 Cartwright St.,* ☎ *604/687–2739.* 🎫 *$7.* ⏲ *Daily 9:30–7 (call for tour times).*

33 **Granville Island Information Centre.** You can pick up maps at the center, and find out about special events. Festivals, outdoor concerts, and dance performances often occur on the island. ✉ *1398 Cartwright St.,* ☎ *604/666–5784.* ⏲ *Daily 8–6.*

36 **Granville Island Museums.** Rods, reels, artwork, and a mounted salmon that at 97 pounds is the largest ever caught with a rod and reel are among the fishing artifacts at this facility. You can try your luck against the large game fish that inhabit the video fish-fighting simulator. The collection of the Model Ships Museum includes exquisitely detailed early 20th-century vessels. One of the museum's highlights is a cast-bronze replica of the HMS *Hood,* the British Royal Navy ship that dealt the final blows that sunk the German warship the *Bismarck* in 1941. Upstairs, the Model Train Museum lays claim to the world's largest toy train exhibit. Shops in the surrounding Maritime Market are all geared to the sea. ✉ *1502 Duranleau St.,* ☎ *604/683–1939.* 🎫 *$3 for all three museums.* ⏲ *June–Aug., daily 10–5:30; Sept.–May, Tues.–Sun. 10–5:30.*

★ 30 **Granville Island Public Market.** Because no chain stores are allowed in this 50,000-square-ft building, each outlet is unique. Most sell high-quality merchandise. You can pick up a snack, espresso, or fixings for lunch on the wharf, and year-round you'll see crafts, exotic foods, and mounds of locally grown produce. There's plenty of outdoor seating on the water side of the market. ✉ *1669 Johnston St.,* ☎ *604/666–6477.* ⏲ *Daily 9–6.*

32 **Granville Island Water Park.** This kids' paradise has slides, sprinklers, and a fire hydrant made for children to shower one another. ✉ *1318*

Cartwright St., ☎ *604/257–8195.* ✉ *Free.* ⊘ *Late May–early Sept., daily 10–6.*

🐸 ㉞ **Kids' Market.** Yet another slice of kids' heaven on Granville Island, the Kids' Market has two floors of small shops that sell toys, arts-and-crafts materials, dolls, records and tapes, chemistry sets, and other items. ✉ *1496 Cartwright St.,* ☎ *604/689–8447.* ⊘ *Daily 10–6.*

㊲ **Net Loft.** In this blue and red building is a collection of high-quality boutiques, including a bookstore, a crafts store–gallery, a kitchenware shop, a postcard shop, a custom-made hat shop, a handmade paper store, a British Columbian native art gallery, and a café. ✉ *1661 Johnston St., across from Public Market.* ⊘ *Daily 10–6.*

Kitsilano

The beachfront district of Kitsilano (popularly known as Kits), south of downtown Vancouver, is among the trendiest Canadian neighborhoods. Originally inhabited by the Squamish people, whose chief, Khahtsahlanough, gave the area its name, Kitsilano began to attract day-trippers from Vancouver in the early part of this century. Some stayed and built lavish waterfront mansions. Others built simpler Craftsman-style houses farther up the slope. After a period of decline in the mid-20th century, Kits, which contains many restored wood-frame Craftsman houses, is once again chic.

Kitsilano is home to three museums, some fashionable shops, and popular pubs and cafés. Kits has hidden treasures, too: rare boats moored at Heritage Harbour, stately mansions on forested lots, and, all along the waterfront, quiet coves and shady paths within a stone's throw of Canada's liveliest beach.

Numbers in the text correspond to numbers in the margin and on the Greater Vancouver map.

A Good Walk

Vanier Park, the grassy beachside setting for three museums and the best kite-flying venue in Vancouver, is the logical gateway to Kits. The most enjoyable way to get here is by False Creek Ferries (☎ 604/684–7781), from Granville Island or behind the Vancouver Aquatic Centre on Beach Avenue. The ferries dock at Heritage Harbour behind the Vancouver Maritime Museum. You can also walk or cycle about 1 km (½ mi) along the waterfront pathway from Granville Island (leave the island by Anderson Street and keep to your right along the waterfront). If you prefer to come by road, drive over the Burrard Street Bridge, turn right at Chestnut Street, and park in either of the museum parking lots, or take Bus 2 or 22 from downtown, get off at Cypress Street and Cornwall Avenue, and walk down to the park.

Vancouver Museum ㊴, which showcases the city's natural and cultural history, shares a building with the **Pacific Space Centre** ㊳, a high-tech museum focusing on outer space. To the west and toward the water is the **Vancouver Maritime Museum** ㊵, which traces the maritime history of the West Coast. Each museum has hands-on exhibits that appeal to kids.

Behind the Maritime Museum, where you'll dock if you come in by ferry, is Heritage Harbour, home to a rotating series of boats of historical interest, including *BCP 45*, the picturesque fishing boat that used to appear on Canada's five-dollar bill. In summer the big tent set up in Vanier Park is the venue for the Bard on the Beach Shakespeare series (☞ Nightlife and the Arts, *below*).

West of the Maritime Museum is a quiet, grassy beach. A wooden staircase leads from the beach up to a paved walkway. Take a moment to look at the huge **Kwakiutl totem pole** in front of the museum, and then follow the walkway west to popular Kitsilano Beach. Ahead is **Point Grey.** Across the water you can see Stanley Park, and behind you is Vancouver's downtown core. Continue past the pool, keep to the water, and you'll enter a shady pathway lined with blackberry bushes running behind the **Kitsilano Yacht Club.** Soon the lane opens up to a viewpoint and gives access to another sandy cove.

About ½ km (¼ mi) from the yacht club, the path ends at another wooden staircase. This leads up to a viewpoint and a park on Point Grey Road. Across the street from the top of the staircase is an Edwardian era, **wood-turreted mansion** (⊠ 2590 Point Grey Rd.) built by a member of Kitsilano's early elite. Double back the way you came—heading east toward Kits Beach—but this time follow Point Grey Road for a look at the front of the waterfront homes you could see from the beach path. The **Logan House** (⊠ 2530 Point Grey Rd.), built in 1909, is an ivory-colored Edwardian dream home with a 180-degree curved balcony.

Follow Point Grey Road as it curves to the right, and cross Cornwall Avenue at the lights at Balsam Street. Turn left on First Avenue and walk two blocks to Yew Street, where in summer you'll find the biggest concentration of sidewalk pubs and cafés in Greater Vancouver. Alternatively, you can hike up the hill to 4th Avenue, once the heart of the hippie district, and explore the shops between Maple and Arbutus streets. You can catch a bus back to downtown Vancouver on Cornwall or 4th Avenue, or cut across Kits Beach Park back to Vanier Park.

TIMING

The walk alone will take about an hour and a half. Add three hours to see the Pacific Space Centre and an hour for each of the other museums. With time out for shopping or swimming, a visit to Kitsilano could easily fill a whole day.

Sights to See

🐚 **Kitsilano Beach.** At Kits Beach (☞ Outdoor Activities and Sports, *below*) are picnic sites, a playground, Vancouver's biggest outdoor pool, and some fine people-watching. Inland from the pool, the Kitsilano Showboat hosts free performances, mostly of the children's dancing variety, during summer. ⊠ *Off Cornwall Ave.,* ☎ *604/738–8535 (summer only).*

🐚 ③⑧ **Pacific Space Centre.** The interactive exhibits and high-tech learning systems at this museum include a kinetic space-ride simulator and a theater showcasing Canada's achievements in space. During the day catch the astronomy show at the **H.R. MacMillan Star Theatre.** When the sky is clear, the half-meter telescope at the **Gordon MacMillan Southam Observatory** (☎ 604/738–2855) is focused on whatever stars or planets are worth watching that night. Admission to the observatory is free, and it's open in the evening, weather permitting (call for hours). ⊠ *Vanier Park, 1100 Chestnut St.,* ☎ *604/738–7827.* 🎫 *$12.* ☼ *July–Aug., daily 10–5; Sept.–June, Tues.–Sun. 10–5.*

🐚 ④⓪ **Vancouver Maritime Museum.** Fully half the museum has been turned over to kids, with touchable displays that provide a chance to drive a tug, build an underwater robot, or dress up as a seafarer. Toddlers and school-age children will appreciate the hands-on displays in Pirates' Cove and the Children's Maritime Discovery Centre. The museum also has an extensive collection of model ships and is the last moorage for the RCMP schooner the *St. Roch,* the first ship to sail in both directions through the treacherous Northwest Passage. Historic boats are moored at **Heritage Harbour,** behind the museum, and a huge Kwak-

iutl totem pole stands out front. ⊠ *Vanier Park, 1905 Ogden Ave.,
north end of Cypress St.,* ☎ *604/257–8300.* ▣ *Museum $6, Heritage
Harbour free.* ☉ *Mid-May–Aug., daily 10–5; Sept.–mid-May, Tues.–
Sat. 10–5; Sun. noon–5.*

🐾 ㉟ **Vancouver Museum.** Life-size replicas of a trading post, a Victorian parlor, and an 1897 Canadian Pacific Railway passenger car, as well as a
real dugout canoe, are the highlights at this museum whose exhibits
focus on the city's natural history, its early history, and on First Nations art and culture. Plans are in place for a major expansion to be
completed by 2001. ⊠ *Vanier Park, 1100 Chestnut St.,* ☎ *604/736–
4431.* ▣ *$8.* ☉ *July–Aug., daily 10–5; Sept.–June, Tues.–Sun. 10–5.*

Greater Vancouver

Some of Vancouver's best gardens, natural sights, and museums, including the renowned Museum of Anthropology, are south of downtown, on the campus of the University of British Columbia and in the
city's southern residential districts. Individual attractions are easily
reached by Buslink buses (☎ 604/521–0400), but you'll need a car to
see them all comfortably in a day.

*Numbers in the text correspond to numbers in the margin and on the
Greater Vancouver map.*

A Good Drive

From downtown Vancouver, cross the **Burrard Street Bridge** and follow the marked scenic route. This will take you along Cornwall Avenue, which becomes Point Grey Road and follows the waterfront to
Alma Street. The little wooden structure at the corner of Point Grey
Road and Alma Street is the **Hastings Mill Museum,** Vancouver's first
retail shop and now a museum.

The scenic route continues south on Alma Street and then west (to the
right) on 4th Avenue. This flows into **Northwest Marine Drive,** which
winds past Jericho, Locarno, and Spanish Banks beaches and up to the
University of British Columbia. At the university are the **Museum of
Anthropology** ㊶, which houses one of the world's best collections of
Westcoast First Nations artifacts, and **Nitobe Memorial Garden** ㊷, a
Japanese-style strolling garden. Three kilometers (2 miles) farther
along Marine Drive is the **University of British Columbia Botanical
Garden.**

For more gardens, follow Marine Drive through the university grounds
and take the left fork onto 41st Avenue. Turn left again onto Oak Street
to reach the entrance of the **VanDusen Botanical Garden** ㊸ on your left.
The complex is planted with an English-style maze, water gardens, herb
gardens, and more. Return to 41st Avenue, continue farther east, and
then turn left on Cambie Street to reach **Queen Elizabeth Park** ㊹,
which overlooks the city. To get back downtown, continue north on
Cambie and over the Cambie Street Bridge.

TIMING

Except during rush hour, it takes about 30 minutes to drive from
downtown to the University of British Columbia. You should add another 30 to 45 minutes' driving time for the rest of the tour, and about
two hours to visit each of the main attractions.

Sights to See

Hastings Mill Museum Vancouver's first store was built in 1865 at the
foot of Dunlevy Street in Gastown and moved to this seaside spot in
1930. The only building to survive the 1886 Great Fire, the site is a
museum, with displays of native artifacts and pioneer household goods.

⊠ *1575 Alma Rd.,* ☎ *604/734–1212.* 🖭 *Admission by donation.* ☉
June–mid-Sept., daily 11–4; mid-Sept.–May, weekends 1–4.

★ ㊶ **Museum of Anthropology.** Arthur Erickson designed the award-winning cliff-top structure that houses the Museum of Anthropology
(MOA). Vancouver's most spectacular museum, the MOA focuses on
the arts of Pacific Northwest First Nations and aboriginal peoples
from around the world, among them the late Bill Reid, one of Canada's
most respected Haida carvers. Reid's *The Raven and the First Men,* a
highlight of the museum's collection, took five carvers more than three
years to complete. In the Great Hall are large and dramatic totem poles,
ceremonial archways, and dugout canoes—all adorned with carvings
of frogs, eagles, ravens, bears, and salmon. You'll also find exquisite
carvings of gold, silver, and argillite (a black stone found in the Queen
Charlotte Islands), as well as masks, tools, and textiles from many other
cultures. The ceramics wing contains several hundred pieces from
15th- to 19th-century Europe. To reach the museum by transit, take
a UBC Bus 4 or UBC Bus 10 from Granville Street downtown to the
university loop, which is a 10-minute walk from the museum. ⊠ *University of British Columbia, 6393 N.W. Marine Dr.,* ☎ *604/822–
3825.* 🖭 *$6, free Tues. 5–9.* ☉ *Memorial Day–Labor Day, Tues. 10–
9, Mon. and Wed.–Sun. 10–5; Labor Day–Memorial Day, Tues. 11–
9, Wed.–Sun. 11–5.*

㊷ **Nitobe Memorial Garden.** This 2½-acre garden is considered one of the
most authentic Japanese tea and strolling gardens outside Japan. The
circular path around the park symbolizes the cycle of life and provides
a tranquil view from every direction. In April and May cherry blossoms are the highlight, and in June the irises are magnificent. ⊠ *University of British Columbia, 1903 West Mall,* ☎ *604/822–9666.* 🖭
Mid-Mar.–mid-Oct. $2.50; mid-Oct.–mid-Mar. free. ☉ *Mid-Mar.–
mid-Oct., daily 10–6; mid-Oct.–mid-Mar., weekdays 10–2:30.*

㊹ **Queen Elizabeth Park.** Besides views of downtown, the park has lavish sunken gardens brimming with roses and other flowers, an abun-
dance of grassy picnicking spots, and illuminated fountains. Other park
facilities include 20 tennis courts, pitch and putt, and a restaurant. In
the **Bloedel Conservatory** you can see tropical and desert plants and
60 species of free-flying tropical birds in a glass geodesic dome. To reach
the park by public transportation, take a Cambie Bus 15 from the corner of Robson and Burrard Streets downtown to 33rd Avenue. ⊠
Cambie St. and 33rd Ave., ☎ *604/257–8570.* 🖭 *Conservatory $3.50.*
☉ *Apr.–Sept., weekdays 9–8, weekends 10–9; Oct.–Mar., daily 10–5.*

University of British Columbia Botanical Garden. Temperate plants—
10,000 trees, shrubs, and flowers from around the world—thrive on
this 70-acre site on the university campus. ⊠ *6804 S.W. Marine Dr.,*
☎ *604/822–9666.* 🖭 *Summer $4.50, winter free.* ☉ *Mid-Mar.–mid-
Oct., daily 10–6; mid-Oct.–mid-Mar., daily 10–2:30.*

㊸ **VanDusen Botanical Garden.** On what was a 55-acre golf course grows
one of the largest collections of ornamental plants in Canada. Displays
from every continent include an Elizabethan maze, five lakes, and a
Sino-Himalayan garden. There's also a shop, a library, and a restaurant (☎ 604/261–0011) on the grounds. The gardens are wheelchair
accessible. An Oak Bus 17 will get you here from downtown. Queen
Elizabeth Park is a ½-mi walk away, on 37th Avenue. ⊠ *5251 Oak
St., at 37th Ave.,* ☎ *604/878–9274.* 🖭 *$6; ½ price Oct.–Mar.* ☉ *June–
mid-Aug., daily 10–9; call for off-season hrs.*

Yaletown and False Creek

In 1985 and 1986 the provincial government cleared up a derelict industrial site on the north shore of False Creek, built a world's fair, and invited the world. Twenty million people showed up at Expo '86. Now the site of the fair has become one of the largest urban redevelopment projects in North America, creating—and, in some cases, reclaiming—a whole new downtown district that Vancouverites themselves are only beginning to discover.

Tucked in among the forest of green-glass, high-rise condo towers is the old warehouse district of Yaletown. First settled by railroad workers who had followed the newly laid tracks down from the town of Yale in the Fraser Canyon, Yaletown in the 1880s and 1890s was probably the most lawless place in Canada. The Royal Canadian Mounted Police complained it was too far through the forest for them to police it. Yaletown is now one of the city's poshest neighborhoods, and the Victorian brick loading docks have become terraces for cappuccino bars. The area, which also holds restaurants, a brew pub, and galleries that sell art and avant-garde home decor, makes the most of its waterfront location, with a seaside walk and cycle path that runs completely around the shore of False Creek.

Numbers in the text correspond to numbers in the margin and on the Greater Vancouver map.

A Good Walk

Start at **Library Square** ㊺ at Homer and Georgia streets. Leave by the Robson Street (east) exit, cross Robson, and continue south on Hamilton Street. On your right you'll see a row of Victorian frame houses built between 1895 and 1900, all painted in candy-box colors and looking completely out of place among the surrounding high-rises. In 1995 these historic homes were plucked from the West End and moved here to protect them from the onslaught of development.

Cross Smithe Street, and continue down Mainland Street to Nelson Street—you're now in the heart of Yaletown. Stop for a coffee at one of Yaletown's loading-dock cafés or poke around the shops on Hamilton and Homer streets.

From the foot of Mainland Street, turn left on Davie Street and cross Pacific Boulevard. This takes you to the **Roundhouse.** Continue to the **waterfront** at the foot of Davie. Here you'll find an intriguing iron and concrete sculpture, with panels displaying archival images of events around False Creek. A few minutes' walk along the waterfront to your right is the Yaletown dock for Aquabus Ferries (☎ 604/689–5858), where you can catch a boat to Granville Island or Science World.

Turn left and follow the waterfront walkway. After about 1 km (½ mi) (possibly with some detours around construction sites), you'll reach the **Plaza of Nations,** the heart of the old Expo site, with pubs and cafés. Cross the plaza toward Pacific Boulevard and take the pedestrian overpass to B.C. Place Stadium. Walk around to Gate A, where you'll find the **B.C. Sports Hall of Fame and Museum** ㊻. To your left as you leave the museum you'll see the Terry Fox Memorial. This archway at the foot of Robson Street was built in honor of Terry Fox (1958–1981), a local student whose cross-Canada run raised millions for cancer research. From here you can walk two blocks north on Beatty Street and take the SkyTrain one stop east or retrace your steps to the waterfront and walk another 1 km (½ mi) east to **Science World** ㊼, a hands-on museum. From Science World, the SkyTrain will take you back downtown, or you can catch a ferry back to Yaletown or to other stops on False Creek.

TIMING

It takes about 1½ hours to walk around all the sights. Allow about an hour for the B.C. Sports Hall of Fame and museum and two hours for Science World. Shoppers may not make it past Yaletown.

Sights to See

⑯ B.C. Sports Hall of Fame and Museum. Inside the B.C. Place Stadium complex, this museum celebrates the province's sports achievers. Visitors can test their own sprinting, rowing, climbing, and throwing prowess in the high-tech participation gallery. ⊠ *B.C. Place, 777 Pacific Blvd. S, Gate A,* ☎ *604/687–5520.* ⊠ *$6.* ☉ *Daily 10–5.*

⑮ Library Square. The spiraling library building, open plazas, waterfall, and shaded atriums of Library Square, which was completed in the mid-1990s, were built to evoke images of the Colosseum in Rome. A high-tech library fills the core of the structure. The outer edge of the spiral houses boutiques, coffeehouses, and a fine book shop. ⊠ *350 W. Georgia St.,* ☎ *604/331–3600.* ☉ *Mon.–Thurs. 10–8, Fri.–Sat. 10–5, Sun. hrs vary.*

Roundhouse. Originally the turnaround point for transcontinental trains reaching the end of the line at Vancouver, this round brick structure was built in 1888. A spirited local campaign helped create a home here for **Engine 374,** which pulled the first passenger train into Vancouver on May 24, 1887. The Roundhouse, a community center, hosts festivals and exhibitions. ⊠ *181 Roundhouse Mews,* ☎ *604/713–1800.* ⊠ *Free; admission may be charged to some events.* ☉ *Weekdays 9 AM–10 PM, weekends 9–5.*

⑰ Science World. In a gigantic shiny dome built over an Omnimax theatre, this hands-on museum contains interactive exhibits. The special Search Gallery is aimed at younger children, as are the fun-filled demonstrations given in Center Stage. The 3-D laser theater appeals to older kids. ⊠ *1455 Quebec St.,* ☎ *604/268–6363.* ⊠ *Science World $11.25, Omnimax $9.75, combination ticket $14.50.* ☉ *July–Aug., daily 10–6; Sept.–June, weekdays 10–5, weekends and holidays 10–6.*

North Vancouver

The mountains that form a stunning backdrop to Vancouver lie in the district of North Vancouver, a bridge or SeaBus ride away on the North Shore of Burrard Inlet. Although the area is part suburb, the mountainous terrain has kept large parts of North Vancouver forested. This is where Vancouverites and visitors go for easily accessible hiking, skiing, and views of the city lights.

Numbers in the text correspond to numbers in the margin and on the Greater Vancouver map.

A Good Drive

From downtown, drive west down Georgia Street to Stanley Park and across the Lions Gate Bridge to North Vancouver. Stay in the right lane, take the North Vancouver exit, then turn left onto Capilano Road. About two miles up Capilano Road is the **Capilano Suspension Bridge and Park** ⑱. Another mile up Capilano Road, in the Capilano Regional Park, is the **Capilano Salmon Hatchery** ⑲. Continuing north, Capilano Road becomes Nancy Greene Way, which ends at the base of **Grouse Mountain** ㊿. From here, a cable car to the summit gives you great city views.

You can also take the SeaBus from Waterfront Station to Lonsdale Quay and then catch a Grouse Mountain Bus 236. This stops at the Capilano Suspension Bridge and near the Salmon Hatchery on its way up to the base of the Grouse Mountain Skyride.

TIMING

You'll need a half day to see the sights, a full day if you want to hike at Grouse Mountain or Capilano Park. You'll save time if you avoid crossing the Lions Gate Bridge during rush hours (from 7 to 9 AM and 3 to 6 PM).

Sights to See

⚙ ㊾ **Capilano Salmon Hatchery.** The hatchery has viewing areas and exhibits about the life cycle of the salmon. The best time of year to see the salmon run is between July and November. The surrounding park has hiking trails and footbridges over the river where it cuts through a dramatic gorge. ⊠ *Capilano Regional Park, 4500 Capilano Park Rd., North Vancouver,* ☎ *604/666–1790.* ⌨ *Free.* ☉ *June–Aug., daily 8–8; call for off-season hrs.*

⚙ ㊽ **Capilano Suspension Bridge and Park.** At Vancouver's oldest tourist attraction (the original bridge was built in 1889), you can get a taste of the mountains and test your mettle on the swaying, 450-ft cedar-plank suspension bridge that hangs 230 ft above the rushing Capilano River. The park also has viewing decks, nature trails, a totem park and carving center, history and forestry exhibits, a gift shop, and a restaurant. Free guided tours and nature walks run throughout the day. ⊠ *3735 Capilano Rd., North Vancouver,* ☎ *604/985–7474.* ⌨ *$10.* ☉ *Apr.–Oct., daily 8:30–dusk; Nov.–Mar., daily 9–5.*

★ ⚙ ㊿ **Grouse Mountain.** The Skyride to the top is a great way to take in city, sea, and mountain vistas, and there's plenty to do when you arrive. A Skyride ticket includes a half-hour video presentation at the Theatre in the Sky. Other mountaintop activities include loggers' sports shows, chairlift rides, walking tours, hiking and, in winter, ice skating, snow-shoeing, skiing, and Sno-Cat-drawn sleigh rides. The mountaintop, which has a café, a pub, and a restaurant, is a popular festival venue, with occasional jazz and Shakespeare performances during the summer. The híwus Feast House (☎ 604/980–9311) presents a traditional Coast Salish feast and entertainment in a mountaintop longhouse. It's open May–October, and reservations are essential. ⊠ *6400 Nancy Greene Way, North Vancouver,* ☎ *604/984–0661.* ⌨ *Skyride and theater $16.95.* ☉ *Daily 9 AM–10 PM.*

OFF THE
BEATEN PATH

LYNN CANYON PARK – With a steep canyon landscape, a temperate rain forest complete with waterfalls, and a suspension bridge 165 ft above raging Lynn Creek, this park provides thrills to go with its scenic views. In the summer, guided walks depart from the Ecology Centre, which distributes maps of area hiking trails and has information about the flora and fauna. To get to the park, take the Lions Gate Bridge and Capilano Road, go east on Highway 1, take the Lynn Valley Road exit, and follow the signs. You can also take the SeaBus to Lonsdale Quay and Westlynn Bus 229 to the corner of Peters and Duval streets. ⊠ *3663 Park Rd., North Vancouver,* ☎ *604/981–3103.* ⌨ *Ecology Centre by donation; suspension bridge free.* ☉ *Apr.–Sept., daily 10–5; Oct.–Mar., weekdays 10–5, weekends noon–4.*

DINING

Vancouver dining is fairly informal. Casual but neat dress is appropriate everywhere except a few expensive restaurants that require men to wear a jacket and tie (indicated in the text). Smoking is prohibited by law in all Vancouver restaurants. A 15% tip is expected. A 10% liquor tax is charged on wine, beer, and spirits. Some restaurants build this into the price of the beverage, but others add it to the bill. *See* the Downtown Vancouver Dining map to locate downtown restaurants and the Greater Vancouver Dining map to locate restaurants in Kitsilano, Granville Island, and other neighborhoods away from downtown.

CATEGORY	COST*
$$$$	over C$40
$$$	C$30–C$40
$$	C$20–C$30
$	under C$20

per person, for a three-course meal, excluding drinks, service, and sales tax

Downtown Vancouver

Cafés

$–$$ ✕ **Bread Garden Bakery, Café & Espresso Bar.** Salads, quiches, elaborate cakes and pies, giant muffins, and fine cappuccinos draw a steady stream of hungry locals to the five branches of this growing, Vancouver-based chain (☞ Greater Vancouver, *below*). All five locations are open six to midnight, and the Yaletown outlet shares space with Milestones, a popular burger bar. ⊠ *812 Bute St.,* ☎ *604/688–3213;* ⊠ *1040 Denman St.,* ☎ *604/685–2996;* ⊠ *1109 Hamilton St.,* ☎ *604/ 689–9500. AE, DC, MC, V.*

Chinese

$$–$$$$ ✕ **Imperial Chinese Seafood.** The two-story floor-to-ceiling windows
★ at this Cantonese restaurant in the Art Deco Marine Building have stupendous views of Stanley Park and the North Shore mountains across Coal Harbour. Any dish with lobster, crab, or shrimp from the live tanks is recommended, as is the dim sum, served from 11 AM to 2:30 PM. ⊠ *355 Burrard St.,* ☎ *604/688–8191. Reservations essential. AE, DC, MC, V.*

$$–$$$$ ✕ **Kirin Mandarin Restaurant.** This upscale restaurant, just two blocks from most of the major downtown hotels, offers a range of northern Chinese cuisines. Dishes include Shanghai-style smoked eel, Peking duck, and Szechuan hot-and-spicy scallops. A second location at Cambie Street and 12th Avenue focuses on milder Cantonese seafood creations. Kirin has a Richmond location as well. ⊠ *102–1166 Alberni St.,* ☎ *604/ 682–8833. Reservations essential. AE, DC, V.*

$ ✕ **Hon's Wun-Tun House.** Mr. Hon has been keeping Vancouver residents in Chinese comfort food since the 1970s. The best bets on the 300-item menu (nothing is over $10) are the pot stickers, the wonton and noodle dishes, and anything with barbecued beef. The shiny new Robson Street outlet has a separate kitchen for vegetarians and an army of fast-moving waitresses keeping your tea topped up. The original Keefer Street location is in the heart of Chinatown. ⊠ *1339 Robson St.,* ☎ *604/685–0871;* ⊠ *268 Keefer St.,* ☎ *604/688–0871. Reservations not accepted. MC, V.*

Contemporary

$$$–$$$$ ✕ **Chartwell.** Named after Sir Winston Churchill's country home, a painting of which hangs over the green marble fireplace, the flagship dining room at the Four Seasons hotel (☞ Lodging, *below*), with its rich wood paneling and deep leather chairs, is the city's top spot for a power

Downtown Vancouver Dining

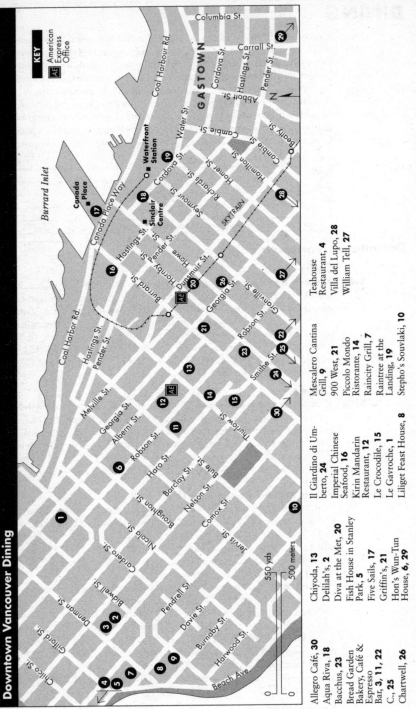

KEY

AE American Express Office

Burrard Inlet

GASTOWN

SKYTRAIN

Allegro Café, **30**
Aqua Riva, **18**
Bacchus, **23**
Bread Garden
Bakery, Café &
Espresso
Bar, **3, 11, 22**
C., **25**
Chartwell, **26**

Chiyoda, **13**
Delilah's, **2**
Diva at the Met, **20**
Fish House in Stanley
Park, **5**
Five Sails, **17**
Griffin's, **21**
Hon's Wun-Tun
House, **6, 29**

Il Giardino di Um-
berto, **24**
Imperial Chinese
Seafood, **16**
Kirin Mandarin
Restaurant, **12**
Le Crocodile, **15**
Le Gavroche, **1**
Liliget Feast House, **8**

Mescalero Cantina
Grill, **9**
900 West, **21**
Piccolo Mondo
Ristorante, **14**
Raincity Grill, **7**
Raintree at the
Landing, **19**
Stepho's Souvlaki, **10**

Teahouse
Restaurant, **4**
Villa del Lupo, **28**
William Tell, **27**

lunch. Menu highlights include a braised Salt Spring Island lamb shoulder served with truffled flageolet cassoulet and grilled salmon with smoked celery root and barley risotto. Men will feel more comfortable in jackets. ✉ *791 W. Georgia St.,* ☎ *604/689–9333. Reservations essential. AE, DC, MC, V. No lunch Sat.*

$$$–$$$$ ✕ **Diva at the Met.** At this multitiered restaurant at the Metropolitan Hotel (☞ Lodging, *below*) the presentation of the innovative contemporary cuisine is as appealing as the modern art deco–style decor. The menu changes seasonally, but top creations from the open kitchen have included smoked Alaska black cod and porcini-crusted veal loin steak. The after-theater crowd heads here for late-evening snacks and desserts: prawn tempura, vegetable chips, fresh sorbet, and Stilton cheesecake are served until midnight. The creative breakfasts and weekend brunches are also popular. ✉ *645 Howe St.,* ☎ *604/602–7788. AE, DC, MC, V.*

$$$–$$$$ ✕ **Five Sails.** The special-occasion restaurant at the Pan Pacific Hotel (☞ Lodging, *below*) commands a sweeping view of Canada Place, Lions Gate Bridge, and the lights of the North Shore. The broad-reaching, seasonally changing menu emphasizes fresh fish and seafood and takes its inspiration from all around the Pacific Rim. Highlights have included ginger marinated salmon, ahi tuna with foie gras, and Dover sole with Portobello mushrooms. ✉ *Pan Pacific Hotel, 300–999 Canada Pl.,* ☎ *604/891–2892 or 604/662–8111. AE, DC, MC, V. No lunch.*

$$$–$$$$ ✕ **900 West.** Half of this lofty, elegant room in the Hotel Vancouver (☞ Lodging, *below*) is the city's most fashionable (to be fair, its only) wine bar. The other half is an elegant dining room serving innovative contemporary cuisine. Using European techniques, fresh, seasonal British Columbia produce, and ideas from around the globe, Chef Dino Renaerts's creations are creative, sometimes complex, and very West Coast. The evolving menu has included roasted lobster and veal medallions with root vegetable gratin and sea urchin sabayon. An extensive wine list includes fifty-five varieties available by the glass. ✉ *900 West Georgia St.,* ☎ *604/669–9378. AE, D, DC, MC, V. No lunch weekends.*

$$–$$$$ ✕ **Raintree at the Landing.** In a beautifully renovated historic building in Gastown, Vancouver's first Pacific Northwest restaurant has waterfront views, fireplaces, a local wine list, and cuisine based on fresh, often organic, regional ingredients. The seasonal menus and daily specials feature innovative treatments of such local bounty as Salt Spring Island lamb and Fraser Valley rabbit, as well as luxurious soups, breads baked in-house, and at least three vegetarian options. A favorite is the Pacific Northwest salmon bounty, featuring several varieties of smoked salmon. The set menus are a good value, offering three courses for less than $30. ✉ *375 Water St.,* ☎ *604/688–5570. Reservations essential. AE, DC, MC, V.*

$$–$$$ ✕ **Aqua Riva.** This lofty, lively modern room just yards from the Canada Place cruise ship terminal affords striking views over the harbor and the North Shore mountains. Food from the wood-fired oven, rotisserie, and grill include thin-crust pizzas with innovative toppings, grilled salmon, spit-roasted chicken, and a good selection of pastas, salads, and sandwiches. There's a long microbrewery beer and martini list, too. ✉ *200 Granville St.,* ☎ *604/683–5599. Reservations essential. AE, D, DC, MC, V.*

$$–$$$ ✕ **Delilah's.** Cherubs dance on the ceiling, candles flicker on the tables, and martini glasses clink during toasts at this popular restaurant. The West Coast Continental cuisine prepared by chef Peg Montgomery is innovative and beautifully presented. Her menu, which changes seasonally, is divided into two- or five-course prix-fixe dinners. Try the pancetta, pine nut, Asiago, and mozzarella fritters with sun-dried tomato aioli and the grilled swordfish with blueberry-lemon compote if they're being served. ⊠ *1789 Comox St.,* ☎ *604/687–3424. AE, DC, MC, V. No lunch.*

$$–$$$ ✕ **Griffin's.** Squash-yellow walls, bold black and white tiles, an open kitchen, and splashy food art keep things lively at this high-energy Hotel Vancouver bistro. The Pacific Northwest buffets—for breakfast, lunch, evening appetizers, and dessert—are the main attractions here. An à la carte menu features burgers, pizza, pasta, and seafood. A traditional afternoon tea, with a pastry buffet, is served from 2:30 to 4:30 daily. ⊠ *900 W. Georgia St.,* ☎ *604/662–1900. AE, D, DC, MC, V.*

$$–$$$ ✕ **Raincity Grill.** This West End hot spot across the street from English Bay is a neighborhood favorite. The sophisticated candlelighted room and views of English Bay play second fiddle to a creative menu that highlights the regional seafood, meats, and produce. Grilled romaine spears are used in the Caesar salad, giving it a delightful smoky flavor. Varying preparations of salmon and duck are usually available, as is at least one vegetarian selection. The exclusively Pacific Northwest wine list offers about 100 choices by the glass. ⊠ *1193 Denman St.,* ☎ *604/ 685–7337. AE, DC, MC, V.*

Continental

$$$–$$$$ ✕ **William Tell.** Silver service plates, embossed linen napkins, and a silver vase on each table set a tone of Swiss luxury at this establishment in the Georgian Court Hotel. Chef Todd Konrad prepares excellent sautéed veal sweetbreads with red-onion marmalade and marsala sauce and Swiss dishes like cheese fondue and thinly sliced veal with mushrooms in a light white-wine sauce. The bar-and-bistro area caters to a more casual crowd than the main restaurant. On Sunday night there's an all-you-can-eat buffet. ⊠ *765 Beatty St.,* ☎ *604/688–3504. Reservations essential. AE, DC, MC, V. Restaurant closed Mon. Lunch served in the bistro section only.*

$$$ ✕ **Teahouse Restaurant.** The former officers' mess in Stanley Park is perfectly poised for watching sunsets over the water, especially if you're in the glassed-in wing, which resembles a conservatory. In summer you can dine on the patio. The West Coast Continental menu includes roasted pear salad, morel-stuffed chicken, and rack of lamb with Dijon cream. ⊠ *7501 Stanley Park Dr., Ferguson Point,* ☎ *604/669–3281. Reservations essential. AE, MC, V.*

Eclectic

$$$–$$$$ ✕ **Mescalero Cantina Grill.** On weekends Mescalero becomes party central, but weekdays are more subdued. Tapas, many with European and Asian Pacific influences, are the main attraction—mussels with sun-dried tomato cream; roast pear puff pastry with Stilton and garlic pesto; and braised rabbit ravioli—but dinner selections, such as salmon fillet on spinach linguine, and grilled pork chops with sweet potato–pear gnocchi, are equally creative. Sunday brunch always draws a crowd. ⊠ *1215 Bidwell St.,* ☎ *604/669–2399. AE, DC, MC, V.*

French

$$$–$$$$ ✕ **Le Crocodile.** Chef and owner Michel Jacob specializes in traditional Alsatian food at this roomy and elegant location on Smithe Street off Burrard. Favorite dishes, many of which also appear at nicer prices at lunch, include caramel–sweet onion tart, Dover sole, calf's liver with garlic spinach butter, and venison with chanterelle mushroom sauce. ⊠ *100–909 Burrard St.,* ☎ *604/669–4298. Reservations essential. AE, DC, MC, V. Closed Sun. No lunch Sat.*

$$$–$$$$ ✕ **Le Gavroche.** Classic French cuisine receives contemporary accents but remains solidly authentic at this restaurant inside a century-old house. The smoked salmon with potato galette is among the simple dishes,

In case you want to see the world.

At American Express, we're here to make your journey a smooth one. So we have over 1,700 travel service locations in over 130 countries ready to help. What else would you expect from the world's largest travel agency?

do more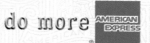

Travel

Call 1 800 AXP-3429 or visit
www.americanexpress.com/travel

In case you want to be welcomed there.

We're here to see that you're always welcomed at establishments everywhere. That's why millions of people carry the American Express® Card – for peace of mind, confidence, and security, around the world or just around the corner.

do more **AMERICAN EXPRESS**

Cards

To apply, call 1 800 THE-CARD
or visit www.americanexpress.com

In case you're running low.

We're here to help with more than 190,000 Express Cash locations around the world. In order to enroll, just call American Express at 1 800 CASH-NOW before you start your vacation.

do more

Express Cash

And in case you'd rather be safe than sorry.

We're here with American Express® Travelers Cheques. They're the safe way to carry money on your vacation, because if they're ever lost or stolen you can get a refund, practically anywhere or anytime. To find the nearest place to buy Travelers Cheques, call 1 800 495-1153. Another way we help you do more.

do more · AMERICAN EXPRESS

Travelers Cheques

but the chefs also prepare complex fare like the grilled pork tender-loin with Calvados and Stilton sauce. The excellent 30-page wine list stresses Bordeaux. ⊠ *1616 Alberni St.,* ☎ *604/685–3924. Reservations essential. AE, DC, MC, V. No lunch weekends.*

Greek

$
★ ✗ **Stepho's Souvlaki.** Regulars swear by, and are quite prepared to wait in line for, Stepho's cheap and tasty roast lamb, moussaka, and sou-vlaki, served in a dark and bustling taverna. **Takis'**, a few doors east at 1106 Davie St. (☎ 604/682–1336) serves equally good value Greek Cypriot food, and there's usually no waiting. Both restaurants have take-out menus—handy for picnics on the beach just down the street. ⊠ *1124 Davie St.,* ☎ *604/683–2555. AE, MC, V.*

Italian

$$$–$$$$ ✗ **Piccolo Mondo Ristorante.** Soft candlelight, bountiful flower ar-rangements, and fine European antiques create an intimate feel at this northern Italian restaurant on a quiet street a block off Robson. Start with an eggplant and tuna tart with pecorino cheese and basil oil, and follow it up with the classic osso buco or the linguine tossed with smoked Alaskan cod, capers, and red onions. In the award-winning wine cel-lar are more than 4,000 bottles (480 vintages). ⊠ *850 Thurlow St.,* ☎ *604/688–1633. Reservations essential. AE, DC, MC, V. Closed Sun. No lunch Sat.*

$$$–$$$$ ✗ **Villa del Lupo.** This Victorian heritage house on the edge of trendy Yaletown is home to one of Vancouver's most established Italian restaurants. Country-house-elegant decor sets a romantic tone, and the contemporary menu takes its inspiration from various regions of Italy. Sea bass wrapped with Parma prosciutto and sage and roasted with braised fennel-savoy cabbage; and osso buco in a sauce of tomatoes, red wine, cinnamon, and lemon are favorites here. ⊠ *869 Hamilton St.,* ☎ *604/688–7436. Reservations essential. AE, DC, MC, V. No lunch.*

$$–$$$$ ✗ **Bacchus.** Low lighting, deep-velvet drapes, and Venetian glass lamps create a mildly decadent feel at this sensuous restaurant inside the Wedge-wood Hotel (☞ Lodging, *below*). Live jazz music, a cigar room, and appropriately ornate northern Italian cuisine round out the mood. Bacchus is open until 1:30 AM six nights a week for after-theater re-freshments, and for weekend brunch. Afternoon tea is served between 2 and 4 daily. ⊠ *845 Hornby St.,* ☎ *604/608–5319. Reservations es-sential. AE, D, DC, MC, V.*

$$–$$$$ ✗ **Il Giardino di Umberto.** This little yellow house at the end of Hornby
★ Street hides an attractive jumble of four terra-cotta tiled rooms and a vine-draped courtyard with a wood-burning oven. For extreme romance, there's a Juliet balcony with its own table for two overlooking the main dining room. The Tuscan food served here features such dishes as smoked salmon with orange, fennel, and leeks; roasted reindeer loin with port peppercorn sauce; osso buco with saffron risotto; and duck with shallots. ⊠ *1382 Hornby St.,* ☎ *604/669–2422. Reservations es-sential. AE, DC, MC, V. Closed Sun. No lunch Sat.*

Japanese

$$–$$$ ✗ **Chiyoda.** A sushi bar and a *robata* (grill) bar curve through Chiy-oda's chic modern main room: on one side are the customers and an array of flat baskets full of the day's offerings; on the other side are the chefs and grills. There are usually more than 35 choices of things to grill, from black cod marinated in miso paste, to squid, snapper, oys-ters, and shiitake mushrooms—all fresh from the market. ⊠ *205–1050 Alberni St.,* ☎ *604/688–5050. Reservations essential. AE, DC, MC, V. Closed Sun. No lunch Sat.*

Mediterranean

$$–$$$ ✕ **Allegro Café.** Cushy curved booths, low lighting, friendly staff, and a long martini menu give this downtown place near Robson Square a romantic—even flirtatious—feel. The menu is playful, too, with such rich and offbeat concoctions as pasta bundles with roasted butternut squash and gorgonzola cream, and roasted breast of chicken with herbs, goat cheese, and peach and fig chutney. The rich daily soups and fair prices make this a good weekday lunch stop. ⊠ *888 Nelson St.,* ☎ *604/683–8485. AE, DC, MC, V. No lunch weekends.*

Native American

$$–$$$$ ✕ **Liliget Feast House.** This intimate downstairs room looks like the
★   interior of a native longhouse, with wooden walkways across pebble floors, contemporary native art on the walls, and cedar plank tables with tatami-style benches. Liliget is one of the few places in the world serving the original Northwest Coast native cuisine. A feast or potlach platter lets you try most of the offerings, which include bannock bread, baked sweet potato with hazelnuts, alder-grilled salmon, toasted sea-weed with rice, steamed fern shoots, barbecued venison, oysters, smoked mussels, and oolican oil, which is prepared from candlefish. ⊠ *1724 Davie St.,* ☎ *604/681–7044 or 888/681–7044. Reservations essential. AE, DC, MC, V. No lunch.*

Seafood

$$$–$$$$ ✕ **C.** With dishes like quince and ginger barbecued eel, roasted fresh-
★   water striped bass with yam and sour cream torte, and octopus-bacon wrapped scallops, C injects a new excitement into Vancouver's seafood scene. Besides the full lunch and dinner menus, there's a raw bar offering sushi, sashimi, oysters, and caviar, an elaborate Sunday brunch and, at weekday lunch, a West Coast seafood dim sum. The interior is done in cool, almost stark grays. Outside, a heated seaside patio has views of Granville Island. ⊠ *2–1600 Howe St.,* ☎ *604/681–1164. Reservations essential. AE, DC, MC, V. No lunch Sat.*

$$–$$$ ✕ **Fish House in Stanley Park.** Tucked between Stanley Park's tennis courts and putting green, this 1930s former sports pavilion with a conservatory, veranda, and fireplace has a relaxed country house ambience. Chef Karen Barnaby writes cookbooks, and the titles—*Pacific Passions* and *Screamingly Good Food*—say a lot about the food here, which is hearty, flavorful, and unpretentious. Good choices are the ahi tuna steak Diane or the cornhusk-wrapped salmon with a maple glaze. Before dinner head straight for the oyster bar, or arrive between 5 and 6 to take advantage of the early bird specials. ⊠ *8901 Stanley Park Dr., near Stanley Park's Beach Ave. entrance,* ☎ *604/681–7275. Reservations essential. AE, DC, MC, V.*

Greater Vancouver

Cafés

$ ✕ **Bread Garden Bakery, Café & Espresso Bar.** The Granville Street and Kitsilano branches of this local chain (☞ Downtown Vancouver, *above*) are open from 6 AM to midnight. ⊠ *1880 W. 1st Ave., Kitsilano,* ☎ *604/738–6684;* ⊠ *2996 Granville St.,* ☎ *604/736–6465. AE, DC, MC, V.*

$ ✕ **Capers.** These casual cafés, tucked into Vancouver's most lavish health food stores, sell light organic and vegetarian meals, treats from the in-store bakeries, and good, strong coffee. The W. 4th location is a self-serve cafeteria, and the West Vancouver store has a full-service restaurant. A third location, at 1675 Robson Street downtown, has outdoor seating and take-out service only. ⊠ *2496 Marine Dr., West Vancouver,* ☎ *604/925–3374;* ⊠ *2285 W. 4th Ave.,* ☎ *604/739–6676. AE, MC, V. No dinner Sun. at the West Vancouver location.*

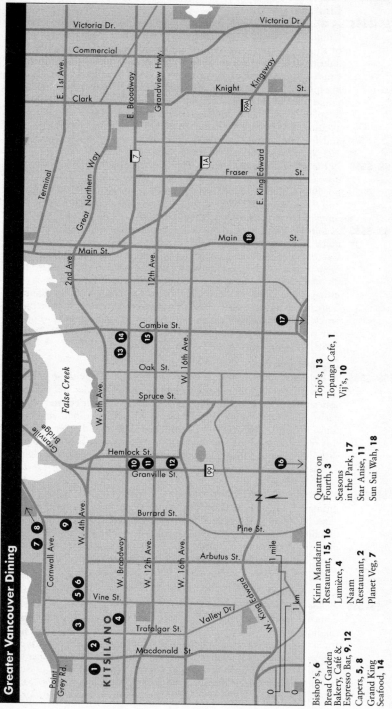

Greater Vancouver Dining

Victoria Dr.
Victoria Dr.
Commercial
E. 1st Ave.
Clark
E. Broadway
Grandview Hwy.
Knight
Kingsway
St.
Great Northern Way
TA
Fraser
St.
E. King Edward
Terminal
2nd Ave.
Main St.
Main
St.
12th Ave.
Cambie St.
W. 16th Ave.
Oak St.
False Creek
W. 6th Ave.
Spruce St.
Granville Bridge
Hemlock St.
Granville St.
99
N
Burrard St.
Pine St.
Cornwall Ave.
W. 4th Ave.
Arbutus St.
W. Broadway
W. 12th Ave.
W. 16th Ave.
Valley Dr.
W. King Edward
Vine St.
KITSILANO
Trafalgar St.
Macdonald St.
Point Grey Rd.

1 mile
1 km
0
0

Bishop's, **6**
Bread Garden
Bakery, Café &
Espresso Bar, **9, 12**
Capers, **5, 8**
Grand King
Seafood, **14**

Kirin Mandarin
Restaurant, **15, 16**
Lumière, **4**
Naam
Restaurant, **2**
Planet Veg, **7**

Quattro on
Fourth, **3**
Seasons
in the Park, **17**
Star Anise, **11**
Sun Sui Wah, **18**

Tojo's, **13**
Topanga Cafe, **1**
Vij's, **10**

Chinese

$$–$$$$ ✕ **Grand King Seafood.** In a city noted for its Chinese restaurants, the Grand King is widely considered one of the best. Decorated like most of the city's upmarket Cantonese establishments—with chandelier lighting and round white tables set for large groups—the Grand King emphasizes seafood from various regions of Southern China, including lobster with black bean sauce and crab claw wrapped in shrimp purée. But the large selection of nonseafood items, like ostrich slices in spicy pepper sauce and sautéed chicken with lily bulbs, is equally exciting. The best bets are the set dinner menus for groups of 2, 4, 6, and 10. The Grand King also has an innovative, popular dim sum. ⊠ *705 West Broadway,* ☎ *604/876–7855, DC, MC, V.*

$$–$$$$ ✕ **Kirin Mandarin Restaurant.** The Greater Vancouver outposts of this upscale operation (☞ Downtown Vancouver, *above*) serve a range of northern Chinese cuisine with a focus on seafood. ⊠ *555 W. 12th Ave., 2nd floor,* ☎ *604/879–8038;* ⊠ *3 West Centre, Suite 200, 7900 Westminster Hwy., Richmond,* ☎ *604/303–8833. AE, DC, V.*

$$–$$$$
★   ✕ **Sun Sui Wah.** Sails in the ceiling reminiscent of Vancouver's landmark Trade and Convention Centre add a lofty elegance to this East Side Cantonese restaurant. An offshoot of a popular Hong Kong establishment, Sun Sui Wah is best known for its dim sum, which ranges from traditional handmade dumplings to some highly adventurous offerings with little Japanese touches thrown in. It's worth coming back for dinner for house specialties like roasted squab and enormous king crab from the live tanks. There's another location in Richmond, the suburban heart of Vancouver's Chinese community. ⊠ *3888 Main St.,* ☎ *604/872–8822.* ⊠ *4940 No. 3 Rd., Richmond* ☎ *604/273–8208. AE, MC, V.*

Contemporary

$$$–$$$$ ✕ **Bishop's.** John Bishop serves West Coast cuisine with an emphasis on organic produce and British Columbia's seafood. Medallions of venison, smoked black cod, or roasted duck breast with dried fruit and ginger are sometimes on the seasonal menu. When they're in town shooting films, Robert De Niro, Glenn Close, Richard Gere, and other stars favor this restaurant, whose small white rooms display selections from Mr. Bishop's extensive local art collection. ⊠ *2183 W. 4th Ave.,* ☎ *604/ 738–2025. Reservations essential. AE, DC, MC, V. Closed 1st wk in Jan. No lunch.*

$$$–$$$$ ✕ **Star Anise.** Pacific Northwest cuisine with French flair shines in this intimate location near Granville Street. The menu varies with the seasons, but highlights, creatively and imaginatively prepared by chef Julian Bond, have included grilled emu set on a torta woven with shiitake mushrooms and potato, tandoori salmon with minted mango chutney, and a ricotta and leek tart. ⊠ *1485 W. 12th Ave.,* ☎ *604/737–1485. Reservations essential. AE, DC, MC, V. No lunch.*

Continental

$$–$$$ ✕ **Seasons in the Park.** Seasons has a commanding view over the gardens in Queen Elizabeth Park and beyond to the city and mountains. Light woods and white tablecloths in the comfortable dining room make for a conservative atmosphere that is mirrored in the Continental menu of herb-crusted sea bass, confit of Muscovy duck, and other standards. Weekend brunch is popular. There's a patio for outdoor dining in summer. ⊠ *Queen Elizabeth Park, 33rd Ave. and Cambie St.,* ☎ *604/874–8008 or 800/632–9422. Reservations essential. AE, MC, V.*

French

$$$$ ✕ **Lumière.** The contemporary French cuisine at this light and airy Kitsilano restaurant isn't so much served as orchestrated. Though you can order á la carte, the idea is to try one of chef Robert Feenie's frequently changing three- to eight-course menus. A tasting menu may take you from lobster bisque with prawn tempura, through roast venison medallions with kumquat and pineapple chutney, to a Valrhona tart with rum and butter chestnuts. A seafood menu makes the most of what's at the docks that day, and a vegetarian selection, with courses like wild mushroom torte and passion fruit sorbet with hibiscus jus, elevates meatless dining to haute cuisine. ✉ *2551 W. Broadway,* ☎ *604/739–8185. Reservations essential. AE, DC, MC, V. Closed Mon. No lunch.*

Indian

$$
★
✕ **Vij's.** Vikram Vij calls his restaurant a curry art gallery, but he's not talking about the bold Klimt-inspired murals on the walls. The art here is on the plate, with such haute-Punjabi creations as cinnamon spiced buffalo meat with sweet corn; tiger prawns with cucumber salsa; and rockfish, spot prawns, and scallops in coconut curry. The dishes on the brief, seasonally changing menu are far from traditional, but the spices are beautifully orchestrated to allow exotic flavors like mango, tamarind, and fenugreek to shine through. Vij's doesn't take reservations, but the inevitable lineups are events in themselves, as the attentive staff serve *papadum* and *chai* (spicy snacks and tea) to the waiting diners. ✉ *1480 W. 11th Ave.,* ☎ *604/736–6664. Reservations not accepted. AE, MC, V. No lunch.*

Italian

$$–$$$$
✕ **Quattro on Fourth.** This Italian restaurant in health-conscious Kitsilano offers light, simple cooking using healthy (often low-fat and low-sodium) ingredients and uncomplicated seasonings. The results—fettuccine with prawns, leeks, and bell peppers; baked sea bass in a pistachio crust; and roast duck breast with grappa, sun-dried cherries, and thyme—are still satisfyingly decadent. The mosaic floor, mustard-color walls, cherry-stained tables, and a wraparound covered porch enhance the Mediterranean atmosphere. ✉ *2611 W. 4th Ave.,* ☎ *604/734–4444. Reservations essential. AE, DC, MC, V. No lunch.*

Japanese

$$$
★
✕ **Tojo's.** Hidekazu Tojo is a sushi-making legend in Vancouver, with more than 2,000 special preparations stored in his creative mind. His handsome tatami rooms, on the second floor of a modern green-glass tower on West Broadway, provide the proper ambience for intimate dining, but Tojo's 10-seat sushi bar provides a convivial ringside seat for watching the creation of edible art. Reserve the seat at the end for the best view. ✉ *202–777 W. Broadway,* ☎ *604/872–8050. Reservations essential. AE, DC, MC, V. Closed Sun. No lunch.*

Tex-Mex

$–$$
✕ **Topanga Cafe.** The Tex-Mex food at this 40-seat Kitsilano classic hasn't changed much since 1978, when the Topanga started dishing up fresh salsa and homemade tortilla chips. Quantities are still huge and prices low. Kids can color blank menu covers while waiting for food; a hundred of their best efforts are framed on the walls. ✉ *2904 W. 4th Ave.,* ☎ *604/733–3713. Reservations not accepted. MC, V. Closed Sun.*

Vegetarian

$
✕ **Naam Restaurant.** Vancouver's oldest natural foods eatery is open 24 hours, so if you need to satisfy a late-night craving for a veggie burger, rest easy. The Naam also serves vegetarian stir-fries, wicked chocolate desserts, and wine, beer, cappuccinos, and fresh juices. Wood tables, an open fireplace, and live blues, folk, and jazz create a homey atmosphere. On warm summer evenings you can sit in the outdoor courtyard. ✉ *2724 W. 4th Ave.,* ☎ *604/738–7151. AE, MC, V.*

$ ✕ **Planet Veg.** The influences on the fare at this fast-food restaurant range as far afield as India, Mexico, and the Mediterranean. Among the most inspired cheap eats to be found in Kitsilano are the roti rolls—spicy treats in Indian flatbread. They're fun, filling, and an excellent value. Eat in, or gather a picnic to take to nearby Kits beach. ✉ *1941 Cornwall St.,* ☎ *604/734–1001. No credit cards.*

LODGING

Vancouver hotels, especially the more expensive properties downtown, contain fairly comparable facilities. Unless otherwise noted, expect to find the following amenities: minibars, in-room movies, no-smoking rooms and/or floors, room service, massage, baby-sitting, laundry service and dry cleaning, concierge, business services, meeting rooms, and parking (there is usually an additional fee). Lodgings in the inexpensive to moderate category do not generally provide much in the way of amenities (no in-room minibar, restaurant, room service, pool, exercise room, and so on). The chart below shows high-season prices, but from mid-October through May, rates throughout the city can drop as much as 50%.

CATEGORY	COST*
$$$$	over C$300
$$$	C$200–C$300
$$	C$125–C$200
$	under C$125

All prices are for a standard double room, excluding 10% room tax and 7% GST.

$$$$ 🏨 **Four Seasons.** This 30-story luxury hotel in downtown Vancouver
★   is famous for pampering guests (kids and pets included). The lobby is lavish, with seemingly acres of couches and a fountain in the lounge. Standard rooms are elegantly furnished, as are the roomier corner rooms with sitting areas. The two opulent split-level suites are handy for putting up visiting royalty. Service at the Four Seasons is top notch, and the attention to detail is outstanding. The many amenities include free evening limousine service. The formal dining room, Chartwell (☞ Dining, *above*), is one of the best in the city. ✉ *791 W. Georgia St., V6C 2T4,* ☎ *604/689–9333,* FAX *604/684–4555. 318 rooms, 67 suites. Restaurant, café, lobby lounge, in-room data ports, indoor-outdoor pool, hot tub, saunas, exercise room, children's programs, business services. AE, D, DC, MC, V.*

$$$$ 🏨 **Hotel Vancouver.** The copper roof of this château-style hotel (☞ Rob-
★   son to the Waterfront *in* Exploring Vancouver, *above*) that opened in 1939 dominates Vancouver's skyline. Even the standard guest rooms have an air of prestige, with high ceilings, mahogany furniture, sitting areas, and down duvets. Rooms on the Entrée Gold floor have extra services and amenities, including a private lounge and their own concierge. A full service salon and day spa add to the pampering. ✉ *900 W. Georgia St., V6C 2W6,* ☎ *604/684–3131 or 800/441–1414,* FAX *604/ 662–1937. 555 rooms, 42 suites. 2 restaurants, lobby lounge, in-room data ports, indoor lap pool, wading pool, beauty salon, hot tub, saunas, spa, health club, car rental. AE, D, DC, MC, V.*

$$$$ 🏨 **Metropolitan Hotel.** The structure was built in 1984 as the Mandarin Oriental Hotel, based on the principles of feng shui, and those precepts have been respected in all renovations since. The spacious, peaceful rooms are decorated in muted colors, and public areas are decorated with Asian art. Business-class rooms come with printers, fax machines, and cordless phones. Standard rooms have bathrobes, newspapers, down comforters, and other luxury amenities. The popular stu-

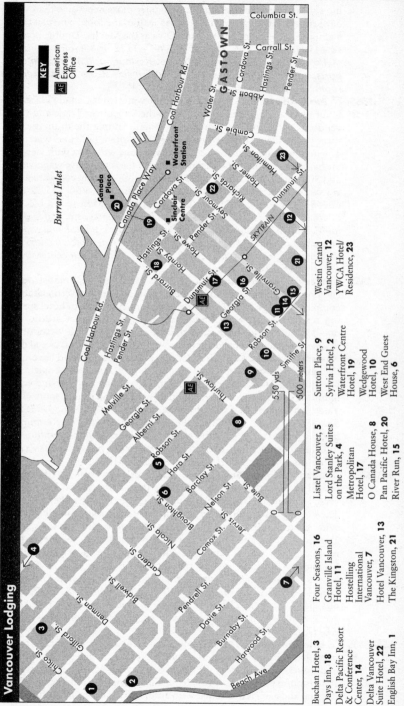

Vancouver Lodging

KEY
AE American Express Office

N

Burrard Inlet

GASTOWN

Canada Place

Waterfront Station

Sinclair Centre

SKYTRAIN

Buchan Hotel, 3
Days Inn, 18
Delta Pacific Resort & Conference Center, 14
Delta Vancouver Suite Hotel, 22
English Bay Inn, 1

Four Seasons, 16
Granville Island Hotel, 11
Hostelling International Vancouver, 7
Hotel Vancouver, 13
The Kingston, 21

Listel Vancouver, 5
Lord Stanley Suites on the Park, 4
Metropolitan Hotel, 17
O Canada House, 8
Pan Pacific Hotel, 20
River Run, 15

Sutton Place, 9
Sylvia Hotel, 2
Waterfront Centre Hotel, 19
Wedgewood Hotel, 10
West End Guest House, 6

Westin Grand Vancouver, 12
YWCA Hotel/Residence, 23

550 yds
500 meters

dio suites are even bigger and only slightly more expensive than standard rooms. Through an etched glass wall in the lobby you can catch a glimpse of the hotel's restaurant, Diva at the Met (☞ Dining, *above*). ✉ *645 Howe St., V6C 2Y9,* ☎ *604/687–1122 or 800/667–2300,* FAX *604/643–7267. 179 rooms, 18 suites. Restaurant, bar, in-room data ports, indoor lap pool, hot tub, saunas, men's steam room, exercise room, racquetball, squash. AE, DC, MC, V.*

$$$$ ⊞ **Pan Pacific Hotel.** A centerpiece of the waterfront Canada Place, the
★ luxurious Pan Pacific is convenient to the Vancouver Trade and Convention Centre and a cruise-ship terminal. Among the dramatic features of the three-story atrium lobby are a totem pole and waterfall. The lounge, restaurant, and café all have huge windows with views of the harbor and mountains. Eighty percent of the rooms have water views, and 30 new Global Office rooms have in-room desktop computers and video-conferencing facilities. ✉ *300–999 Canada Pl., V6C 3B5,* ☎ *604/ 662–8111; 800/663–1515 in Canada; 800/937–1515 in the U.S.;* FAX *604/685–8690. 466 rooms, 40 suites. 3 restaurants, café, coffee shop, lobby lounge, in-room data ports, in-room safes, pool, beauty salon, hot tubs, outdoor hot tub, saunas, steam rooms, aerobics, health club, indoor track, racquetball, squash, billiards, convention center, travel services. AE, DC, MC, V.*

$$$$ ⊞ **Westin Grand Vancouver.** With its strikingly minimalist decor, cherry-wood and marble lobby, and all-suite layout, the Westin Grand— completed in April 1999—sets the tone for a new style of hotel springing up in fast-growing Vancouver. All the compact studio and one-bedroom suites have floor-to-ceiling windows with views of the skyline, and fully equipped kitchenettes, including microwaves and dishwashers, tucked into armoires. Corner suites are larger and have small balconies. Office suites come equipped with fax, photocopier, and laser printer. The hotel is close to Vancouver's main sports and entertainment district and to the fashionable shops and dining spots of the Yaletown district. ✉ *433 Robson St., V6B 6L9,* ☎ *604/684–9393 or 888/680–9393,* FAX *604/684–9396. 23 rooms, 184 suites. Restaurant, bar, in-room data ports, kitchenettes, outdoor lap pool, outdoor hot tub, sauna, steam room, exercise room, nightclub, piano, children's programs (ages 0–12), travel services. AE, DC, MC, V.*

$$$–$$$$ ⊞ **Delta Vancouver Suite Hotel.** Vancouver's newest luxury hotel, attached to the city's newest conference center (the Simon Fraser University Centre for Dialogue) is a nice example of early millennial chic. The striking marble and cherry-wood lobby soars four stories high. The suites have blonde art deco furnishings, floor-to-ceiling windows, movable work tables, and sliding doors or Japanese screens to hide the bedroom. Slightly pricier Signature Club suites offer a private lounge, Continental breakfast, evening refreshments, and turndown service. The hotel's cozy restaurant, Manhattan, is hidden away from the madding crowd. ✉ *550 W. Hastings St., V6B 1L6,* ☎ *604/689–8188,* FAX *604/ 605–8881. 7 rooms, 219 suites. Restaurant, lobby lounge, in-room data ports, indoor pool, hot tub, sauna, exercise room, convention center. AE, D, DC, MC, V.*

$$$–$$$$ ⊞ **Listel Vancouver.** This hotel on Vancouver's most vibrant shopping
★ street has reinvented itself as something of an art gallery. About half of the guest rooms display the original or limited-edition works of such contemporary artists as Carmelo Sortino, Bernard Cathelin, and Otto Rogers, and each is decorated with antiques or custom-made furniture to complement the art. Gallery-room guests are invited to a reception at the nearby Buschlen Mowatt Gallery (☞ Shopping, *below*) each evening. There's also live jazz and occasional opera performances in O'Doul's lounge downstairs. ✉ *1300 Robson St., V6E 1C5,* ☎ *604/ 684–8461 or 800/663–5491,* FAX *604/684–7092. 119 rooms, 10 suites.*

Restaurant, lobby lounge, in-room data ports, indoor pool, hot tub, exercise room. AE, D, DC, MC, V.

$$$-$$$$ ★ 🖭 **Sutton Place.** The feel here is more exclusive European guest house than large modern hotel. Guest rooms are furnished with rich, dark woods reminiscent of 19th-century France, and the service is gracious and attentive. The hotel's Fleuri Restaurant is known for its Continental cuisine, Sunday brunch, and weekend evening chocoholic bar. La Grande Residence (part of Sutton Place), a fully equipped apartment hotel, suitable for stays of at least a week, is next door at 855 Burrard. ⊠ *845 Burrard St., V6Z 2K6,* ☎ *604/682–5511 or 800/961–7555,* FAX *604/682–5513. 350 rooms, 47 suites, 162 apartments. Restaurant, bar, indoor lap pool, hot tub, ladies' sauna, spa, men's steam room, health club. AE, D, DC, MC, V.*

$$$-$$$$ 🖭 **Waterfront Centre Hotel.** An underground walkway leads from this striking 23-story glass hotel to Canada Place. Views from the lobby and from 70% of the guest rooms are of Burrard Inlet and Stanley Park. Other rooms look onto a terraced herb garden. The spacious rooms have big picture windows and are attractively furnished with blonde wood furniture and contemporary Canadian artwork. Large corner rooms have the best views. Rooms on the Entrée Gold floor have extra amenities, including in-room safes, a private lounge, and their own concierge. ⊠ *900 Canada Pl. Way, V6C 3L5,* ☎ *604/691–1991 or 800/ 441–1414,* FAX *604/691–1999. 460 rooms, 29 suites. Restaurant, lobby lounge, pool, hot tub, sauna, steam room, exercise room, car rental. AE, D, DC, MC, V.*

$$$-$$$$ ★ 🖭 **Wedgewood Hotel.** The small, elegant Wedgewood is run by an owner who cares fervently about her guests. The lobby and guest rooms are decorated in a traditional European style with original artwork and antiques selected by the proprietor on her European travels. Guest rooms are spacious and each has a balcony, a bar, and a desk. The four penthouse suites have fireplaces. All the extra touches are here, too: afternoon ice delivery, dark-out drapes, robes, and a morning newspaper. The turndown service incudes homemade cookies and Evian water. In the lobby is the sensuous Bacchus restaurant and lounge (☞ Dining, *above).* ⊠ *845 Hornby St., V6Z 1V1,* ☎ *604/689–7777 or 800/663– 0666,* FAX *604/608–5348. 51 rooms, 38 suites. Restaurant, lobby lounge, in-room data ports, in-room safes, sauna, exercise room. AE, D, DC, MC, V.*

$$$ 🖭 **Granville Island Hotel.** Granville Island (☞ Exploring Vancouver, *above)* is one of Vancouver's more entertaining neighborhoods, but unless you've moored up in your own houseboat, the only overnight option is the Granville Island Hotel. This modern water's-edge hotel looks from the outside like it's made of Lego toy blocks. Inside, the decor is more elegant, with marble floors and Persian rugs in the lobby and guest rooms. Most rooms have water views, and all have big soaking tubs. Those on the top floor, the third, have small balconies. Step into the corridor and you'll overlook the vats brewing away for the fashionable brew pub and restaurant downstairs. Rooms not overlooking the pub's summertime patio are the quietest. ⊠ *1253 Johnston St., V6H 3R9,* ☎ *604/683–7373 or 800/663–1840,* FAX *604/683–3061. 54 rooms. Restaurant, pub, in-room data ports, hot tub, sauna, billiards. AE, MC, V.*

$$-$$$ 🖭 **Delta Pacific Resort & Conference Center.** The recreational facilities make this 14-acre site a resort: swimming pools (one indoor, with a three-story tubular water slide), tennis courts with a pro, aqua-exercise classes, outdoor volleyball nets, a play center and summer camps for children, and a playground. The hotel, near the airport and about a 30-minute drive south of downtown Vancouver, is large but casual and friendly. Guest rooms are modern, with contemporary decor and a pleasant blue-and-green color scheme. Business-class rooms, with print-

ers and fax machines, are also available. ✉ *10251 St. Edwards Dr.,
Richmond V6X 2M9,* ☎ *604/278–9611 or 800/268–1133,* FAX *604/
276–1121. 434 rooms, 2 suites. 2 restaurants, lobby lounge, indoor
pool, 2 outdoor pools, barbershop, beauty salon, hot tub, saunas, 4
indoor tennis courts, exercise room, squash, bicycles, children's programs (ages 5–12), convention center, airport shuttle, car rental. AE,
DC, MC, V.*

$$–$$$ 🏨 **English Bay Inn.** This renovated 1930s Tudor-style house one block
   ★   from the ocean and Stanley Park is elegantly furnished with museum-
quality antiques. The parlor has wing chairs, a fireplace, a gilt Louis
XV clock, and French doors overlooking the front garden. The guest
rooms are equally sumptuous. Three have sleigh beds and one has a
romantic four-poster. The suite has a loft bedroom with its own fireplace. Two double rooms in an equally beautiful house across the
street have their own sitting and breakfast room. ✉ *1968 Comox St.,
V6G 1R4,* ☎ *604/683–8002,* FAX *604/899–1501. 6 rooms, 1 suite. Free
parking. Full breakfast. No smoking. AE, MC, V.*

$$–$$$ 🏨 **West End Guest House.** This Victorian house, built in 1906, is a true
   ★   "painted lady," from its front parlor, cozy fireplace, and early 1900s
furniture to its bright-pink exterior. Most of the handsome rooms
have high brass beds, antiques, and gorgeous linens, as well as TVs
and phones; two larger rooms have gas fireplaces. The inn is in a residential neighborhood, a two-minute walk from Robson Street. Book
by March for summer. ✉ *1362 Haro St., V6E 1G2,* ☎ *604/681–
2889,* FAX *604/688–8812. 8 rooms. Bicycles, free parking. Full breakfast. No smoking. AE, D, MC, V.*

$$ 🏨 **Days Inn.** This six-story hotel, which opened as the Abbotsford in
1920, is one of the few moderately priced hotels in the business dis-
trict. Rooms are bright, clean, and utilitarian, with phones, TVs, and
refrigerators. The two-bedroom/one-bathroom units are a good value
for groups and families. There is no room service or air-conditioning,
although in-room data ports and voice mail are available. Guests have
free use of the YWCA pool and fitness facilities, a half block away. ✉
921 W. Pender St., V6C 1M2, ☎ *604/681–4335,* FAX *604/681–7808.
80 rooms, 5 suites. Restaurant, lounge, pub, fans, in-room data ports,
in-room safes, billiards, coin laundry. AE, D, DC, MC, V.*

$$ 🏨 **Lord Stanley Suites on the Park.** Here's a secret: these small, attractive,
fully equipped suites built in 1998 on the edge of Stanley Park are pri-
vately owned and thus charge less than a comparable hotel for a
nightly stay; the weekly rates are even better. Each suite incorporates
an office nook as well as a sitting room, one or two bedrooms, a gal-
ley kitchen, and a washer/dryer. Those overlooking busy Georgia Street
have an enclosed sunroom. Those backing onto quieter Alberni Street
have balconies. You'll find many good restaurants on Denman Street,
just a block away. The only catch: the vacant lot next door may, or
may not, be under construction in 2000. Check before booking. ✉ *1889
Alberni St.,* ☎ *604/688–9299 or 888/767–7829,* FAX *604/688–9297.
98 one-bedroom suites, 4 two-bedroom suites. In-room data ports, in-
room VCRs, saunas, exercise room. AE, DC, MC, V.*

$$ 🏨 **O Canada House.** Beautifully restored, this 1897 Victorian within
   ★   walking distance of downtown was where the first version of *O
Canada,* the national anthem, was written in 1909. Each spacious
bedroom is appointed with late-Victorian antiques. Modern comforts,
like in-room TVs, VCRs, phones, and bathrobes, help make things
homey. The top-floor room is enormous, with two double beds and a
private sitting area. A separate one-bedroom coach house in the gar-
den is the most romantic option. Guests also have the use of a guest
pantry and two parlors, both with fireplaces. ✉ *1114 Barclay St., V6E*

1H1, ☎ *604/688–0555,* FAX *604/488–0556. 6 rooms. Free parking. Full breakfast. No smoking. MC, V.*

$$ 🏠 **River Run.** A unique bed-and-breakfast, River Run sits in the serene
★ Fraser River delta in the village of Ladner, a 30-minute drive south of
downtown Vancouver, 10 minutes north of the ferry terminal, and near
Highway 99 on the way from Seattle. The accommodations include a
little gem of a floating house; a net loft (complete with Japanese soak-
ing tub on the deck and a cozy captain's bed); and two river's-edge
cottages, each with a fireplace and deck over the water. ✉ *4551 River
Rd. W, Ladner V4K 1R9,* ☎ *604/946–7778,* FAX *604/940–1970. 2
rooms, 2 suites. Refrigerators, microwave ovens, TV and VCR on re-
quest, bicycles, free parking. Full breakfast, afternoon refreshments.
No smoking. MC, V.*

$ 🏠 **Buchan Hotel.** The three-story Buchan, built in the 1930s, sits on a
tree-lined residential street a block from Stanley Park. The hotel's
rooms have basic furnishings, ceiling fans, and color TVs but no tele-
phones or air-conditioning. The lounge has a fireplace, and there's stor-
age for bikes and skis. The 35 pension-style rooms with shared baths
may be the most affordable accommodations near downtown. The
Buchan has no elevator. ✉ *1906 Haro St., V6G 1H7,* ☎ *604/685–5354
or 800/668–6654,* FAX *604/685–5367. 65 rooms, 30 with bath. Coin
laundry. No smoking. AE, DC, MC, V.*

$ 🏠 **Hostelling International Vancouver.** Vancouver has two Hostelling
★ International locations: a big barracklike hostel at Jericho Beach in Kit-
silano, and a smaller, downtown hostel near English Bay and Stanley
Park. Each has private rooms for two to four people; bunks in men's,
women's, and coed dorms; a shared kitchen and dining room, coin laun-
dry, TV lounge, bicycle rental, luggage and bike storage, and a range
of low-cost tours and activities. The downtown hostel also has a meet-
ing room, a games room, a library, and is wheelchair accessible. The
Jericho Beach hostel has a licensed café open April–November. A free
shuttle bus runs between the hostels and the bus and train station. ✉
Downtown, 1114 Burnaby St., V6E 1P1, ☎ *604/684–4565,* FAX *604/
684–4540. 23 rooms, 44 4-bed dorms. Jericho Beach 1515 Discovery
St., V6R 4K5,* ☎ *604/224–3208,* FAX *604/224–4852. 10 rooms, 58 4-
bed dorms.*

$ 🏠 **The Kingston.** Convenient to shopping, the Kingston is an old-style
four-story building with no elevator—the type of establishment you'd
find in Europe. Small and immaculate, the spartan rooms all have phones;
some rooms have TVs and private baths. Guests with cars will have
to find their own parking. ✉ *757 Richards St., V6B 3A6,* ☎ *604/684–
9024 or 888/713–3304,* FAX *604/684–9917. 56 rooms, 8 with bath. No-
smoking floor, coin laundry. Continental breakfast. AE, MC, V.*

$ 🏠 **Sylvia Hotel.** To stay at the Sylvia from June through August you'll
need to book six months to a year ahead. This ivy-covered 1912 build-
ing is popular because of its low rates and near-perfect location: about
25 ft from the beach on scenic English Bay, 200 ft from Stanley Park,
and a 20-minute walk from Robson Street. The unadorned rooms all
have private baths, phones, and TVs. Some suites are huge, and all have
kitchens. ✉ *1154 Gilford St., V6G 2P6,* ☎ *604/681–9321,* FAX *604/
682–3551. 97 rooms, 22 suites. Restaurant, bar, room service, dry clean-
ing, laundry service, parking (fee). AE, DC, MC, V.*

$ 🏠 **YWCA Hotel/Residence.** A secure, 12-story building in the heart of
★ the entertainment district, the YWCA has bright comfortable rooms,
some big enough to sleep five. All have cheery floral bedspreads, night-
stands and desks, minirefrigerators, telephones, and sinks. Some share
a bath down the hall, some share a bath between two rooms, and others
have private baths. The hotel is open to men and women and offers
discounts for seniors, students, and YWCA members. Rates include

use of the YWCA pool and fitness facility at 535 Hornby Street (☞ Health and Fitness Clubs *in* Outdoor Activities and Sports, *below*). ⊠ *733 Beatty St., V6B 2M4, ☎ 604/895–5830; 800/663–1424 in Western Canada and the Pacific Northwest;* FAX *604/681–2550. 155 rooms. 3 shared kitchens, 2 shared kitchenettes, no-smoking floors, refrigerators, 3 shared TV lounges, 3 coin laundries, meeting rooms, parking (fee). MC, V.*

NIGHTLIFE AND THE ARTS

For **events information,** pick up a copy of the free *Georgia Straight* (available at cafés and bookstores around town) or look in the entertainment section of the *Vancouver Sun* (Thursday's paper has listings in the "Queue" section). Call the **Arts Hotline** (☎ 604/684–2787) for the latest entertainment information. Book tickets through **Ticketmaster** (☎ 604/280–4444).

Nightlife

Bars and Lounges

DOWNTOWN

Musicians at the chic **Bacchus Lounge** (⊠ Wedgewood Hotel, 845 Hornby St., ☎ 604/608–5319) play mellow tunes to sip cocktails by. A waterfall and soft, comfy chairs make the airy **Garden Terrace** (⊠ Four Seasons, 791 W. Georgia St., ☎ 604/689–9333) a peaceful place to relax. The fireplaces, wing chairs, dark wood, and leather at the **Gerard Lounge** (⊠ Sutton Place Hotel, 845 Burrard St., ☎ 604/682–5511) provide a suitably stylish setting for the film-industry types who hang out here. The tenders of the wine bar at the **Hotel Vancouver** (⊠ 900 W. Georgia St., ☎ 604/669–9378) pour 55 wines by the glass.

GRANVILLE ISLAND

The **Backstage Lounge** (⊠ 1585 Johnston St., ☎ 604/687–1354) is a loud and popular hangout behind the main stage at the Arts Club Theatre. The after-work crowd heads to **Bridges** (⊠ 1696 Duranleau St., ☎ 604/687–4400), near the Public Market overlooking False Creek. **The Creek** (⊠ Granville Island Hotel, 1253 Johnston St., ☎ 604/685–7070) is a popular microbrewery lounge.

Brew Pubs

The brewmasters at **Steam Works** (⊠ 375 Water St., ☎ 604/689–2739), on the edge of Gastown, use an age-old steam process and large copper kettles (visible through glass walls in the dining room downstairs) to fashion several brews, including espresso ale. The **Yaletown Brewing Company** (⊠ 1111 Mainland St., ☎ 604/681–2739) occupies a renovated warehouse. The microbrewery turns out eight tasty concoctions and includes a darts and billiards pub and a restaurant.

Casinos

Vancouver has a few casinos; proceeds go to local charities and arts groups. No alcohol is served. The **Great Canadian Casino** (⊠ 1133 West Hastings St., ☎ 604/682–8415) is in the Renaissance Hotel. The **Royal Diamond Casino** (⊠ 106B-750 Pacific Blvd. S, ☎ 604/685–2340) is in the Plaza of Nations Expo site downtown.

Coffeehouses

A large European population and the shortage of pubs mean that coffeehouses play an even bigger role in Vancouver's social life than they do in Seattle's. The Starbucks invasion is nearly complete—there are blocks in town with two branches—but there are other, more colorful places to have a cappuccino, write that novel, or watch the world go by.

There are many coffee places on Granville Island but only the **Blue Parrot Café** (✉ Granville Island Public Market, 1689 Johnston St., ☎ 604/688–5127) provides such sweeping views of the boats on False Creek. The Blue Parrot, like the public market, gets madly crowded on weekends. Cushy couches and wholesome goodies make **Bojangles Café** (✉ 785 Denman St., ☎ 604/687–3622) a good place to rest up after a walk around Stanley Park. **Blake's on Carrall** (✉ 221 Carrall St., ☎ 604/899–3354) is an atmospheric Gastown hangout, doubling as a mini-art gallery and performance space. Everyone seems to know everyone else at **Delaney's** (✉ 1105 Denman St., ☎ 604/662–3344), a friendly and often crowded coffee bar near English Bay. Cozy wooden booths and stacks of magazines will tempt you to spend a rainy afternoon here.

Comedy Clubs

The **TheatreSports League** (☎ 604/738–7013), a hilarious improv troupe, performs at the Arts Club New Review Stage on Granville Island. The **Vancouver International Comedy Festival** (☎ 604/683–0883), held in late July and early August, brings an international collection of improv, stand-up, circus, and other acts to Granville Island. **Yuk Yuks** (✉ 750 Pacific Blvd. S, in the Plaza of Nations Expo site, ☎ 604/687–5233) is Vancouver's main stand-up venue.

Gay and Lesbian Nightlife

Celebrities (✉ 1022 Davie St., ☎ 604/689–3180) is a multilevel space with dancing, billiards, and Wednesday drag shows. **Denman Station** (✉ 860 Denman St., ☎ 604/669–3448), a friendly and low-key pub, is patronized by gay men and lesbians. **Odyssey** (✉ 1251 Howe St., ☎ 604/689–5256) is one of Vancouver's most popular gay discos.

Music

DANCE CLUBS

The Gate (✉ 1176 Granville St., ☎ 604/608–4283) is a popular place with a big dance floor, live music on weekends, and Top 40 during the week. **Richard's on Richards** (✉ 1036 Richards St., ☎ 604/687–6794) is one of Vancouver's most established dance clubs, with live bands on weekdays. **Sonar** (✉ 66 Water St., ☎ 604/683–6695) in Gastown, has international dance sounds and frequent touring guest DJs.

FOLK

The **Vancouver Folk Music Festival** (☎ 604/602–9798 or 800/883–3655), one of the world's leading folk- and world-music events, takes place at Jericho Beach Park on the third weekend of July. For folk and traditional Celtic concerts year-round, call the **Rogue Folk Club** (☎ 604/736–3022).

JAZZ AND SOUL

The hot line of the **Coastal Jazz and Blues Society** (☎ 604/872–5200) has information about concerts and clubs. The society also runs the Vancouver International Jazz Festival, which lights up 37 venues around town every June.

BaBalu (✉ 654 Nelson St., ☎ 604/605–4343) leads the local lounge revival with its house band, *The Smoking Section*. The DJ at **Bar None** (✉ 1222 Hamilton St., ☎ 604/689–7000) in Yaletown favors funk and soul. Bands perform on Monday and Tuesday. The **Cellar Jazz Café** (✉ 3611 W. Broadway, ☎ 604/738–1959) presents everything from acid jazz to mainstream quartets, both live and recorded. Beatnik poetry readings would seem to fit right in at the **Chameleon Urban Lounge** (✉ 801 W. Georgia St., ☎ 604/669–0806) in the basement of the Crowne

Plaza Hotel Georgia, but it's the sophisticated jazz, R&B, and Latin tunes that draw the crowds. A big band dance sound carries into the night at the **Hot Jazz Club** (✉ 2120 Main St., ☎ 604/873–4131).

ROCK

The **Rage** (✉ 750 Pacific Blvd. S, ☎ 604/685–5585) hosts touring acts on weeknights and has DJs on weekends. Two spots for local and alternative live bands are the **Railway Club** (✉ 579 Dunsmuir St., ☎ 604/681–1625) and the **Starfish Room** (✉ 1055 Homer St., ☎ 604/682–4171).**The Vogue Theatre** (✉ 918 Granville St., ☎ 604/331–7909), a former movie palace, hosts a variety of concerts by visiting performers.

Pool Halls

Most of the city's "hot" pool halls are in Yaletown, including the **Automotive Billiards Club** (✉ 1095 Homer St., ☎ 604/682–0040), **Cutters Billiard** (✉ 1011 Hamilton St., ☎ 604/669–3533) , and **Soho Café and Billiards** (✉ 1144 Homer St., ☎ 604/688–1180).

The Arts

Dance

The **Dance Centre** (☎ 604/606–6400) has information about dance in British Columbia.

Ballet British Columbia (☎ 604/732–5003), based at the **Queen Elizabeth Theatre** (✉ 600 Hamilton St.), mounts productions and hosts out-of-town companies from November through April. A few of the many modern dance companies in town are Karen Jamieson, DanceArts Vancouver, and JumpStart; among the venues they perform at include **Firehall Arts Centre** and the **Vancouver East Cultural Centre** (☞ Theater, *below*).

Film

Tickets are half price on Tuesday at most Vancouver movie theaters. The **Vancouver International Film Festival** (☎ 604/685–0260) is held in late September and early October in several theaters around town.

FOREIGN/INDEPENDENT

Fifth Avenue Cinemas (✉ 2110 Burrard St., ☎ 604/734–7469). **Park Theater** (✉ 3440 Cambie St., ☎ 604/876–2747). **Pacific Cinématèque** (✉ 1131 Howe St., ☎ 604/688–8202). **Ridge Theatre** (✉ 3131 Arbutus St., ☎ 604/738–6311).

Music

CHAMBER MUSIC AND SMALL ENSEMBLES

Early Music Vancouver (☎ 604/732–1610) performs medieval, Renaissance, and Baroque music throughout the year and hosts the Vancouver Early Music Summer Festival. Concerts by the **Friends of Chamber Music** (☎ 604/437–5747) are worth watching for. Programs of the **Vancouver Recital Society** (☎ 604/602–0363) are always of excellent quality.

CHORAL GROUPS

Choral groups like the **Bach Choir** (☎ 604/921–8012), the **Vancouver Cantata Singers** (☎ 604/921–8588), and the **Vancouver Chamber Choir** (☎ 604/738–6822) play a major role in Vancouver's classical music scene.

ORCHESTRAS

The **Vancouver Symphony Orchestra** (☎ 604/876–3434) is the resident company at the **Orpheum Theatre** (✉ 601 Smithe St.).

Opera

Vancouver Opera (☎ 604/682–2871) stages several productions a year from October through May at the **Queen Elizabeth Theatre** (✉ 600 Hamilton St.).

Theater

Arts Club Theatre (✉ 1585 Johnston St., ☎ 604/687–1644) operates two stages on Granville Island and presents theatrical performances all year. **Bard on the Beach** (☎ 604/739–0559) is a summer series of Shakespeare's plays performed under a huge tent on the beach at Vanier Park. **Carousel Theatre** (☎ 604/669–3410) performs theater for children and young people at the **Waterfront Theatre** (✉ 1412 Cartwright St.) on Granville Island.

The **Chan Centre for the Performing Arts** (✉ 6265 Crescent Rd., on the University of British Columbia campus, ☎ 604/822–2697) contains a 1,400-seat concert hall, a theater, and a cinema. The **Firehall Arts Centre** (✉ 280 E. Cordova St., ☎ 604/689–0926) showcases Canadian works in an intimate downtown space. **The Fringe** (☎ 604/257–0350), Vancouver's annual live theatrical arts festival, is staged in September at various venues in Vancouver's east end.

The **Queen Elizabeth Theatre** (✉ 600 Hamilton St., ☎ 604/665–3050) is a major venue for ballet, opera, and other events. **The Stanley Theatre** (✉ 2750 Granville St., ☎ 604/687–1644), an elegant 1930s movie palace, reopened in 1998 as a live theater. **Theatre Under the Stars** (☎ 604/687–0174) performs musicals at Malkin Bowl, an outdoor amphitheater in Stanley Park, during July and August. **Vancouver East Cultural Centre** (✉ 1895 Venables St., ☎ 604/254–9578) is a multipurpose performance space. **Vancouver Playhouse** (✉ 649 Cambie St., ☎ 604/665–3050) is the leading venue in Vancouver for mainstream theatrical shows.

OUTDOOR ACTIVITIES AND SPORTS

Beaches

An almost continuous string of beaches runs from Stanley Park to the University of British Columbia. The water is cool, but the beaches are sandy, edged by grass. All have lifeguards, washrooms, concession stands, and limited parking, unless otherwise noted. Liquor is prohibited in parks and on beaches. For information, call the **Vancouver Board of Parks and Recreation** (☎ 604/738–8535, summer only).

Kitsilano Beach, over the Burrard Bridge from downtown, has a lifeguard and is the city's busiest beach. In-line skaters, volleyball games, and sleek young people are ever present. The part of the beach nearest the Vancouver Maritime Museum is the quietest. Facilities include a playground, tennis courts, a heated pool, concession stands, and nearby restaurants and cafés.

The **Point Grey beaches** provide a number of options. Jericho, Locarno, and Spanish Banks, which begin at the end of Point Grey Road, have huge expanses of sand, especially in summer and at low tide. The shallow water, warmed slightly by sun and sand, is good for swimming. Farther out, toward Spanish Banks, the beach becomes less crowded. Past Point Grey is Wreck Beach, Vancouver's nude beach.

Among the **West End beaches,** Second Beach and Third Beach, along Beach Drive in Stanley Park, draw families. Second Beach has a guarded pool. A water slide, kayak rentals, street performers, and artists keep things interesting all summer at English Bay Beach, at the foot of Denman Street. Farther along Beach Drive, Sunset Beach is a little too close to the downtown core for safe swimming.

Participant Sports

Biking

One of the best ways to see the city is to cycle along at least part of the **Seaside Bicycle Route.** This 15-km (10-mi), flat, car-free route starts at Canada Place downtown and follows the waterfront around **Stanley Park** (☞ Stanley Park *in* Exploring Vancouver, *above*) and continues, with a few detours, all the way around False Creek to Spanish Banks beach. Rentals are available from a number of places near Stanley Park, including **Bayshore Bicycles** (✉ 745 Denman St., ☎ 604/688–2453), the **Westin Bayshore Hotel** (✉ 1601 W. Georgia St., ☎ 604/689–5071), and **Spokes Bicycle Rentals & Espresso Bar** (✉ 1798 W. Georgia St., ☎ 604/688–5141). Cycling helmets, a legal requirement in safety-conscious Vancouver, come with the rentals.

For guided biking and mountain bike tours, *see* Ecology Tours *in* Contacts and Resources, *below.*

Boating

Blue Pacific Yacht Charters (✉ 1519 Foreshore Walk, Granville Island, ☎ 604/682–2161) is one of several boat charter companies on Granville island. **Cooper Boating Centre** (✉ 1620 Duranleau, Granville Island, ☎ 604/687–4110) has a three-hour introduction to sailing around English Bay, as well as longer cruise-and-learn trips lasting from five days to two weeks.

Fishing

You can fish for salmon all year in coastal British Columbia. **Sewell's Marina Horseshoe Bay** (✉ 6695 Nelson Ave., Horseshoe Bay, ☎ 604/921–3474) organizes a daily four-hour trip on Howe Sound and has hourly rates on U-drives. **Westin Bayshore Yacht Charters** (✉ 1601 W. Georgia St., ☎ 604/691–6936) operates fishing charters. For fly fishing day trips, contact **L. H. I. Trout Fishing Adventures** (✉ 1995 West 19th Ave., ☎ 604/838–5873).

Golf

For a spur of the moment game, call **Last Minute Golf** (☎ 604/878–1833). The company matches golfers and courses at substantial greens-fee discounts. The half-day packages of **West Coast Golf Shuttle** (☎ 604/878–6800) include the greens fee, power cart, and hotel pickup.

The challenging 18-hole, par-72 course (closed between mid-November and mid-March) at **Furry Creek Golf and Country Club** (✉ Hwy. 99, Furry Creek, ☎ 604/922–9576), a 45-minute drive north of Vancouver, has a greens fee that ranges from $45 to $90 and includes a mandatory cart. The facilities of the 18-hole, par-71 public **McCleery Golf Course** (✉ 7188 McDonald St., ☎ 604/257–8191) include a driving range. The greens fee is $34–$37; an optional cart costs $25. **Northview Golf and Country Club** (✉ 6857 168th St., Surrey, ☎ 604/576–4653) has two Arnold Palmer–designed 18-hole courses (both par 72) and is the home of the Air Canada Championship (a PGA tour event). The greens fee for the Ridge course, where the PGA tour plays, ranges from $45 to $80, the fee for the Canal course from $35 to $60; an optional cart at either course costs $30. At the 18-hole, par-72 course (closed November–March) at the **Westwood Plateau Golf and Country Club** (✉ 3251 Plateau Blvd., Coquitlam, ☎ 604/552–0777) the greens fee, which includes a cart, ranges from $90 to $125.

Health and Fitness Clubs

The **Bentall Centre Athletic Club** (✉ 1055 Dunsmuir St., lower level, ☎ 604/689–4424), has racquetball and squash courts and weight rooms; aerobics classes are also given here. The **YMCA** (✉ 955 Burrard St., ☎ 604/681–0221) downtown has daily rates. Facilities include a pool and weight rooms, as well as racquetball, squash, and handball courts. The **YWCA** (✉ 535 Hornby St., ☎ 604/895–5800) has a pool, weight rooms, and fitness classes.

Hiking

Stanley Park, the more rugged Pacific Spirit Park near the University of B.C., and the seaside Lighthouse Park in West Vancouver all have fairly flat, forested trails. In the mountains of North Vancouver, **Capilano Regional Park** (☞ North Vancouver *in* Exploring Vancouver, *above*) and the **Seymour Demonstration Forest** (✉ at the end of Lillooet Rd., North Vancouver, ☎ 604/432–6286) have some easy rainforest walks. **Mount Seymour** and **Cypress** provincial parks (☎ 604/924–2200) offer more challenging mountain trails for experienced, well-equipped hikers.

A number of companies conduct guided walks and hikes in nearby parks and wilderness areas (☞ Ecology Tours *in* Contacts and Resources, *below*).

Jogging

The **Running Room** (✉ 1519 Robson St., ☎ 604/684–9771) is a good source for information about fun runs in the area.

The seawall around **Stanley Park** (☞ Stanley Park *in* Exploring Vancouver, *above*) is 9 km (5½ mi) long. Running it provides an excellent minitour of the city. You can take a shorter run of 4 km (2½ mi) in the park around Lost Lagoon.

Skiing

CROSS-COUNTRY

The best cross-country skiing, with 16 km (10 mi) of groomed trails, is at **Cypress Bowl Ski Area** (✉ Cypress Bowl Ski Area Rd., Exit 8 off Hwy. 1 westbound, ☎ 604/922–0825).

DOWNHILL

Whistler/Blackcomb (☞ Chapter 5), a top-ranked ski destination, is a two-hour drive from Vancouver.

The **North Shore mountains** hold three ski areas. All have rentals, lessons, and night skiing. **Cypress Bowl** (✉ Cypress Bowl Ski Area Rd., Exit 8 off Hwy. 1 westbound, ☎ 604/926–5612; 604/419–7669 snow report) has 25 runs (serviced by four chairlifts) and a vertical drop of 1,750 ft. The mountain also has a tobogganing and snow tubing area. **Grouse Mountain** (✉ 6400 Nancy Greene Way, ☎ 604/984–0661; 604/986–6262 snow report) has four chairlifts, a vertical drop of 1,300 ft, extensive night skiing, restaurants, bars, cross-country ski trails, an ice rink, a snowshoeing park, and great city views from the runs. **Mount Seymour** (✉ 1700 Mt. Seymour Rd., ☎ 604/986–2261; 604/718–7771 snow report) has three chairlifts and a vertical drop of 1,042 ft. You can also try snowshoeing and snow tubing here.

Tennis

There are 180 free public courts around town. Contact the **Vancouver Board of Parks and Recreation** (☎ 604/257–8400) for locations. **Stanley Park** has 15 well-surfaced outdoor courts near English Bay Beach. Many of the other city parks have public courts as well.

Water Sports

KAYAKING

Kayaks are a fun way to explore the waters of False Creek and the shore-line of English Bay. **Ecomarine Ocean Kayak Center** (⊠ Granville Island, 1668 Duranleau St., ☎ 604/689–7575) and **Ocean West Expeditions** (⊠ English Bay Beach, ☎ 800/660–0051) rent kayaks and offer lessons and tours.

For guided kayak trips, *see* Ecology Tours *in* Contacts and Resources, *below.*

RAFTING

The **Canadian Outback Adventure Company** (⊠ ☎ 604/921–7250 or 800/565–8735) runs white-water rafting and scenic (non–white-water) floats on day trips from Vancouver.

WINDSURFING

Sailboards and lessons are available at **Windsure Windsurfing School** (⊠ Jericho Beach, ☎ 604/224–0615). The winds aren't very heavy on English Bay, making it a perfect locale for learning the sport. You'll have to travel north to Squamish for more challenging high-wind conditions.

Spectator Sports

Vancouver's professional basketball and hockey teams play at **General Motors Place** (⊠ 800 Griffiths Way, ☎ 604/899–7400). **Ticketmaster** (☎ 604/280–4400) sells tickets to many local sports events.

Basketball

The **Vancouver Grizzlies** (☎ 604/899–7400) of the National Basketball Association play at General Motors Place.

Football

The **B.C. Lions** (☎ 604/930–5466) of the Canadian Football League play at B.C. Place Stadium (⊠ 777 Pacific Blvd. S, ☎ 604/661–7373).

Hockey

The **Vancouver Canucks** (☎ 604/899–7400) of the National Hockey League play at General Motors Place.

SHOPPING

Unlike many cities where suburban malls have taken over, Vancouver is full of individual boutiques and specialty shops. Antiques stores, ethnic markets, art galleries, high-fashion outlets, and fine department stores abound. Store hours are generally from 9:30 to 6 on Monday, Tuesday, Wednesday, and Saturday, from 9:30 to 9 on Thursday and Friday, and from noon to 5 on Sunday.

Shopping Districts and Malls

About two dozen high-end art galleries, antiques shops, and Oriental rug emporiums are packed end to end between 6th and 15th avenues on Granville Street, in an area known as **Gallery Row. Oakridge Shopping Centre** (⊠ 650 W. 41st Ave., at Cambie St., ☎ 604/261–2511) has chic, expensive stores that are fun to browse through. The immense **Pacific Centre Mall** (⊠ 550–700 W. Georgia St., ☎ 604/688–7236), on two levels and mostly underground, in the heart of downtown, connects Eaton's and the Bay department stores, which stand at opposite corners of Georgia and Granville streets. **Robson Street,** stretching from Burrard to Bute streets, contains boutiques and cafés. A commercial center has developed around **Sinclair Centre** (⊠ 757 W. Hastings St.),

RAINY DAYS

I T'S NO SECRET THAT IT RAINS in Vancouver. Easterners call it the Wet Coast, film types call it Brollywood, and those courtesy umbrellas distributed by some hotels are not meant to shield you from the sun. The secret is that some people quite like it.

For many it's the atmosphere. Bobbing among the harbor freighters on the SeaBus or taking a rare solitary stroll on the **Stanley Park Seawall** (☞ Stanley Park) gain a certain nautical cachet in bad weather. The **Museum of Anthropology** (☞ Greater Vancouver) is best seen on a wet day, when dark skies and streaming windows evoke the storm-lashed northern rain forest from which the artifacts came. It's not cheerful, sunny art. It's mystical, spiritual, and so elemental that it's best seen on a gray and stormy day. The weather sets the proper mood.

If denial is more your thing, you can escape to the tropics in the conservatory at **Queen Elizabeth Park** (☞ Greater Vancouver) or into the wet but warm rain-forest display at the **Vancouver Aquarium** (☞ Stanley Park). Since you're already wet, head outside to see the resident whales do their high-splash dives in the pool. They don't mind the rain.

The best thing about rain, though, is that it forces many normally frenetic Vancouverites to slow down. This is probably why the city has so embraced the coffeehouse culture—sipping a cappuccino is the only way to look even marginally cool while a puddle forms at your feet.

Favorite places to let your umbrella drip (☞ Coffeehouses *in* Nightlife and the Arts for the first three) include **Delaney's,** quite the social center, and **Blake's on Carrall,** which doubles as an art gallery and performance space in Gastown. The wraparound windows at Granville Island's **Blue Parrot Café** afford views of people and boats. Vancouver's two Chapters mega-bookstores (☞ Shopping) have their own in-house **Starbucks.** If you must have an urban-outdoorsy ambience, try the concourse at Library Square, which holds Vancouver's only indoor-outdoor sidewalk café.

Or you could take tea—that's proper tea, with cakes and sandwiches and none of those silly modern tea bags. If you're uncertain of the proper tea etiquette, simply observe the other guests and follow their lead. The **Empress Hotel** (☞ Victoria *in* Chapter 5) in Victoria is an institution, but tea can be taken (if a little tongue in cheek) in Vancouver as well. Try **Bacchus** in the Wedgewood Hotel, or **Griffin's** in the Hotel Vancouver (☞ Lodging). You don't have to wear hats and gloves, and you don't have to discuss the weather.

You could wear rubber boots, though. Large ones with ducks on them are very fashionable in Vancouver, as are resigned yet cheerful expressions and daft comments like: "At least you don't have to shovel it."

which caters to sophisticated and upscale tastes (☞ Robson to the Waterfront *in* Exploring Vancouver, *above*).

Ethnic Districts

Bustling **Chinatown**—centered on Pender and Main streets—holds restaurants and markets (☞ Gastown and Chinatown *in* Exploring Vancouver, *above*). **Commercial Drive** north of East 1st Avenue is the center of Vancouver's Italian and Latin American communities. You can sip cappuccino in coffee bars, or buy sun-dried tomatoes or an espresso machine. **Little India** is on Main Street around 50th Avenue. Curry houses, sweetshops, grocery stores, discount jewelers, and silk shops abound.

Department Stores

Holt Renfrew (⊠ 633 Granville St., ☎ 604/681–3121) focuses on high fashion for men and women.

Auction Houses

Love's (⊠ 1635 W. Broadway, ☎ 604/733–1157) holds auctions of collectibles and antiques on the last Wednesday and Thursday of each month at 6 PM. **Maynard's** (⊠ 415 W. 2nd Ave., ☎ 604/876–6787) auctions home furnishings every second Wednesday at 7 PM and holds occasional art and antiques auctions as well.

Specialty Stores

Antiques

Two key hunting grounds for antiques are Gallery Row on Granville Street (☞ Shopping Districts, *above*), and the stretch of antiques stores along Main Street from 16th to 25th avenues. **The Vancouver Antique Center** (⊠ 422 Richards St., ☎ 604/669–7444) has two floors of antiques and collectibles dealers under one roof.

Treasure hunters enjoy the vintage clothing and curio shops clustered along the 300 block of **West Cordova Street,** between Cambie and Richards streets near Gastown.

Art Galleries

Buschlen Mowatt (⊠ 1445 W. Georgia St., ☎ 604/682–1234), one of the city's best galleries, exhibits the works of Canadian and international artists. **Diane Farris** (⊠ 1565 W. 7th Ave., ☎ 604/737–2629) often showcases hot new artists. **The Inuit Gallery of Vancouver** (⊠ 345 Water St., ☎ 604/688–7323) exhibits Northwest-coast native and Inuit art. The **Marion Scott Gallery** (⊠ 481 Howe St., ☎ 604/685–1934) specializes in Inuit art. The **Douglas Reynolds Gallery** (⊠ 2335 Granville St., ☎ 604/731–9292) has one of the city's finest collections of Northwest-coast native art.

Books

Vancouver's two **Chapters** stores (⊠ 788 Robson St., ☎ 604/682–4066; ⊠ 2505 Granville St. at Broadway, ☎ 604/731–7822) are enormous, with a café in each location and a series of author readings and other performances. **Duthie Books** (⊠ 2239 West Fourth Ave., ☎ 604/732–5344) is a long-established homegrown favorite. The store fell on hard times in 1999 and closed all branches but this one. **MacLeod's Books** (⊠ 455 W. Pender St., ☎ 604/681–7654) is one of the city's best antiquarian bookstores. Despite its name, **Manhattan Books and Magazines** (⊠ 1089 Robson St., ☎ 604/681–9074) specializes in European books and periodicals.

Clothes

For unique women's clothing, try **Dorothy Grant** (✉ 757 W. Hastings St., ☎ 604/681–0201), where traditional Haida native designs meld with modern fashion. **Dream** (✉ 311 W. Cordova, ☎ 604/683–7326) is where up-and-coming local designers sell their wares. European fashions for men and women meet locally designed furs at **Lauren Paris** (✉ 377 Howe St., ☎ 604/681–6391). Handmade Italian suits and other upscale menswear is sold at stylish **E. A. Lee** (✉ 466 Howe St., ☎ 604/683–2457). There are also a few women's items to browse through. **Leone** (✉ 757 W. Hastings St., ☎ 604/683–1133) is an ultrachic boutique, dividing designer collections in themed areas. If your tastes are traditional, don't miss **Straith** (✉ 900 W. Georgia St., ☎ 604/685–3301) in the Hotel Vancouver, offering tailored designer fashions for men and women. At **Versus** (✉ 1008 W. Georgia St., ☎ 604/688–8938) boutique, ladies and gents sip cappuccino as they browse through fashionable Italian designs.

Gifts

Museum and gallery gift shops are among the best places to buy high-quality souvenirs—West Coast native art, books, music, jewelry, and other items. Four noteworthy stores are the **Clamshell Gift Shop** (✉ Vancouver Aquarium, ☎ 604/659–3413) in Stanley Park, the **Gallery Shop** (✉ 750 Hornby St., ☎ 604/662–4706) in the Vancouver Art Gallery, the **Museum of Anthropology Gift Shop** (✉ 6393 N.W. Marine Dr., ☎ 604/822–3825) on the University of British Columbia campus, and the **Museum Shop**(✉ 639 Hornby St., ☎ 604/687–8266) in the Canadian Craft Museum.

Hill's Indian Crafts (✉ 165 Water St., ☎ 604/685–4249), in Gastown, sells Northwest native art. **Leona Lattimer Gallery** (✉ 1590 W. 2nd Ave., ☎ 604/732–4556), near Granville Island and built like a longhouse, is full of native arts and crafts in all price ranges. At the **Salmon Shop** (☎ 604/669–3474) in the Granville Island Public Market you can pick up smoked salmon wrapped for travel.

VANCOUVER A TO Z

Arriving and Departing

By Bus

Greyhound Lines (☎ 604/482–8747; 800/661–8747 in Canada; 800/231–2222 in the U.S.) is the largest bus line serving Vancouver. **The Pacific Central Station** (✉ 1150 Station St.) is the depot for Greyhound. **Quick Shuttle** (☎ 604/940–4428 or 800/665–2122) bus service runs between downtown Vancouver, Vancouver Airport, Seattle (Seatac) Airport, and downtown Seattle five times a day in winter and up to eight times a day in summer. The downtown Vancouver depot is at the **Sandman Hotel** (✉ 180 W. Georgia St.).

By Car

Interstate 5 in Washington State becomes **Highway 99** at the U.S.–Canada border. Vancouver is a three-hour drive (226 km/140 mi) from Seattle. It's best to avoid border crossings during peak times such as holidays and weekends. Highway 1, the **Trans-Canada Highway,** enters Vancouver from the east. To avoid traffic, arrive after rush hour (8:30 AM).

By Ferry

B.C. Ferries (☎ 250/386–3431; 888/223–3779 in British Columbia only) serves Vancouver, Victoria, and other parts of coastal British Columbia. For more information about the system and other ferries that serve the area, *see* Ferry Travel *in* Smart Travel Tips.

By Plane

Vancouver International Airport (✉ Grant McConachie Way, Richmond, ☎ 604/276–6101) is on Sea Island, about 14 km (9 mi) south of downtown off Highway 99. An airport improvement fee is assessed on all flight departures: $5 for flights within British Columbia or the Yukon, $10 for other flights within North America, and $15 for overseas flights. Alaska, America West, American, British Airways, Continental, Northwest, Reno, and United serve the airport. The two major domestic carriers are Air Canada and Canadian Airlines. *See* Air Travel *in* Smart Travel Tips for airline numbers.

Air B.C. (☎ 604/688–5515 or 800/663–3721) serves destinations around the province including Vancouver airport and Victoria airport. **West Coast Air** (☎ 604/688–9115 or 800/347–2222) and **Harbour Air** (☎ 604/688–1277 or 800/665–0212) both operate 35-minute harbor-to-harbor service (downtown Vancouver to downtown Victoria) several times a day. Planes leave from near the **Pan Pacific Hotel** (✉ 300–999 Canada Pl.). **Helijet Airways** (☎ 604/273–1414 or 800/665–4354) has helicopter service between downtown Vancouver, downtown Seattle, and downtown Victoria. The heliport is near Vancouver's Pan Pacific Hotel (☞ *above*).

BETWEEN THE AIRPORT AND DOWNTOWN

The drive from the airport to downtown takes 20 to 45 minutes, depending on the time of day. Airport hotels provide free shuttle service to and from the airport. If you're driving, go over the Arthur Lang Bridge and north on Granville Street (also signposted as Highway 99). Signs will direct you to Vancouver City Centre.

The **Vancouver Airporter Service** (☎ 604/946–8866) bus leaves the international and domestic arrivals levels of the terminal building about every half hour, stopping at major downtown hotels. It operates from 5:23 AM until midnight. The fare is $10 one way and $17 round-trip.

Taxi stands are in front of the terminal building on domestic and international arrivals levels. The taxi fare to downtown is about $22. Area cab companies include **Black Top** (☎ 604/681–2181) and **Yellow** (☎ 604/681–1111).

Limousine service from **Airlimo** (☎ 604/273–1331) costs a bit more than the taxi fare to downtown, about $30.

By Train

The **Pacific Central Station** (✉ 1150 Station St.), at Main Street and Terminal Avenue, near the Main Street SkyTrain station, is the hub for rail service. **Amtrak** (☎ 800/872–7245) operates the *Mt. Baker International* train between Seattle and Vancouver, and in late 1999 is scheduled to begin its *Cascades* high-speed train service between Vancouver and Eugene, Oregon. **VIA Rail** (☎ 800/561–8630 in Canada; 800/561–3949 in the U.S.) provides transcontinental service through Jasper to Toronto three times a week. Passenger trains leave the **BC Rail Station** (✉ 1311 W. 1st St., ☎ 604/631–3500; 800/339–8752 in British Columbia; 800/663–8238 from outside British Columbia) in North Vancouver for Whistler and the interior of British Columbia.

Getting Around

Ride a bike, walk, take a cab, or take the bus, SeaBus, SkyTrain, or False Creek Ferry, but if at all possible avoid using a car in downtown Vancouver. The congested downtown core is all of about 2 square mi. There is very little parking and many one-way streets, all of which makes driving difficult. There's really no advantage to bringing a car downtown, unless you're staying there, in which case your hotel will have parking. Even then, you'll still be better off using public transportation to tour the area.

By Bus

Exact change is needed to ride **Translink** (☎ 604/521–0400) buses. Buslink buses are run by Translink. The fare is $1.50 for normal rides, and $2.25 for weekday trips to the suburbs, including the SeaBus to the North Shore. Books of 10 tickets are sold at convenience stores and newsstands; look for a red, white, and blue FARE DEALER sign. Day passes, good for unlimited travel all day, cost $6. They are available from fare dealers and at any SeaBus or SkyTrain station. Transfers are valid for 90 minutes, allow travel in both directions, and are good on buses, SkyTrain, and SeaBus. A guide called "Discover Vancouver on Transit" is available free at the Tourist Info Centre (☞ Visitor Information *in* Important Contacts, *below*).

By Car

Vancouver rush-hour traffic can be horrendous. The worst bottlenecks outside the city center are the North Shore bridges, the George Massey Tunnel on Highway 99 south of Vancouver, and Highway 1 through Coquitlam and Surrey. Parking downtown is expensive and tricky to find; metered street parking is scarce. Two large underground pay parking lots that usually have space are at **Library Square** (⊠ 800 block of Hamilton St., off Robson St.) and **Pacific Centre** (⊠ 700 block Howe St., east side). Parking fees vary, running from about $6 to $10 a day. Don't leave anything in your car, even in the trunk. Car break-ins are quite common downtown (hotel parking tends to be more secure than public lots). Parking outside the downtown core is an easier proposition. Right turns are allowed on most red lights after you've come to a full stop.

By Ferry

The **SeaBus** is a 400-passenger commuter ferry that crosses Burrard Inlet from the foot of Lonsdale (North Vancouver) to downtown. The ride takes 13 minutes and costs the same as the Buslink bus (and it's much faster). With a transfer, connection can be made to any Buslink bus or SkyTrain. **Aquabus Ferries** (☎ 604/689–5858) and **False Creek Ferries** (☎ 604/684–7781), which are not part of the Translink system, connect several stations on False Creek including Science World, Granville Island, Stamp's Landing, Yaletown, Vanier Park, and the Hornby Street dock. Aquabus Ferries can take bicycles.

By Rapid Transit

Vancouver has a one-line, 25-km (16-mi) rapid transit system called **SkyTrain,** which travels underground downtown and is elevated for the rest of its route to New Westminster and Surrey. Trains leave about every five minutes. Tickets, sold at each station from machines (correct change is not necessary), must be carried with you as proof of payment. You may use transfers from SkyTrain to SeaBus (☞ *above*) and Buslink buses and vice versa. The SkyTrain is convenient for transit between downtown, BC Place Stadium, Pacific Central Station, and Science World.

By Taxi

It is difficult to hail a cab in Vancouver. Unless you're near a hotel, you'll have better luck calling a taxi service. Try **Black Top** (☎ 604/683–4567) or **Yellow** (☎ 604/681–1111).

Contacts and Resources

B&B Reservation Agencies

Super, Natural British Columbia (✉ 601–1166 Alberni St., V6E 3Z3, ☎ 604/663–6000 or 800/663–6000) can book accommodation anywhere in British Columbia. **Town & Country Bed and Breakfast Reservation Service** (✉ Box 74542, 2803 W. 4th Ave., V6K 1K2, ☎ FAX 604/731–5942) specializes in B&Bs.

Car Rental

Avis (☎ 604/606–2847 or 800/331–1212). **Budget** (☎ 604/668–7000 or 800/527–0700). **Thrifty Car Rental** (☎ 604/606–1666 or 800/367–2277).

Consulates

Australia (✉ 1225-888 Dunsmuir St., ☎ 604/684–1177). **New Zealand** (✉ 1200-888 Dunsmuir St., ☎ 604/684–7388). **United Kingdom** (✉ 800-1111 Melville St., ☎ 604/683–4421). **United States** (✉ 1095 W. Pender St., ☎ 604/685–4311).

Emergencies

Ambulance (☎ 911). **Fire** (☎ 911). **Police** (☎ 911).

Medicentre (✉ 1055 Dunsmuir St., lower level, ☎ 604/683–8138), a drop-in clinic in the Bentall Centre, is open weekdays. Doctors are on call through the emergency ward at **St. Paul's Hospital** (✉ 1081 Burrard St., ☎ 604/682–2344), a downtown facility open around the clock.

Guided Tours

Tour prices fluctuate, so inquire about rates when booking tours. Kids are generally charged half the adult fare.

AIR

Tour Vancouver, the harbor, or the mountains of the North Shore by helicopter. For around $200 per person (minimum of three people) for 45 minutes, **Vancouver Helicopters** (☎ 604/270–1484) flies from the Harbour Heliport downtown. You can see Vancouver from the air for $72 for 30 minutes, or take a 90-minute flight over nearby mountains and glaciers with **Harbour Air Seaplanes** (☎ 604/688–1277), which leaves from beside the Pan Pacific Hotel.

BOAT

Aquabus Ferries (☎ 604/689–5858) and **False Creek Ferries** (☎ 604/684–7781) both operate 25-minute minicruises around False Creek for about $6. You can also take a 1-hour tour of False Creek on a vintage wooden ferry with **Aquabus Ferries.** The tours cost $10 and leave hourly from the Aquabus dock on Granville Island.

Harbour Cruises (✉ 1 N. Denman St., ☎ 604/688–7246), at the foot of Denman Street on Coal Harbour, operates a 1¼-hour narrated tour of Burrard Inlet aboard the paddle wheeler MPV *Constitution*. Tours, which cost less than $20, take place from April through October. Harbour Cruises also offers sunset dinner cruises, four-hour lunch cruises up scenic Indian Arm, and links with the Royal Hudson Steam Train (☞ Train Tours, *below*) to make a daylong boat-train excursion to Howe Sound.

Paddlewheeler River Adventures (✉ 810 Quayside Dr., New Westminster, ☎ 604/525–4465), in the Information Centre at Westminster Quay, will take you out on the Fraser River in an 1800s-style paddle wheeler. Choose from a three-hour tour of the working river, a day trip to historic Fort Langley, a sunset dinner cruise, or a Friday night martini cruise.

ECOLOGY

By Cycle Tours (✉ ☎ 604/936–2453) runs bicycle tours around Vancouver. A unique way to see the heights of the city is the Grouse Mountain downhill mountain-biking trip operated by **Velo-City Cycle Tours** (☎ 604/924–0288).

Hike B.C. (☎ 604/540–2499) conducts guided hikes and snowshoe trips to the North Shore mountains. Another good operator with a number of interpretive day hikes around Vancouver is **Path of Logic Wilderness Adventures** (☎ 604/802–2082). **Rockwood Adventures** (☎ 604/926–7705) conducts various guided hikes through the rain forests and canyons surrounding the city, including a popular day trip to Bowen Island in Howe Sound.

From May through October, **Lotus Land Tours** (☎ 604/684–4922 or 800/528–3531) runs an easygoing four-hour sea kayak trip that includes a salmon barbecue lunch. The trip visits Twin Island (an uninhabited provincial marine park) to explore marine life in the intertidal zone. Experience is not required. The kayaks are easy for beginners to handle.

A number of companies offer multiday sea kayaking trips out of Vancouver, including **Canadian Outback Adventure Company** (☎ 604/921–7250 or 800/565–8735), which offers river rafting as well, **Ecosummer Expeditions** (☎ 604/214–7484 or 800/465–8884), which also runs sailing trips, and **Ocean West Expeditions** (☎ 604/898–4979 or 800/660–0051). Most trips offer a good chance of spotting orca whales, and some are suitable for first-timers.

In December and January, bald eagles gather at Brackendale, about an hour north of Vancouver. With **Canadian Outback Adventures** (☎ 604/921–7250 or 800/565–8735) you can watch and photograph the eagles from a slow-moving raft on the river. **Lotus Land Tours** (☎ 604/684–4922 or 800/528–3531) also offers eagle-watching trips, as well as sea lion viewing tours in April and May. **Vancouver All-Terrain Adventures** (☎ 604/434–2278 or 888/754–5601) runs a variety of four-wheel-drive trips into the mountains near Vancouver, including an eagle-viewing trip.

FIRST NATIONS

West Coast City and Nature Sightseeing (☎ 604/451–1600) offers a daily, four-hour Native Culture tour, with expert guides offering insights into the history and culture of Vancouver-area First Nations peoples. The tours take in the Stanley Park totem poles, the Museum of Anthropology, and two First Nations community facilities: the First Nations House of Learning and the Native Education Centre. The $41 fee includes admission to the Museum of Anthropology.

ORIENTATION

Gray Line (☎ 604/879–3363 or 800/667–0882) offers a 3½-hour Grand City bus tour year-round. The tour picks up at all major downtown hotels and includes Stanley Park, Chinatown, Gastown, English Bay, and Queen Elizabeth Park. The fee is about $39. From May through October, Gray Line also has a narrated city tour aboard double-decker buses. Passengers can get on and off as they choose and can travel free the next day. Adult fare is about $22. The one-hour **Stanley Park Horse Drawn Tours** (☎ 604/681–5115) cost about $14 per person ($43 for a family of four). The tours leave every 20 to 30 minutes from the information booth on Stanley Park Drive. The **Vancouver Trolley Company** (☎ 604/801–5515 or 888/451–5581) runs old-style trolleys through Vancouver from mid-March through October on a two-hour narrated tour of Stanley Park, Gastown, English Bay, Granville

Island, and Chinatown, among other sights. A day pass allows you to complete one full circuit, getting off and on as often as you like. Start the trip at any of the 16 sights and buy a ticket on board. The adult fare is $22. **West Coast City and Nature Sightseeing** (☎ 604/451–1600) runs a four-hour City Highlights tour for about $40. Pickup is available from all major hotels downtown.

North Shore tours usually include any or several of the following: a gondola ride up Grouse Mountain, a walk across the Capilano Suspension Bridge, a stop at a salmon hatchery, a visit to the Lonsdale Quay Market, and a ride back to town on the SeaBus. North Shore tours are offered year-round by **Landsea Tours** (☎ 604/255–7272) and **West Coast City and Nature Sightseeing** (☎ 604/451–1600). The half-day tours cost between $45 and $55.

PERSONAL GUIDES

Early Motion Tours (☎ 604/687–5088) will pick you up at your hotel for a spin through Vancouver in a Model-A Ford convertible. Individualized tours in six European languages are available from **VIP Tourguide Services** (☎ 604/214–4677).

TRAIN

You can sample West Coast cuisine in the vintage rail coaches of the **Pacific Starlight Dinner Train** (☎ 604/631–3500; 800/339–8752 in British Columbia; 800/663–8238 from outside British Columbia), which leaves the North Vancouver BC Rail station at 6:15 PM, stops at scenic Porteau Cove on Howe Sound, and returns to the station at 10 PM. The train runs from Wednesday through Sunday May–October. Fares, including a three-course meal, are $71 for salon seating, $86 for the dome car. Reservations are essential.

The Royal Hudson (☎ 604/631–3500; 800/339–8752 in British Columbia; 800/663–8238 from outside British Columbia), Canada's only functioning main-line steam train, leaves the North Vancouver BC Rail station for a trip along the mountainous coast up Howe Sound to the logging town of Squamish. After a break there, you can return by train or sail back to Vancouver on the MV *Britannia*. The trip runs from Wednesday through Sunday June–late September. The round-trip train fare is $46.50 or $85 with a three-course meal. By train and boat the trip costs about $75. Reservations are advised.

WALKING

During the summer, students from the **Architectural Institute of British Columbia** (☎ 604/683–8588) lead free walking tours of the city's top heritage sites. The **Gastown Business Improvement Society** (☎ 604/683–5650) sponsors free 90-minute historical and architectural walking tours daily June–August. Meet the guide at 2 PM at the statue of "Gassy" Jack in Maple Tree Square. Ninety-minute walking tours of Chinatown leave from the **Chinese Cultural Centre** (⌂ 50 E. Pender St., ☎ 604/687–0729) daily, on the hour from 10 to 4 and cost $5. **Rockwood Adventures** (☎ 604/926–7705) has guided walks around Vancouver neighborhoods, including Gastown, Granville Island, and Chinatown, and a special walk for art lovers. Guides with **Walkabout Historic Vancouver** (☎ 604/720–0006) take on the costume and the character of early residents for their two-hour historical walking tours around Downtown and Gastown or Granville Island. Tours run year-round.

Late-Night Pharmacy

Shopper's Drug Mart (⌂ 1125 Davie St., ☎ 604/669–2424) is open around the clock.

Road Emergencies

The **British Columbia Automobile Association** (☎ 604/293–2222) provides 24-hour emergency road service for members of the American
Automobile Association and the Canadian Automobile Association.

Visitor Information

Super, Natural B.C. (☎ 800/663–6000). **Vancouver Tourist Info Centre**
(✉ 200 Burrard St., V6C 3L6, ☎ 604/683–2000).

5 SIDE TRIPS FROM VANCOUVER

Victoria, the capital of British Columbia, is one of several destinations within easy reach of Vancouver. Long known as the most British city in Canada, Victoria has shed its tea-cozy image and reemerged as a Pacific Rim metropolis that celebrates its native, Asian, and European roots. Also near Vancouver are the rustic Gulf Islands and Whistler, one of North America's premier ski resorts.

OSMOPOLITAN VANCOUVER IS BRITISH COLUMBIA'S urban star, but to appreciate the province's most dramatic natural attractions you'll need to travel beyond the city limits. No matter how modern British Columbia may appear, evidence remains of the earliest settlers: Pacific Coast first nations peoples (Haida, Kwakiutl, Nootka, Salish, and others) who occupied the land for more than 12,000 years before the first Europeans arrived en masse in the late 19th century. British Columbia's heritage is on display throughout the province, in art galleries and restaurants, in the totems and petroglyphs on Vancouver Island, and in the striking collections at the Royal British Columbia Museum in Victoria and the Cowichan Native Village in Duncan.

Revised by Sue Kernaghan

Pleasures and Pastimes

Dining

Restaurants are generally casual in the region. A bylaw bans smoking in all public places, including restaurants and bars, in Greater Victoria and the southern Gulf Islands. For price ranges on Vancouver Island and the Gulf Islands refer to the chart below. A separate chart in the coverage of Whistler outlines meal costs in that resort town.

CATEGORY	COST*
$$$$	over C$35
$$$	C$25–C$35
$$	C$15–C$25
$	under C$15
*per person, excluding drinks, service, and 7% GST	

Lodging

Accommodations across the province range from bed-and-breakfasts and rustic cabins to deluxe chain hotels. Most small inns and B&Bs in Victoria and the Gulf Islands are entirely no-smoking, and virtually all hotels in the area offer no-smoking rooms. For price ranges on Vancouver Island and the Gulf Islands refer to the chart below. A separate chart in the coverage of Whistler outlines room costs in that resort town.

CATEGORY	COST*
$$$$	over C$250
$$$	C$170–C$250
$$	C$90–C$170
$	under C$90
*All prices are for a standard double room, excluding 10% provincial accommodation tax, service charge, and 7% GST.	

VICTORIA

Victoria was the first European settlement on Vancouver Island. In 1843 the city, originally known as Fort Victoria, was made the westernmost trading outpost of the British-owned Hudson's Bay Company. Victoria became the capital of British Columbia in 1868. The city is 71 km (44 mi) south of Vancouver and a 2½-hour ferry ride from Seattle.

Exploring Victoria

Numbers in the text correspond to numbers in the margin and on the Downtown Victoria map.

Southern Vancouver Island

A Good Walk

Begin on the waterfront at the **Visitors Information Centre** ①. Across the way on Government Street is the majestic **Empress** ② hotel. A short walk south on Government Street leads to the **Parliament Buildings** ③ complex on Belleville Street. Cross Government to reach the **Royal British Columbia Museum** ④. Behind the museum and bordering Douglas Street is Thunderbird Park, where totem poles and a ceremonial longhouse stand in one corner of the garden of **Helmcken House** ⑤. A walk south on Douglas Street leads to **Beacon Hill Park** ⑥. A few blocks west of the park on Government Street is **Emily Carr House,** the birthplace of British Columbia's best-known painter. From the park, walk north on Douglas Street to Blanshard Street, where, just past Academy Close, you'll see the entrance to **St. Ann's Academy,** a former convent school with parklike grounds. (There's also a footpath to the academy from Southgate Street). From St. Ann's, follow Belleville Street west. The next stop, at the corner of Douglas and Belleville, is the glass-roofed **Crystal Gardens Conservatory** ⑦.

From Crystal Gardens, continue north on Douglas Street to View Street, then west to **Bastion Square** ⑧. Stop in at the **Maritime Museum of British Columbia** ⑨ to learn about an important part of the province's history. Around the corner on Wharf Street is the **Victoria Bug Zoo,** a creepy crawly attraction popular with kids. West of Government Street between Pandora Avenue and Johnson Street is the **Market Square** ⑩ shopping district. Around the corner from Market Square is Fisgard Street, the heart of **Chinatown** ⑪. A 25-minute walk or a short drive east on Fort Street will take you to Joan Crescent and lavish **Craigdarroch Castle** ⑫. Down the hill on Moss Street is the **Art Gallery of Greater Victoria.** In summer, a ride on Harbour Ferries (☞ Victoria, A to Z, *below*), from the Inner Harbour will take you to **Point Ellice House,** an historic waterside home and garden.

Downtown Victoria

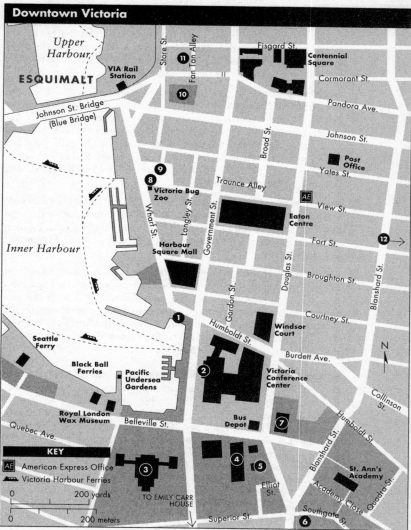

KEY

AE American Express Office
Victoria Harbour Ferries

0   200 yards
0   200 meters

Upper Harbour

ESQUIMALT

VIA Rail Station

Johnson St. Bridge (Blue Bridge)

Inner Harbour

Seattle Ferry

Black Ball Ferries

Pacific Undersea Gardens

Royal London Wax Museum

Quebec Ave.

TO EMILY CARR HOUSE

Store St.

Fan Tan Alley

Fisgard St.

Centennial Square

Cormorant St.

Pandora Ave.

Broad St.

Johnson St.

Post Office

Yates St.

Trounce Alley

View St.

Eaton Centre

Fort St.

Blanshard St.

Wharf St.

Langley St.

Government St.

Victoria Bug Zoo

Harbour Square Mall

Douglas St.

Broughton St.

Courtney St.

Gordon St.

Humboldt St.

Windsor Court

Burdett Ave.

Victoria Conference Center

Belleville St.

Bus Depot

Collinson St.

Humboldt St.

Blanshard St.

St. Ann's Academy

Academy Close

Quadra St.

Elliot St.

Southgate St.

Superior St.

N

TIMING

Many of the attractions in downtown Victoria are within easy walking distance of one another. You can walk this tour in a day, but there's so much to see at the Royal British Columbia Museum and the other museums that you could easily spend two. This would allow time for some shopping and a visit to Craigdarroch Castle.

Sights to See

Art Gallery of Greater Victoria. This fine museum houses large collections of Chinese and Japanese ceramics and contains the only authentic Shinto shrine in North America. A permanent exhibit of British Columbian artist Emily Carr's work is on display. The gallery is a few blocks west of Craigdarroch Castle, off Fort Street. ⊠ *1040 Moss St.,* ☎ *250/384–4101.* ⊡ *$5, Mon. by donation.* ☉ *Mon.–Wed., Fri., and Sat. 10–5, Thurs. 10–9, Sun. 1–5.*

❽ Bastion Square. James Douglas, the fur trader and former colonial governor for whom Douglas Street was named, chose this spot for the original Fort Victoria and Hudson's Bay Company trading post. Fashion boutiques and restaurants occupy the old buildings. ⊠ *Off Wharf St., at the end of View St.*

★ ☜ **❻ Beacon Hill Park.** The southern lawns of this spacious park have great views of the Olympic Mountains and the Strait of Juan de Fuca. Also here are lakes, jogging and walking paths, abundant flowers and gardens, a wading pool, a petting zoo, and an outdoor amphitheater for Sunday afternoon concerts. The park is home to the world's tallest freestanding totem pole and Mile Zero of the Trans-Canada Highway. ⊠ *East of Douglas St., south of Southgate St.*

OFF THE
BEATEN PATH

BUTCHART GARDENS – Originally a private estate and still family-run, this stunning 50-acre garden has been drawing visitors since it was planted in a limestone quarry in 1904. The site's Japanese, Italian, rose, and sunken gardens grow 700 varieties of flowers in a setting that's beautiful year-round. From mid-June to mid-September many of the exhibits are illuminated at night, and musicians and other entertainers perform in the afternoons and evenings. In July and August, fireworks light the sky over the gardens on Saturday nights. Bring a picnic if you'd like. ⊠ *800 Benvenuto Ave., Brentwood Bay,* ☎ *250/652–5256 or 250/652–4422; 250/652–8222 for dining reservations.* ⊡ *$15.75; discounts in winter.* ☉ *June 15–Sept. 4, daily 9 AM–10:30 PM; Sept. 5–Sept. 15, daily 9–9; Sept. 16–June 14, call for hrs.*

⓫ Chinatown. Chinese immigrants built much of the Canadian Pacific Railway in the 19th century, and their influence still marks the region. If you enter Chinatown from Government Street, you'll pass under the elaborate **Gate of Harmonious Interest,** made of Taiwanese ceramic tiles and decorative panels. Along the street, merchants display paper lanterns, embroidered silks, imported fruits, and vegetables. Mahjongg, fan-tan, and dominoes were among the games of chance played on narrow **Fan Tan Alley.** Once the gambling and opium center of Chinatown, it's now lined with offbeat shops. Look for the alley on the south side of Fisgard Street between Nos. 545½ and 549½.

⓬ Craigdarroch Castle. This castlelike mansion was built as the home of one of British Columbia's wealthiest men, coal baron Robert Dunsmuir, who died in 1889, just a few months before the castle's completion. Converted into a museum depicting life in that period, the castle has ornate Victorian furnishings, stained-glass windows, carved woodwork—precut in Chicago for Dunsmuir and sent by rail—and a beautifully restored ceiling frieze in the drawing room. A winding staircase climbs four floors to a ballroom and a tower overlooking Victoria and the Olympic Mountains. ✉ *1050 Joan Crescent,* ☎ *250/592–5323.* ▣ *$7.50.* ☉ *Mid-June–early Sept., daily 9–7; mid-Sept.–mid-June, daily 10–4:30.*

👋 ❼ **Crystal Gardens Conservatory.** Opened in 1925 as the largest saltwater swimming pool in the British Empire, this glass-roof building houses exotic flora and a variety of endangered tropical mammals, reptiles, and birds, including flamingos, tortoises, macaws, lemurs, bats, and, in summer, butterflies. ✉ *713 Douglas St.,* ☎ *250/381–1213.* ▣ *$7.* ☉ *July–Aug. daily 8:30–8; call for hrs rest of yr.*

Emily Carr House. Emily Carr (1871–1945), one of Canada's most celebrated artists—and a respected writer as well—was born and raised in this very proper wooden Victorian house before abandoning her middle-class life to live in, and paint, the wilds of British Columbia. ✉ *207 Government St.,* ☎ *250/383–5843.* ▣ *$5.* ☉ *Mid-May–mid-Oct., daily 10–5; Dec. 1–Dec. 24 and Dec. 27–Dec. 31, daily 11–4. At other times, tours by arrangement.*

★ ❷ **The Empress Hotel.** A symbol of the city and the Canadian Pacific Railway, the Empress was designed by Francis Rattenbury, who also designed the Parliament buildings. The ingredients that made the 483-room, château-style structure a tourist attraction in the past—Old World architecture, an ornate decor, and a commanding view of the Inner Harbour—are still here. You can stop in for afternoon tea (the dress code calls for smart casual wear and reservations are recommended). Hotel staff run tours daily at 10 AM in summer. The archives, an historical photo display, are open to the public anytime. **Miniature World** (☎ 250/385–9731), a display of doll-size dioramas, is on the Humboldt Street side of the complex. ✉ *721 Government St.,* ☎ *250/384–8111.* ▣ *Free; historical tours $6; afternoon tea $21; Miniature World $8.*

❺ **Helmcken House.** The oldest house in British Columbia was erected in 1852 for pioneer doctor and statesman John Sebastian Helmcken. Audio tours of the house, whose holdings include early Victorian furnishings and an intriguing collection of 19th-century medical tools, last 20 minutes. The building next door to Helmcken House (but not open for tours) is **St. Ann's Schoolhouse,** one of the first schools in British Columbia. **Thunderbird Park,** with totem poles and a ceremonial longhouse constructed by Kwakiutl chief Mungo Martin, occupies one corner of the Helmcken House's garden. ✉ *10 Elliot St.,* ☎ *250/361–0021.* ▣ *$4.* ☉ *May–Sept., daily 10–5; Feb.–Apr. and Oct.–mid.-Nov. Thurs.–Mon. 11–4. Closed Jan. and late Nov.*

👋 ❾ **Maritime Museum of British Columbia.** The dugout canoes, model ships, Royal Navy charts, photographs, uniforms, and ship's bells at this museum inside Victoria's original courthouse chronicle the city's seafaring history. A seldom-used 100-year-old cage lift, believed to be the oldest in North America, ascends to the third floor, where the original admiralty courtroom looks set for a court-martial. ✉ *28 Bastion Sq.,* ☎ *250/385–4222.* ▣ *$5.* ☉ *Daily 9:30–4:30.*

❿ **Market Square.** During the late 19th century, this two-level square, built like an old inn courtyard, provided everything a sailor, miner, or lumberjack could want. Restored to its original architectural, if not commercial, character, it's a pedestrian-only, café- and boutique-lined hangout. As in the days of yore, it's a great spot for people-watching. ✉ *West of Government St., between Pandora Ave. and Johnson St.*

★ ❸ **Parliament Buildings.** These massive stone structures, completed in 1898, dominate the Inner Harbour. Two statues flank them, one of Sir James

Douglas, who chose the site where Victoria was built, the other of Sir Matthew Baille Begbie, the man in charge of law and order during the gold-rush era. Atop the central dome is a gilded statue of Captain George Vancouver, the first European to sail around Vancouver Island. A statue of Queen Victoria reigns over the front of the complex. More than 3,000 lights outline the buildings at night. Another of Francis Rattenbury's creations (☞ The Empress, *above*), the Parliament Buildings typify the rigid symmetry and European elegance of much of the city's architecture. When the legislature is in session, you can sit in the public gallery and watch British Columbia's often polarized democracy at work (custom has the opposing parties sitting two-and-a-half sword lengths apart). Informative half-hour tours are obligatory on summer weekends and optional the rest of the time. ⊠ *501 Belleville St.,* ☎ *250/387–3046.* ▣ *Free.* ☉ *June–Aug., daily 9–5; Sept.–May, weekdays 8:30–5.*

OFF THE BEATEN PATH

POINT ELLICE HOUSE – The O'Reilly family home, an 1867 Italianate villa overlooking the Upper Harbour, has been restored to its original splendor, with the largest collection of Victorian furnishings in Western Canada. Tea and home-baked goodies are served on the lawn. Visitors can also take an audio tour of the house, stroll in the gardens, or try their hand at croquet. Point Ellice house is a few minutes' drive north of downtown, but it's much more fun to come by sea. Harbour Ferries (Getting Around, in Victoria A to Z, *below*) leave from a dock in front of the Empress Hotel. ⊠ *2616 Pleasant St.,* ☎ *250/380–6506 or 250/387–4697.* ▣ *$4; $13 for tea.* ☉ *Mid-May–mid-Sept., daily 10–5. Tea served noon–4.*

★ ☙ ❹ **Royal British Columbia Museum.** At the best attraction in Victoria, you can spend hours wandering through the centuries, back 12,000 years. The First Peoples exhibit includes a genuine Kwakwaka'wakw longhouse and provides insights into the daily life, art, and mythology of coastal and lesser-known interior groups. The Modern History Gallery re-creates most of a frontier town, complete with cobblestone streets, silent movies, and the rumbling of a train. The Natural History Gallery reproduces the sights, sounds, and smells of many of the province's natural habitats, and the Open Ocean mimics, all too realistically, a submarine journey. An IMAX theater shows National Geographic films on a six-story-high screen. ⊠ *675 Belleville St.,* ☎ *250/387–3701 or 800/661–5411.* ▣ *$8, some surcharges for special events; IMAX theater $9.* ☉ *Museum daily 9–5, theater daily 10–8.*

St. Ann's Academy. This former convent and school, founded in 1858, played a central role in Victoria's pioneer life. Closed in 1974, it was carefully restored and reopened as an historic site in 1997. The academy's little chapel—the first Roman Catholic cathedral in Victoria—now looks just as it did in the 1920s. The six-acre grounds, with their fruit trees and herb and flower gardens, are also being restored as historic landscapes. ⊠ *835 Humboldt St.,* ☎ *250/386–1428.* ▣ *Free.* ☉ *July–Aug., daily 10–4; May–June and Sept.–Oct., Wed.–Sun. 10–4. Call for winter hrs.*

☙ **Victoria Bug Zoo.** This offbeat, two-room minizoo draws plenty of children and their parents. Many of the bugs—mostly large tropical varieties such as stick insects, scorpions, and centipedes—can be held, and staff members are on hand to dispense scientific information. ⊠ *1107 Wharf St.,* ☎ *250/384–2847.* ▣ *$6.* ☉ *Daily 9:30–6.*

❶ **Visitor Information Centre.** You can get the lowdown on Victoria's tourist and other attractions at this facility near the harbor ferries. The staff

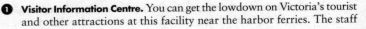

here can help you out with maps, theater and concert tickets, accommodation reservations, and outdoor adventure day trips. ✉ *812 Wharf St.,* ☎ *250/953–2033.* ⊙ *July–Aug., daily 8:30–8; May–June and Sept., daily 9–7; Oct.–Apr., daily 9–5.*

Dining

Chinese

$$–$$$$ ✕ **Don Mee's.** A large neon sign invites you inside this traditional Chinese restaurant that's been in business for 70 years. The entrées served in the expansive dining room include sweet-and-sour chicken, Peking duck, and bean curd with broccoli. Dim sum is served at lunchtime. ✉ *538 Fisgard St.,* ☎ *250/383–1032. AE, DC, MC, V.*

Contemporary

$$$$ ✕ **Empress Room.** Beautifully presented Pacific Northwest cuisine vies
★   for attention at the elegant Empress Room, where candlelight dances on tapestried walls beneath a carved mahogany ceiling. Fresh local ingredients go into imaginative seasonal dishes like the wild-mushroom-and-chicken terrine, the veal tenderloin with a crust of wild rice and herbs, and Fraser Valley smoked marinated duck breast. The wine list is excellent, as are the table d'hôte menus. ✉ *Empress, 721 Government St.,* ☎ *250/389–2727 or 800/644–6611. Reservations essential. AE, D, DC, MC, V. No lunch.*

$$$–$$$$ ✕ **Camille's.** The menu at quiet and intimate Camille's emphasizes fresh local products and regional exotica like ostrich, quail, and emu. These and favorites like the lamb with a crust of mint and Dijon mustard and the roast venison with wild-mushroom polenta are served in generous portions. ✉ *45 Bastion Sq.,* ☎ *250/381–3433. AE, MC, V. No lunch.*

$$$–$$$$ ✕ **The Victorian Restaurant.** This small, formal restaurant in the Ocean Pointe Resort has striking views over the Inner Harbour and a seasonally changing menu of fine Pacific Northwest cuisine. Chef Craig Stoneman offers such elegantly presented regional dishes as wild mushroom and truffle soup, roast rack of lamb with maple and juniper glaze, and pheasant breast with goat cheese and sun-dried cranberry mousse. The wine list has won a number of awards, including Wine Spectator's Award of Excellence in 1999. ✉ *45 Songhees Rd., (across the Johnson Street bridge from downtown Victoria,* ☎ *250/360–5800. Reservations essential. AE, D, DC, MC, V. Closed Sun.–Mon. Nov.–Apr. No lunch.*

$$–$$$$ ✕ **Café Brio.** In an Italian Villa–style building, a little north of the Inner
★   Harbour, candlelight, hardwood floors, lush Modigliani nudes, and rich gold walls create a warm glow. The daily menu depends on what's fresh that day—very fresh. The café works in partnership with a local organic farm and serves the produce the same day it's harvested. Favorites have included confit of duck with three bean, pancetta, and tomato braise, and a melt-in-the-mouth lamb sirloin served with leeks and chanterelles. There are always good vegetarian options, and the extensive wine list goes easy on the markups. ✉ *944 Fort St.,* ☎ *250/383–0009. AE, MC, V. No lunch weekends.*

$$–$$$$ ✕ **Herald Street Caffe.** Intriguing combinations are the hallmarks of
★   this art-filled bistro in Victoria's warehouse district. The menu, which changes seasonally, always lists fresh local cuisine, daily fish grills, great pastas, and good vegetarian selections. Try, if available, a starter of East Coast mussels steamed in a lemon Szechuan peppercorn pesto, followed by calamari in tomato-dill ratatouille with crumbled feta, or free-range beef tenderloin stuffed with a wild mushroom chestnut paté. The wine list is excellent. ✉ *546 Herald St.,* ☎ *250/381–1441. Reservations essential. AE, DC, MC, V. No lunch Mon.–Tues.*

Indian

$$ ✕ **Bengal Lounge.** Buffet lunches in the elegant Empress Hotel include curries with extensive condiment trays of coconut, nuts, cool *raita* (yogurt with mint or cucumber), and chutney. Popular with cabinet ministers and bureaucrats, the curry lunches are almost as much a Victorian tradition as high tea. ⊠ *721 Government St.,* ☎ *250/384–8111. AE, D, DC, MC, V. No dinner buffet Fri.–Sat.*

Italian

$$$–$$$$ ✕ **Il Terrazzo.** The locals' choice for romantic outdoor dining prepares
★   scallops dipped in roasted pistachios and garnished with arugula, Belgian endive, and mango salsa; grilled lamb chops on angel-hair pasta with tomatoes, garlic, mint, and black pepper; and other hearty northern Italian dishes. ⊠ *555 Johnson St., off Waddington Alley (call for directions),* ☎ *250/361–0028. Reservations essential. AE, MC, V. No lunch Sun. No lunch Sat. Oct. –Apr.*

Seafood

$$–$$$$ ✕ **The Marina Restaurant.** The Marina, a prime spot for Sunday brunch, has a 180-degree view over Oak Bay. The extensive menu usually lists creative appetizers like warm salmon and spinach salad, and a variety of pastas, grills, and seafood entrées. There's also a sushi bar. Downstairs is a more casual café-deli.⊠ *1327 Beach Dr.,* ☎ *250/598–8555. AE, DC, MC, V.*

$ ✕ **Barb's Place.** Funky Barb's, a blue-painted take-out shack, sits out where the fishing boats dock, west of the Inner Harbour off Erie Street. Locals consider the authentic fish-and-chips to be the best in town. You can catch a ferry to Fisherman's Wharf from the Inner Harbour, pick up an order, and take another ferry to Songhees Point for a picnic. ⊠ *Fisherman's Wharf, 310 St. Lawrence St.,* ☎ *250/384–6515. No credit cards. Closed Nov.–Mar.*

Thai

$$–$$$ ✕ **Siam Thai.** The chefs at Siam work wonders with hot and mild Thai dishes that you can wash down with any of several good beers. The *pad Thai goong* (fried rice noodles with prawns, tofu, peanuts, eggs, bean sprouts, and green onions) and *satay* (grilled, marinated cubes of meat served with a spicy peanut sauce) are particularly good options. ⊠ *512 Fort St.,* ☎ *250/383–9911. AE, DC, MC, V. No lunch Sun.*

Vegetarian

$–$$ ✕ **Re-Bar Modern Foods.** This bright and casual, kid-friendly café in Bastion Square is *the* place for vegetarians in Victoria. The almond burgers, wild mushroom ravioli, decadent home-baked goodies, and big breakfasts will keep omnivores happy, too. An extensive tea and fresh juice selection shares space with espresso, microbrews, and local wines on the drinks list. ⊠ *50 Bastion Square,* ☎ *250/361–9223. AE, DC, MC, V.*

Vietnamese

$$–$$$ ✕ **Le Petit Saigon.** The fare is Vietnamese with French influences at this intimate café-style restaurant. The crab, asparagus, and egg swirl soup is a house specialty, and combination meals are cheap and tasty. ⊠ *1010 Langley St.,* ☎ *250/386–1412. AE, MC, V. No lunch Sun.*

Lodging

$$$$ ▥ **Coast Victoria Harbourside.** West of the Inner Harbour, the Coast Victoria has marine views but is away from the traffic on Government Street. Serene relaxation in modern comfort is a theme here, from the mahogany-panel lobby and soothing shades in average-size guest rooms to an extensive health club. Fishing and whale-watching charters and the harbor ferries stop at the hotel's marina. Guests ride on the hotel's downtown shuttle for free. The hotel's **Blue Crab** restaurant, with its seafood and harbor views, is a popular dining spot. ⊠ *146 Kingston St., V8V 1V4,* ☎ *250/360–1211 or 800/663–1144,* FAX *250/360–1418. 126 rooms, 6 suites. Restaurant, bar, minibars, no-smoking rooms, room service, indoor-outdoor pool, hot tub, sauna, exercise room, business services, dock, laundry service and dry cleaning, meeting rooms, free parking. AE, DC, MC, V.*

$$$$ 🏨 **The Empress.** For titled ladies, empire builders, movie stars, and a
★ great many others, the exquisitely comfortable Empress is the only place to stay in Victoria. Opened in 1908, this Canadian Pacific château has aged gracefully, with sympathetically restored Edwardian decor, discreet modern amenities, and service standards that recall a more gracious age. A concierge floor, called Entrée Gold, provides boutique hotel intimacy within the larger hotel. ⊠ *721 Government St., V8W 1W5,* ☎ *250/384–8111 or 800/441–1414,* FAX *250/381–4334. 474 rooms, 36 suites. 2 restaurants, bar, fans, minibars, no-smoking rooms, room service, indoor pool, wading pool, hot tub, sauna, spa, exercise room, laundry service and dry cleaning, concierge, concierge floor, business services, convention center, parking (fee). AE, D, DC, MC, V.*

$$$$ 🏨 **Ocean Pointe Resort Hotel and Spa.** Across the "blue bridge" (John-
★ son Street Bridge) from downtown Victoria, the waterfront Ocean Pointe has a resort's worth of facilities, including a full spa. The hotel's striking two-story lobby and half of its guest rooms offer romantic views of the Inner Harbour and the lights of the Parliament Buildings across the water. Standard rooms are spacious and airy, and the apartment-sized suites have kitchenettes and separate living and dining areas. The Victorian Restaurant serves fine Pacific Northwest cuisine in a scenic setting. ⊠ *45 Songhees Rd., V9A 6T3,* ☎ *250/360–2999 or 800/667–4677,* FAX *250/360–5856. 212 rooms, 34 suites. 2 restaurants, bar, wine shop, in-room data ports, minibars, room service, indoor pool, hot tub, sauna, 2 tennis courts, health club, jogging, racquetball, squash, shops, baby-sitting, laundry service and dry cleaning, concierge, business services, meeting rooms, travel services, airport shuttle, parking (fee). AE, DC, MC, V.*

$$$–$$$$ 🏨 **Abigail's Hotel.** A Tudor-style inn built in 1930, Abigail's is within
★ walking distance of downtown. The guest rooms are attractively furnished in an English arts and crafts style. Down comforters, together with whirlpool tubs and fireplaces in many rooms, add to the pampering atmosphere. Six large rooms in the Coach House building are especially lavish, with whirlpool tubs, four-poster king beds, and wood-burning fireplaces. All of Abigail's rooms have telephones, but no TVs. ⊠ *906 McClure St., V8V 3E7,* ☎ *250/388–5363 or 800/561–6565,* FAX *250/388–7787. 22 rooms. Breakfast room, library, laundry service and dry cleaning, concierge, free parking. Full breakfast, evening sherry. AE, MC, V.*

$$$–$$$$ 🏨 **The Aerie.** The million-dollar view of Finlayson Arm and the Gulf
★ Islands persuaded Maria Schuster to build her luxury resort, 30 km (19 mi) north of Victoria. Most of the plush rooms in the Mediterranean-style villa have a patio, a fireplace, and a whirlpool tub. The dining room is open to the public after 6 PM for stunning views and cuisine. The herb-crusted pheasant breast and the chanterelle, potato, and rosemary bisque are worth the drive from Victoria. A full-service Aveda Spa adds to the pampering. ⊠ *600 Ebedora La., Box 108, Malahat V0R 2L0,* ☎ *250/743–7115 or 800/518–1933,* FAX *250/743–4766. 11 rooms, 12 suites. Restaurant, bar, fans, no-smoking rooms, indoor pool, indoor and outdoor hot tubs, sauna, spa, tennis court, exercise room, hiking, library, meeting room, helipad. Full breakfast. AE, DC, MC, V.*

$$$–$$$$ 🏨 **Beaconsfield Inn.** Built in 1905 and restored in 1984, the Beacons-
★   field has retained its Old World charm with dark mahogany wood
throughout the house. Down comforters and canopy beds adorn some
of the rooms, reinforcing its Edwardian style. Some of the rooms have
fireplaces and whirlpool tubs. Added pluses are the guest library and
the conservatory-sunroom. The inn is on a quiet residential street nine
blocks from the Inner Harbour. The owners also operate a one-bed-
room beach cottage about 10 minutes away. ⊠ *998 Humboldt St., V8V
2Z8,* ☎ *250/384–4044,* FAX *250/384–4052. 5 rooms, 4 suites. Break-
fast room, library, free parking. Full breakfast, afternoon tea. MC, V.*

$$$–$$$$ 🏨 **A Haterleigh Heritage Inn.** This 1901 mansion two blocks from the
Inner Harbour was opened as a bed-and-breakfast after an arduous
restoration. Leaded- and stained-glass windows and ornate plasterwork
on 11-ft ceilings transport guests back in time. Mounds of pillows and
plush down comforters dress the beds, and several rooms have whirl-
pool tubs. ⊠ *243 Kingston St., V8V 1V5,* ☎ *250/384–9995,* FAX *250/
384–1935. 5 rooms, 1 suite. Free parking. Full breakfast and afternoon
tea. MC, V.*

$$$ 🏨 **Admiral Motel.** This small, friendly motel along the Inner Harbour
is a good choice for families. About half the rooms have kitchens or
kitchenettes, and all have a balcony or patio. Breakfast is included, and
there's a guest lounge with a fireplace. Small pets are permitted. Kids
under 12 stay free in their parents' room. ⊠ *257 Belleville St., V8V
1X1,* ☎ *250/388–6267 or 888/823–6472. 22 rooms, 10 suites. Refrigerators, bicycles, coin laundry, free parking. AE, D, MC, V.*

$$$ 🏨 **Prior House Bed & Breakfast Inn.** In a beautifully restored 1912 manor
★   home on a quiet residential street near Craigdarroch Castle, this B&B
has a pretty garden, a guest library, two parlors, antique furniture, leaded-
glass windows, and oak paneling throughout. All the rooms have TVs
and fireplaces, and some have whirlpool tubs and private balconies.
The Garden Suite, with a private entrance, two bedrooms, and a full
kitchen, is an especially good value. ⊠ *620 St. Charles St., V8S 3N7,*
☎ *250/592–8847,* FAX *250/592–8223. 4 rooms, 2 suites. Breakfast
room, refrigerators, library, free parking. Full breakfast, afternoon
tea. MC, V.*

$$$ 🏨 **Swans.** When English-born shepherd Michael Williams bought
supplies for his kennel at the Buckerfield Company Feed Store during
the 1950s, he never dreamed he would one day own the building and
turn it into a waterfront hotel. There's a brewery, bistro, and pub on
the first floor, and a jazz bar in the cellar. Apartmentlike suites, all with
kitchens and decorated with Pacific Northwest art, fill the upper floors.
⊠ *506 Pandora Ave., V8W 1N6,* ☎ *250/361–3310 or 800/668–7926,*
FAX *250/361–3491. 29 suites. Restaurant, pub, beer and wine shop, no-
smoking rooms, room service, nightclub, coin laundry, meeting rooms,
parking (fee). AE, DC, MC, V.*

$$–$$$ 🏨 **Bedford Regency.** This European-style hotel in the heart of down-
town is reminiscent of San Francisco's small hotels. Many of the earth-
tone rooms have goose-down comforters, fireplaces, and whirlpool
bathtubs. Four rooms on the west side have views of the harbor and
are quieter than those facing Government Street. ⊠ *1140 Government
St., V8W 1Y2,* ☎ *250/384–6835 or 800/665–6500,* FAX *250/386–8930.
40 rooms. Pub, no-smoking rooms, laundry service and dry cleaning,
meeting rooms, business services, parking (fee). AE, DC, MC, V.*

$$–$$$ 🏨 **Holland House Inn.** This stylish art- and antiques-filled Italian Re-
★   naissance–style home is in a quiet residential neighborhood just two
blocks from the Inner Harbour and the Victoria Clipper terminal. The
guest rooms all have sitting areas, and many have fireplaces, balconies,
and canopied four-poster beds. A 1998 arts-and-crafts-style addition,
linked to the main building through a conservatory, has four large rooms

with fireplaces and double soaking tubs. ⊠ *595 Michigan St., V8V 1S7,* ☎ *250/384–6644 or 800/335–3466,* FAX *250/384–6117. 14 rooms. Breakfast room, no-smoking rooms, free parking. Full breakfast. AE, MC, V.*

$$–$$$ 🏨 **Laurel Point Inn.** Every room has water views at this modern resort and convention center on a 6-acre peninsula in the Inner Harbour. The decor, especially in the newer Arthur Erickson–designed suites, is light and airy, with a strong Asian influence. Chinese art decorates many public areas, and the Terrace Room lounge looks out over a Japanese garden. All the rooms have balconies, hair dryers, and coffeemakers. ⊠ *680 Montreal St., V8V 1Z8,* ☎ *250/386–8721 or 800/663–7667,* FAX *250/386–9547. 120 rooms, 80 suites. Restaurant, 2 lounges, air-conditioning, no-smoking floors, room service, indoor pool, sauna, hot tub, laundry service and dry cleaning, business services, meeting rooms, free parking. AE, DC, MC, V.*

$$–$$$ 🏨 **Mulberry Manor.** The last building designed by Victoria architect ★ Samuel McClure has been restored and decorated to shelter magazine-cover perfection with antiques, sumptuous linens, and tile baths. The Tudor-style mansion sits behind a high stone wall on an acre of carefully manicured grounds. The inn is a five-minute drive from the Inner Harbour, among the mansions of the Rockland neighborhood. ⊠ *611 Foul Bay Rd., V8S 1H2,* ☎ *250/370–1918,* FAX *250/370–1968. 2 rooms, 1 suite. Breakfast room, no-smoking rooms, free parking. Full breakfast. MC, V.*

$$ 🏨 **Chateau Victoria.** Wonderful views from the upper-floor suites and rooftop restaurant are a plus at this centrally located 19-story hotel. All suites have balconies and sitting areas; some have kitchenettes. The rooms are comfortable and standard in size. ⊠ *740 Burdett Ave., V8W 1B2,* ☎ *250/382–4221 or 800/663–5891,* FAX *250/380–1950. 60 rooms, 118 suites. 2 restaurants, lounge, no-smoking floors, in-room data ports, room service, indoor pool, hot tub, exercise room, babysitting, laundry service and dry cleaning, concierge, business services, meeting rooms, free parking. AE, D, DC, MC, V.*

$ 🏨 **The Cherry Bank.** This 1897 Victorian house with a modern restaurant attached must defy every zoning law in the book. Inside, a warren of red wallpapered corridors gives the place the look of a wholesome Wild West brothel. This wacky-looking budget hotel a few blocks from the Inner Harbour is clean, friendly, and a good value—especially for groups and families. One room has a kitchenette, and another is large enough to sleep six. There are no telephones or TVs in the rooms, but a traditional bacon and egg breakfast is included in the rate. ⊠ *825 Burdett Ave., V8W 1B3,* ☎ *250/385–5380,* FAX *250/383–0949. 25 rooms, 6 with shared bath, 1 suite. Restaurant, pub, free parking. Full breakfast. AE, MC, V.*

$ 🏨 **Hostelling International Victoria.** This hostel, in a beautifully restored heritage building, is right in the thick of things near the waterfront and Market Square. The accommodations include private rooms with shared baths, as well as beds in men's and women's dorms, a game room, TV lounge, private lockers, laundry and cooking facilities, and loads of information for onward journeys. ⊠ *516 Yates St., V8W 1K8,* ☎ *250/385–4511,* FAX *250/385–3232. 110 beds in 10 single sex dorms; 6 private rooms sleep 2 to 8 people. 2 shared kitchens, coin laundry, travel services. MC, V.*

Nightlife and the Arts

For entertainment listings, pick up a free copy of "Monday Magazine" (it comes out every Thursday) or call the Talking Yellow Pages at 250/953–9000.

Bars and Clubs

Chic and arty **Hugo's** (✉ Magnolia Hotel, 627 Courtney St., ☎ 250/ 920–4844) serves lunch, dinner, and four of its own brews. Bands, from big band to funk, bebop to rumba, perform at the **Millennium Jazz Club** (✉ 1601 Store St., ☎ 250/360–9098), under Swan's Hotel. **The Planet** (✉ 15 Bastion Sq., ☎ 250/385–2626) hosts rock, blues, and jazz performers. In addition to live music, darts, and brewery tours, **Spinnakers Brew Pub** (✉ 308 Catherine St., ☎ 250/386–2739) pours plenty of British Columbian microbrewery beer. **Steamers Public House** (✉ 570 Yates St., ☎ 250/381–4340) has four pool tables and live music every night. The **Strathcona Hotel** (✉ 919 Douglas St., ☎ 250/383–7137) is something of an entertainment complex, with the Sticky Wicket Pub on the main floor and Legends nightclub in the basement. Its biggest draw, though, is the beach volleyball played on the roof in the summertime.

Swan's Pub (✉ 1601 Store St., ☎ 250/361–3310) is a popular brew pub and café that hosts folk and jazz performers on most nights. For dancing, head to **Sweetwater's** (✉ Market Square, 27-560 Johnson St., ☎ 250/383–7844). **Uforia** (✉ 1208 Wharf St., ☎ 250/381–2331) is a waterfront spot for dancing.

Music

The **Victoria Symphony** (☎ 250/385–6515) plays in the **Royal The-atre** (✉ 805 Broughton St., ☎ 250/386–6121) and at the **University Centre Auditorium** (✉ Finnerty Rd., ☎ 250/721–8480).

The **TerriVic Jazz Party** (☎ 250/953–2011) showcases internationally acclaimed musicians every April. The **Victoria Jazz Society** (☎ 250/ 388–4423) organizes an annual JazzFest International in late June and the Vancouver Island Blues Bash in Victoria every Labour Day weekend.

Opera

The **Pacific Opera Victoria** (☎ 250/385–0222) performs three productions a year in the 900-seat McPherson Playhouse (✉ 3 Centennial Sq., ☎ 250/386–6121), adjoining the Victoria City Hall.

Theater

An old church houses the **Belfry Theatre** (✉ 1291 Gladstone Ave., ☎ 250/385–6815), whose resident company specializes in contemporary Canadian dramas. **Langham Court Theatre** (✉ 805 Langham Ct., ☎ 250/384–2142), a small theater in a residential neighborhood, is the home stage of the Victoria Theatre Guild, known for musicals, dramas, and comedies. **McPherson Playhouse** (✉ 3 Centennial Sq., ☎ 250/ 386–6121) presents some big-scale musicals, along with opera and dance. The students of the University of Victoria mount productions on campus at the **Phoenix Theatre** (✉ Finnerty Rd., ☎ 250/721–8000).

Outdoor Activities and Sports

Golf

The **Cordova Bay Golf Course** (✉ 5333 Cordova Bay Rd., ☎ 250/658– 4075) is an 18-hole, par-72 course set on the shoreline. The greens fee is $45 weekdays and $48 weekends. An optional cart costs $27.

Whale-Watching

To see the pods of orcas that travel in the waters around Vancouver Island, you can take charter boat tours from Victoria from May through October. These Zodiac (motor-powered inflatable boat) excursions cost from $75 to $80 per person and take about three hours: **Great Pacific Adventures** (☎ 250/386–2277), **Ocean Explorations** (☎ 250/383–

6722), and **Seacoast Expeditions** (☎ 250/383–2254) are among the many operators.

To book almost any kind of marine activity, including whale-watching cruises, seaplane tours, fishing, and kayaking expeditions, contact the **Victoria Marine Adventure Center** (✉ 950 Wharf St., ☎ 250/995–2211 or 800/575–6700).

Shopping

Antique Row, on Fort Street between Blanshard and Cook streets, is home to more than 60 antiques, curio, and collectibles shops. **Market Square** (✉ 560 Johnson St., ☎ 250/386–2441) has two floors of specialty and offbeat shops. You'll find many specialty stores on **Government Street** downtown, particularly in the blocks between 800 and 1400.

Victoria Essentials

Arriving and Departing

BY BOAT

BC Ferries (☎ 250/386–3431; 888/223–3779 in British Columbia only) operates daily service between Vancouver and Victoria. The Vancouver terminal is in Tsawwassen, 38 km (24 mi) southwest of downtown at the end of Highway 17. In Victoria, ferries arrive at and depart from the Swartz Bay Terminal at the end of Highway 17 (the Patricia Bay Highway), 32 km (20 mi) north of downtown Victoria. Sailing time is about 1½ hours. The tickets cost about $9 per passenger, and $32 per vehicle each way. Rates fluctuate depending on the season.

There is year-round passenger-only service between Victoria and Seattle on the **Victoria Clipper** (☎ 206/448–5000 in Seattle; 800/888–2535 elsewhere). The fare between Seattle and Victoria is $109 (U.S. dollars). You'll receive a discount if you order 14-day advance tickets, which have some restrictions.

Washington State Ferries (☎ 250/381–1551; 206/464–6400 in the U.S.; 888/808–7977 in WA only) travel daily between Sidney, north of Victoria, and Anacortes, Washington. **Black Ball Transport** (☎ 250/386–2202; 360/457–4491 in the U.S.) operates between Victoria and Port Angeles, Washington.

Direct passenger and vehicle service between Victoria and Seattle is available from mid-May to mid-September on the *Princess Marguerite III,* operated by **Clipper Navigation** (☎ 206/448–5000 in Seattle; 800/888–2535). The boat departs from Ogden Point in Victoria at 7:30 AM and arrives at Seattle's Pier 48 at 12 noon. It departs from Seattle at 1 PM, arriving back at Odgen Point at 5:30. Reservations are advised if you're traveling with a vehicle.

BY BUS

Pacific Coach Lines (☎ 800/661–1725) operates daily connecting service between Victoria and Vancouver on BC Ferries.

BY CAR

Highway 17 connects the Swartz Bay ferry terminal on the Saanich Peninsula with downtown Victoria. The **Island Highway** (Highway 1, also known as the Trans-Canada Highway) runs south from Nanaimo to Victoria. **Highway 14** connects Sooke and Port Renfrew, on the west coast of Vancouver Island, with Victoria.

BY HELICOPTER

Helijet Airways (☎ 800/665–4354, 604/273–1414, or 250/382–6222) helicopter service is available from downtown Vancouver and downtown Seattle to downtown Victoria.

BY PLANE

Victoria International Airport (✉ Willingdon Rd. off Hwy. 17, Sidney, ☎ 250/953–7500) is served by Air B.C., Canadian, and Horizon airlines. *See* Air Travel *in* Smart Travel Tips for airline phone numbers. Air B.C. provides airport-to-airport service from Vancouver to Victoria at least hourly. Flights take about 35 minutes.

West Coast Air (☎ 604/688–9115 or 800/347–2222) and **Harbour Air** (☎ 604/688–1277 or 800/665–0212) provide 35-minute harbor-to-harbor service (downtown Vancouver to downtown Victoria) several times a day. **Kenmore Air** (☎ 425/486–1257 or 800/543–9595) operates direct daily floatplane service from Seattle to Victoria's Inner Harbour.

Airport Transfers: To drive from the airport to downtown, take Highway 17 south. A taxi ride costs between $35 and $40, plus tip. The **Airporter** (☎ 250/386–2525) bus service ($13 one-way; $23 round-trip) drops off passengers at most major hotels.

BY TRAIN

VIA Rail's **Esquimalt & Nanaimo Rail Liner** (☎ 800/561–8630 in Canada; 800/561–3949 in the U.S.) serves Duncan, Chemainus, Nanaimo, and Courtenay from Victoria's **VIA Rail Station** (✉ 450 Pandora Ave., at the east end of the Johnson Street Bridge).

Getting Around

BY BUS

BC Transit (☎ 250/382–6161) serves Victoria and the surrounding areas. An all-day pass costs $5.50.

BY FERRY

Victoria Harbour Ferries (☎ 250/708–0201) serve the Inner Harbour, with stops that include the Empress Hotel, Point Ellice House, Spinnaker's Brew Pub, Ocean Pointe Resort, and Fisherman's Wharf. Fares start at $3. Harbor tours cost $12 to $14. Boats make the rounds every 12 to 20 minutes, daily from mid-March through October and on sunny weekends the rest of the year. If you're by the Inner Harbour at 9:45 on a summer Sunday morning, you can catch the little ferries performing a water ballet—they gather together and do maneuvers set to classical music that's blasted over loudspeakers.

BY TAXI

Empress Taxi (☎ 250/381–2222). **Victoria Taxi** (☎ 250/383–7111).

Contacts and Resources

CAR RENTAL

Avis (☎ 250/386–8468). **Budget** (☎ 250/953–5300). **Enterprise** (☎ 250/475–6900)). **Island Autos** (☎ 250/384–4881). **National Tilden** (☎ 250/386–1213). **Rent-a-Wreck** (☎ 250/413–4638).

EMERGENCIES

Ambulance (☎ 911). **Fire** (☎ 911). **Police** (☎ 911).

Victoria General Hospital (✉ 1 Hospital Way, off Helmcken Rd., ☎ 250/727–4212).

GUIDED TOURS

Gray Line (☎ 250/388–5248) conducts tours on double-decker buses that visit the city center, Chinatown, Antique Row, Oak Bay, and Beacon Hill Park; a combination tour stops at Butchart Gardens as well. **Tally-Ho Horsedrawn Tours** (☎ 250/383–5067) operates a get-acquainted tour of downtown Victoria that includes Beacon Hill Park. **Victoria Carriage Tours** (☎ 250/383–2207) has horse-drawn tours of the city. The best way to see the sights of the Inner Harbour is by **Victoria Harbour Ferry** (☎ 250/708–0201).

Island Outings (☎ 250/642–4469 or 888/345–4469) conducts soft adventure trips year-round, including hikes, river tours, and whale-watching excursions. **Nature Calls Eco-Tours** (☎ 250/361–4453) conducts half- and full-day guided hikes in wilderness areas near Victoria. Experts from the **Royal British Columbia Museum** (☎ 250/387–5745) lead day trips to study Vancouver Island's natural and cultural history.

LATE-NIGHT PHARMACY

London Drugs (✉ 911 Yates St., ☎ 250/381–1113) is open daily until 10 PM.

LODGING RESERVATION SERVICES

Garden City B&B Reservation Service (✉ 660 Jones Terrace, Victoria V8Z 2L7, ☎ 250/479–1986). **Super Natural B.C.** (☎ 800/663–6000). **Tourism Victoria** (☎ 800/663–3883).

VISITOR INFORMATION

Discover B.C. (✉ 601–1166 Albernie St., Vancouver, V6E 3Z3, ☎ 800/663–6000). **Tourism Victoria** (✉ 812 Wharf St. V8W 1T3, ☎ 250/953–2033, FAX 250/382–6539).

SOUTHERN VANCOUVER ISLAND

The largest island on Canada's west coast, Vancouver Island stretches 450 km (279 mi) from Victoria in the south to Cape Scott in the north. Thick conifer forests blanket it down to soft, sandy beaches on the eastern shoreline and rocky, wave-pounded grottoes and inlets along the western shore. The cultural heritage of the island is from the Kwaki-utl, Nootka, and Coastal Salish native groups. Arts and other centers flourish throughout the region, enabling you to catch a glimpse of contemporary native culture.

Mining, logging, and tourism are the important island industries. Environmental issues, such as the logging practices of British Columbia's lumber companies, are important to islanders—both native and non-native. Residents are working to establish a balance between the island's wilderness and its economy.

Sooke

42 km (26 mi) west of Victoria on Hwy. 14.

Rugged beaches, hiking trails through the surrounding rain forest, and views of the Olympic mountains across the strait of Juan de Fuca make the village of Sooke a peaceful seaside escape.

East Sooke Park, on the east side of the harbor, has 350 acres of beaches, hiking trails, and wildflower-dotted meadows. Another popular hiking and biking route is the **Galloping Goose Regional Trail,** a former railway line that runs all the way to Victoria. The trail runs past the **Sooke Potholes** (at the end of Sooke River Rd. off Hwy 14), a series of swimming holes carved out of the sandstone by the Sooke River.

The **Sooke Region Museum and Visitor Information Centre** exhibits Salish and Nootka crafts and artifacts from the 19th century. ✉ *2070*

Phillips Rd., Box 774, V0S 1N0, ☎ *250/642–6351.* ✉ *Donations accepted.* ☉ *July–Aug., daily 9–6; Sept.–June, Tues.–Sun. 9–5.*

Victor and Carey Newman, a father and son team of Kwakiutl and Salish artists, display traditional and modern prints, masks, and jewelry at the **Blue Raven Gallery** (✉ 1971 Kaltasin Rd., ☎ 250/881–0528).

Dining and Lodging

$$–$$$ ✕ **Seventeen Mile House.** Stop here on the road between Sooke and Victoria for pub fare, a beer, or fresh local seafood. The 1894 structure is a study in late-19th-century island architecture. ✉ *5126 Sooke Rd.,* ☎ *250/642–5942. MC, V.*

$$$$ ✕▥ **Sooke Harbour House.** The restaurant at this oceanfront 1929 clap-
★   board country inn is one of the finest in British Columbia. Nonguests can come to dinner, which generally includes just-caught fish and dishes made with herbs, produce, and fresh flowers grown on the property. The romantic guest rooms, each with a sitting area and fire-place, are individually decorated and photo-shoot perfect. The inn offers massage and other spa treatments. ✉ *1528 Whiffen Spit Rd., V0S 1N0,* ☎ *250/642–3421 or 800/889–9688,* ⨳ *250/642–6988. 28 rooms. Restaurant, in-room data ports, refrigerators, room service, massage, hiking, snorkeling, kayaking, bicycles, piano, laundry service and dry clean-ing, business services, meeting room. Full breakfast. Lunch included May–Oct. and all weekends. No smoking. AE, DC, MC, V.*

$$–$$$ ▥ **Point No Point.** Here's a place that will satisfy the longings of your inner Robinson Crusoe. Twenty-two cabins sit on a cliff edge, over-looking a mile of private sandy beach and the open Pacific. The one and two-bedroom cabins, in single, duplex, and quad units, range from rustic to romantic. Seven newer cabins have tall windows, loft bedrooms, and hot tubs. The older, cheaper cabins are basic, with the original 1960s furniture; pets are allowed in two of the rooms. Every unit has a kitchen, a fireplace or wood stove, and a cliff-edge deck. The restaurant in the lodge serves lunch, afternoon tea, and dinner from a seafood-oriented menu. There's a pair of binoculars at each table for spotting whales and ships on the open sea. ✉ *1505 West Coast Rd. (915 mi west of Sooke), V0S 1N0,* ☎ *250/646–2020,* ⨳ *250/646–2294. 22 cabins. Restaurant, hiking. AE, MC, V. Restaurant closed for din-ner Mon.–Tues.; call for winter hrs.*

Duncan

60 km (37 mi) north of Victoria on the Trans-Canada Hwy. (Hwy. 1).

Duncan is nicknamed City of Totems for its many totem poles. The two carvings behind the City Hall merit a short trip off the main road.

★ ☉ The **Cowichan Native Village,** covering six acres on the banks of the tree-lined Cowichan River, is one of Canada's leading First Nations cultural facilities. You can see the work (including a stunning whaling canoe diorama) of Northwest artists in a longhouse-style gallery, learn about the history of the Cowichan people in a multimedia show, and sample traditional foods at the Riverwalk Café. You can also watch artisans at work in the world's largest carving house, and even try your hand at carving on a visitor's pole. There are craft demonstrations and performances throughout the summer. ✉ *200 Cowichan Way,* ☎ *250/ 746–8119.* ✉ *$8.* ☉ *Daily 9–5; café closed Nov.–Apr.*

☉ The **British Columbia Forest Museum,** more a park than a museum, spans 100 acres, combining indoor and outdoor exhibits that focus on the history of forestry in the province. In the summer you can ride an orig-inal steam locomotive around the property and over an old wood tres-tle bridge. ✉ *2892 Drinkwater Rd. (Trans-Canada Hwy.),* ☎ *250/715–*

1113. ✉ *$8.* ⊘ *May–early Sept., daily 9:30–6; Sept.–Apr., call for seasonal hrs.*

Shopping

A large selection of Cowichan wool sweaters is available at the Cowichan Native Village and from **Hill's Indian Crafts** (☎ 250/746–6731) on the main highway, about 1½ km (1 mi) south of Duncan.

En Route At Crofton, about halfway between Duncan and Chemainus, there's a tiny BC Ferries (☎ 250/386–3431 or 888/223–3779 in B.C.) terminal, with service to Salt Spring Island and connecting service to other southern Gulf Islands (☞ Gulf Islands, *below*).

Chemainus

85 km (53 mi) north of Victoria, 27 km (17 mi) south of Nanaimo.

About three dozen outdoor murals depicting local historical events decorate the town of Chemainus, which was dependent on the lumber industry but had to retool in the 1980s after its mill closed down. Footprints on the sidewalk lead you on a self-guided tour of the murals, which were painted by international artists. Restaurants, shops, tearooms, coffee bars, art galleries, antiques dealers, restored Victorian homes, and the **Chemainus Theater** (☎ 250/246–9820 or 800/565–7738), which presents live theater (matinees and shows with dinner included), are among the town's lures.

Lodging

$$–$$$ 🏨 **Bird Song Cottage.** This whimsical white and lavender Victorian cottage has been playfully decorated with antiques and collectibles. Breakfast (often with piano accompaniment) is served on the sunporch, evening tea and cookies in front of the fire in the lounge. All rooms have fresh-cut flowers, pure cotton sheets, and window seats. There's also a one-bedroom medieval-themed castle just behind the inn, with a kitchen, a two-sided fireplace, and a balcony with an ocean view. ✉ *9909 Maple St., Box 1432, V0R 1K0,* ☎ *250/246–9910,* 🆂 *250/246–2909. 3 rooms. Full breakfast. No smoking. AE, MC, V.*

Nanaimo

110 km (68 mi) northwest of Victoria, 115 km (71 mi) southeast of Courtenay, 155 km (96 mi) southeast of Campbell River, 23 km (14 mi) on land plus 38 nautical mi west of Vancouver.

Nanaimo is the primary commercial and transport link for the mid-island, with direct ferry service to the mainland.

Nanaimo District Museum (✉ 100 Cameron Rd., ☎ 250/753–1821) has reproductions of the petroglyphs, representing human and animal spirit figures, that have been found in the area. Trails at **Petroglyph Provincial Park** (✉ Hwy. 1, ☎ 250/391–2300), 8 km (5 mi) south of town, lead from the parking lot to designs carved thousands of years ago.

Dining and Lodging

$$$ ✕ **Mahle House.** Set in a 1904 farmhouse about 12 km (8 mi) south
★ of Nanaimo, this spot serves innovative Northwest cuisine, much of it raised on site or in the neighborhood. Highlights on the seasonal menu include different versions of rabbit, venison, mussels, salmon, and good vegetarian options. ✉ *South of Nanaimo on Cedar Rd., at Hemer Rd.,* ☎ *250/722–3621. AE, MC, V. Closed Mon.–Tues. No lunch. Closed Jan.*

$$–$$$$ ✕ **The Grotto.** This offbeat seafood and sushi place near the Departure Bay ferry terminal looks like a sea shanty, full of driftwood, fishing floats, and weathered pillars borrowed from a dock somewhere. The five-page Japanese-Canadian-seafood menu has enough options to keep everyone happy. Try the sushi, charred tuna, teriyaki spareribs, Cajun pasta, or the Japanese platter for two. ✉ *1511 Stewart Ave.,* ☎ *250/753–3303. AE, MC, V. Closed Mon. No lunch.*

$$ 🏨 **Best Western Dorchester Hotel.** Though it now looks like a modern hotel, this 1889 building in the city center was once the Nanaimo Opera House. Rooms are comfortably furnished with rich cherry wood furniture, TVs, and coffeemakers. Many have air-conditioning. Most rooms have views of the harbor, and there's a view of the city from the rooftop patio. ✉ *70 Church St., V9R 5H4,* ☎ *250/754–6835 or 800/661–2449,* FAX *250/754–2638. 59 rooms, 6 suites. Restaurant, lounge, no-smoking floors, library, laundry service and dry cleaning, business services, meeting rooms, free parking. AE, DC, MC, V.*

$$ 🏨 **Yellow Point Lodge.** This lodge, on a spit of land 24 km (15 mi) south
★   of Nanaimo, has been an adults-only summer camp since the 1930s. Everything's included, from the kayaks, bicycles, tennis, and other sports, to the three meals and snacks served communally in the dining room. The accommodations range from comfortable lodge rooms and cozy new cottages to some very basic summer-only cabins with no running water and a shared bathhouse. The main lodge, with its great stone fireplace and ocean views, is a wonderful place to unwind. You can also stroll the resort's 165 acres, lounge on its secluded beaches, or take a tour on the owner's cutter. Guests must be over 16. ✉ *3700 Yellow Point Rd., Ladysmith V0R 2E0,* ☎ *250/245–7422,* FAX *250/245–7411. 9 lodge rooms, 12 private cabins, 10 units in shared cabins, 25 rustic rooms with no running water. Dining room, outdoor saltwater pool, outdoor hot tub, sauna, 2 tennis courts, badminton, jogging, volleyball, boating, mountain bikes. AP. AE, MC, V.*

Southern Vancouver Island Essentials

Arriving and Departing

BY BUS

Island Coach Lines (☎ 250/385–4411) serves most towns on Vancouver Island. **Greyhound** (☎ 604/482–8747; 800/661–8747 in Canada; 800/231–2222 in the U.S.) serves Nanaimo from Vancouver (☞ By Ferry, *below*).

BY CAR

The Island Highway (Highway 1), which becomes Highway 19 in Nanaimo, is the main road up the east side of Vancouver Island.

BY FERRY

BC Ferries (☎ 250/386–3431; 888/223–3779 in British Columbia) provides service from outside Vancouver to Victoria and Nanaimo. There are two ferry terminals serving Nanaimo. Ferries from Tsawwassen, south of Vancouver, arrive at Duke Point, south of Nanaimo. Ferries from Horseshoe Bay, north of Vancouver, arrive at Departure Bay north of the Nanaimo town center.

BY TRAIN

VIA Rail (☎ 800/561–8630) provides service between Victoria and Nanaimo.

Getting Around

BY CAR

To reach Nanaimo from the Departure Bay ferry terminal, take Stewart Avenue south to Terminal Avenue, which intersects with the downtown core. From Duke Point, take Highway 19 west then turn right on the Trans Canada Highway.

Contacts and Resources

CAR RENTAL

Most major agencies, including **Avis, Budget, Hertz,** and **National Tilden** serve cities throughout the province. *See* Car Rental *in* Smart Travel Tips for company numbers.

EMERGENCIES

Ambulance (☎ 911). **Fire** (☎ 911). **Police** (☎ 911).

GOLF BOOKINGS

Golf Central (☎ 250/380–4653) provides a transportation and booking service for golfers all over southern Vancouver Island.

VISITOR INFORMATION

Tourism Vancouver Island (✉ 302–45 Bastion Sq., Victoria, V8W 1J1, ☎ 250/382–3551).

THE GULF ISLANDS

A temperate climate, scenic beaches, rolling pastures, and virgin forests are common to all of the Gulf Islands, of which Galiano, Mayne, and Salt Spring are among the most popular. Marine birds are numerous, and unusual vegetation such as arbutus trees (also known as madrones, a leafy evergreen with red peeling bark) and Garry oaks differentiate the islands from other areas around Vancouver.

Galiano Island

20 nautical mi (almost 2 hrs by ferry due to interisland stops) from Swartz Bay (32 km/20 mi north of Victoria), 13 nautical mi (a 50-min ferry ride) from Tsawwassen (39 km/24 mi south of Vancouver).

Galiano's long, unbroken eastern shoreline is perfect for leisurely beach walks, while the numerous coves and inlets along the western coast make it a prime area for kayaking. **Montague Harbour Provincial Marine Park** has camping and boating facilities. Miles of trails through forests of Douglas fir beg for exploration by foot or bike. Hikers can climb to the top of **Mount Galiano** for a view of the Olympic Mountains in Washington or trek the length of **Bodega Ridge.** The best spots to view **Active Pass** and the surrounding islands are Bluffs Park and Bellhouse Park. These are also good areas for picnicking and bird-watching.

Biological studies show that the straits between Vancouver Island and the mainland of British Columbia are home to the largest variety of marine life in North America. The frigid waters offer superb visibility, especially in winter. Alcala Point, Porlier Pass, and Active Pass are top locations for scuba diving. Fishermen head to the point at Bellhouse Park to cast for salmon from shore, or head by boat to Porlier Pass and Trincomali Channel.

Go Galiano (☎ 250/539–0202) provides year-round taxi, bus, ferry pick-up, and sightseeing services on the island. In summer, **Dionisio Express** (☎ 250/539–3109) runs a boat service to Dionisio Marine Park.

Lodging

$$–$$$ **Woodstone Country Inn.** This serene inn sits on the edge of a forest overlooking a meadow that's fantastic for bird-watching. Tall windows bring the pastoral setting into spacious bedrooms furnished in a mixture of wicker, antiques, and English country prints. Most rooms

have fireplaces, patios, and oversize tubs. Guests and nonguests can have three-course dinners (reservations essential). The menu changes daily, but past offerings include yam soup with toasted almonds, rack of lamb, and warm bread pudding with rum sauce. ⊠ *Georgeson Bay Rd., R.R. 1, V0N 1P0,* ☎ *250/539–2022 or 888/339–2022,* FAX *250/539–5198. 13 rooms. Restaurant, piano, meeting room. Full breakfast, afternoon tea. No smoking. AE, MC, V. Closed Jan.*

$–$$ ⊞ **Sutil Lodge.** This 1928 bungalow overlooking Montague Harbour ★ has some of the most beautiful sunset views on the islands. The simple guest rooms have throw rugs on hardwood floors and beds tucked under window nooks. A hearty breakfast is served in the lodge's old dance hall. The kayak center on the property attracts folks from around the world who want to paddle the still coves of the Gulf Islands. The innkeepers can take you exploring on a catamaran cruise. ⊠ *637 Southwind Rd., Montague Harbour V0N 1P0,* ☎ *250/539–2930 or 888/539–2930,* FAX *250/539–5390. 7 rooms share 3 baths. Breakfast room, boating, hiking. Full breakfast. No smoking. AE, MC, V. Closed Oct.–Mar.*

Outdoor Activities and Sports

BICYCLES

Galiano Bicycle (☎ 250/539–9906) rents bikes a short walk from the Sturdies Bay ferry terminal.

BOATING, DIVING, AND FISHING

Call **Bert's Charters** (☎ 250/539–3181), **Mel-n-i Fishing Charters** (☎ 250/539–3171), or **Retreat Cove Charters**(☎ 250/539–9981) to charter a fishing boat. For dive charters contact **Galiano Diving** (☎ 250/539–3109) or **Gulf Islands Diving & Boat Charters** (☎ 250/539–5341).

KAYAKING

Gulf Islands Kayaking (☎ 250/539–2442) rent kayaks and arrange tours. **Galiano Island Seakayak and Catamaran** (☎ 250/539–2930 or 888/539–2930) has kayak rentals and tours and also offers catamaran cruises.

Mayne Island

28 nautical mi from Swartz Bay (32 km/20 mi north of Victoria), 22 nautical mi from Tsawwassen (39 km/24 mi south of Vancouver).

Middens of clam and oyster shells give evidence that tiny Mayne Island—only 21 square km (13 square mi)—was inhabited as early as 5,000 years ago. It later became the stopover point for miners headed from Victoria to the gold fields of Fraser River and Barkerville, and by the mid-1800s it had developed into the communal center of the inhabited Gulf Islands.

Mount Parke was declared a wilderness park in 1989. A 45-minute hike leads to the highest point on the island and a stunning, almost 360-degree view of Vancouver, Active Pass, and Vancouver Island.

The village of **Miners Bay** is home to Plumbers Pass Lockup (closed September–June), built in 1896 as a jail but now a minuscule museum chronicling the island's history. You can stop for a drink at the seaside **Springwater Lodge,** one of the oldest hotels in the province. From Miners Bay head north on Georgina Point Road to **St. Mary Magdalene Church,** a stone chapel built in 1898. Across the road, a stairway leads down to the beach.

At the end of Georgina Point Road is the **Active Pass Lighthouse,** built in 1855, which still signals ships into the busy waterway. The grassy grounds are great for picnicking. There's a pebble beach for beach-combing at shallow (and therefore warmer) **Campbell Bay.**

Dining and Lodging

$$–$$$$ ✕🏨 **Oceanwood Country Inn.** This Tudor-style house on 10 forested
★ acres overlooking Navy Channel has English country decor through-out. Fireplaces, ocean-view balconies, and whirlpool or soaking tubs make several rooms deluxe. The waterfront dining room, which is open to the public, serves outstanding regional cuisine for dinner. You may find grilled salmon, tomato and Dungeness crab soup, or wild mush-room and goat cheese ravioli on the prix-fixe menu. ⊠ *630 Dinner Bay Rd., V0N 2J0,* ☎ *250/539–5074,* ℻ *250/539–3002. 12 rooms. Restaurant, hot tub, sauna, hiking, jogging, bicycles, library, meeting room. Full breakfast, afternoon tea. No smoking. MC, V. Closed Dec.–Feb.*

$$ 🏨 **Fernhill Lodge.** Constructed of wood from the property, this 1983 West Coast cedar structure has fantastical theme rooms—Moroccan, East Indian, and Jacobean. Two have outdoor hot tubs. On the 5-acre grounds are an herb garden and a rustic gazebo with a meditation loft. Hosts Mary and Brian Crumblehulme offer, on request, historical four-course dinners (Rome, Medieval, and Renaissance, to name a few themes) for guests and nonguests. ⊠ *Fernhill Rd., R.R. 1 C-4, V0N 2J0,* ☎ ℻ *250/539–2544. 3 rooms. Dining room, sauna, piano, library. Full breakfast. No smoking. MC, V.*

Outdoor Activities and Sports

For bike rentals on Mayne island, contact **Bay View Bike Rentals** (☎ 250/539–2924). **Mayne Island Kayaking**(☎ 250/539–2667) have kayak rentals.

Salt Spring Island

28 nautical mi from Swartz Bay (32 km/20 mi north of Victoria), 22 nautical mi from Tsawwassen (39 km/24 mi south of Vancouver).

Named for the saltwater springs at its north end, Salt Spring is the largest and most developed of the Gulf Islands. Among its first nonnative set-tlers were black Americans who came here to escape slavery in the 1850s. The agrarian tradition they and other immigrants established remains strong, but tourism and art now support the local economy. A gov-ernment wharf, three marinas, and a waterfront shopping complex at Ganges serve a community of more than 10,000 residents.

In **Ganges,** a pedestrian-oriented seaside village and the island's cul-tural and commercial center, you'll find dozens of smart boutiques, gal-leries, and restaurants. **Mouat's Trading Company** (⊠ Fulford–Ganges Rd.), built in 1912, was the original village general store. Now a hard-ware store, it has a display of historical photographs. At the Visitor Information Centre (☎ 250/537–5252) on Lower Ganges Road you can pick up a map of the dozens of artists' studios that are open to the public. More than 200 artisans participate in the summer-long **ArtCraft** sale of arts and crafts. The **Salt Spring Festival of the Arts** brings in-ternational music, theater, and dance to the island in July.

From Ganges, you can circle the northern tip of the island by bike or car (on Vesuvius Bay Road, Sunset Road, North End and North Beach roads, Walker Hook Road, and Robinson Road) past fields and peek-aboo marine views. You can take a shortcut on North End Road past **St. Mary Lake,** or drive south of Ganges to **Cusheon Lake.** Both lakes are good bets for warm-water swimming.

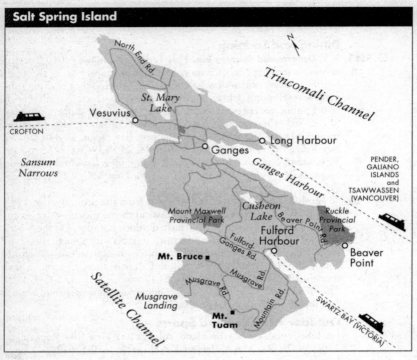

Near the center of Salt Spring, the summit of **Mount Maxwell Provincial Park** (⊠ Mt. Maxwell Rd., off Fulford–Ganges Rd.) affords spectacular views of south Salt Spring, Vancouver Island, and other of the Gulf Islands. It's also a great picnic spot. The last portion of the drive is steep, winding, and unpaved.

From Mount Maxwell, follow Fulford–Ganges Road south, then turn east on Beaver Point Road to reach **Ruckle Provincial Park,** site of an 1872 heritage homestead and extensive fields still being farmed by the Ruckle family. The park has camping and picnic spots, 11 km of coastline, a beach, and trails leading to rocky headlands.

Dining and Lodging

$$$–$$$$ ✕ **House Piccolo.** Broiled sea-scallop brochette, roasted British Columbia venison with juniper berries, and the salmon du jour are good choices for dinner at this casual restaurant in Ganges village. But save room for homemade ice cream or the signature chocolate terrine. ⊠ *108 Hereford Ave., Ganges,* ☎ *250/537–1844. Reservations essential. AE, DC, MC, V. No lunch.*

$$$$ ✕🏠 **Hastings House.** The centerpiece of this luxurious 25-acre seaside farm estate is a Tudor-style manor built in 1939. Guest quarters are in the manor or the farmhouse, in garden cottages and in suites in the reconstructed barn. All are furnished with fine antiques in an English country theme. Dinners in the manor house are open to the public (reservations essential): the five-course prix-fixe menu might include grilled eggplant with goat cheese, peppered sea bass on wilted spinach with nasturtium butter, and Salt Spring lamb loin with rosemary. Dinner guests can eat in the formal dining room (jacket required), the more casual lower-floor dining area, or the kitchen, where chef Marcel Kauer provides the entertainment. ⊠ *160 Upper Ganges Rd., Ganges, V8K 2S2,* ☎ *250/537–2362 or 800/661–9255,* FAX *250/537–5333. 3 rooms, 7*

suites. Restaurant, minibars, massage, croquet, mountain bikes. AE, MC, V. Full breakfast. Closed Jan.–early Mar.

$$–$$$ ⚅ **Anne's Oceanfront Hideaway.** Atop a steep slope above the sea, 6 km (4 mi) north of the Vesuvius ferry terminal, this modern waterfront home has panoramic ocean views, a cozy library, a sitting room, two covered verandas, and an elevator. Every room has a hydromassage tub and water view; three have private balconies. The Douglas Fir and Garry Oak rooms have the best views. Robes, a bottle of wine upon your arrival, and morning coffee in your room are among the amenities that make this a comfortable place to unwind. ✉ *168 Simson Rd., V8K 1E2,* ☎ *250/537–0851 or 888/474–2663,* FAX *250/537–0861. 4 rooms. Breakfast room, air-conditioning, outdoor hot tub, boating, bicycles, library. Full breakfast. No smoking. AE, MC, V.*

$$ ⚅ **Old Farmhouse Bed and Breakfast.** This gray-and-white saltbox farmhouse sits in a 3-acre meadow near St. Mary Lake. The style of the main house, a registered historic property built in 1894, is echoed in the four-room guest wing added in 1989, which has country-comfortable guest rooms furnished with pine bedsteads, down comforters, lace curtains, and wicker chairs. Each room has a private balcony or patio. ✉ *1077 Northend Rd., V8K 1L9,* ☎ *250/537–4113,* FAX *250/537–4969. 4 rooms. Breakfast room, boating. Full breakfast. No smoking. MC, V.*

Outdoor Activities and Sports

For guided day paddles, kayak lessons, and kayak and bike rentals, try **Salt Spring Kayaking** (✉ 2923 Fulford–Ganges Rd., Ganges, ☎ 250/653–4222). For kayak rentals, tours, and lessons, try **Sea Otter Kayaking** (✉ 1186 North End Rd., Ganges, ☎ 250/537–5678). **Salt Spring Marine Rentals** (✉ at the head of Ganges Harbour, ☎ 250/537–9100) conducts fishing charters and nature cruises and rents boats, bicycles, and scooters.

For post-sport pampering, the day spa at the **Salty Springs Spa Resort** (☎ 250/537–4111) offers treatments using the island's natural mineral springs.

Shopping

There are bargains galore at Ganges' **Market in the Park,** held every Saturday from April through October in Centennial Park. Fresh produce, seafood, crafts, clothing, herbs and aromatherapy mixtures, candles, toys, home-canned items, and more are available.

Gulf Islands Essentials

Smoking is banned in all Southern Gulf Island public places, including lodgings, restaurants, and pubs. Accommodations on all the islands can book up in the summer—reserve ahead. Services like bank machines, car rentals, and liquor stores are available in Ganges, but limited or nonexistent elsewhere in the islands.

Arriving and Departing

BY BOAT

BC Ferries (☎ 250/386–3431; 888/223–3779 in British Columbia only) provides service from outside Vancouver and Victoria to Galiano Island, Mayne Island, and Salt Spring Island. If you're traveling from the mainland, vehicle reservations are recommended (and required on some sailings).

BY PLANE

Harbour Air Ltd. provides regular service from Victoria, Nanaimo, and Vancouver Airport to Salt Spring, Thetis, Mayne, Saturna, Galiano, and South Pender Islands. **Pacific Spirit Air** provides scheduled floatplane service from Vancouver Harbour and Vancouver Airport to all southern Gulf Islands. *See* Air Travel *in* Smart Travel Tips for airline phone numbers.

Contacts and Resources

CAR RENTAL

Car rentals are available on Salt Spring Island through **Heritage Rentals** (☎ 250/537–4225).

EMERGENCIES

Ambulance (☎ 911). **Fire** (☎ 911). **Police** (☎ 911).

Lady Minto Hospital (⊠ Ganges, Salt Spring Island, ☎ 250/538–4800).

OUTDOOR AND ECOLOGICAL ADVENTURE TOURS

Ecosummer Expeditions (⊠ Unit 130, 5640 Hollybridge Way, Richmond V7C 4N3, ☎ 604/214–7484 or 800/465–8884), the **Canadian Outback Adventure Company** (⊠ 100–657 Marine Dr., West Vancouver V7T 1A4, ☎ 604/921–7250 or 800/565–8735), and **Island Escapades** (⊠ 118 Natalie Lane, Salt Spring Island, ☎ 250/537–2537 or 888/529–2567) operate kayaking and other outdoor adventure trips on and around the Gulf Islands.

VISITOR INFORMATION

Galiano Island Visitor Information Centre (⊠ Box 73, Sturdies Bay V0N 1P0, ☎ 250/539–2233. **Mayne Island Chamber of Commerce** (⊠ General Delivery, Mayne Island V0N 2J0, ☎ no phone). **Salt Spring Island Visitor Information Centre** (⊠ 121 Lower Ganges Rd., Ganges V8K 2T1, ☎ 250/537–5252).

WHISTLER

Whistler and Blackcomb mountains, part of the Whistler Resort (☎ 800/944–7853), are the two largest ski mountains in North America and are consistently ranked as the first- or second-best ski destinations on the continent. There's winter and summer glacier skiing, the longest vertical drop in North America, and one of the most advanced lift systems in the world. Whistler has also grown in popularity as a summer destination, with a range of outdoor activities and events.

Whistler Village

120 km (74 mi) north of Vancouver, Hwy. 1 to Hwy. 99.

At the base of the mountains are Whistler Village, Village North (also called Marketplace), and Upper Village—a rapidly expanding, interconnected community of lodgings, restaurants, pubs, gift shops, and boutiques. Locals generally refer to the entire area as Whistler Village. With dozens of hotels and condos within a five-minute walk of the mountains, the site is frenzied with activity, though all on foot: Whistler Village is a pedestrian-only community.

Dining

Dining at Whistler is informal though pricey. Casual dress is appropriate everywhere.

CATEGORY	COST*
$$$$	over C$40
$$$	C$30–C$40
$$	C$20–C$30
$	under C$20

per person for a three-course meal, excluding drinks, service, and sales tax

$$$-$$$$ ✕ **Il Caminetto di Umberto, Trattoria di Umberto.** Umberto prepares home-style Italian dishes in a relaxed atmosphere. He specializes in pastas like seafood and spinach-stuffed cannelloni and lasagna al forno. Il Caminetto is known for its veal, osso buco, and game dishes. The Trattoria is the more casual of the two (there are ski racks outside). ✉ *Il Caminetto, 4242 Village Stroll,* ☎ *604/932–4442.* ✉ *Trattoria, Mountainside Lodge, 4417 Sundial Pl.,* ☎ *604/932–5858. Reservations essential. AE, DC, MC, V. No lunch at Il Caminetto.*

$$$-$$$$ ✕ **La Rúa.** One of the brightest lights on the Whistler dining scene is on the ground floor of Le Chamois (☞ Lodging, *below*). Reddish flagstone floors and sponge-painted walls, a wine cellar behind a wrought-iron door, modern oil paintings, and sconce lighting give the restaurant an intimate, Mediterranean ambience. Favorites from the Continental menu include charred rare tuna, loin of deer, rack of lamb, and baked sea-bass fillet in a red-wine and herb sauce. ✉ *4557 Blackcomb Way,* ☎ *604/932–5011. Reservations essential. AE, DC, MC, V. No lunch.*

$$$-$$$$ ✕ **Val d'Isère.** Chef and proprietor Roland Pfaff satisfies a skier's craving for fine French food with traditional dishes from his native Alsace. Highlights served in this elegant but welcoming room overlooking the Town Plaza include goat's cheese and roasted chestnut salad, braised duck legs with endives, and roast rabbit with dried fruit crumbs and polenta. ✉ *8–4314 Main St.,* ☎ *604/932–4666. Reservations essential. AE, DC, MC, V. No lunch in winter.*

$$-$$$ ✕ **Zeuski's.** At this friendly taverna in Village North, wall murals of the Greek islands surround candlelighted tables, helping create a Mediterranean atmosphere. There's a patio for alfresco dining. It's hard to pass on the spanakopita, souvlaki, and other standards, but the house special, *kotapoulo* (chicken breast rolled in pistachios and roasted), is not to be missed, nor are the tender, herb-battered calamari. ✉ *4314 Main St.,* ☎ *604/932–6009. Reservations essential. AE, DC, MC, V.*

Lodging

Accommodations in Whistler, including hundreds of time-share condos, can be booked through the **Whistler Resort Association** (☎ 604/ 932–4222 or 800/944–7853).Price categories are based on January– April ski season rates. Rates are higher during Christmas and spring holidays, and they can be slightly lower in the summer. Many Whistler lodgings have a minimum stay requirement, especially over the holidays. Whistler Village has some serious nightlife. If peace and quiet are important to you, ask for a room away from the main pedestrian thoroughfares or consider staying outside the village in one of Whistler's residential neighborhoods.

CATEGORY	COST*
$$$$	over C$300
$$$	C$200–C$300
$$	C$125–C$200
$	under C$125

*All prices are for a standard double room for two, excluding 10% provincial accommodation tax, 15% service charge, and 7% GST.

$$$$ ⊞ **Chateau Whistler Resort.** Canadian Pacific built and runs this ★ friendly looking fortress at the foot of Blackcomb Mountain. Though built and expanded during the 1990s, it has, with its grand stone fireplace and warm Canadiana craft decor, the ambience of an earlier era. The largest hotel in Whistler, the Chateau is a self-contained ski-in, ski-out resort with a spa, health club, and golf course. Rooms and suites on the Entrée Gold concierge floors have fireplaces and whirlpool baths. ✉ *4599 Chateau Blvd., V0N 1B4,* ☎ *604/938–8000 or 800/ 606–8244,* FAX *604/938–2099. 558 rooms, 47 suites. 2 restaurants, lobby*

lounge, some in-room safes, indoor-outdoor pool, beauty salon, hot tubs, saunas, spa, steam rooms, 18-hole golf course, 3 tennis courts, health club, ski shop, ski storage, shops, children's programs (ages 5–12), concierge, concierge floor, convention center. AE, D, DC, MC, V.

$$$$ **Le Chamois.** This hotel has a prime location in the Upper Village at the foot of the Blackcomb ski runs. Of the spacious guest rooms with convenience kitchens, the most romantic are the executive studios with whirlpool tubs set in front of the living room's windows overlooking the slopes and lifts. The one-bedroom suites with kitchenettes and two full baths are great for families. The three- and four-bedroom suites with gas fireplaces, fully equipped kitchens, and washer/dryers are a good bet for groups. ⊠ *4557 Blackcomb Way, V0N 1B4,* ☎ *604/932–8700 or 800/777–0185,* FAX *604/905–2576. 47 suites, 6 studios. Restaurant, café, room service, pool, hot tubs, exercise room, coin laundry, meeting rooms. AE, DC, MC, V.*

$$$ **Pan Pacific Lodge Whistler.** This eight-story lodge is tucked in at the base of both mountains, just steps from either the Whistler or Blackcomb gondola. Accommodations include studios with pull-down queen beds, and one- and two-bedroom units, all with kitchens, balconies, gas fireplaces, and tall windows that make the most of the mountain or valley views. In the evenings, there's live traditional Irish music at the Dubh Linn Gate pub. ⊠ *4320 Sundial Crescent, V0N 1B4,* ☎ *604/905–2999 or 888/905–9995,* FAX *604/905–2995. 76 suites, 45 studios. Pub, in-room data ports, in-room safes, 24-hr room service, pool, outdoor hot tubs, exercise room, steam room, ski shops, ski storage, coin laundry, meeting rooms. No smoking. AE, DC, MC, V.*

$$–$$$ **Delta Whistler Resort.** The resort at the base of Whistler Mountain is a large complex, complete with shopping, dining, and fitness facilities. Rooms are very generous in size (almost all will easily sleep four). There are a few standard rooms, but most have fireplaces, whirlpool bathtubs, balconies, and kitchens. ⊠ *4050 Whistler Way, V0N 1B4,* ☎ *604/932–1982 or 800/515–4050,* FAX *604/932–7332. 268 rooms, 24 suites. Restaurant, sports bar, in-room data ports, minibars, no-smoking floors, room service, pool, beauty salon, indoor and outdoor hot tubs, massage, steam room, 2 indoor/outdoor tennis courts, health club, ski shop, ski storage, shops, baby-sitting, children's programs (ages 0–12), coin laundries, concierge, business services, meeting rooms. AE, DC, MC, V.*

$$–$$$ **Durlacher Hof.** Custom fir woodwork and doors, exposed ceiling beams, a *kachelofen* (a traditional farmhouse fireplace–oven), and antler chandeliers hung over fir benches and tables carry out the rustic European theme of this fancy Tyrolean inn a few minutes' walk outside the village. The green and maroon bedrooms, all named for European mountains, contain more fine examples of custom-crafted wooden furniture. Four rooms have whirlpool tubs. ⊠ *Box 1125, 7055 Nesters Rd., V0N 1B0,* ☎ *604/932–1924,* FAX *604/938–1980. 8 rooms. Breakfast room, outdoor hot tub, massage, sauna, ski storage. Full breakfast, afternoon tea. No smoking. MC, V.*

$$ **Edgewater.** All rooms at this simple cedar lodge on Green Lake have private entrances and water and mountain views. You can do everything from sleigh riding and cross-country skiing to canoeing, kayaking, bird-watching, and horseback riding. Highly regarded evening meals are served. ⊠ *8841 Hwy. 99, Box 369, 3 km (2 mi) north of the village, V0N 1B0,* ☎ *604/932–0688 or 888/870–9065,* FAX *604/932–0686. 6 rooms, 6 suites. Restaurant, bar, outdoor hot tub, hiking, meeting rooms. Continental breakfast. No smoking. AE, MC, V.*

$ **Hostelling International Whistler.** Bunks in men's or women's dorms, a shared kitchen, and a games room make up the basic accommodations of this hostel overlooking Alta Lake. The hostel is next to the swimming beach at Rainbow Park and 15 km (9 mi) by road, or 4 km

(2½ mi) by footpath, from the village. About 4 BC Transit buses a day serve the hostel, and BC Rail will make a request stop here. Reservations are recommended. ⊠ *5678 Alta Lake Rd., V0N 1B0,* ☎ *604/932–5492,* FAX *604/932–4687. 32 beds in 7 dorms, 1 private room (no bath). Kitchenette, ski storage. MC, V.*

Outdoor Activities and Sports

At the **Whistler Activity and Information Center** (⊠ 4010 Whistler Way, in the Whistler Conference Centre, ☎ 604/932–2394) you can book activities, and pick up hiking and biking maps.

CANOEING AND KAYAKING

Canoe and kayak rentals are available at **Alta Lake** at Lakeside Park and Wayside Park. A spot that's perfect for canoeing is the **River of Golden Dreams,** from Alta Lake to Green Lake. For guided canoeing and kayaking trips, sailing, and waterskiing, call **Whistler Outdoor Experience** (☎ 604/932–3389).

FISHING

Whistler Backcountry Adventures (⊠ ☎ 604/932–3474) or **Whistler Fishing Guides** (☎ 604/932–4267) will take care of anything you need—equipment, guides, and transportation. All five lakes around Whistler are stocked with trout.

GOLF

Robert Trent Jones II designed the championship, 18-hole, par-72 course at the **Chateau Whistler Golf Club** (⊠ 4612 Blackcomb Way, ☎ 604/938–2092). The scenery at the 18-hole, par-71 course at the **Whistler Golf Club** (⊠ 4010 Whistler Way, ☎ 604/932–4544 or 800/376–1777) is as beautiful as the back nine is difficult. Jack Nicklaus designed the challenging 18-hole, par-71 **Nicklaus North Golf Course** (⊠ 8080 Nicklaus North Blvd., ☎ 604/938–9898 or 800/386–9898).

RAFTING

Whistler River Adventures (☎ 604/932–3532 or 888/932–3532) operates half- and full-day rafting and jet boating trips.

Skiing

CROSS-COUNTRY

The meandering trail around the Whistler Golf Course is an ideal beginners' route. For more advanced skiing try the 28 km (17 mi) of track-set trails that wind around Lost Lake, Chateau Whistler Golf Course, and the Nicklaus North Golf Course and Green Lake. Trail maps and equipment rental information are available at the **Whistler Activity and Information Center** (☎ 604/932–2394) in the village.

DOWNHILL

The vertical drops and elevations at **Blackcomb and Whistler** (☎ 604/932–3434 or 800/766–0449) mountains are perhaps the most impressive features here. The resort covers 7,071 acres of skiable terrain in 12 alpine bowls on three glaciers and on more than 200 marked trails, served by the most advanced, high-speed lift system on the continent. Blackcomb has a 5,280-ft vertical drop, North America's longest, while Whistler comes in second, with a 5,020-ft drop. The top elevation is 7,494 ft on Blackcomb and 7,160 ft on Whistler. Blackcomb and Whistler each receive an average of 360 inches of snow per year. Blackcomb is open from June to early August for summer glacier skiing. **Whistler/Blackcomb Ski and Snowboard School** (☎ 800/766–0449 for both) provide lessons to skiers of all levels.

HELI-SKIING

Whistler Heli-Skiing (☎ 604/932–4105 or 888/435–4754) conducts guided day trips with up to three glacier runs. The cost is about $430.

Whistler Essentials

Arriving and Departing

BY BUS

Greyhound buses (☎ 604/482–8747; 800/661–8747 in Canada) leave every few hours for Whistler Village from the depot in downtown Vancouver. The fare is about $34 round-trip. **Perimeter Whistler Express** (☎ 604/266–5386 in Vancouver; 604/905–0041 in Whistler) has daily year-round service from Vancouver International Airport to Whistler. Perimeter has a ticket booth at domestic arrivals level 2, and one at the airport's international receiving lounge. The fare is around $47 one-way and reservations are recommended. **West Coast City and Nature Sightseeing** (☎ 604/451–1600 in Vancouver) operates a sightseeing tour ($57) to Whistler that allows passengers to stay over and return on their date of choice to Vancouver.

BY CAR

Whistler is 120 km (74 mi), or 2½ hours, north of Vancouver on winding Highway 99, the Sea-to-Sky Highway.

BY TRAIN

B.C. Rail (☎ 604/631–3500; 800/339–8752 in British Columbia; 800/663–8238 from outside British Columbia) has one train a day leaving its North Vancouver Station (✉ 1311 W. 1st. St., North Vancouver) at 7 AM and arriving at Whistler at 9:10 AM. The $59 round-trip fare includes a full meal each way. The B.C. Rail station is about a 30-minute drive from downtown Vancouver. It's connected to the Vancouver bus and train terminal by shuttle during the summer.

Getting Around

Streets in Whistler Village, Village North, and Upper Village are all pedestrian-only. Pay parking is readily available on the village outskirts. A **free public transit system** loops throughout the village and paid public transit serves the whole valley. Call ☎ 604/932–4020 for information and schedules. For a cab, call **Sea to Sky Taxi** (☎ 604/932–3333).

Contacts and Resources

CAR RENTAL

Budget (☎ 604/932–1236). **Thrifty Car Rental**(☎ 604/938–0302 or 800/367–2277).

EMERGENCIES

Ambulance (☎ 911). **Fire** (☎ 911). **Police** (☎ 911).

GUIDED TOURS

Blackcomb Helicopters (☎ 604/938–1700 or 800/330–4354) is one of several operators that fly year-round flightseeing tours over Whistler's mountains and glaciers.

For guided hikes and snowshoeing trips, contact **Outdoor Adventures@Whistler** (☎ 604/932–0647) or **Whistler Outdoor Experience** (☎ 604/932–3389). Whistler Outdoor Experience also runs trail rides, sleigh rides, and cross-country ski trips.

A number of companies, including **Outdoor Adventures@Whistler** (✉ ☎ 604/932–0647) and **Whistler ATV Tours** (☎ 604/932–6681) offer backcountry tours on all-terrain vehicles.

VISITOR INFORMATION

Whistler Resort Association (✉ 4010 Whistler Way, Whistler V0N 1B4, ☎ 604/932–4222; 604/664–5625 in Vancouver; 800/944–7853 in the U.S. and Canada).

INDEX

L@@king © FOR A great place to go?

We know just the place. In fact, it attracts more than 125,000 visitors a day, making it one of the world's most popular travel destinations. It's previewtravel.com, the Web's comprehensive resource for travelers. It gives you access to over 500 airlines, 25,000 hotels, rental cars, cruises, vacation packages and support from travel experts 24 hours a day. Plus great information from Fodor's travel guides and travelers just like you. All of which makes previewtravel.com quite a find.

Preview Travel has everything you need to plan & book your next trip.

air, car & hotel reservations

vacation packages & cruises

destination planning & travel tips

24-hour customer service

previewtravel.com

preview travel SM

aol keyword: previewtravel

www.previewtravel.com